Herman Grimm

Life Of Michael Angelo

Vol. II

Herman Grimm

Life Of Michael Angelo
Vol. II

ISBN/EAN: 9783348008785

Printed in Europe, USA, Canada, Australia, Japan

Cover: Foto ©ninafisch / pixelio.de

More available books at **www.hansebooks.com**

LIFE·OF MICHAEL ANGELO·

BY
HERMAN·GRIMM·
TRANSLATED·BY
FANNY·ELIZABETH
BVNNÈTT·
VOLVME·II·

NEW·EDITION·WITH·AD-
DITIONS·ILLVSTRATED
WITH·PHOTOGRAVURE
PLATES·FROM·WORKS
OF·ART * * * *

BOSTON·
LITTLE·BROWN·AND·CO·
MDCCCXCVII·

University Press:
JOHN WILSON AND SON, CAMBRIDGE, U.S.A.

CONTENTS OF VOLUME II.

CHAPTER TENTH.

1525—1530.

I.

CHAPTER ELEVENTH.

1530—1534.

[v]

CHAPTER FIFTEENTH.

1542—1547.

CHAPTER SIXTEENTH.

1547—1564.

CONCLUSION.

LIST OF ILLUSTRATIONS.

VOLUME II.

LIFE OF MICHAEL ANGELO.

CHAPTER TENTH.

1525—1530.

THE year 1525 was not a propitious one. The plague appeared repeatedly in Rome and Florence. There was war in Lombardy. A comet was seen in the heavens, which excited the fear that the entire world would be again destroyed by a new deluge. In the same year also there was a jubilee in Rome; but the plague interfered with the assembling of the pilgrims, with the ceremonies, and the receipts.

Clement VII.—such was the name assumed by Medici, after having expended much thought on the

selection — summoned Michael Angelo to him in
the year 1525. A more accurate statement of the
time is lacking.   Michael Angelo had applied himself with all his energy to the sacristy and library
of San Lorenzo ; and, on the other hand, the heirs
of Julius II. had again brought a complaint against
him. They insisted that some agreement should be
made. For this reason the pope now summoned
Michael Angelo ; and the latter presented himself
before him. The affair was left to the will of the
pope. The Duke of Urbino, the representative of
the Rovere in this matter, asserted even then that
Michael Angelo had received more than he would
confess ; but the disputes on this point did not break
out openly till later. For the present it was enough
that the pope desired, that, for the sake of his personal plans, the further prosecution of the matter
should be given up.*

Condivi says that Michael Angelo did not like
being in Rome, and returned again quickly to Florence, because he foresaw subsequent events. This
is as inaccurate as if Vasari had written it ; for no
man could at that time anticipate what would happen two years later. The plague may far rather
have decided him not to remain there longer than
necessary ; but that he did not like being in Rome,
may be explained perhaps by the manner in which
matters of art were treated at the papal court. For
the position which Michael Angelo had himself formerly held with Julius II., and afterwards Raphael
with Leo X., Bandinelli now held with Clement

* See Appendix, Note I.

VII.; and at this very time he was using this favor to inflict a sensitive offence upon Michael Angelo.

Vasari devotes a long biography to Bandinelli, because he was on terms of intercourse with him, and Bandinelli exerted an influence upon affairs in Florence. In himself he was nothing. His name would never be mentioned at the present day, had not that false suspicion of having destroyed Michael Angelo's cartoon made him famous. No single work of his calls forth an inquiry as to the name of the artist who executed it; except that one might perhaps wish to know who could have produced any thing so cold, and at the same time so full of pretension.

Still his long-continued intrigues against Michael Angelo make Bandinelli important. If any thing characterizes the leap downwards from Leo to his successor, it is his making a favorite of this man, who, although raised into the class of nobility, remained all his life a servile nature; and though he has produced works that hold a place, and even gained praise from his contemporaries, he was nothing after all but a bungling slave to routine. But his father, one of the most skilful goldsmiths in Florence, had been a confidant of the Medici; and at their flight, in the year 1494, many valuable things had been intrusted to him, which he justly delivered up again on their return. This favor passed to the son. Leonardo da Vinci had acknowledged Bandinelli's drawings to be important; he had encouraged him to pursue the career of an artist, and had had him instructed by Rustici, his friend and pupil. His wonderful hatred of Michael Angelo, and his fixed idea that he was called upon to excel him, was early formed in him. By passionate work and conspicuous skill in the technical part of his profession, by neglecting no opportunity of testifying his devotion to the ruling family, he succeeded in advancing himself. He never allowed himself to waver in his demands, in his complaints at being put in the background, and in his accusations of others. Such characters are often more acceptable at court than men who rarely demand any thing, but who, when it comes to them, claim it as a right. The former, burdensome as they are at times, show themselves as they are, and allow themselves to be converted by gold into submissive friendship; the latter seem always concealing something, and take what they receive silently, as due acknowledgment. Bandinelli had been about Clement as long as the latter had ruled in Florence as cardinal, and had followed him to Rome. He suited him as a dog suits his master. He might bark and snarl, and was trod upon or caressed accordingly.

But he did not desire only to surpass Michael Angelo. He considered him as the one to blame for his misfortune in being ill appreciated. He regarded his mere existence as a malicious trick of fate. Himself he considered as the true sun of art: Michael Angelo had basely risen before him on the horizon; and, when he came afterwards, it was already day, and no one marvelled. But the world should be compelled to chose between them; and hence, with him as with many other artists who feel

Statue of David.

MICHAEL ANGELO.

themselves offended and unappreciated by the mere existence of a higher, arose the desire to bring his own works into immediate vicinity with those of his enemy.

Michael Angelo's most important work in Florence was the David at the gate of the palace. Bandinelli wished to place a work in marble at the other side of the entrance, to show people to whom so much praise truly belonged. Soderini had already, in 1507, ordered a second statue for this place, from Michael Angelo; and the block for it lay ready at Carrara. The execution of it had only been deferred because Michael Angelo never found time for it. After the fall of the gonfalonier, Bandinelli endeavored to get the block for himself. At the entrance of Leo X., he knew how to gain his point so far, that his model of a Hercules was placed as a festive ornament in front of the palace, as a counterpiece to the David. He boasted openly, at that time, of wishing to annihilate Michael Angelo's fame; now, at last, in the year 1525, he accomplished the matter with the new pope.

Michael Angelo had enemies in the Vatican. At the order for the sacristy of San Lorenzo, the pope's treasurer wished that the blocks intended for the building of the façade, and used in the new sacristy, should be again placed to the pope's account. Michael Angelo rejected this, and the man became his adversary. Besides this, the younger Florentine sculptors were little disposed towards him. Leo X. had desired, as has before been related, that Michael Angelo should make a model of the statues intended for the façade, as large as they were to be executed subsequently; so that others might work after his pattern, and the whole be completed more speedily. Michael Angelo was not to be induced to do this; he prepared nothing but the small models, after which he alone was able to work. This was considered by the younger artists as intentional malevolence. They imagined that he wished to do all alone, that he might merit all alone, and that he might cut them off from the opportunity of learning his art. Lesser talents always believe that every thing depends upon tricks, which great masters have casually discovered. With Leo, however, such slander produced very little effect. Much as he delighted in fools, he knew, however, occasionally how to distinguish them from superior natures. Clement was moderate, and liked his equals. They represented to him that it was too much to give this work also to Michael Angelo. He had not yet finished the mausoleum; and, if he now began the Hercules, the sacristy and library would suffer from it. Clement's mind was of too low an order to feel the impossibility of a dispute for precedency between Michael Angelo and Bandinelli. They represented to him, that, in employing both, he would be served doubly well.

Bandinelli had just completed a copy of the Laocoon for the King of France. He was working in the immediate neighborhood of the pope; and his task pleased Clement so well, that he not only ordered Bandinelli to restore in wax the arm missing in the original group, but he had the copy, instead of being sent to France, placed in Florence, in the palace of his family. We need only see this group in the Uffici, at the present day, to have an idea of Bandinelli's style, — a weak, awkward imitation of the antique. And as regards the arm, which is stiff and inharmonious, it would be well if the marble arm, subsequently executed after his model, as well as the newly added hand of the Apollo Belvedere, were again removed, and the antique works purified from the additions of the false judgment of modern times.[*]

Bandinelli now produced his model of a counterpiece to the Buonarroti David; and the pope gave him the commission. In July, 1525, the marble arrived at Florence. Every one felt the injustice done to the great Michael Angelo by this decision. In conveying the block from the vessel, the ropes broke; and it fell into the Arno, from which it was again raised with great difficulty. A lampoon in rhyme was circulated about it, in which it was said that the marble, out of sorrow at being delivered from Michael Angelo's hands to those of Bandinelli, had wished to drown itself.

It was indeed a disgrace for Michael Angelo. It was no longer a Raphael or a Leonardo who disputed with him the place of honor. Perugino, Francia, Signorelli, and all the greater earlier masters, who, once working with him, had won just fame, were either dead or nearing death. He stood alone, a new generation round him, not one of whom practised the art independently in the old manner, the

[*] See Appendix, Note II.

best among them being only imitating pupils; and, to one of the poorest among these, the honor was awarded of producing, in the place of Michael Angelo himself, a counterpiece to that work from which he dated the beginning of his fame.

It was natural that under these circumstances Michael Angelo gladly turned his back upon Rome. With the exception of Sebastian del Piombo, none were at work there who were intimate with him. Next to him, Penni, a pupil of Raphael's, was the most important; but he was without any peculiar characteristic, and was only eminent among the more modern. Giulio Romano, Raphael's greatest pupil and imitator, had already gone to Mantua, where he was honorably employed by the duke in every branch of artistic power. Penni, too, also soon left. Roman art had well-nigh drawn to an end; while in Florence, where it was no outward luxury dependent on the will of a single master, but the fruit of a native culture, it advanced alike in good or evil times.

2.

The cupola of the sacristy of San Lorenzo must have been completed in the year 1525. In the construction of the rough building, Michael Angelo had tolerably adhered to Brunelleschi. The sacristy is a space of moderate extent. The light falls from above. Piloto the goldsmith, a Florentine, well known in the city, esteemed for his iron work and feared for his evil tongue, made the knob with seventy-two facets, — the perforated work over the opening in the middle of the dome. When they said to Michael Angelo that he would make his lanterns far better than Brunelleschi, he is said to have replied, "Different certainly, but not better."

In the year 1525, Michael Angelo was also at Carrara. His name is to be found with the date below on a bas-relief hewn out of the rock there; but I have not seen it myself. When and why he went to Carrara is not known. This year and that which followed were among the quietest in Michael Angelo's life.

Matters in Italy were becoming all the more agitated. In the year 1525, an event also took place, which in its consequences put an end to the building before it was completed. The King of France, at that time an ally of the pope, was taken prisoner at Pavia by Charles V., and carried to Madrid. Scarcely had Clement, who had no other course left him, become the ally of the emperor, than, by a natural process of crystallization, a union of all the other princes in Europe against the latter was brought about; and the pope, in spite of the alliance just concluded with Charles, allowed himself to be implicated in their plans. It is one of the most brilliant passages in Guicciardini, where he represents the pope between his two ministers, one of whom, the imperial disposed Schomberg, was honored and feared by Clement, who loved and could not do without Ghiberti, the advocate of the French policy; how both, counteracting each other, drew him hither and thither; and how he himself, fearful and irresolute, but self-willed and jealous of his

1*

own deciding word, at length, after the unceasing
discussion over matters had filled him with the
deluding comfort that he had seriously deliberated
on the point,* announced that the declaration of
war against the emperor was to be joined.

The emperor, however, was no longer the young
man from whom little was expected, and in ridicule
of whom it had once been written in the streets of
Spires, "We will be ruled by no boy;" he was no
longer the youth who was preferred by the German
princes at the time of the election, before the King
of France, because the powerful energy of Francis I.
was dreaded.   In the six years of his rule, Charles
had formed himself into a prince who understood
how to hold together his immense empire, and who
kept the pope in as great a strait between Naples and
Milan, as he did the King of France between Burgundy and Spain.   He favored the Lutherans in
Germany, however this might be regarded in Italy.
To oppose the emperor was perhaps still possible
to England or Venice; but the pope must have
seen, that no other course was left to him than
that of affecting voluntary, hearty devotion, to conceal the necessity to which he was obliged to submit.

What gave Charles personally such great superiority over Francis, was the coolness with which he
acted, and the appearance of legitimacy which he
knew how to impress upon all his measures.   Only
with reluctance did he at any time sacrifice his love
of peace by entering upon war.   Compelled by his

* See Appendix, Note III.

enemies to defend the most distinct right, he pitied
those who misunderstood it, and obliged him to take
up arms. Francis, on the other hand, who was not
inferior to him in cunning, did not possess this de-
liberation, and lacked perseverance in following out
what he undertook. He came like a thunder-storm,
but was satisfied if his lightning struck nothing.
He was capricious, sensitive, and incapable of har-
boring tormenting thoughts. It is characteristic of
him, though the event happened long subsequent to
this time, that, at the death of his eldest son, he
would not allow the court to go into mourning, or
any one to remind him of his loss. Now, as a prisoner in Madrid, he would have died of grief, had
not the negotiations for his liberty led to a result.
Two millions of ready money, his two sons as hostages, the surrender of his right to Burgundy, his
marriage with Charles's sister Eleanor, — these were
the conditions sanctioned by solemn oaths. All this;
however, could not prevent Francis, as soon as he
saw himself at liberty, from joining the alliance
against the emperor.

The latter, on the other hand, prepared himself
slowly. In the year 1526, he gave the pope a slight
foretaste of what was impending upon him in Rome,
in case he did not keep quiet. Cardinal Colonna, the
most powerful enemy of the Medici after Soderini,
left Naples for Rome, with an armed force. The
pope alone was the object. The Vatican suburb, and
above all the papal palace, was plundered. Clement
fled to the Castle of St. Angelo, and was obliged to
come to terms with the imperial governor in Naples,

to get rid of molestation. Yet this was only for the moment. The efforts of the allies progressed, and the pope remained in league with them. Then, in the autumn of 1526, the army raised by the emperor in Germany crossed the Alps into Italy; those soldiers under Frundsperg and Bourbon, who brought such immense misery upon Rome. For it was a matter of course that Italy was to be the theatre of this war.

By sea, the Venetian, French, Papal, and Genoese fleets united, were five times superior to the Span-ish-Neapolitan naval force. By land, however, the emperor could come forward with more terrible and enduring power. United masses did not here strike great premeditated blows. What most distinguishes the warfare of that day from the present, is the slow-ness of the movements and the want of connection. Commands and tidings might come too late, or might be omitted; the constant uncertainty allowed of no vast and rapidly executed plans. The contingencies of supplies; the influence of climate; the abundance or lack of pay for the troops; the dependence upon the means of transporting the artillery; the malig-nant sicknesses which were almost unavoidable from the impurity prevalent in camps, and from the alter-nations of want and plenty; and, lastly, the good-will of the troops, who often gave the decisive word to their generals for striking or not striking, for remain-ing or advancing,—all this made the results of a campaign uncertain. Where victories were gained, a chance might snatch every advantage from him who had carried the day; and, on the other side, the annihilation of an army might not make him who had sent it forth waver in his obstinacy. Princes, accustomed to these circumstances, began war as readily as they concluded peace; and from this arose a mixture of war and peace, which was the perpetual and ordinary state of things.

For this reason there was no alarm felt in Rome, when, in the autumn of 1526, the Germans appeared in Lombardy, and settled themselves there through the winter. In the spring of 1527, apprehension for Florence was awakened. A bad state of feeling had arisen in the city since the Government had been in the hands of the Cardinal of Cortona. Not one of the expectations which had been excited by Clement as cardinal, had been fulfilled by him as pope. Both in Florence and Rome, they regarded the time of Leo, whose death had been welcomed as a deliverance, as the good old days. There was no trace left of his generosity, and of his richly dispensed favors. The Cardinal of Cortona, an avaricious, severe man, burdened citizens and ecclesiastics with taxes. His coarse appearance made him soon as much hated by his own party as he had been at first by the enemies of the Medici alone. Added to this, he was no born Florentine. Like Piero, however, after the death of the old Lorenzo, Cortona maintained his ascendency in Florence so long as he was not compelled to seek support in the adherence of all. He was lost as soon as outward disturbances united all parties; and the matter at stake was no longer the fighting-out of internal disputes, but the safety of the country itself.

The troops of the allied powers — that is, the united Papal-Venetian army — encountered the imperial army on the borders of the kingdom of Naples, but was unable to impede the approach of the foe now advancing in the north. Bourbon was drawing nearer Tuscany. The pope became suddenly alarmed. Without allowing himself to be disturbed by the consideration that he himself was one of those leagued against the emperor, he negotiated with the Spanish governor in Naples, and an agreement was effected. Bourbon received orders to discontinue his march. But the troops pressed forward, and carried him with them. Florence and Rome were the baits upon which the army had been raised. Frundsperg is said to have carried at his girdle a golden knife with which he intended killing the pope, and red silk cord for the necks of the cardinals. Slowly the columns of the army moved on, past Ferrara and Bologna, towards Tuscany; and, in proportion as the danger increased without, within the city it grew more and more threatening. Greater and greater became the union among the citizens; more and more precarious became the friends of the Medici.

For, as at Piero's overthrow, it was the nobles of the same rank with the Medici who now favored the movement against their ascendency.

These nobles, who, when the maintenance of their privileges was concerned, had sided with the Medici, and formed generally the party of the Palleski, fell into two divisions. The one adhered to them at any price. Known as declared enemies of the people,

and more Medicæan often than the Medici themselves, they cared little about the hatred which this
position brought upon them. They felt themselves
powerful as participators in the supreme power.
The other party, on the contrary, would have gladly
consented to the precedence of the Medici; but they
would not accept the position of inferiors. They,
the first families of the city, came forward all the
stronger, because, closely related for the most part
to the Medici, they reckoned among their members
those who considered themselves, with respect to succession, entitled to more than Clement, Ippolito, and
Alessandro, — those illegitimate scions whose only
title consisted in the possession of power.

This part of the nobility favored the revolt. They
demanded that arms should be given to the citizens,
because the danger threatened too closely, and the
Government alone was not able to avert it. When,
in the Medici palace, this and other proposals were
one day discussed with Cortona, Niccolo Capponi,
the son of that man who had once so boldly opposed
Charles VIII. in the same house, rose with the declaration, that matters thus referring to the State
ought not to be discussed here, but in the palace
of the Government. These words produced no effect
at the moment; but, repeated abroad and carried
about the city, they served to heighten the discord.
The arming of the citizens was unnecessary; there
were mercenaries enough in the city to defend it
against Bourbon. Besides, the army advancing from
the south for the protection of Florence was expected
every hour. But the current of public opinion was

too strong.　On the 26th April, arms were to be distributed.

Early in the morning of this day, however, the cardinal received tidings, that the army of the allies was approaching the city.　He immediately gave orders to withhold the arms, and rode with the two Medici to meet the Duke of Urbino, under whose command the troops stood.　In the evening, it was decided that he was to enter Florence.　All danger for the Medici was over.

The feeling, however, was strong in the city. While the cardinal was deliberating with the duke without the city, the citizens, who had expected the promised arms, and saw themselves disappointed, had gathered together in front of the palace of the Government.　Again rose the cry, "Popolo, popolo! libertà!"　The palace was stormed without any resistance being offered by the soldiers who garrisoned it; the noblest citizens, among them acknowledged friends and associates of the Medici, called together a meeting of the council, and four decrees were passed.　The political prisoners were to be set at liberty; the State was to be re-established as it had been under Soderini; the Medici were to be banished; and the people were summoned armed to the parliament.

The news of these events was immediately conveyed to the cardinal.　Cortona, accompanied by Ippolito and Alessandro, took a thousand men from the army, and returned at once to Florence.　Their friends there took care that the gate by which they must enter should be kept open; and just as the nobles had assembled to decree further that the city should adhere to the Italian league against the emperor, and that their proscription of the Medici was in nowise to interfere with their reverence for Clement as pope, Ippolito and Alessandro appeared with the troops before the palace. Many of the citizens who had heard the cry, "Palle, palle!" which accompanied their entry, fled even before the troops had appeared in sight; those who remained behind had bolted the gate of the palace.

A sort of contest now arose. The soldiers endeavored to force open the gates by inserting their pikes; the citizens hurled down from the windows whatever was at hand, in order to drive them away. A bench, falling from above, struck the David of Michael Angelo, which towered above the throng at the gate, and broke off its arm. They succeeded in driving the soldiers off. The night approached. The Medici proposed mounting cannons; but the Venetian ambassador and other men of influence effected an agreement. Every thing was to be regarded as if nothing had occurred; and it was to be forgotten for ever. Upon these conditions, the besieged left the palace, which was again taken possession of by the soldiers.

3.

On the same day, the Duke de Bourbon, with his German soldiers, — for thus his army was called in spite of the Spanish troops which it numbered, — arrived in the neighborhood of Florence. Both armies stood so near each other, that a battle could

have been fought; but no encounter followed. Turning suddenly round, Bourbon left Florence, and
hastened by forced marches towards Rome, whither
Urbino slowly followed him. With such rapidity
did the Germans advance, that they formed chains
across the river by men holding each other, and so
they passed over. On the 5th May, they arrived
before the walls of the city, and Bourbon demanded
a free passage to Naples.

So little had they thought of danger in Rome,
that the pope, trusting to the last agreement, had
even dismissed his troops. Every preparation was
wanting. The citizens were hurriedly gathered together on the Capitol, and arms were distributed.
On the 6th, at dawn of day, the Germans began the
attack. Bourbon fell at the first assault; but by
evening the Vatican suburb was in the hands of the
enemy. Clement, who was even best informed of
the state of things, had not anticipated such an issue.
He scarcely saved himself by flight from the Vatican
to the Castle of St. Angelo, whither the fugitive
population hurried, as the shipwrecked crew of an
entire fleet hastens to a single boat which cannot
receive them. In the midst of the thronging stream
of men, the portcullis was lowered. Whoever remained without was lost. Benvenuto Cellini was at
that time in Rome, and was among the defenders of
the walls. He boasted that his ball had destroyed
Bourbon. He stole fortunately into the citadel,
before it was closed, and entered the pope's service
as bombardier.

Even at this last moment, Clement might have

saved Rome itself, which, situated on the opposite
shore of the river, had not yet been entered by the
enemy. They offered to spare it for a ransom; but
finding this too high, and awaiting hourly Urbino's
army, to which, though nothing was yet to be seen
of it, he looked as a deliverer in the time of need,
he would hear nothing of it. And thus the unde-
fended city fell into the hands of the imperialists.
Almost without resistance, they entered Trastevere,
a small quarter of the city lying to the west of the
Tiber; and then crossing the bridges, which no one
had demolished, they pressed forwards into the heart
of Rome.

It was the depth of the night. Benvenuto Cellini
was stationed on the tower of the Castle of St. Angelo, at the foot of the colossal angel, and saw the
flames bursting forth in the darkness, and heard
the sorrowful cry all around. For it was late before
the soldiers began to cast off all restraint. They
had entered quietly. The Germans stood in battalions. But, when they saw the Spaniards broken up
and plundering, the desire was aroused in them also;
and now a spirit of emulation appeared, as to which
nation could outdo the other in cruelty. The Spaniards, it is asserted by impartial Italians, carried the
day.

There had been no siege, no bombardment, no
flight of any great extent; but as if the earth had
opened, and had disgorged a legion of devils, so
suddenly came these hosts. Every thing was in a
moment abandoned to them. We must endeavor to
conceive what kind of men these German soldiers

were. They formed an intermediate class between the prime and the refuse of the people. Gathered together by the hope of booty; indifferent what end was assigned them; rendered wild by hunger and tardy pay; left without a master after the death of their commander, — they found themselves unrestrained in the most luxurious city of the world, — a city abounding with gold and riches, and at the same time decried for centuries in Germany, as the infernal nest of the popes, who lived there as incarnate devils in the midst of their Babylonian doings. The opinion that the pope of Rome, and Clement VII. in particular, was the devil, prevailed not only in Germany; but in Italy and in Rome the people called him so. In the midst of plague and famine, he had doubled the taxes, and raised the price of bread. What with the Romans, however, was an invective arising from indignation, was an article of faith among the Germans. They believed they had to do with the real antichrist, whose destruction would be a benefit to Christendom. We must remember, if we would understand this fury of the German soldiery, in whose minds, as in those of all Germans, Lutheran ideas at that time prevailed, how Rome had been preached and written upon in the north. The city was represented to people as a vast abyss of sin; the men as villains, from the lowest up to the cardinals; the women as courtesans; the business of all as deceit, theft, and murder; and the robbing and deluding of men that had for centuries been emanating from Rome, was regarded as the universal disease from which the world was languishing. Thither for centuries the gold of Germany had flowed; there had emperors been humbled or poisoned; from Rome every evil had sprung. And thus, while satiating themselves with rapine and murder, they believed a good work was being done for the welfare of Christendom, and for the avenge of Germany. Never, however,—this we know,—does the nature of man exhibit itself more beast-like, than when it becomes furious for the sake of ideas of the highest character.

Before the Castle of St. Angelo, which, carefully fortified with walls and fosses, alone afforded resistance, the German soldiers proclaimed Martin Luther as pope. Luther's name was at that time a war-cry against pope and priestcraft. The rude multitude surmised not what Luther desired when he attacked the papacy. In front of St. Peter's Church, they represented an imitation of the papal election with the sacred garments and utensils. They compelled one priest to give extreme unction to a dying mule. One protested that he would not rest until he had consumed a piece of the pope's flesh. It is true, Italians for the most part relate, this; but the German reports themselves do not deny the excessive barbarity which was permitted.

Ten millions of precious metal was carried away. How much blood did this money involve; and what was done to those from whom it was taken? Fewer were put to death than were plundered, says one of the records; but what does that imply? It is true, the Germans often quarrelled with the Spaniards, because the horrors which they saw them practise

were too terrible for them. Otherwise the sparing
of human life was less an act of clemency than of
covetousness. Prisoners of war were at that time
regarded as slaves; they were carried away as personal property, or a ransom was extorted. When
the French came to Florence in the year 1494,
differences arose between the citizens and soldiers,
from the fact that the Florentines could not endure
the sight of their captive countrymen driven like
cattle with halters through the streets; and they set
them free by force. This appeared to the French a
plunder of what they had lawfully obtained.

This system was carried to a great pitch in Rome.
The possessors of palaces were obliged to purchase
their ransom, the Spanish cardinals as well as the
Italian,—no difference was made. Thus at least
escape was possible. And here, too, it occurred
that the German soldiers took those prisoners who
had purchased their life under their protection,
against those who wished to force them to settle the
business again.

And as the people were treated, so were the
things. Upon the inlaid marble floor of the Vatican, where the Prince of Orange took up his abode,
—the command of the army devolving upon him
after Bourbon's death,—the soldiers lighted their
fire. The splendid stained glass windows, executed
by William of Marseilles, were broken for the sake
of the lead. Raphael's tapestries were pronounced
excellent booty; in the paintings on the walls the
eyes were put out; and valuable documents were
given as straw to the horses which stood in the

Sistine Chapel. The statues in the streets were thrown down; the images of the Mother of God in the churches were broken to pieces. For six months the city thus remained in the power of the soldiery, who had lost all discipline. Pestilence and famine appeared. Rome had more than ninety thousand inhabitants under Leo X.; when Clement VII. returned a year after the conquest, scarcely a third of that number then existed, — poor, famished people, who had remained behind, because they knew not whither to turn.

All this lay on the conscience of the man who now for months had been condemned to look down upon this misery from the Castle of St. Angelo, in which the Spaniards held him completely blockaded, and where pestilence and want of provisions appeared just as much as down below in Rome. At last, after waiting day after day, he saw Urbino's army approaching from afar: their watch-fires were to be perceived; and every moment he expected that the duke would attack and deliver the city. But he moved not. It is thought he intended now to avenge the rapine which the Medici under Leo X. had carried on against him. For Lorenzo's daughter was still styled officially the Duchess of Urbino; and he had only just succeeded in Florence in effecting the surrender of the fortresses, which had been always withheld from him. The duke asserted, that strategical considerations would not have permitted an assault at that time. After having rested for some time in sight of the city, in which the imperialists had opened their intrenchments round the

Castle of St. Angelo for a regular siege, he withdrew back again to the north, and left the pope to his fate.

4.

On the 12th May, the tidings of the events in Rome reached Florence.

Immediately after the departure of Urbino, the citizens there had risen for a new commotion. The men who had originated the occurrences of the 26th April, held secret conferences; and Cortona began to feel himself uneasy, in spite of his three thousand soldiers. He was obliged to consent, that the assembly of the citizens, which had always regulated the form of the government of the city, should be remodelled into an actual government; and that they should debate over things of importance, without concerning themselves about his opinion. There were, besides Cortona, two other cardinals in Florence, sent by Clement; but these also knew not whether to yield, or to exert their power with energy. Thus it was, that, when the evil tidings from Rome arrived, the opposition to the Medici in Florence might be considered as having already broken forth; and, instead of being driven away by a sudden blow from the people, they were able to withdraw in peace upon favorable conditions. Nothing was to happen either to them personally, or to any of their servants or adherents. Ippolito retained the capacity which had been awarded to him of holding any office. Their property remained exempt from taxes. Cortona's attendants also were to be safe from every act of spiteful enmity. Thus they left the city, as it were, only for an indefinite time, because their own welfare rendered this necessary for the moment.

Scarcely were they gone, than the people became conscious of what had happened. Florence had only been committed temporarily to the care of the remaining party of the Medici. The rumor spread that the pope had escaped from the Castle of St. Angelo, and was marching towards Florence. They demanded arms. The palace of the Medici was to be stormed. The consiglio grande was to assemble. A disorder arose, from which there would have been no way of escape, had not Niccolo Capponi proved himself the man in whom the general confidence was concentrated. On the 17th May, 1527, the Medici had departed; on the 20th, the Government, under the direction of Capponi, decided on opening the consiglio grande on the day following. It seemed scarcely possible to prepare the great hall in the palace of the Government for it. It had been given up as a residence to the soldiers, and with wise forethought had been divided into a series of smaller apartments. Every one, however, set to work to remove these impediments; the noblest vied with the lowest; the partition-walls were broken down, the stones carried away; and the hall was restored in the course of one night to what it had been in Savonarola's times. Then came the clergy, sprinkled it with holy water, and gave it its old dignity by celebrating mass there. Two thousand five hundred citizens gathered together. Capponi was elected gonfalonier for a year.

Thus Michael Angelo saw freedom return to his

native city. His name is not mentioned; but he was in Florence, and took part in these things. Nothing but an unimportant mention of those days is to be found in his papers in the British Museum. "Some days ago," it says there, "Piero Gondi came to me, and begged for the key of the new sacristy of San Lorenzo, as he wished to conceal there various matters belonging to him, on account of the danger-ous position in which we stand; and to-day, the 29th April, he began to bring some packets there. He said it was linen, and that it belonged to his sister; and that I might not see further what it was, and where he concealed it, I have this evening con-signed to him the key of the sacristy."* Piero Gondi is mentioned as one of those who took part in the insurrection on the 26th April; otherwise he was not a person of any importance. We see how little secure seemed the state of things in spite of the mutual pardon.

Before these last events had taken place, little progress had been made in the sacristy of San Lor-enzo, on account of the plague; now, of course, it was no longer thought of. It is uncertain whether Michael Angelo was among those in the palace on the 26th; but there is no doubt that he now sat in the consiglio grande. I could not, moreover, assert that he voted against Capponi at the election; for his aversion to him was certainly caused by the sub-sequent policy of the gonfalonier.

Niccolo Capponi is treated with a certain respect by those who give an account of him. That he

* See Appendix, Note IV.

wished to act for the best is denied by none; but it cannot also be denied that he wished differently to what he did. In the circle of his intimates, he was the temperate man, who knew the end of all popular excitement, who understood how to estimate the resources of the Medici, and who considered enough had been obtained if the city appeared indifferent to her old masters; to the people he came forward as the man of confidence, full of hope for the advent of true liberty and the most glorious future. He soon reached such a pitch, that he must have esteemed himself fortunate in succeeding in keeping up the appearance to the people, by whom he was urged forward step by step, of having independently taken the lead, and at the same time of holding the pope convinced that he could not have done otherwise.

The first step was one to which he had allowed himself to be urged: it had never been his intention to have convoked the consiglio grande. He was obliged to do so, because the Piagnoni and Arrabiati desired it,—two parties, which arose again as in the days of Savonarola. And between these, again, here stood the Palleski, as at that time; and all the old game was repeated. Arrabiati and Piagnoni would not have the Medici for any thing; but they hated each other like poison. The casting vote, therefore, was in the hands of the Palleski.

In the consiglio grande, Capponi was supported by the Piagnoni; and he cast into oblivion the fact that he had been hitherto a Palleski. In secret he debated with his old companions, whose severe criticism at the untenableness of the new state of things he understood only too well. The Arrabiati, however, who watched every step he took, endeavored so to turn things as to do away with the assent of the Piagnoni to resolutions, which, contrary to Capponi's own feeling, he was nevertheless obliged to carry out. Still, in 1527, nothing decisive happened by which the alternative was placed before the gonfalonier, of opposing his will to the majority, or of laying down his office. Outward circumstances allowed matters to go on thus for a long time. The plague raged so terribly through the summer, that whoever could, left the city, and went into the country. The pope was all this time in the Castle of St. Angelo. It was not till the November of the year that a French army appeared in Tuscany with assistance. Florence, which had joined the Italian league, sent a contingent to it. Capponi, who wished to hold himself free with regard to the emperor, was of opinion that they should compound with money for the city's share; the Arrabiati, however, enforced that they should march out troops. At last, in December, Clement regained his freedom, not through the French, but by an agreement with Spain; and, leaving the Castle of St. Angelo, he went suddenly, as if in flight, to Orvieto, a small and strong city in the papal territory to the north of Rome, and in the neighborhood of Tuscany. From here, where he united his scattered adherents round him in a kind of court, the nets were again thrown over Florence, and negotiations with Capponi were entered into.

In a certain respect it must have been even agreeable to the pope that his family should be at this time driven out of Florence, and not answerable for the policy of the city. He stood on terms of tenderness with both beloved sons,—that of France as well as of Spain; but he was cautious of drawing nearer either. He must first wait to see which gained the ascendency in Italy, that he might make common cause with the conqueror. And so he contented himself with concealing every bad feeling towards his native city, and exhibiting good-will towards it. He told them that he cherished no other wish than that the members of the Medici family should be allowed to live and die in Florence as simple citizens. And he added to this the request that they should send him his little niece, who had retired into a convent under the guardianship of her aunt Clarice Strozzi, a daughter of the old Lorenzo, and who, when that lady had died, had been detained there alone.

Capponi, in the meanwhile, in order to remove beforehand any ground of mistrust which they had sought to excite against him among the Piagnoni, attached himself more closely than ever to the Piagnoni. It is singular to hear how the adherents of Savonarola, who had been dead now for thirty years, should have preserved themselves as a sect, sometimes secretly making their way, sometimes tolerated by the Government; and how their belief had grown into a system, which might be called a national Florentine pietism. Savonarola had been transformed into a true saint. His remains—bones, ashes, and the like—performed miracles; his prophecies of the terrible fall of Rome and the revival of the Florentine republic had been confirmed by late events in every particular, and were regarded as articles of faith.

We see Michael Angelo strangely entangled in these affairs. In an old Florentine manuscript belonging to that period,* we find how, in the year 1513, he had seen a meteor in Rome, and had at once sketched it, — a three-tailed star, one ray of which had pointed to Rome, a second to Florence, and a third to the east. Any one, it says, might see the sheet from Michael Angelo himself; and what it indicated was clear, — fearful fates impending upon Rome and Florence and the Catholic Church, and this from the Turkish emperor, or from some great Christian ruler. In Rome and Florence, the barbarians would riot worse than in Prato in the year 1512. These sayings were current among the people; and that they might prepare, by repentance and atonement, for these fearful things, Savonarola's teachings were again introduced into practical life with ardent zeal. The inclination to the outward observances of religion, which is often seen in manufacturing cities, was favorable to these things. Again civil laws were to help the maintenance of religious austerity. Hence, immediately, there were decrees of the consiglio grande against the adornment of females, against Jews and their usury, against gamblers, swearers, tavern-keepers, and against want of chastity. Processions were prohibited. Once, in the midst of a sitting of the consiglio, the whole assembly fell on their knees with the cry, Misericordia! And, with all this enthusiasm, no tinge of Lutheran, anti-

* See Appendix, Note V.

Roman taste was mingled : it was publicly forbidden
to discuss religious matters ; and one of the conspira-
tors of 1521, who had now returned after long travels,
bringing back with him from Germany ideas as to
the uselessness of numerous monks and priests, was
banished. With difficulty he was rescued by his
friends from the brethren of San Marco, who demanded that he should be put to the rack. So
completely had Capponi the Piagnoni in his power,
that, on the last of May, 1528, he obtained the majority, and was appointed gonfalonier for the second
year on the 1st July. He had left nothing untried
in gaining over Savonarola's adherents to himself ;
and yet, in spite of this, he was wavering at the
beginning of the year. What, however, regained
him his popularity, at one stroke, was the proposal
he made in February to proclaim Jesus Christ King
of Florence. The unanimous applause of the consiglio was bestowed on this proposal. An inscription
over the hall confirmed the acceptance of the new
ruler. Thus were the old romantic ideas of a sect,
so narrow in its views, used in effecting an election.
The Palleski saw through Capponi, although they
supported him ; the Arrabiati saw through just as
much, but were powerless. And so, urged on one
side, and restrained on the other, matters continued
through 1527, and no party had reason to regard his
cause as the succumbing one.

5.

The years 1527 and 1528 are also extremely
scanty in their information respecting Michael An-

gelo. We have no intimation whether he was involved in party affairs, or what occupied him. Perhaps he worked at Julius's mausoleum, and, as is
related of all these years of disorder, secretly at the
statues for the tombs of the Medici. The Florentine
papers, it is to be hoped, will one day fill up the gap
which here, for a time, is still left open in Michael
Angelo's life. Until then, we must be satisfied with
the narrative of what was going on around him in
Florence, and was certainly experienced by him.

According to his character, he held himself aloof
from political life, until his practical energy was
urgently required. He had never yet filled any
public office. In the year 1521, he was to have been
a member of the Government; but he thought himself obliged to refuse the post, because he could not
accept it according to his lawful vocation. The
letter to his brother on this subject, which is still
preserved, shows how conscientiously he acted in the
matter.* All excitement over trifles was contrary
to his nature. For this reason, he may even now
have played no part in the consiglio. There, as
ever, different opinions existed among the three
great parties, whose members voted according to
their conviction at the time, rather than according
to their given word; and it is most probable that he
belonged to these. We only once catch a glimpse
of Michael Angelo in 1528, in the biography of Benvenuto Cellini, who met with him in Florence in the
summer of this year, when he was himself but a
young goldsmith, who had gained but little fame.

* See Appendix Note VI.

Released with the pope in December, 1527, from the Castle of St. Angelo, Cellini had gone to Mantua, where Giulio Romano, who was engaged in building the famous Palazzo del T, received him kindly. Returning from thence to Florence, he settled himself there for some time as a goldsmith; and Michael Angelo, who was interested in him and his mode of working, sent a young Florentine to him as a proof of it.

"My intention was to go again to Rome," says Cellini; "but, at the request of my brother and sister, I remained in Florence. Piero Landi, too, an old friend who had truly helped me in early difficulties, advised me to remain in Florence. The Medici had been expelled; and Piero thought I should wait for a time to see what would happen. And so I began to work on the new market-place, and set a number of precious stones, for which I gained much money.

"At this time there came to Florence a Sienese, by name Marretti, a man of active mind, who had lived for a long time in Turkey; and he ordered of me a gold medal to wear on his hat. I was to fashion on it a Hercules wrenching open the jaws of a lion. While I was engaged upon it, Michael Angelo Buonarroti came from time to time to look at the work. And as I had harassed myself much with it, and had conceived the Hercules and the rage of the animal very differently to any thing that had been produced before in representing this scene, and because this kind of work was new to the divine Michael Angelo, he praised my work, and excited in

me such a desire to do something superior, that
something very successful was indeed produced.

"The setting of precious stones now no longer
satisfied me. I gained richly by such work; but my
mind aimed at producing somewhat that required
greater art. And so it happened that a certain Federigo Ginori, a young man of noble mind (he had
lived long in Naples, and was so beautiful in form,
and so attractive in manner, that a princess there
fell in love with him), wished to have a medal made,
with an Atlas bearing the world on his back; and he
begged the great Michael Angelo to design the thing
for him. The latter told him to apply to a goldsmith named Benvenuto, who would serve him well,
and would need no design from himself. 'But,' he
continued, 'that you may not imagine that I will
not gladly do you the small favor, I will make a
sketch for it. Speak, meanwhile, with Benvenuto,
that he may also model something to show you how
he thinks of doing it. Whichever succeeds best shall
be executed.'

"Federigo Ginori came to me, and told me what
his wish was, — how much the wonderful Michael
Angelo had praised me; and how I was to model
something in wax, while the marvellous man himself had promised to draw a sketch. These words
from the great man incited me so much, that I at
once began with the greatest care to make a model.
When I was ready with it, a painter named Giuliano
Bugiardini, very intimate with Michael Angelo, came
and brought me the drawing of the Atlas.* I

* See Appendix, Note VII.

showed Bugiardini at once my little wax model,
which was very different from Michael Angelo's
design; and both Federigo and Bugiardini came to
the conclusion that the thing must be done after my
model. And so I began; and the most excellent
Michael Angelo saw and praised my work as in-
valuable. It was a figure embossed in silver; the
celestial sphere on its back being a ball of crystal,
and the ground *lapis lazuli*."

Cellini subsequently relates how the beautiful
Ginori died of consumption; the medal came into
the hands of a Florentine, through whom the King
of the French saw it; and the latter by this means
had his attention first drawn to him. His connection with Francis I., however, was the most important part of his life. And thus it may be said, if we
attach the value of a chain of destiny to any such
connection of events, that the meeting with Michael
Angelo had a decided influence upon Cellini's entire
future.

How freshly the Florentine life of that period
comes before us in his narrative, in which Michael
Angelo is brought for a moment out of obscurity into
bright light! The mausoleum may still have been
his principal work. He must have discussed the
matter with the Duke of Urbino, when he was in
Florence in April, 1527. This inference seems natural, although we find no mention made of it.

One thing more, however, occurred in this year.
The new Government endeavored to compensate for
the injustice which Michael Angelo had suffered
by the transfer of the block of marble to Bandinelli.

The latter had left the city with the Medici. The block, twenty-one feet high, stood in his atelier. By a decree of the 22d August, the consiglio grande awarded it to Michael Angelo, and, with the most flattering expressions, consigned the work to him. He was to begin it, if agreeable to him, on the 1st November, and to remain occupied with it until the figure was completed, — an arrangement which was probably not without a double signification, inasmuch as he received a pension as long as the work lasted.

I know not whether Michael Angelo touched the marble himself. The sketch of what he intended to do is preserved in a small model, which is now in the Kensington Museum, and which I have not seen myself. But I will quote an extract from a letter of my friend Joseph Joachim, who communicated with me respecting it. " The Hercules and Cacus are powerful. The whole thing is only roughly sketched on a small scale. In the former, the head and arm are wanting. The body seems to me to stand there in conscious power, ready for action; and, by the movement of the shoulders, and the bending of the strong back, we see how well able he was to wield the club, which was to give the death-stroke to Cacus, who lies there, held down by the right knee of the demi-god, vainly endeavoring by the movements of his left leg to entangle the left leg of Hercules, while his right arm involuntarily tries to avert the death-stroke from his head. The whole figure is like a coil, — a striking contrast to the powerful, victorious hero who had cast him on the ground."

This representation was intended, like the David, to signify symbolically the victory of the Florentine republic over her enemies, in the same sense as Donatello had before executed his Judith, and Benvenuto Cellini subsequently produced his Perseus conquering the Medusa.

6.

Events, however, interrupted such thoughts. The decree of the consiglio of the 22d August, 1527, may be considered as one of the last tokens of good faith in the successful issue of affairs. For, at the very time when they were thus debating in Florence upon the adornment of the palace, the army of the allies was defeated before Naples. Two days after the 28th, Lautrec, the French general-in-chief, died of a pestilential sickness which had broken out in the camp; and the greatest part of his soldiers followed him. Naples had just been on the point of submitting to the French, when by a sudden turn the Imperialists became victorious, if we can so call the fact of no enemy being any longer there. The cause of the emperor gained the ascendency in Italy. The pope began to feel that Spain was the side to which he must turn; and the citizens of Florence were again in the position of deliberating whether they would join Spain or France.

The resolve which was now taken was decisive: the parties stood closely opposed to each other. The pope, to whom it was deeply mortifying to re-instate his family in Florence, with the help of those Spaniards who had been just mistreating him so shamefully, left no means untried to regain the city without their assistance. His efforts were noiseless: with gentle application he demanded little; but they knew what lay behind. Capponi urged that they should negotiate direct with the emperor, or that they should rely on the pope. Neither the one nor the other was effected. It was resolved that they should adhere to the league with France.

The alliance with France was inseparable from the idea of the old Florentine freedom. There was a saying, that, if the heart of a Florentine were cut in two, a golden lily would be found in it. Luigi Alamanni, one of the noblest citizens of the town, who, having shared in the conspiracy of the year 1521, had been obliged to live abroad, and had become a friend of the great Doria, who at that time passed with the Genoese fleet from the service of Francis 1. into that of Charles, returned in the autumn of 1528, only for the sake of making it plain to the citizens, that there was now but one way of safety, — direct negotiation with the emperor. Doria himself was willing to conduct the negotiations. Nothing, he urged, would afford the city such great security against the Medici as such a step; and that this was indeed the truth, was the cause of the pope's fear that such a resolution might be taken in Florence. But Clement need not have feared danger on this side. Alamanni's words were in vain: so little could he prevail, that his own sentiments were doubted, and he was pointed at as an enemy to liberty. They would adopt no middle course.

It proved Capponi's ruin, that he notwithstanding attempted this; and it was for this reason that Michael Angelo must have belonged to his adversaries. For the gonfalonier could have managed the different parties; but above the parties there was a set of men, whom Busini enumerates as the flower of the citizens when he records these divisions of the city: these he could not deceive. They desired liberty; nothing more. Enthusiastically adhering to the idea, rather than understanding by it any thing definite and practically attainable, their sincere desire was to awaken, as it were, the good spirit of Florence. Unfortunately, fate decreed that a demon should arise instead; and no verdict of ours can deny this.

Michael Angelo's family did not belong to the nobility of the city. He himself was not rich; he was no open adherent of Savonarola, nor was he one of the Arrabiati. He had no defined course; he stood forth on any side which manifested an inclination to that ideal of freedom which filled his heart, but the nature of which he could have as little translated into words, as we can any feeling deeply rooted in the heart. It can only be shown by occasional actions.

Capponi's principles were not equally high. He was reckoned among the nobility of the city. They said the pope had rendered him submissive by having promised Caterina, the Duchess of Urbino, to his eldest son. He had wished to make the other a cardinal. It would have been unnatural if the gonfalonier had not paid regard to this, or had left unnoticed the claims of the other noble families, whose anger against the Medici only proceeded from the fact that they had curtailed their privilege of co-operation in acting the tyrant. Capponi, who had grown up in these pretensions, was obliged at first to accommodate himself to them.

And thus it was. The real Government of the city consisted of eighty citizens, the assembly of the highest magistrates. To these the foreign ambassadors addressed themselves; and the reports of their own were first brought before them. Capponi summoned the nobles of the city to this assembly, as if it were a matter of course, as though access belonged to them as lords by birth. They did not vote; but they took part in the sessions, — men of experience, trained in the art of making their opinions plausible. Biassed by them, the eighty ventured not to speak as they thought, often even not to vote as they intended. Then, again, the eighty changed in short intervals, as the majority of the high offices were always held only for a short time; the nobles remained ever the same. Instead of soliciting offices, they even declined them. They did not require them; they would have been a hinderance to them. And thus the Government centred in this one fixed, and at the same time independent body, to whom the ambassadors of foreign powers involuntarily turned, and by whom thus indirectly the fate of the city was decided.

The Arrabiati would have put an end to this, had it not been for the Piagnoni, who were fawned upon by the nobles, with Capponi at their head. Besides,

the bulk of the population — the lower class of inhabitants, possessing no political rights, and without
a share in the consiglio grande — was dependent on
the nobles, most of them being in their employ.
And thus the Arrabiati remained in the minority
between two powers, against both of which their
weapons failed.

With the year 1529, the strife of parties began.
Hitherto within the city the plague had depressed
the public life, whilst from without no danger had
threatened. France and Venice held their ground
against the emperor, and carried on the war. When
the plague had now disappeared, and the approxi-
mation of pope and emperor had become a public
matter, Capponi's doubtful sentiments were soon put
to the test.

Was Florence to defend herself with arms, if she
were attacked by the Medici? The nearer the spring
approached, the more urgent became the necessity
of coming to a decision. Scarcity prevailed. One of
those moments was again at hand, when undefined
anxiety bursts forth, and parties intermingle. Apprehensions arose without any one knowing why
the aspect of things just now looked so much worse.
Each was suspiciously observed by the other; and
secret alliances with the pope were everywhere conjectured. The gonfalonier was forbidden by the
State to negotiate in any way with the Medici.
Then, on the 15th April, the letter escaped him,
revealing secret correspondence with the agents of
the pope. One of his worst enemies, an Arrabiate,
was the successful discoverer. After the utmost

scandal in the palace of the Government, Capponi
was obliged at once to lay down his office. His defence, pleaded in the consiglio grande, saved him
from the charge of high treason. There was an
end, however, to his mild, palliating manner of
directing public affairs. Carducci, who had been
twice proposed in vain by the Arrabiati, was elected
in the excitement of the moment,—a man whom, in
other times, neither birth nor ability would have
raised so high; a political upstart, whose hatred to
the Medici furnished his best guarantee for useful-
ness, whose opinions compensated for what he lacked
in statesmanlike keenness, and whose honesty the
city seemed more in need of than the suspicious
dexterity of Capponi. A decided step was made in
his election. The pope could not have been told
more plainly what he might have to expect. He
saw himself now for the first time in truth ejected,
and driven almost by force to the emperor, to be
obliged to seek help of whom was the hardest thing
that fate could have laid upon him. And, like him,
the city also, who, however energetically under Capponi she had refused the return of the Medici, now
for the first time treated the proscription of the family as an actual thing.

The new gonfalonier, when he entered upon his
office, was in perfect accordance with the majority
of the citizens. Nothing, however, could compensate
for the help of a party working for him secretly, as
the Palleski had done for Capponi. Even he had
been obliged to yield so far as to take the diplomatic
representatives at foreign courts from the popular

party, and to let the nobles who had hitherto held these posts change places with them. Now, when a democrat, without rank and name, occupied the first place in the State, and the aristocrats in Florence were allowed only their strict legal measure of participation even at the deliberations of the Government, the direction of things was left to the energy of well-inclined but unskilful citizens.

Carducci, of course, endeavored at once to pacify the nobles and the Piagnoni, and to propitiate them. With his own party he did his utmost to bring about Capponi's acquittal, who left the palace as if in triumph. But Carducci's power was still less than Capponi's. If, as a good citizen, he endeavored to secure the eighty from all unlawful influence, he was soon obliged to be so far subordinate to them, that he was nothing but the receiver of their votes. While decrees had formerly been passed under the influence of the Palleski, these were not only now excluded by Carducci, but he admitted the sixteen standard-bearers of the people; citizens whose office consisted in bearing the standards in times of need, under which the citizens were divided, for the defence of the palace at the summons of the gonfalonier,—men who understood affairs of State less than any one else. It was now almost impossible to preserve secrecy. They recounted in the streets what had been propounded or decreed in the secret conferences of the Government, and what was contained in the dispatches of the ambassadors. The Palleski, on the other hand, assembled among themselves. No one knew what was going on with them. They were observed and feared. Men began to perceive that it might occur, that, forsaken by France, they would have to oppose the emperor alone. Without knowing why, they felt things were going downwards; and the defence of the city, which had before stood before them only as a general probability, forced itself upon them with greater and greater certainty, as a contingency that might surely be expected, and which rendered the prosecution of the fortification works a matter of the utmost importance and urgency.

Capponi had been against the fortification of the city. He was of opinion that it was not possible to approach near; but that, if they did approach, the best works would fail to defend her. Through all the years of Clement's rule, fortifications had been made, for which one of the first generals of the time had designed extensive plans. Under Capponi, too, these had been slowly carried on. In the autumn of 1528, the matter had been a little more seriously thought of; but it had not much advanced. In April, 1529, Michael Angelo was appointed superintendent of the fortifications of Florence and the cities of the Florentine territory; while they endeavored to obtain Malatesta Baglioni, the head of the ruling family in Perugia, as commander-in-chief of the army.

Michael Angelo's energy had been one of those things which ran counter to Capponi's mind, and which he, however, could not prevent. The gonfalonier had endeavored to counteract it indirectly. On the occasional absence of Michael Angelo, who could not always be in Florence, he either ordered works already begun to remain untouched, or even to be demolished. But the days of his office were at that time numbered; and, with Carducci's appearance, the sluggishness of the Government was changed into an activity and animation, which Michael Angelo, unusual as was his power for work, could now scarcely satisfy.

Florence is divided into two parts,—the real Florence, the city situated to the north of the Arno; and the smaller part built to the south of the river, which lies, with regard to the larger, much as Sachsenhausen does to Frankfort-on-the-Maine. The attack might first be expected here. Here the surrounding heights were most contiguous to the walls, so that whoever possessed himself of them commanded the whole of Florence with his artillery. For this reason a fortification of the most adjacent height appeared necessary; and Michael Angelo began with that of San Miniato; while, with regard to the country surrounding the northern city, he undertook at first only an accurate survey and estimate of the buildings lying outside the city walls, the destruction of which was to ensue when the danger became more urgent.

Florence was at that time surrounded with suburbs, consisting of churches, monasteries, and palaces, to which numerous country houses to a vast extent were attached. These, too, would have to be destroyed, as affording accommodation to a hostile army. So valuable was this girdle of buildings, that for that reason the siege of the city had been hitherto considered impossible in Italy. The citizens would never have resolved thus to rage against their own property. It seems therefore natural that they should now at least delay their destruction. All the more expeditiously were the works at San Miniato carried on. Michael Angelo rejected the old plan of the Medici, which had also had this height in view. He drew the lines closer together. The peasants of the surrounding country were summoned; and the work was carried on by him with such zeal, that his brick bastions rose from the ground with wonderful rapidity.

Four places were intended for defence besides the capital, — Pisa, Livorno, Cortona, and Arezzo. The two first indispensably so, because by them communication with the sea was kept open; the two others because they lay in the way of the army approaching from the south. From the north, for a time, nothing was to be feared. In that direction they had only to keep some mountain-passes occupied. Besides, the Duke of Ferrara stood as general-in-chief in the service of the Florentine republic; and united with Venice, who might like himself be depended on as an irreconcilable enemy of the pope, he would allow nothing to approach the frontiers of Tuscany. Ferrara as well as Venice possessed papal cities, which, if ever an alliance should be effected between pope and emperor, must have been defended as well as Florence.

In April, May, and June, 1529, we see Michael Angelo partly in Florence, and partly employed in person with the fortifications of Pisa and Livorno.

Letters are still extant, in which his presence is required, and which contain records of his subsequent journeys of inspection. He received plans, and sent them back revised. From the urgency with which he is written about, and the repeated answer that he could not get away, we may conclude how much he was occupied with his office, and that he was the soul of general activity.

The dispatches of the Venetian ambassadors, however, show at the same time that more and more the hope was vanishing, that King Francis would come with an army to Italy. The two French princes were hostages in Madrid. The king could not bear to be deprived of his children any longer. He had intended to appear with forty thousand foot, two thousand horse, and four hundred knights. His coming was held as certain as the arrival of the emperor was considered doubtful; but the indications of having been deceived became stronger and stronger.

In the meanwhile, nothing decisive had taken place, and all was conjecture. In Lombardy, the united French and Venetian power kept the Imperialists besieged in Milan. In Naples, the troops of the allies had again the advantage over the Spaniards. The pope, too, was ill; and the tidings respecting him made a breaking-up of things at Rome seem possible. Clement, exhausted by the events of the last few years, had been very near death in December, 1528; and, since then, had not regained his strength. His malady increased again in the spring, and his death was expected. Instead of this, on the 13th June, the disheartening intelligence arrived of the defeat of the French in Lombardy, and at the same time a dispatch from France respecting the impending reconciliation between the emperor and the king.

If matters had been thus with Francis I. before the disaster in Lombardy, they knew now that no hope remained of his assistance. He would be obliged to leave the Italian allies to their fate. Affairs had so changed their aspect, that, on the Genoese coast, the landing of Spanish troops was expected, and the inhabitants of Spezia fled with their property to Genoa. They were soon also informed that the pope had recovered, the contract between him and the emperor for the common subjection of the city was concluded, and the Prince of Orange had arrived in Rome to prepare for the campaign.

The same German soldiery and Spaniards who had made Rome a desert, and had carried their defiance of the pope himself to extreme lengths, entered the papal service; and Orange, who resided at the Vatican, was stimulated to greater energy by Clement, through the hope of Caterina's hand. Guicciardini writes at that time, that the strongest he could say, respecting the papal court, must appear too weak, — that the life at the Vatican was infamous, and a type of every thing condemnable. Is it to be wondered at, if the people of that day strove to free themselves from the rule of these priests; and if Luther's doctrines, after having for a time diffused themselves in Germany like a secret fire, now burst forth in all lands? Throughout Europe an echo was awakened of that which had been preached in Germany for ten years. For every one saw how things were going at Rome. Charles needed the pope, because he wished to be crowned; Clement needed Charles, because he would rather have his own native city destroyed, than not see his family ruling there. Charles's, however, were at least the grand, extensive plans of a circumspect and slowly advancing ruler; Clement's was the avengeful, capricious policy of a furious, narrowminded man, to whom falsehood and treachery were as daily bread. I cannot find a single trait in this pope, which allows a higher feeling to arise than that of pity. There is something effeminately sickly in his nature, which makes him insufferable; and this is rendered uncomfortably striking in his portraits.

Still no open proceedings against Florence were taken at Rome. The preparations nominally aimed at the war against Perugia. Malatesta Baglioni was to be chastised for having undertaken the command of the Florentine troops against the will of the pope. Siena also was to receive chastisement. Malatesta would, perhaps, now have joined the pope, had he not been convinced, that not a single point of the promises by which he was allured would be kept. The Sienese also would have regarded with delight the misfortune of the Florentines, whom they hated, but that the old tyranny would have been again established among them by the Medici. For a time, therefore, Tuscany held together against the pope; even the tyrant of Piombino offered his troops for money. But, in this union of the entire land, there was not a touch of uniting national feeling. It was alone brought about by the calculations of individual members, whose common advantage was opposed to any other course. We must observe this, to feel how active, free, and natural was the position of Florence. Here, too, there was a selfish policy; but the actions of the citizens acquire a mixture of child-like simplicity, which calls forth our deepest sympathy. They carried in their heart an ideal, to which they were willing to sacrifice themselves.

7.

On the 20th July, the importation of supplies into the city began. Every one was to fill the storerooms of his house as full as possible. The year had been a good one, and favored the laying-up of provisions. Three thousand men worked on the walls; ten thousand soldiers were in the pay of the republic; there were, besides, four thousand armed citizens, and new troops were daily enlisted. On the 24th, the destruction of the suburbs began. The houses were broken down with battering rams such as the ancients used; trees and underwood in the gardens were hewn down and manufactured into fascines. Houses, palaces, and churches fell to the ground; all lent a hand, and helped in the work of destruction. Like sailors on board ship, says Varchi, they kept time when the cords were drawn back and again loosened, as they moved the heavy beams. The possessors of the buildings often helped most eagerly in their ruin. So thoroughly did the spirit of freedom dwell in the

The Last Supper.

ANDREA DEL SARTO.

mass of the people; and only in a few of the richest families was any resistance manifested in sacrificing what belonged to them.

In this work of destruction, there occurred one of those little natural marvels which witness to the power of art over men. A number of peasants and soldiers were engaged in demolishing the monastery of San Salvi. A part of the building lay already in ruins, when they reached the refectory, where, as was usual, the Last Supper was painted on the large wall. This work, which is still standing at the present day on the half-destroyed walls, fresh and in good preservation, as if all had only just occurred, is a fresco painting of Andrea del Sarto, and is one of the finest things he has produced.

Del Sarto would have been mentioned as one of the most important of the Florentine artists, had he not stood so utterly unconnected with his contemporaries. A few years younger than Raphael, he yet belongs to those masters who would be styled modern in comparison with Michael Angelo and Leonardo; but, compared with those who formed the majority at about 1529, must be styled old. With regard to the intrinsic value of his works, he stands somewhat on a level with Fra Bartolomeo: he possessed superior gifts; but there is a lack of that comprehensive intellectual culture, which, at the beginning of the sixteenth century, was indispensable in keeping pace with Raphael, Michael Angelo, and Leonardo. His drawing is noble, and often grand in its simplicity. His coloring is never brilliant; but it is harmonious to the most delicate shades. It

has that peculiar paleness or light which belongs
especially to Florentine coloring, and may be explained by the influence of fresco painting. Andrea del Sarto wanted but little to have been a
genius of the first rank ; but this little he lacks all
the more perceptibly. Vasari thus expresses his
own opinion concerning him. If there had been any
thing prouder and bolder in Andrea's nature, he
says, he would have been without an equal ; but a
certain timidity of mind, a pliability of character,
and a desire not to render himself conspicuous, prevented that living fire of conscious independence
from infusing itself into his works, by which he
might have attained to the greatest heights in his
art : he lacked grandeur and exuberance. Vasari,
however, measures him by the highest standard.

Del Sarto was only once in Rome : but he soon
left ; and, except a short sojourn in France, he never
quitted Florence, where, during twenty years, he held
the same rank which Sebastian del Piombo maintained in Rome. When Michael Angelo was summoned to the pope in 1525, he consigned to him the
young Vasari, who had been his own pupil. But
that Michael Angelo should have said, with regard
to Del Sarto, that he knew one in Florence who
would compete with Raphael, is one of the many
opinions which subsequent writers have placed in
his lips without having any other source than hear-
say. Had he expressed this, it would have been
only in derision.

Del Sarto died when he was scarcely forty years
old. He has produced much. Florence is rich in

his works, and we find them in many galleries: but
the finest are in his native city, where we can alone
arrive at a just conception of his manner of painting; for he is most bold and natural in his fresco
paintings.

It is possible that his painting in the monastery
of San Salvi was saved by Michael Angelo's express
command. For he directed the demolition of the suburbs; and, without his consent, no exception could
have been made. Many other works of art met
with no forbearance; and, even within the walls,
much was at that time lost. Gold and silver works
were melted down; pictures and statues were sold
by the possessors in their distress, and were carried
abroad, especially to France. Francis I. had his
agent for these in Florence, — a man named Batista
della Palla, who, turning to advantage the distress
for money of the citizens, purchased on all sides
works of art, and sent them away.

Vasari relates one of these cases. That Borgherini, who was so intimate with Michael Angelo, —
one of the richest of the noble Florentine bankers,
— had left the city when the siege began, and had
repaired to Lucca. There was in his palace a room,
painted by the first masters, and furnished with
artistic magnificence to the smallest article. Puntormo, a pupil of Michael Angelo's, had been especially engaged in it, — an artist best known at the
present day from having executed some paintings
after the cartoons of his master.* This valuable
room seemed a real booty to the agent of the king.

* See Appendix, Note VIII.

It was the property of one of those who had fled,
and was outlawed. The Government knew how to
represent to Batista della Palla, that no more suitable gift from the republic to the king could be
found than the complete contents of this apartment;
and he received permission to place himself in possession of it.

Borgherini's consort had been left in the palace.
She was to receive in money whatever had been paid
for the works. With a patent of absolute authority,
Batista presented himself to her. She, however, did
not allow herself to be intimidated. "Do you venture, wretched broker, to penetrate here," she called
to him, "and to rob the palaces of the nobles of their
ornaments, that you may fill the houses of foreigners
with them, for the sake of your own miserable gain?
Yet I am less astonished at you, plebeian soul and
enemy of my country, than I am at the Government
which favors such crimes. This bed here, which
you wish to carry off to procure gain for your covetousness, although you assume the appearance of
doing it with regret, is my bridal-bed, for the adornment of which the father of my husband had these
regal ornaments made, and which I honor for his
sake and for the sake of my husband; and I will
defend it with my blood before you shall touch it.
Away with your accomplices! Tell them who gave
you authority to rob me, if they wish to present gifts
to King Francis, they may plunder their own houses
and apartments; and, if you venture to return, you
shall learn how I will then send you back!" It
does not seem that Della Palla made a second at-

tempt. Others defended their property with less
energy; many thanked Heaven that in such evil
times there were those who gave money for their
goods; whilst others, as the Medici themselves had
done before they departed, melted down their gold
and silver utensils, which in almost all houses were
of artistic value in their form. Not only did they
wish to win money for themselves, but that the State
might not be in distress for want of it.

The houses that had been thrown down were now
to be transformed into fortifications. The Government sent Michael Angelo to Ferrara, to see the
famous fortifications there, and to confer with the
duke. He left the city on July 20th, and arrived
in Ferrara in the evening of the 2d August, where
he at once presented his letters to the Florentine
ambassador. He declined taking up his abode with
the latter, as the ambassador expressly mentions in
his dispatch announcing Michael Angelo's arrival.
Accurate account was at that time kept, by diploma-
tists, of all these trifles; and, just as the ambassador
would have set down the expenses accruing to him
from Michael Angelo's accommodation, the latter
without doubt was repaid on his return whatever he
had spent at an inn.

Ferrara was at that time the real military State in
Italy; and the duke was considered a perfect adept
as regarded politics and the direction of war. His
rule had been a continuous chain of difficulties, all
of which he overcame, and none of which he allowed
to prevent him from advancing his country and his
own family to the utmost.

"We hope," thus it was written from Florence to the ambassador,[*] "that nothing will be neglected to evidence to the duke what a man Michael Angelo is, and what a high opinion of him is cherished by the Government." Every thing was at once vouchsafed to him. When in company with the ambassador he had had a view of the city and fortifications, he repeated the survey in company with the duke himself. Riding with him, he received information upon every point from his lips. "His Excellency," says the ambassador, "has received Michael Angelo with the utmost friendliness."

He remained more than a week in Ferrara. When he took leave of the palace, the duke detained him. Jestingly he declared him to be his prisoner, and, as a ransom, required from him the promise that he would paint a picture for him. Michael Angelo agreed, and again set out for Florence, where they had been working at the fortifications day and night during his absence, the feast-days not excepted. With longing they awaited his arrival, and the result of the conferences with the duke.

For it was just during his absence that the position of things had taken the worst turn possible for Florence. Positive tidings had arrived of the peace which had been concluded at Cambray.[†] It was now certain that the Florentines were forsaken by France, and were given up to the pope. Francis I. had submitted to Spanish superiority. Venice and Ferrara now also struck sail. The last hope for Florence rested on the possibility of her offering

---

[*] See Appendix, Note IX.   [†] *Ibid.*, Note X.

resistance long enough for affairs, at that time so variable, to assume a more favorable aspect. Now, when matters so stood that the choice lay before them of adopting this extreme course, and, as the Palleski thought, of madly challenging fate, the latter effected that an embassy should be sent to the emperor to negotiate directly with him. Capponi had always desired this, but at times when it was not possible. For now, when fixed treaties existed between the pope and emperor, nothing more could issue from it.

But the embassy only served to furnish a sort of pretext to Ferrara and Venice for abandoning Florence. They declared the conduct of the city to be an act of faithlessness; and while Charles, it is true, received the ambassadors in Genoa, he gave an indefinite reply to their indefinite proposals, and advanced to Bologna; Alessandro and Ippolito in his immediate suite; Spanish troops, which had accompanied his fleet, slowly following; and a German army approaching from the north, having for the time no other destination than, united with the Spaniards, to form an imposing power in Italy.

At the same time, south of Perugia, the union of the army took place, which, under Orange, as was now openly declared, was to march against Florence. The Duke of Ferrara forbade his son to accept the command assigned him by the Florentines. How matters stood with Venice is shown by a clause in the treaty of Cambray, according to which the king had engaged to let his own fleet co-operate against the republic in case the cities on the Nea-

politan eastern coast, which has been taken possession of, were not surrendered within a fixed term.
The Florentines wished to make resistance; and,
with that strange cheerfulness which, in times of
need, breaks forth in all minds when every power is
strained, the arrival of the enemy was awaited.

He appeared sooner than they had thought. In
the second week of September, Perugia was given
up. They had intended to defend it; but Malatesta
yielded his city to the prince, with the permission
of the Florentine Government, and withdrew to
Arezzo. This gave a blow to the citizens, coura-
geous as they were. They suggested sending ambassadors to the pope, the mere proposal of which
had been before declared treason. But it was not
carried. The man most opposed to it was Capello,
the Venetian ambassador. For what reason, his
dispatches tell us. He had neglected no means,
he there says, in making plain to the nobles in the
palace that such a step would be their sure ruin;
for it is clear, these are his words, that, if an agreement now took place between Clement and the city,
the army of the prince would throw itself upon
Apulia, Urbino, and the Romagna, or unite in
Lombardy with the troops of the emperor, to operate
against Venice. Whilst Capello, therefore, feigned
the most solicitous friendship for the Florentines, all
that he did was only for the advantage of his own
Government.

On the 16th September, Malatesta came to Florence to inspect the fortifications. Arezzo was to be
held at any price. On the 8th, Michael Angelo had

been required there to give good advice. On the 18th, however, the Florentine troops had marched away. The day before, Cortona had fallen. Within a few days, the war, which was to have been carried on and fought on the remote frontiers of Tuscany, was brought close to the walls of Florence, and a tone of feeling was excited in the city, which threatened momentarily to bring about some decisive act before arms were resorted to.

For until now the Medici party had held their ground in Florence. They would not give up their influence upon the resolutions of the Government. They hoped for a settlement of things which might allow of the return of the Medici, without forfeiting too much of their independence. They so far succeeded that the ambassadors to the pope were chosen; and, in order to effect an immediate check to the movements of the imperial army, a citizen was dispatched before the embassy to announce its arrival. Clement, however, would now hear of nothing but unconditional and immediate subjection; and he ordered the command to be communicated at once to the heads of the Medicæan party, that they should leave Florence, and appear in Rome.

The position of affairs was of such a nature, that the Palleski might now have succeeded in bringing about a revolution in favor of the Medici. They had already carried matters so far, that a part of the authorities were convinced of the necessity of sending a citizen to Rome, furnished with unlimited power. Yet the gonfalonier kept his ground in opposing them. Had, however, the Prince of Orange been one day's journey nearer the city on the 18th September,* nothing would have stopped the general feeling, and a capitulation would have been concluded. For a panic of fear seized the citizens. The sudden arrival of Malatesta's soldiers had given rise to the idea that he himself was in the pope's pay, and would deliver up the city which was in his power. Many left Florence. The Palleski, who had been summoned by the pope, fled for the greater part to the court at Bologna; many others, driven away by fear alone, took refuge in the surrounding cities. And among those who thus sought safety by flight, we find Michael Angelo.

He had especial grounds for regarding the cause of the city as lost. He fancied he had observed intentional carelessness in the behavior of the general in his arrangements for arming the walls. The height of San Miniato, as the best of the fortifications before the southern city, had been specially assigned to Malatesta; and the manner in which he had placed the cannons there astonished Michael Angelo so much, that he questioned Mario Orsini, one of the other principal people in the pay of the republic, about it.

"You must know that these are all traitors of Baglioni's," he replied. Michael Angelo hastened to the palace, and expressed his apprehensions. They heard him, derided him, and reproached him with want of courage. The lords of the Government had been too often on that day informed of similar things; and they cut short the suspicions and

* See Appendix, Note XI.

Portrait of the Artist.

ANDREA DEL SARTO.

apprehensions brought before them. Their first duty was to appear strong and secure, and to allow no doubts to arise.

Agitated and offended, Michael Angelo left the palace. In the street he met a friend, Rinaldo Corsini, who assured him that within a few hours the Medici would be in the city, and invited him to fly with him. And so convinced was Michael Angelo of the truth of what Corsini imparted to him, that he resolved to leave the city.

Many have endeavored to exculpate Michael Angelo; and the decision has been arrived at, that, although his weakness may be pardoned as a natural feeling, which might completely master any one, yet nothing frees him from the reproach of not having done his duty as a citizen. Nothing, however, was more natural than his flight. It was evident to him that Malatesta was a traitor. Instead of being listened to by the Government, he had been requited with scorn, and was offended. He foresaw how, on the following day, those who still so energetically set aside every interposition and precaution, would be silenced by Malatesta or Orange. He would be no witness to the destruction. He had his old father, his brothers, and their families, who could not exist without him. He must preserve his life for them. He had three thousand ducats sewn up in his clothes; he mounted his horse, called his servant Antonio Mini to mount likewise, and endeavored to escape from the city with Corsini.* The gates were closed. They tried one after another;

* See Appendix, Note XII.

at last they found a passage through the Porta di
Prato. A voice rose from the guard keeping watch
there, inquiring whether it was Michael Angelo,
one of the Nine, who demanded egress. As chief
superintendent of the fortifications, Michael Angelo
belonged to the committee of the " Nine Men super-
intending military affairs," who, as a sort of staff,
were under the orders of the " Ten Men regulating
matters of war and peace." And so, when the
watch heard his name at the gate, they allowed him
and his companions to pass through freely.

II.

The object of their flight was Venice. They rode
towards the north, where, on this side the Apennines,
there is a point of the territory of Ferrara. They
came to a halt at Castelnuovo in the Carfagnana;
for thus the tract of land is called, belonging to the
Duke of Ferrara. Here a tragic meeting took place.
They were met by Tommaso Soderini, the brother of
the cardinal, and Niccolo Capponi, members of the
embassy sent to the emperor, who, after having been
kept for a time in suspense, and consoled with uncertain words, were at length convinced of the vanity
of their efforts, and had come as far as Castelnuovo
on their return journey. They hesitated to go to
Florence. Michael Angelo refused to see Capponi;*
but, through Corsini, the latter learned how things
stood at home; and the tidings he heard so completely

---

* See Appendix, Note XIII.

disheartened the broken-down old man, that they
terminated his career. He lay down and died; while
Soderini went to Pisa, and from thence, when threatened with proscription, he proceeded to Florence.
The Soderini had had their downfall in 1523, when
the cardinal failed at the papal election; the events
of 1530 gave the final blow to the family.

From the Carfagnana they continued their flight
across the mountains to Ferrara. Immediately behind Ferrara, Polisella lies on the Po; and, from
here, Venice is reached most easily by water. Just
as they were embarking from here, Corsini begged
Michael Angelo to stop. He wished to return to
the city once more, and asked Michael Angelo to wait
for him. Corsini, however, did not return. The
Florentine ambassador had persuaded him so urgently, that he resolved to turn the other way.
Michael Angelo proceeded to Venice alone with his
servant. He sailed down the Po, if he chose that
route, then along the coast of the Adriatic towards
the north, and reached the city, — the only one at
that time of all Italy which had preserved its old
freedom, in the true sense of the word.

The history of the destinies of Venice appears
like a poem of the imagination in the midst of the
great records of human events. Wherever elsewhere
great occurrences shape themselves, we see a people,
a country, a political development of the State alternating almost necessarily in various transitions from
its commencement to its fall. Here there is nothing
of all this. There is no people; for an assembly of
men with no distinct origin formed the State: there

is no country; for on a swampy soil in the middle of
the sea they built a city without walls, and the territory that they conquered in addition consisted of
parts lying widely separated,—a piece of Lombardy,
a couple of seaports in Italy, Greek islands, Greek
continent; nests everywhere clinging to the rocks
on the sea-shore, each of which is only a chance
possession, which is either exchanged or dispensed
with. It is as if England at the present day consisted
only of Corfu, Gibraltar, Ireland, India, Australia,
and Canada, with London as the ruling centre of all,
but without England,—the city lying alone in the
middle of the ocean. Thus was it with the Venetians;
the sea and the deck of their vessels was their country. And, lastly, there was no progress; for what
the Venetians have been as a State they have been
just as much from the first: an aristocracy entwined
together with iron rivets, and drawn closer and closer
together, formed the ruling element. Never has the
domination of parties been permitted; never has there
existed a popular political life; never have men appeared, who, upraised from the masses, have placed
themselves at the head of affairs: and when, after a
thousand years' existence, her fall took place, it was
a sudden breaking-down and disappearance. There
was no echo of the old magnificence. There is no
one in the present day in whose mind dwells the idea
of the old splendor of the Venetian State; for the
Venetians of our own time have nothing in common
with the spirit of those families whose names stand
registered in the golden book. The city herself
alone remains,—her palaces empty, like beautiful

blown eggs, from which no young ones can any more be hatched. Florence and Rome and Genoa are no longer what they were; but the change of centuries has never extinguished their active life, and a moving multitude ever fills their streets. But Venice stands there like a theatre, on whose scenes the bright sun is shining, while the heroes who acted within her walls have departed or disappeared for ever.

Even at that time, in the year 1530, when Michael Angelo came to Venice, the growth of her power stood still, or retrograded, which means the same; but still, wherever the fleets of the Republic appeared, they were more powerful than all the others of the Mediterranean. And this sea was at that time what the ocean is at the present; and Italy was the land of civilization, and the centre of the world. It is true, the Turks had destroyed the Indian commerce of the Venetians through Egypt; and Spain and Portugal had begun to ransack India and America by more circuitous routes. But Venice still formed the centre of communication. For as England's power at the present day depends on the political condition of all the five divisions of the globe, the States of which she surpasses by the immense energy with which she concentrates her powers; so the strength of Venice lay in the relations of European countries, over which she had the advantage.

The most brilliant period for Venice was that when, after the fall of the German empire, Europe separated into infinite fragments, and common co-operation for great ends seemed no longer possible. Princes had their hands fettered by their nobles; cities held back;

money was difficult to procure: if it were at last
raised, it was by many streams meeting together, and
was no constantly flowing source. In moments of
the greatest political importance, it was wanting.
Deaths in princely houses, family alliances, insur-
rections at home, caused inactivity or a change of
system, and prevented the pursuance of great plans.
There were nothing but sudden storms, which dis-
charged themselves now here and now there; and in
their chance recurrence there was no sure connection.
In Venice there was none of these disturbances. A
great immortal corporation sits on their rocks like
a flock of eagles looking out for prey. Money under
all circumstances was ready; men were never lacking.
There was no other hinderance in the resolutions of
the Government than the repose and precaution with
which they formed them: where it was necessary to
strike, they were able to do so. With admirable
acuteness affairs were considered, and the advantages
and disadvantages of undertakings weighed; personal passion was compelled to be silent; the influence
of events even was controlled; and absolute authority
was averted by the most accurate instructions. In
the election of the doge, out of thirty nobles chosen
by lot, nine were selected. These chose forty, twelve
of whom were again selected; these chose twenty-
five, and so on: the doge, who at last came forth,
was obliged to be confirmed again by the assembly of
all. It was impossible for him to elevate his family
as the popes could, or to cherish tyrannical desires
like the Medici; but it was impossible also for him
to meet with opposition like the Kings of Germany,

France, and Spain, in whose kingdoms rebellion knew no end. All the nobles united formed the one Republic, for the advantage of which every desire was abandoned, and which never was divided in its opinion respecting foreign countries.

We possess a beautiful letter of Aretino's, in which, comparing Rome and Venice, he exhibits the contrast which existed between these two heads of the world. "He who has not seen them," he writes, "knows not the two wonders of the world, — how, in Rome, fortune is pursued with presumptous bounds; whilst, in Venice, the Government advance step by step with serious and solemn dignity. There can be no stranger sight than the opposing confusion of the Roman court, compared with the quiet unity of the Republic of Venice. We could imagine the aspect of things in paradise without having seen it; but no mortal man who did not see Rome with his own eyes could have an idea of the intricate ways there, and of the grand simple path adopted by us. In both there are vast works interpenetrating each other; but in the one they advance with violent noise, in the other with imperceptible quietness.

"To him who comes to Venice," he continues, "all other cities must appear like miserable, poor houses. I could not help laughing recently at a Florentine, as he looked at a magnificently decorated gondola, with a bridal train in it, and the velvet, the gold, and the jewels which the bride presented to view. 'We are a heap of rags compared to it!' he cried out: and he was not wrong; for with us the wives of bakers and shoemakers appear as the wives of nobles scarcely do in other cities. We live here like Turkish pashas. And what provisions are to be had in Venice! Here, and not to Cyprus, the kingdom of Venus and Cupid should be transported; for every day is a holiday, and satiety and pain never follow. No one thinks of death and the end of things; and liberty appears with flying colors!"

Even this last phrase contains nothing untrue. For although the aristocracy in Venice had all power in their hands, and no shadow of direct influence fell to the lot of those who did not belong to them, such a division of authority was not only customary everywhere, but it was nowhere less felt than in Venice. For, in other countries and cities, the ruling aristocracy were obliged to maintain their high position amid continual disputes: in Venice, however, they soared safely above; and, while by this means the feeling of a decided contrast between high and low was removed, the masses of those who possessed mind and intelligence without high birth naturally adhered to the powerful families, who yielded freely and unreservedly to this influence. Woe to him who might have wished to act against the Government! But the Government was so sensitive, on the other hand, to the public feeling, and in all its endeavors aimed so entirely at meeting the general advantage, that an opposition, if it ever manifested itself, could only be the fruit of personal ambition or hatred against those who were casually in authority. Whatever then happened was the affair of the nobles among themselves, and did not affect the policy of the State. The people lived unconstrained and securely. In religious matters, they were more independent of Rome than elsewhere. Venice was the refuge of the exiled and the persecuted. If in those days the idea of one united free Italy had been possible, in connection with this city alone could it have been accomplished. But, when we speak of this, we must take into consideration how biassed every one at that time was by the laws which everywhere regulated the ordinary habits of life. Bygone ages still exercised all their charm. Universal right, awarded alike to each, was an idea which no one would have conceived. Transported into such circumstances at the present day, we should believe ourselves cast into fearful slavery, which, leaving none unfettered from his birth, dictated a path to the lowest as well as the highest, — a path from which it would only be possible for extraordinary natures to deviate.

2.

Such had been the condition of Venice when Michael Angelo went there for the first time thirty years before, although perhaps at that period he was too young to understand it perfectly. One thing, however, must have been new to him: a peculiar art had developed there during the interval. The commencement of it, which he had then seen, had been followed by wonderful improvement. For there had been painting in Venice, as elsewhere, even in the fifteenth century; and she had possessed distinguished masters, but they belonged to the old school, — sharply drawn outlines, rather filled up

with color than any absolute harmony of tone traceable in the picture itself from the first; severe con-
trasts of light and heavy opaque shadows were in
especial favor.   Giovanni Bellini worked in this
manner; he was the best painter in Venice when
Michael Angelo came there in the year 1494.   Since
then, two men of genius had appeared, who, like
Raphael and Michael Angelo in Florence and Rome,
took their own path, and called into being an art,
which, wonderful and peculiar as the city herself,
forms a new phenomenon.

Venice was modern.   She stood on no soil out of
which statues were brought to light; she had no
antique buildings telling of an old and venerable
civilization; nothing was there which, as a pattern
of old and perfect work, presented itself as a model
for that newly to be created.   There was no writer
giving information respecting the ancient Venetians,
and whose words rested in men's minds.   Secluded
and solitary, like a vast fleet lying at anchor in the
midst of the sea, the city had nothing but herself;
the feeling of the moment was that which filled her.
They spoke her own musical-sounding *patois;* and
in this her citizens sang and wrote, or spoke of war
and commerce, and affairs of State.   In the foreign
lands of the East, they saw strange buildings; and
after these they constructed their churches and palaces.   In the remote distance they saw indeed the
mainland and the chain of the Alps, but close around
them there was nothing but sky and sea; and more
familiar to their eyes than the charm of cultivated
plains, woods, and mountains, were the ever-chang-

ing, purer tints of waves and clouds. And as all art is a copy of that which fills the soul of man, so the painting which sprung up in Venice, disdaining the strong lines of the Romans and Florentines, took the brilliant coloring which played around the city for the expression of its ideas.

As music stands in relation to poetry, so does Titian's art to that of Raphael and Michael Angelo; just as life in Venice was music compared with the noise of Rome and the Florentine streets. There, running, riding, the clanking of swords, and bustle prevailed; while, in the canals of Venice, the gondolas flew hither and thither like twittering swallows. Once again I will let Aretino speak in a letter to Titian : —

"I leaned against the parapet of the window," — thus he writes, — "and looked down on the innumerable vessels with foreigners and Venetians in them, the Canal Grande furrowed with them, and the people on the banks looking on at the race of the gondolas, and crying 'Bravo!' I had all beneath me as far as the Rialto.

"And then I raised my eyes to the sky; and, since God created it, I never have seen it so beautiful, — such colors, such shadows, such light. It was just as those artists would delight in painting it, who envy you what you can do, and they cannot. First, the mass of buildings, the stone of which seemed changed by the evening glow into a nobler material created by art; then the clear atmosphere above, — a broad streak of light; then clouds hanging dark and gray, as if just going to burst forth, and seeming to touch the points of the houses, and so losing themselves in the distance, lighted up in front by the declining sun, and melting away into a softer, less burning red. What a mistress was nature at this moment! with what touches did she paint the atmosphere, making it recede far behind the palaces! There were places in the sky where it was blue with touches of green, places where it was green with streaks of blue, — one set off the other, one blended into the other. Titian, I was compelled to exclaim, where are you to paint it?"

I have never met with any trace of such enthusiastic contemplation of surrounding nature among the Romans or Florentines. Among them, there was rather aversion to the picturesque. The piercing sun made the light too glaring to them, the shadows too deep; they lacked the medium of the transparent mist, which subdued the lights, and did not rob the shadows of their coloring. Their painting inclines to sculpture-like conceptions. They endeavored to make things appear round and tangible, and not merely to give the indefinite coloring, in which objects seemed to resolve themselves under the humid sunshine of Venice. Raphael and Michael Angelo looked at the bodies of things, as geologists do mountains, the innermost structure of which is apparent through the outward lines. Both, it is true, may have looked with admiring soul when the evening glow passed over the Campagna, or lay on the towers and pinnacles of Florence; but their art was not able to retain this indefinite brilliancy. What they represented was the harmony of lines in the movements of human figures. Titian saw further. He perceived in things the relative position of colors, and then obtained the lines; the others, on the contrary, went from the lines to the coloring. As Aretino says, that it seemed as if the stones had been transformed by the declining sun into a more ideal material, so Titian elevated the substance of every thing he represents. He makes an inner light breathe through it. His color has something of a dim brightness in it. When the clear sun touches things, there is a colorless light-reflecting brilliancy, and in hard contrast to it colorless shadows; but what the sun on the sea illuminates, seems, as it were, to absorb light, and to become luminous of itself.

Giorgione first imparted this property to his pictures. His outlines disappear into something almost unessential. As, when living beings approach us, we see only colors and movement, so in his pictures: there is none of the fixed, statue-like appearance; the living, moving character alone seems produced by magic. This power in its perfection was, however, possessed by Titian. There is something unfathomable in his coloring. He alone has produced paintings before which we stand, as before many of Raphael's, as though they were unsolvable enigmas, the mystery of which seems ever renewing itself, — as though the figures were living, and were ever fostering other thoughts, just as thoughts alternate with ourselves. I call to mind his picture of the Tribute Money, which Michael Angelo must have seen in Ferrara when the duke showed him the palace. As in the Madonna della Sedia, there is here an arrangement of colors which can be classified by no name, and can be described by no language.

And in this coloring what a countenance! There is no praise of human beauty, which is not suitable to it. He who has never heard of Christ, must feel that the noblest, finest human countenance is represented here. Or, to mention something which is painted, as we are accustomed to say, more in Titian's manner, the portrait of the young girl in the Pitti palace at Florence. What life! We stand before it with a feeling as if it were impossible that this charming creature should have been dead for now three hundred years, and should not be at the present time as fresh and beautiful as ever; and we seek to fathom the means which art has here employed. We observe the delicate, almost trembling, glimpse of the slightest redness in the white of the eye; the fair points of the darker plaits; the golden chain which falls over her neck and youthful bosom, covered with a stiff brocade garment, as if her hand had just thrown it over her with its small and somewhat extended fingers. It is as if she had been suddenly called by her mother; had quickly wiped away a tear from her eye, which she had wept, no one knows wherefore (no sorrow was necessarily the cause of it), and had so appeared before Titian to sit for the first time for her portrait. And this was the moment which he had preserved as the most charming.

Giorgione had been dead for years when Michael Angelo now came to Venice; but Titian was in full vigor, and at the height of his fame. Whether, however, they met at that time, we know not. I should almost think it was not the case. For Michael

La Bella, Pitti Palace.

TITIAN.

Angelo's natural inclination to solitude must have held him away from men more strongly at that time than ever. Just as little may he have seen Sansovino again, his old adversary at Rome, who, since his flight in the year 1527, had obtained a position in Venice. He held the first rank there as a sculptor and architect; but he was still evil-disposed towards Michael Angelo, as Benvenuto Cellini bears witness, who spoke to him severely about it, when he visited Venice. What, however, must at this time have prejudiced all Venetian artists, and Sansovino especially, against Michael Angelo, was the wish of the Government to take advantage of the opportunity, and to retain the great man in Venice. If he remained, it was calling upon them all to stand back, and take a lower position.

But Michael Angelo felt that there was no terrain for him here. The first nobles of the city visited him, and persuaded him to take up his permanent abode with them. He declined. His idea was to go on to France, perhaps to influence the king respecting Florence, perhaps because Florentine art was represented there with distinguished power, and the way had been prepared for his own activity. Francis I. is the first among modern kings who endeavored to transplant into his country, not only individual artists, but the energy of an entire school. Through his means, there arose in France, by a blending of Florentine conception with French skilfulness, that art so fruitful in all three branches, which, without denying its origin, developed still further, and the productions of which cannot be contemplated without pleasure, little as nature is purely imitated in them. France was at that time to the Florentine painters what Russia was about twenty years ago to German musicians, — a half-civilized foreign land, where, however, men gladly accepted exile for some years, for the sake of gaining great sums of money. Michael Angelo would have been splendidly received. Francis I. honored in him one of the founders of that art which placed him above all; but, besides this, he honored him as he had done Leonardo, as the famous man. In after-years, the king repeated his proposals; and three thousand ducats always lay ready with his banker in Rome, in case Michael Angelo might ever resolve to use it as travelling money.

For a time, Michael Angelo lived in Venice perfectly retired. He had hired a house on the Giudecca, one of the islands to the west of the Canal Grande, and just that on which Aretino had looked down when he wrote to Titian; and thus, after the immense excitement he had recently gone through, he had suddenly fallen into a quiet more profound than any thing that can be imagined, and found time and repose to reflect upon his position.

What he was offered, if he would remain, is not accurately stated: in later times, when similar proposals were repeated from Venice, they were six hundred ducats annually, and especial payment for every work.* In gratitude for the good feeling with which they had met him, he made a design for the rebuilding of the Rialto, the principal bridge in

* See Appendix, Note XIV.

Venice, which had been burnt down. He gave the
sketch to the doge; but the bridge was executed subsequently after other plans. Still, to remain there
himself, and to build the Rialto, perhaps, and palaces, and begin new statues, while in Florence and
Rome works were lying which he had completed or
begun, seemed impossible. It was something in
those days to change one city for another. He must
have lived in Venice as an exile, apart even from the
few Florentines who dwelt there, or passed through
in their journeys; for, even in foreign lands, intercourse with the proscribed was not permitted, and
there were means of secretly observing whether the
command was attended to. He would have been a
stranger here, separated from his family; at home,
he was a noble taking part in the State; in Venice,
he was a paid celebrity without rights or influence.
Rome or Florence were the two only places in Italy
where he could live and work. Rather than Venice,
there was France, where the exiles formed an entire
colony; where the sound of the Florentine language
was no rarity; and where the freshest tidings from
Tuscany arrived uninterruptedly, almost as quickly
as at Venice.

I place at this period the origin of Michael
Angelo's sonnets on Dante, which perhaps were the
direct result of the tone of feeling which must have
been excited in his mind by the tidings of the
proclamation in Florence of the proscription against
him. The official document, drawn up in Latin,
was published there on the 30th September, 1529;
and thirteen citizens were in it declared to be reb-

els, provided they did not appear before the 6th of October. Michel Angelus Lodovici de Bonarrotis is the eighth name; Rainaldus Filippi de Corsinis is the first. The proscription, however, no longer affected the latter, as he had returned before the 6th October; and, in the copy of the edict preserved to the present day, we find his name erased. Michael Angelo, however, had not appeared, and had forfeited all that which, by such a sentence, might be taken from a citizen of Florence.

This is one of his sonnets upon Dante : —

> "How shall we speak of him? for our blind eyes
> Are all unequal to his dazzling rays.
> Easier it is to blame his enemies,
> Than for the tongue to tell his highest praise.
> For us he did explore the realms of woe;
> And, at his coming, did high heaven expand
> Her lofty gates, to whom his native land
> Refused to open hers. Yet shalt thou know,
> Ungrateful city, in thine own despite,
> That thou hast fostered best thy Dante's fame;
> For virtue, when oppressed, appears more bright,
> And brighter, therefore, shall his glory be,
> Suffering of all mankind most wrongfully,
> Since in the world there lives no greater name."
>
> SOUTHEY.[*]

> "Quanto dirne si dee non si può dire,
>   Chè troppo agli orbi il suo splendor s'accese,
>   Biasmar si può più 'l popol' che l'offese,
>   Ch'al minor pregio suo lingua salire.
>
> Questi discesi a' regni del fallire
>   Per noi 'nsegnare, e poscia a Dio n'ascese,
>   E le porte che 'l ciel non gli contese
>   La patria chiuse al suo giusto desire.

---

[*] I have selected Southey's translation, as better than any I could offer.—F. E. B.

Ingrata patria, e della sua fortuna
A suo danno nutrice! e n'è ben segno,
Ch' a più perfetti abbondi di più guai.

E fra mille ragion vaglia quest' una,
Ch'egual non ebbe il suo esilio indegno,
Com' uom maggior di lui non nacque mai." *

This may have been written by Michael Angelo when the term allowed for return had elapsed. For his peculiar passionateness bursts forth in these verses; and that he twice said almost the same, though in other words, shows how the one poem was not sufficient completely to disburden his feeling. He was constrained to repeat it, as Raphael wrote his three sonnets; because, when he fancied he had assuaged the storm by one, his heart rose again, and new verses were required to describe the ardor with which he was filled : —

"I speak of Dante, — him whose mighty mind
Was ill-conceived by that ungrateful race
With whom the great no recognition find.
Oh! were I he, then the same fate were mine,
His exile and his power alike to share ;
Happiest of all that earth could me assign." †

This concludes the second sonnet, which, in these last verses, indicates the period of its origin more plainly than the first.

It was natural that Michael Angelo should, at that time, read Dante, and think of him. Not merely on account of politics. Dante stands in relation to Michael Angelo's times, as Goethe or Shakespeare do to our own. His works formed a kind of second Bible, both in their characters and language: Chris-

---

* From MS. in British Museum. † See Appendix, Note **XV**

tian heroes appearing in heathenish aspect, and heathenish poets and thinkers half warmed by the light of Christianity, were well known and familiar to the minds of that day. For three centuries it lasted, — as long as Italian art and cultivation prevailed in Europe. With the end of the sixteenth century it ceased. "If you examine Italian art," said Cornelius to me, "its decline begins when painters ceased·to carry Dante in their minds."

Nor does this relate to art alone. Dante's mind was the fruit of an elevated view of all natural and supernatural matters, a feeling of the even balance of things in the sight of the highest Creator and Prime Mover. There is nothing which Dante does not include in his system. From politics, history, morals, nature, and all the heavenly mysteries, he draws the oil with which he feeds his light. He gives those who study him a complete theory of life. Every one finds in his nature and in his destiny whatever he needs to warm, to enlighten, to console, and to animate his mind.

Looking at the outward aspect of things, it might appear that Dante and Michael Angelo had fostered different political views, — that Dante had gone into exile as a Ghibelline, and Michael Angelo as a Guelf. But the position of things was such, that the Guelfs in Florence, in Michael Angelo's time, desired the same as the Ghibellines had done in the days of Dante. Dante's characteristic is truly, not that he pledged himself to the nobles and the emperor, but, glorifying a past which had never existed as his enthusiasm saw it, he opposed the admission of those new elements, which would have established, on the mere ground of superiority, a new power, which they called liberty, in the place of that which he regarded as the old order of things founded by God, and which he called liberty. Equally so, Michael Angelo stood between the past and the future. Like Dante, he too was a partisan, animated by idea alone; fighting for the old liberty, which he deemed the only legitimate one. For centuries had sanctioned, in this old liberty, what was regarded by Dante, in its origin, as a new, unauthorized power. And, as Dante deceived himself by considering the continuance of the old empire possible through an ideal renovation, so Michael Angelo erred in his dream of the revival of Florentine liberty. For the observation must have forced itself upon any one who hated tyranny and the satisfying of common personal love of power, as Michael Angelo hated them, that the attempts of the Medici to form, out of a free city, a capital subject to themselves, were obviated by the desire of her inhabitants, as well as of those of other Tuscan cities, — a desire almost stronger than the obstinate craftiness of the Medici, and without which the subjection of Florence would have been impossible.

For their best abettors consisted of Florentines. This was felt in Florence. Still it seemed too dishonorable to those who fought against the Medici to believe in this, or to give way on account of it. And this rendered these final contests so desperate, that the feeling of being obliged to succumb secretly accompanied the immense efforts with which they

endeavored not only to save, but to stupefy themselves.

For such was the condition of things. All these
heads of families hostile to the Medici, who, united
by common distress, opposed the one superior house,
worked involuntarily against each other in secret
or open enmity, however closely they appeared
united. All wished to rule. The upper societies
wished to oppress the lower. All the members of
the consiglio grande wished to oppress those who
were entitled to take part in the State. Lastly, all
Florentines united wished to oppress the inhabitants
of the other cities of Tuscany, the citizens of Pisa,
Lucca, Arezzo, Volterra, Livorno, Prato, and Pistoia,
whom they styled inferiors (*sudditi*). Fifty wished
to rule over twenty-five hundred, twenty-five hundred over a hundred thousand; and these hundred
thousand wished to act the tyrant over all the other
inhabitants in the territory of the Republic. If they
had desired liberty, the first thing necessary would
have been to have a more just idea of its meaning.
But there was no mention of this. Far rather, that
which most stirred up the citizens of Florence was,
that the Medici, without paying regard to birth or
wealth, had brought into the city, and employed in
the government, talented Tuscans from all parts, if
they only seemed available; so that the lower classes
found through the Medici a path to offices, dignities,
wealth, and influence. Without the city, whoever
was not a Florentine was to be oppressed; within
the city, whoever had not a seat in the consiglio;
within the consiglio, whoever was not belonging to

the oldest nobility. Michael Angelo himself is said to have had enemies, only because he belonged to the Nine, and his family was not among the nobles of the city.

He contested for the maintenance of this state of things, just as Dante had once struggled for the rule of the incapable Ghibelline nobles. Both of them, however, had not the men in view, but the idea. Dante regarded the Guelfic liberty, Michael Angelo the Medicæan, as an unauthorized, peace-destroying element. To the greater mass of the inhabitants of Florence and Tuscany at that time, that, however, was liberty which was brought by the Medici. The country would rather have allowed itself to be ruled by one single, free, generous, easily accessible family, than by a body of arrogant, cold, ambitious citizens. This had driven Benvenuto Cellini, whose poor family had no seat in the consiglio to lose, to the pope at Rome, instead of defending his native city; and had made Vasari of Arezzo a servant of the Medici: and similar motives had influenced a number of Tuscans and Florentines, to whom the old liberty presented no means of rising. Thus considered, the Medici appeared less as a house coming forward with unjust desires for authority; as a power growing up on a natural soil, which, in the course of things, was at last compelled to seize upon the monarchy.

But still, even thus considered, what happened in Florence between 1527 and 1530 appeared of little account. The last contest of the citizens against tyranny possesses a higher importance.

As early as the beginning of the sixteenth century,
when Julius II. stood between France, Spain, and
the emperor, the policy at work among these powers
began to be a rule of conduct for other States, and
to constrain them to follow it. At that time, however, Europe was split into so many parts, that the
will of following whom he chose was not wholly
taken from individual members. Since the appearance of Charles V., an end had been put to this.
The union of the immense masses of land under
one hand acted authoritatively upon the policy of
the portions not ruled by him; and the alliance
of all of them, after the battle of Pavia, for mutual
co-operation against the preponderating power of the
emperor, appears as natural as the gathering together
of a flock of low beasts of prey against the single
lion that threatens to kill them. The power of the
Hohenstauffens had once been broken, while all
drew back; and they, forsaken by princes and cities,
had sunk down into sovereigns of Naples, whom an
unsuccessful war had ruined. Now an emperor had
arisen, into whose power so much had fallen as
private possession, that he was able, with new resources, to assert the old ideal claim of being lord
of the whole. And, by so doing, there was an end
to the part the pope was playing, who desired not
only to be the first spiritual power in Europe, but
at the same time to be a temporal prince in Italy.
If Clement VII. had been the hereditary possessor
of the States of the Church, he might perhaps have
been able to unite France, England, North Germany,
and Venice against the emperor; but, dependent on

his revenues, which flowed to him most richly from the lands which were subject to Hapsburg, no choice remained for him: he was compelled to take the side of the emperor. Again and again, urged by the longing to preserve his freedom, he endeavored to approach France by secret paths: each time, however, a mighty blow pointed out the right way. Now at length he yielded. Rome's independence was given up. He would at least save Florence for his family. And thus the subjugation of this city by the army of the emperor is marked at the same time by the subjugation of Rome, and the complete advent of the new powers in Europe.

For, as the emperor endeavored to fashion all within his lands to forward his higher objects, he did so now also with the princes who had opposed him. Like him, they must seek to concentrate their power. There must be an end to the opposition of the nobles, who would only acknowledge their sovereigns as the first among those possessing equal rights, and an end to the independence of the cities who claimed as a right to open their gates to him, or to shut them at will. Princes required subjects, over whose highest right the right of the emperor or king swayed with unapproachable superiority. It was no longer good-will, but obedience, which they required. And thus in the stream of time there floated no point of deliverance, no blade of straw to which the declining liberty of Florence could have clung. The old rights, in defence of which the citizens hoped to rise anew, were like stones fastened to their necks. With the same in-

exorable consistency, the old state of things was at
that time broken up, and the new gained the ascendency; as, in our own days, this new, which was
fashioned at that time, dies away of itself as old
and unfruitful, and again a new must step into its
place, which times to come will destroy as obsolete.

Never, however, have men a thoroughly clear
sense of their position. They see only the separate
parts. Neither they who sink know what thrusts
them deeper and deeper, nor those who rise know
quite the secret help which allows them to conquer
from step to step. For the future is not unveiled,
and every day seems to contain a possibility. A
vague presentiment alone shows at times the inevitable fate awaiting us.

For this reason it would be too much to suppose,
that Michael Angelo had perceived why the cause
of the city was a lost one. But that a gentle voice
told him that the contest was in vain, and that the
feeling thrilled through him many a time, that his efforts were fruitless, may be conjectured from his
character and his inclination to see things gloomily.
He and the best round him never doubted what
must happen, as in Homer's Iliad the Trojans from
the first seemed to bear in them the certainty of
their defeat. It is just that, however, which makes
them greater in our sight. Like the characters of
some vague Florentine epic, which no poet would be
called upon to conceive in words, they awaken in us
a higher feeling than the daily pity we experience
when a good soldier falls at length by a ball or a
blow. They excite the sympathy in our hearts, that

we feel when we see the hero of a tragedy perish.
It is as if Florence assumed the nature of a noble,
unique form, — a woman with helmet and shield
and lance, just like united Germany in the single
figure of Germania; and as if she stood there, and
defended the place to which her life was chained.
And thus it is no empty image, when we say that
the heroic city, at length struck to the ground, only
desisted from the contest when she had no more
blood in her veins to shed.

Florence stands so far behind Carthage or Jeru-
salem, that she can scarcely be named at all by the
side of these. Compared with the powers that were
at war there, and drove the blockaded to desperation,
the efforts of the Florentines were of small extent.
Wars of annihilation were fought against those cities;
here only an insurrection was crushed. But the
comparison does not diminish the greatness of that
which occurred in Florence. The feeling was the
same. Men were capable of the same desperate
courage. Life and property were, as then, regarded
as nothing. They felt that without freedom all was
lost; and at that very period which followed the
discouragement, under the influence of which Michael Angelo had fled, the grand feeling burst forth
purely for the first time, and courage changed to
enthusiasm.

The letters of Michael Angelo's friends must have
shown him how the city, now purified of those under
whose influence divided opinion and want of confidence had arisen, had regained a trustful unity and
courage. They wanted Michael Angelo. His posi-

tion was not to be supplied by others. They conjured him to return; and, if the messages to this effect were not able to induce him, the dispatches of the Venetian ambassador, which the latter forwarded the day after his flight, and the purport of which could not have been concealed from Michael Angelo, owing to his high connections in Venice, must have increased his home-longing into an urgent yearning to hasten back to Florence.

Rather would they give the city with their own hands to the flames, and surrender themselves to death, was the reply of the Signiory to the pope, when he had demanded, as the basis of negotiations, that they should allow his ambassador to remodel affairs at his own discretion. However sure Clement might be of his cause, and thus demand the impossible with imperious pertinacity, in Florence also they knew at length what they desired: they would defend themselves to the last drop of blood, and at the end transform the city into a heap of ruins. The smoking stones alone should be the victor's booty. If Michael Angelo had been capable of the feeling which commonly is called fear, as a milder expression for cowardice, he would not have resolved to return now to Florence, instead of going to France.

Far away, unbiassed by the enthusiasm which was rising at home, he was able to review the future more coolly. They may have talked to him in Venice ever so consolingly of help, or of a revolution of affairs; he must have perceived what was possible and impossible, and what was probable. One thing was certain, — that, if the proud Venetian Republic

entered into a peaceful agreement with the emperor,
on the conditions held out to her at Cambray, she
herself lost enough in possession and importance
not to be compelled to strike, if she were able to
afford assistance, far rather in her own behalf than
in defence of Florence. Venice no longer felt the
power within her to pursue the bold policy which
the Florentines desired of her. Had she helped, it
would have been, not out of love for them, but out
of hatred of the Spaniards. The moment was long-
ingly expected when they could avenge themselves.
If Florence held her ground; if the position of the
Imperialists in Tuscany thus became critical; if
the pope's money failed; if the Turks were victorious
in Hungary; if only a glimmer of success appeared,
— then France, Ferrara, and Venice remained the
old allies. But the contrary to all this was far more
probable; and in Venice this was most dispassion-
ately perceived, because her ambassadors were most
skilful in observation. They knew how desperately
the pope united his interests with those of the emperor; and equally so how the latter, even if he himself
wished otherwise, was bound to deliver Florence into
the hands of the Medici.

Amid such thoughts Michael, Angelo received the
letter of the Florentine ambassador at Ferrara, in
which he begged him to meet him there, on account
of an important matter. The Ten who consulted
upon war and peace had chosen this way to induce
Michael Angelo to return, without being obliged to
take steps in it personally, as such authorities could
not negotiate with an exile. The ambassador, Gale-

otto Giugni, an older, experienced man; similar in character to Michael Angelo; a furious Guelf; passionate; belonging to the old nobility, and beloved by the people; unselfish, and, when he spoke, fiery in his language; and endowed with the talent of infusing his whole nature into the soul of him whom he wished to convince, — this man knew so well how to treat Michael Angelo, that he not only induced him to return home, but he carried his point so far as to make him take the first step. On the 13th October, Giugni was able to inform the Government that he had been requested by Michael Angelo to make intercession for him. If they would pardon him, and promise him security, he was ready to receive the orders of the Signiory in Florence. On the 20th, the repeal arrived: he was to come, and again to occupy his post.

Michael Angelo had returned to Venice; and the letter in which free return was promised him reached him there. One of his own workmen in marble had been selected as the messenger. How much they reckoned on his return, and had striven to bring it about, is seen from the fact, that when, on the 6th October, the fugitives who had not appeared at the first summons were once more formally declared to be rebels, and the confiscation of their goods proclaimed, Michael Angelo, although he remained away, was not named among them, nor is his name found on the list sent by the Venetian ambassador on the 15th. The punishment imposed on him was exclusion from the consiglio for three years, under condition that every year he should himself petition the consiglio for the repeal of this measure, admission being again awarded him by two-thirds of the votes. The wording of this sentence may have attested the possibility of at once making a motion for his re-admission; and it appears, therefore, a mere formal punishment which was awarded, because complete exemption would have been an insult to the law.

The pass issued at Ferrara on the 10th November, with the duke's signature, is still extant, and shows the route to have been by Modena, and through Carfagnana.* It was available for fifteen days. On his first passage through Ferrara, Michael Angelo had again met the duke. Alfonso had a list of the strangers who had arrived presented to him every evening; and, when he found Michael Angelo among them, he sent some of his nobles to him in the hotel, who invited him with the most honorable expressions to repair to the palace. Michael Angelo thanked him, but went in quest of the duke, who offered him money; upon which he replied, that he was himself richly provided for, and was at his excellency's service with this sum. I know not whether it is allowable to see in this expression, after Michael Angelo's fashion, who often delighted in vague ironical utterance of his thoughts, an allusion to the scarcely honorable behavior of the duke, who, when his son laid down the command of the Florentine troops, refused to give back the money he had received beforehand, and therefore, strictly speaking, had deceived the Republic.

* See Appendix, Note XVI

That Michael Angelo adhered to the route laid down in the pass is evidenced by his meeting, in Modena, with the sculptor Begarelli, whose works he saw and praised highly. Begarelli did not understand how to handle marble; but he made clay statues, which he baked, and to which, by coloring, he gave an almost marble-like appearance. Michael Angelo is said to have exclaimed, "Alas for the statues of the ancients, if this clay were changed into marble!" I have never seen Begarelli's works in Modena; those that are left of them are highly prized, though such praise from such lips appears to me scarcely credible.*

Between the 15th and 20th November, Michael Angelo must have arrived once more in his native city.

III.

On the 5th November, 1530, Charles V. arrived at Bologna, whither the pope, for the sake of etiquette, had repaired some days before. As a happy welcome to both, came the tidings of the retreat of the Turks from Vienna. This alone had still clogged them. They could now employ all their powers for the undertaking against Florence. On the 15th, the army of the Prince of Orange arrived before the city, simultaneously with the return of Michael Angelo. On the same day, the tidings of the taking of Vienna by Soliman had been spread abroad. This was indeed a deception, as were, from henceforth, almost

* See Appendix, Note XVII.

all the promises of help from abroad. But no one thought any more of surrender; and, well provided with soldiers, supplies, and money, they awaited the attack.

During Michael Angelo's absence, the work had been carried on at the height of San Miniato. The citizens had divided themselves into battalions, and had worked. The richest people, splendidly equipped, had taken part: distinctions of class were forgotten.* Of the exiles of former years, six hundred men capable of bearing arms had returned. Whatever yet remained undestroyed in the suburbs, now entirely perished. Country houses and palaces in the neighborhood were set fire to by the enemy's soldiers, and equally often by their own proprietors. They emulated each other in sacrificing their possessions for their country, — an emulation which excited the admiration of Italy, who again, as in the times of Savonarola, watched the solitary struggles of the beautiful city with that anxious feeling of sorrowful curiosity with which we see a palace in flames, and its walls holding their ground in the midst of the conflagration.

The first attack, as had been foreseen, was directed against San Miniato. Michael Angelo's fortifications, however, left no doubt as to the capability of the place for affording resistance. But the foes were not merely outside the walls. A Franciscan was seized, as he was on the point of spiking the guns on San Miniato. He was at the same time accused of endeavoring to smuggle hostile soldiers

* See Appendix, Note XVIII.

into the city in the garb of monks. Little ceremony was made with him. Shortly before, a man had lost his head in Florence for having expressed himself contemptuously of the Government; just at the time of Michael Angelo's return, the Franciscan followed him. A grandson of the famous old Marsilio Ficino, himself a scholar, had said that the Medici, who had ruled so long, and had beautified the city with so many buildings, seemed to him more entitled to govern than any one else; the assertion cost him his life. And others also shared a similar fate, against whom nothing further was to be proved than that they had cursed or offended the moral laws of the Piagnoni.

On the day when all was in order on San Miniato, and troops as well as guns were in their places, Malatesta appeared on the bastions with the morning light. Surrounded with drummers, pipers, and other musicians, he greeted the foe on the opposite heights with an immense flourish. Then, as nothing was stirring abroad in the camp, he sent out a trumpeter, and challenged to the contest. And, when this also was ineffectual, all the cannons on the hill thundered forth at once; the drums and trumpets joined; and, when a mighty echo answered on all sides, the whole of Florence, says Varchi, trembled with joy and anxiety.

The besieging army had obtained its artillery from Siena. It was difficult to get it from the city, and then to convey it across the mountains before Florence. Four cannons, a culverin,* and three smaller

* A long slender piece of ordnance or artillery used in those days.

pieces, had arrived. The cannons were old booty, taken from the Florentines. The° pope furnished three pieces of ordnance from the Castle of St. Angelo; and Lucca, which, like Siena, was inclined to the Imperialists, did its part. Early on the 29th October, the bombardment began.

San Miniato is closely contiguous to the southern part of Florence, and commands the surrounding heights; but it could be just as easily swept by them, as it was within reach of their cannons. The battle at that time waged there would, in the present day, be child's play. The Imperialists fired from their position over San Miniato into the heart of the city, and beyond. At that day, provided with badly cast pieces, of little range and uncertain aim, the attack was less strong. For two days, Orange fired upon San Miniato. One hundred and fifty shots were fired in all. On the second day, two cannons burst. He had never once stopped the fire from the height of the church-tower, from whence a daring gunner, with two small cannons, had invited the bombardment by the injury he had inflicted on the camp. Michael Angelo had had woolsacks suspended from the projecting parapet of the tower, which, floating freely, and hurled here and there by the balls, without touching the walls, kept the tower uninjured. In front of the façade, an earthwork was thrown up at his order, in which the shot was received. This church, one of the oldest in the city, a charming masterpiece of pre-Gothic architecture of the best Hohenstauffen period, in the style of which we see the transition from the ancient to the modern, was a favorite of Michael Angelo's. He called it his bride, and successfully carried it through these evil days. And unattacked since then, and well preserved, it still stands at the present day as one of the most glorious works in that most glorious region.

The successful beginning of the defence seemed to promise well for the position of the city. Damp, and want of provisions, as well as that of forage, tormented the army without; their artillery and horse stuck fast in the ground, which was rendered soft by violent rain; while the empty walls of the burnt-down country houses afforded no shelter. On the same day as that on which Orange's cannons burst, the Florentine horse broke from the walls, cut off the road to Arezzo from the Imperialists, and took away a large mass of supplies. Hope on the steadfastness of Venice and Ferrara rose anew. They saw the most glorious victory before them. Successful sorties, and the discontinuance of the bombardment, made the hope become almost a certainty; and a confidence arose among the citizens, which increased to an impatient desire for contest. In the churches, the brethren of San Marco strengthened the old belief in the invincibility of the city. All contradiction of this doctrine was silenced as a crime against the State; energetic men of different parties were regardlessly brought into offices which seemed to require such occupants; and the sway of one party gave way to a vehement longing for action in all minds. When Jacopo Salviati, one of the recalled fugitives, did not appear, and was declared guilty of high treason, a body of Florentines marched out, and set fire to his summer palace, some miles from the city, and which had been spared hitherto as belonging to a relative of the Medici. It was a magnificent building. And, having once begun the work of conflagration, they prepared a similar fate for the villa of the Medici in Carreggi. Had the Government not interfered, all the possessions of the Medici would have shared alike. The proposal is said to have originated with Michael Angelo, of levelling with the ground the principal palace of the family in the city, and of making in its stead a public square, which should receive the name of the "mule square," because the Medici at that time were all of illegitimate descent. This was subsequently brought against him as a capital crime; yet his friends assert that he never thought of such a thing. If the idea were not incredible on account of the destruction of the noble building, we might be inclined to impute it to him. But this also speaks against it, — that he had received so much kindness in the house, and had begun his career there.

But mercy was not known in those days. The prisoners on both sides were put to death. Voices had grown loud in asserting that they must avenge the injustice suffered from the Medici on the young Caterina, who had been detained in the convent as a hostage; and her fate — she was scarcely ten years old — sounds scarcely less barbarous than the atrocities practised in Rome by the Spaniards in 1527.

During these preliminaries, the pope and emperor were at Bologna. Besides the Spaniards he had brought from Spain, Charles had with him the troops which had been victorious before Milan. His intention was to have himself crowned, and then set forth to Germany with the whole army, in order to establish his authority there, where the north of the country, according to the treaty of Cambray, could no longer be supported by France.

The pope also would have been obliged to sanction this, as the Lutherans would have been at last subdued; but Florence took precedence with him. Charles, on the contrary, had it not been of such importance to him to appear in Germany as a crowned emperor, would have withdrawn his army from the city, and at once have started for the north with all his forces. But he was thus compelled to stop. The pope effected that Milan should be given back to Sforza, and that the Venetians should restore to the latter the part of Lombardy conquered by them, while Ravenna should fall to himself. The emperor, on the contrary, desired that Modena should be left, for a time, to the Duke of Ferrara, who had succeeded in establishing the most cordial relations with him, in spite of his intimate connection with France. He promised anew what Clement, hitherto, could not have hindered, — to enter into no negotiations with Florence for himself alone. It became politically settled at that time, that Florence, in her present state of defence, was no longer Florence, but only the city withheld by a seditious minority from her lawful inhabitants. The lawful possessors were the citizens to be found as fugitives, partly in Rome, partly in other cities, partly in the camp of the Imperialists before Florence; and these were to be again re-instated in their possessions. This view was subsequently adopted, even by the King of France; a perfidy which appears just as pitiable as the treachery he practised at Cambray. For the pope thus really considered the matter. To the emperor all opinions stood open; he had pledged himself to nothing: but, with Francis I., it was a cloaking of his weakness, which he made appear still more pitiable by such a denial of his friends.

It lay in the interest of the emperor, now that the attack of the city had been once undertaken, to use every effort to carry it through. The Genoese were forbidden to carry on commerce with Florence. Thus the greatest part of their supplies was cut off. The Duke of Ferrara was compelled to recall the Ferrarese who had enlisted in the Florentine army. He was obliged to assist Orange, who complained in Bologna of insufficient means. He gave him cannons, which he had obtained from Bourbon in 1527, when they hindered the latter in his march. With eight thousand new troops, besides twenty-five cannons of the heaviest calibre, which were conveyed with immense labor across the Apennines in the middle of winter, Orange arrived in the camp from Bologna. The cardinals themselves were obliged to give their mules as beasts of burden. As soon as he arrived, the bombardment was carried on. On the 19th and 21st November, the Imperialists fired upon San Miniato from morning till night. Their balls were fruitless. On the 1st December, however, they succeeded in setting fire to the tower.

It burned the whole night through : the wood-work in it was consumed, and the woolsacks took fire. The damage, however, was repaired immediately, and the fire again reduced. But, on the 6th December, an important loss occurred. La Lastra was stormed on the road to Pisa, and two hundred Florentine citizens lost their lives. On the 11th, a sortie took place. Six hundred men left the city at midnight. In order to recognize each other in the darkness, they had drawn their shirts over their coats of mail. The camp was attacked opposite San Miniato ; and, while the Florentines did not lose a man, two hundred hostile Italians were cut down. The Imperial army was divided according to nations: Spaniards, Germans, and Italians were encamped in separate intrenchments. And, at the same time, Ferruccio, the commander of the city forces outside the walls, whose duty it was to keep the road to Livorno open, defeated the enemy so successfully in open fight, that he destroyed an entire division, and carried off six standards.

The whole contest was still nothing but a chain of separate skirmishes. In the country lying between Florence and the sea, to the north of the Arno, the citizens had free scope. Florence herself was not blockaded. Young men were hunting there, and ascending the heights of Fiesole without encountering the enemy. And even towards San Miniato and the southern city, in which Malatesta was stationed, and where lay the quarters of the foreign troops, there was no systematic course of action. They were bombarding one day, then again they paused, and at times began again. The supplies in the camp became more and more difficult to obtain, and money often began to ebb; while in Florence there was plenty everywhere. And so, while the prince's army was disturbed by the jealousy of three nations, who were more disposed for mutual internal contest than for an attack against Florence, the city appeared in every respect superior to the foe; and, the longer the siege was prolonged, the more advantageous was the form which the position of things assumed. France secretly gave the fairest promises. The king only desired to have his sons restored, and he would at once appear in their aid. Ferrara and Venice made similar assurances. The emperor, who wanted his army elsewhere, became impatient. The pope saw the moment approaching, when no more money was to be raised for Orange; for that he bore the whole expense of the war, was a matter of course.

Clement, resolved as he was for extremities, did not yet break entirely with the Florentine Government. He still held a finger stretched out: a secret interchange of mutual proposals never ceased. Not only the worse it went with the siege, the more freely the constitution and such things were talked of, but he even offered to enlarge the territory of the Republic, if they would come to an agreement with him. Cervia and Ravenna were to be joined to it; a masterly move for separating Venice and Florence, and to which, as soon as it was rumored abroad, the Venetian ambassador did not fail to draw the attention of his Government. Yet this was carried on in profound secrecy. The public opinion was in favor of a struggle of life and death; and the new gonfalonier, who had entered on office January 1, 1530, was a man to adhere to these extreme measures. This was Rafael Girolami, who had sprung from one of the oldest families, formerly a Palleski, but now the bitterest foe of the Medici; a man of a quick, versatile nature, beloved by the people on account of his brilliant gifts, and the only one of the four ambassadors sent to Genoa who had immediately returned to Florence.

Girolami would have perhaps been able to save Florence; but the subjection in which he was kept as gonfalonier was too great for the wisest head to have been able to obtain any thing in this position. A statesman standing at the head of the Government, must, in certain things, act according to discretion, and be able to exclude all co-operation. The consiglio, however, interfered in every thing; and the people, through whom the resolutions of the majority were brought about, based their decisions neither according to fixed rules, nor, often enough, even upon distinct information. The resolutions lacked the impress that gives effect to the words of a monarch acting for himself. Where one single man says firmly what he wills, the people feel that there is a necessity either to obey or to resist; where a majority commands, every one knows that the next day the decree may be again abolished. Thus, in the consiglio, matters were talked over again and again; opinion changed; jealousy was never at rest; mistrust kept on the alert; and the gonfalonier, instead of giving the casting vote, yielded to the will of the citizens, who to-day from casual circumstances voted in one way, and to-morrow in another. And, worst of all, opposed to this civil, many-headed Government, there was within the walls, in spite of it, an independent power, standing alone without control, and with plans in his head, for the secrets of which none possessed the key. This was Malatesta Baglioni.

When the son of the Duke of Ferrara had resigned the command, Malatesta had asked for his position for himself, and had gained it. The form of Malatesta stands ever like the shadow of a devil in the background, when we speak of the decline of Florentine liberty. He cannot be reproached, however, with having deceived an unsuspecting friend.

These military lords were at that time all the same. Florence perished not through Malatesta, but through the system of which he was the representative. He was considered as nothing particular. What had induced the citizens to place confidence in him, was their estimation of his political position. Malatesta's fate was connected with that of Florence. He was a son of that Baglioni whom Macchiavelli once reproached with not having seized Julius II. with the cardinals, and who was subsequently allured to Rome by Leo. X., and was beheaded there. The son of such a man, it was thought, would never have confidence in the Medici, least of all in Clement,

under whose advice Leo had at that time acted.
It was known that in Rome they were only waiting
opportunity to remove the Baglioni from Perugia,
as the Bentivogli had once been from Bologna. All
the small tyrants were to be uprooted in the cities
of the States of the Church, and set aside. This was
what Malatesta had to expect, however favorable the
conditions held out to him for the moment from
the Vatican. On the other hand, if freedom were
established in Florence, he would gain by this means
a support against Rome, such as no friendship of
the pope's afforded.

Still, they mistrusted him. For the opposite case
might be also calculated on. But this case was
viewed in Florence with more ardor than by Malatesta himself. He must have thought indeed of
covering his retreat, in any possible issue, at a time
when such a policy on his side must have seemed
to the Florentines less imposed upon him. To conceive Malatesta's position, no display or considera
tion of the particular qualities of the man are
needed. If he wished to come to an agreement
with the pope, he must seize him at the point where
he could hold him. Clement had made promises to
Orange, which he knew that the prince would force
him to fulfil. If the Imperialists took Florence,
Orange might have negotiated with the citizens without the pope; and who knows upon what they might
have resolved, from hatred to the Medici, and in hope
of a better turn of affairs to come? Hence the efforts
of the pope to remain in connection with the citizens.
And here Malatesta took his position. Under any

circumstances he must prevent the city falling into
foreign hands. In this there was no treachery. But
it was also necessary, that, when Florence should
have been brought to such a pitch as not to be able
to offer resistance any longer to Orange, Malatesta
should be sufficiently strong within the walls to
prevent their entrance. For this end, however, he
must spare his soldiers. In this lies the despicable
part of his double game. Favorable sorties were
possible, which he either hindered for this reason,
or which he seems to have carried out with too little
energy. As soon as he observed that there was
nothing more to hope for in France, Ferrara, and
Venice, it was no longer important for him to
strengthen the resistance of the Florentines, and
to cut off his men by contests, the favorable results
of which would not now afford him any advantage.

And so we may say, that Malatesta betrayed and
deceived those to whom he had sworn faithful service; whilst we cannot spare the citizens the reproach
of having at the same time betrayed and deceived
themselves, by conceding to a man, whom they so
well saw through, that power which at last grew
above them.

On the 26th January, 1530, the supreme command
was consigned to him. The solemn act took place
in front of the palace of the Government. The
marble lion on the platform erected in the square,
where the Signiory had their seat, was crowned with
a wreath of gold; the armed citizens filled the open
space around; Malatesta appeared with a medal on
his cap, on which stood the word *libertas*, and he

received the baton from the gonfalonier, who deliv-ered a flourishing oration. The showers of rain which interrupted the ceremony were interpreted both into good or evil. The mercenary troops were scarcely ten thousand men strong. Malatesta, how-ever, drew payment for them as if they were fourteen thousand; the number of armed citizens may have amounted to an equal number. Continual reduc-tion and addition made these numbers vary. Some-times the troops from the smaller fortresses that had surrendered came into the city; sometimes soldiers or citizens went into the enemy's camp. From without, also, deserters presented themselves. On the whole, the number of combatants slowly in-creased; while in the camp a constant increase of the active forces took place on a larger scale. The pope levied troops wherever he could. The forces sent by the emperor from Bologna were especially important, because a part consisted of old experi-enced Spaniards.

At the end of January, the first tokens appeared in the city which indicated the necessity of a deci-sion: meat began to prove scarce. In the camp, on the other hand, bread and wine were lacking. Cattle could be driven in from abroad; but the laden wagons stuck fast. The Imperialists, at this time, established themselves at length on the northern bank of the Arno. Maramaldo, a famous Neapolitan soldier, led across the river two thousand of the Spaniards who had come from Bologna. The city was in nowise completely blockaded by this; but the supplies had to be conveyed into it with more caution. Varchi, however, observes that neither the beginning of scarcity nor the advance in the movements of the enemy had any influence on the feelings of the citizens. None, he says, would have imagined from the life in the streets that they were in a besieged city. Money was in abundance, although the taxes were heavy. Michael Angelo had given fifteen hundred ducats for himself alone. A spirit of conciliatory kindness in intercourse, such as never had been experienced in Florence, had an elevating effect. " Poor, but free," was everywhere written on the houses with chalk or charcoal. " Let it be till the danger is over," was the common expression when strife appeared. At the same time, the work in the fortifications was uninterrupted; for there were symptoms that soon greater masses of troops would be ordered to this side of the shore, and little had been done hitherto for the defences here.

By degrees the northern side was completely surrounded. On the 13th February, German troops under the Count of Lodron arrived in the camp, — troops which had become unnecessary in Lombardy, owing to the peace with Venice. They posted themselves on the northern bank, where they erected a battery of twenty-two cannons. From henceforth it was not merely San Miniato which was the aim of the imperial guns. And even on the 2d February, when the connection with Pisa and Livorno had been far more open than after the arrival of the Germans, the Venetian ambassador had sent tidings home, that meat was so rare that soon none at all would be procurable.

In consideration of the increasing danger, the Government resolved to arm five thousand six hundred artisans and six thousand countrymen; and to imprison fifteen citizens, who were not quite free from suspicion of connection with the Medici. These measures only appear natural, when we know the often strangely ingenious manner with which, in spite of all precaution, intelligence of the most secret plans of the Government found its way to those Florentines in the camp who expected the victory of the pope. Pope and emperor still tarried in Bologna. In the year 1527, Clement had secretly had a model of Florence made for him by Tribolo, a sculptor, a pupil of Michael Angelo; and this made him acquainted with the city, even as to the different houses. With this before him, he studied events. On the 24th February, the crown was placed on the head of the emperor. Spring was approaching. Day by day, matters assumed a more favorable aspect for the besiegers; within, however, the citizens began to feel, that, with all their vigorous enthusiasm, the air was oppressive, and that a decisive blow must take place.

3.

In the beginning of March, the emperor advanced northwards, while Clement returned to Rome. So completely were his resources drained, that he was not able to procure pay for the army. The number of deserters in the city increased in consequence; but meat had almost disappeared, and sickness was on the increase. In April, Malatesta's ten thousand men had diminished to half the number ; while altogether, from the 15th March to the 15th April, five thousand eight hundred persons had perished. The citizens wished to fight, and importuned Malatesta to lead them forth. The Imperialists, however, avoided any encounter. When the Florentines came close to their intrenchments, and challenged them, they called scornfully out, that they had no idea of fighting with them. "You shall suffer hunger," they cried, "until you can be led like dogs by a cord."

Michael Angelo was occupied at this time day and night on San Miniato. He saw Maria Orsino, who had been the first to declare to him Malatesta's treachery, killed there by a ball from the enemy. The whole city felt it with him. In such times, when man is defending his highest blessings, all private interests flow into the great general feeling which is shared by each, as on some burning vessel the same pulsation seems to unite every one. No one, at such a time, experiences any feeling which does not at the same moment convulse the heart of another. Every transition from the deepest anxiety to hope, and from hope back again to the old misery, — moments respecting which Capello's letters to Venice day by day furnish an account, — all these Michael Angelo must have gone through, like the other citizens ; and the history of all contains his, without the necessity of mentioning him especially.

Grown old amid the uninterrupted pursuance of art, it was impossible for him to abstain entirely from his wonted work. There were days in which San Miniato seemed less threatened by danger ; and these he spent in quiet among his marble figures. Whilst without he was fighting against the Medici, he was secretly working on still at his monuments; for it might have brought him into suspicion of adherence, had he made no secret of it. But the continuance of this work may perhaps be regarded as a proof, that at the bottom of his heart he thought less hopefully of the future than he ventured publicly to show, and that he gave himself up to the illusions with which the nobles in the palace so readily, day by day, disposed of their cares.

He also began to paint again, after having laid his brush aside for nearly twenty years; for, after having completed the Sistine Chapel, he seems to have entirely given up that branch of art. He now began the painting intended for the Duke of Ferrara, Leda with the Swan, a painting *a tempera*, of which he had first made a cartoon. This latter is said to be in England; but I have not seen it. The original also, which is asserted by some to have been burnt by Louis XIII., is said to have been rescued in a sad condition. On the other hand, there are old engravings and copies, some of which were made very early. That in the museum at Dresden is easily accessible: it is large, powerful, and in good preservation, the work perhaps of some Netherland painter, and well fitted to give an idea of the design and the painting.*

I will not describe the picture here. As there are things which cannot be mentioned without portraying themselves to the mind, so there are

* See Appendix, Note XIX.

paintings which allow of no description, because that which we see in them seems to change while we are speaking of it. This alone we will say: While other artists, in painting Leda with the Swan, would have been able to produce nothing but the charming form of a woman approached by a swan, — so that, if the old legend were lost, its deeper purport would scarcely be guessed from the composition of the picture, — Michael Angelo makes the form of Leda, and the occurrence to which she is subjected, appear so great and so historical in the highest sense, that we are astonished at his ability in conceiving things as well as in reproducing them. None of his female figures are so thoroughly colossal as this Leda. She lies there like an outstretched giantess; and the eye, dreamily fixed on her bosom, seems, in one foreboding glance, to see in fancy all the immense evil which her brood of swans have brought upon Troy and Greece. She is beautiful enough to be the mother of Helena, and of those dissimilar twins Castor and Polydeukos, who are all three the children of this moment. No one thinks on those heroic forms, who sees the representation of this scene by Correggio and other painters, who, by portraying the descent of Jupiter in the form of a swan, lose all grandeur of idea, and treat it in a pretty, genre-like manner. Like a snow-white range of clouds descending on a chain of mountains, Michael Angelo's swan comes down. We cannot but feel, that, as long as he was painting this picture, his mind was far away from Florence, absorbed in thoughts of the old Greeks, and freed from the burden of events

which would otherwise have weighed down upon
him with a uniform mournful oppression.

Yet many a time a gleam of true hope passed over
the city. A turn in their fate seemed taking place
at Easter. As happiness and evil are wont to cling
to distinct persons, and to return with their appearance; so, in opposition to the fatal presence of Malatesta, another man now seemed to appear without
the walls as the bearer of safety and deliverance for
Florence, — Francesco Ferrucci. Next to Michael
Angelo, he is the most gifted character distinguished
in those contests, and almost more striking as having perished miserably in the season of youth and
vigor. Francesco Ferrucci is a man whose name at
the present day is known by every child in Florence,
and whose marble statue has been erected there by
the side of that of Dante, Michael Angelo, and other
great citizens.

Ferrucci sprang from a family whose military
ability had been acknowledged for generations. In
the year 1528, he had returned to Florence as the
only one of the higher officers who had marched to
Naples with the French army under Lautrec. All
the others, and two-thirds of the Florentine troops,
were left there as victims to the plague. Ferrucci
had so ably understood how to lead those who remained to Tuscany, and had gained such respect by
his severe discipline, that, promoted from post to
post by the Government, he had at length, in the
year 1529, received the supreme command in Empoli, a highly important place between Florence and
Livorno, through which the supplies of gunpowder

and meat reached the city. From this time he resolved, on his own account, to pursue other plans than Malatesta and the nobles of the Government had ever intended; and the beginning of these plans was, that he reconquered Volterra, which had just revolted against the Florentines, and had submitted to the pope.

He demanded re-inforcements from Florence. Five hundred foot set out to join him in the midst of the hostile camps; and, amid continual contest with five hundred imperial horse, they gained their end so well, that, while they had only lost four men and one of their leaders, the enemy was obliged to give up the pursuit, with a loss of eighty horse and three captains. Indeed, had they had with them, says Capello, the two hundred mounted Florentines, who left the city at the same time to reach Empoli by another route, the entire cavalry of the enemy would have perished.

This had happened on the 24th March; on the 29th, the tidings were received in Florence of the taking of Volterra. Four hundred Spaniards had been cut down there; and the heavy artillery sent by the Genoese to the pope had been carried off. At the same time, letters arrived from France that the king would receive his sons back in a few days, and that then at once he would come to the help of the Florentines. Nor was this all: in the camp without the city, matters had long been in a state of ferment; the money arriving from Rome was insufficient; differences arose between the different nationalities; each division thought itself slighted; and

when, on the 1st May, the taking of Volterra became
rumored about, and, besides this, the report spread
that the whole of Tuscany would in a short time rise
in favor of the Florentines, the Spaniards rebelled,
seized all the guns as a pledge for the pay they had
never received, and wished to withdraw. The prince
quieted them with difficulty by instalments. On
the day following, it was known in the city that the
mounted nobles had left the camp to go to Naples,
where the Turks were in earnest at length with their
long-expected attack. The firm conviction was cherished, that in fourteen days the rest of the army
would follow, and Florence would be rid of her
misery.

At the same time, however, the mortality increased
from day to day. Bread was baked of the most inferior materials, because there was no more wheat.
Oil and wine were entirely wanting; horses, asses,
and cats were slaughtered. The good tidings, however, helped through every privation. Re-inforcements were dispatched to Ferrucci; they resolved to
raise six thousand men for him, and the Imperialists
themselves furnished the best troops. The desire
for combat increased to such an extent, that, in spite
of Malatesta's opposition, a grand attack was to take
place on the 5th May. The enemy was, of course,
informed of it beforehand. Three thousand men
stormed the enemy's intrenchments on the southern
bank; and the contest was so vehement, that the
troops on the opposite side were called to assist;
while, on the Florentine side, Malatesta himself
wished to rush into the throng, and was only re

strained with difficulty by his party, on account of
his age and feebleness. Towards evening he gave
the signal for retreat. One of his best officers, who
had taken the command instead of him, was mortally
wounded; otherwise the enemy lost more men than
the Florentines. Had they brought all their strength
to bear, it was afterwards decided, the camp would
have been conquered, and the enemy destroyed.

The tidings meanwhile arriving from Ferrucci
consoled them for their failure in this contest. Now,
for the first time, they learned to estimate at its full
extent what had been gained by him in the taking
of Volterra, and what, with regard to the enemy,
had been frustrated. At Volterra, an army formed
of the Palleski was to have united, to have operated
with the Spaniards stationed there under Maramaldo
against Pisa, Pistoja, and Arezzo, where the citadels
were still Florentine; while Florence was to have
remained closely surrounded. The centre of this
intended enterprise was lost by the taking of Volterra. Instead of attacking the other places, the
enemy was obliged to endeavor to regain the principal one, which Ferrucci now armed for resistance
as quickly as he could. Wine, oil, and corn was to
be found in abundance : he knew how to procure
money, and men were not wanting. Every thing indicated the most brilliant success.

Florence, on the contrary, had been completely
blockaded from the 12th May. The two hundred
sheep which had been brought in on that day, formed
the last meat that had reached the city. In spite of
this, on the 15th, the anniversary of the restoration

of liberty was celebrated with magnificence. In the cathedral, Baccio Cavalcanti, one of the most zeal-ous citizens, delivered, after mass, a flourishing oration, the purport of which was freedom or death. On the following day, every citizen to a man took the oath in the square before the Church of San Giovanni, in the presence of the magistrates, that, true to the Government, he would either conquer or die. New taxes were added. All the deposited capital that existed, all foundation stock, ecclesiasti-cal property, and money belonging to hospitals and guilds, was monopolized.

But in the midst of this very enthusiasm lay the change of fortune.

Ferrucci, when he advanced to Volterra, had left behind him, as a commissioner in Empoli, a Floren-tine citizen, well known as a valiant man. His coadjutors seemed equally trustworthy. Neverthe-less, some Florentines in the Imperial camp suc-ceeded in inducing them to treachery. On the 28th May, Empoli was occupied and plundered by the Spaniards; and, two days after, the citizens of Florence beheld the noble wives and maidens—of whom Ferrucci had said, that they alone could have defended Empoli — on the ramparts of the camp, where they were exposed in defiance. The citadel of Arezzo fell at the same time through treachery. Tidings came from France, that the king would not have his sons restored to him until Florence was conquered. And while, besides all this, the distress for food and drink daily increased, the Imperialists were supplied with the twelve thousand bushels of corn and thirty thousand gallons of wine seized at Empoli. Miserable bread and water served the citizens for food. There was no longer a thought of importation. The streets were full of corpses. Instead of the attack of the Turks in Naples, the Imperialist cavalry returned to the camp. And, in Malatesta's house, a confidant of the pope was suddenly discovered with proposals for an accommodation. He was met, however, by the reply that Clement might apply to the Government of the city; that they had no desire to negotiate either through their own envoys, or through Malatesta. Every hope rested on Ferrucci, who was opposed to Maramaldo in Volterra.

The latter was now joined by the Spaniards who had taken Empoli, and by a division from the camp under the Marquis del Guasto. These re-inforcements arrived on the 12th June. Wearied with marching, they encamped before Volterra, without caring for the necessary intrenchments. They were at once attacked by Ferrucci; but he was obliged to retire before their superior power. On the day following, Del Guasto raised the batteries; on the third, he stormed the place. But Ferrucci, although twice wounded, had himself carried on a litter; and the Spaniards were driven back. On the next day, Del Guasto received four new cannons; and the fire was now opened from fourteen guns. Again the Spaniards stormed; again Ferrucci, though ill with fever, was in the midst of the throng. Not only was the city defended with arms, but boiling oil and baskets full of stones were hurled against the besiegers;

and so devastating was the effect of this defence, that the besiegers withdrew the next day with a loss of six hundred men.

Orange, however, did not agree to this: he sent Del Guasto two thousand infantry, and cavalry to correspond, with orders to take the city on any condition. The Florentines, encouraged by Ferrucci's success, and by the weakness of the army before the city, ventured a sortie, scaled the walls of the camp, cut down five hundred of the German soldiery, and retired victorious with a loss of scarcely fifty. At the same time, Ferrucci, for the third time, defeated the Marchese del Guasto before the walls of Volterra; and the siege was again raised. The loss of the Spaniards was large. The pope, who had sold and removed all his treasures, could procure no more money; while the citizens were for ever finding gold and silver vessels, which they changed into coin. On both sides they were straining every nerve.

July began. We know what Florence is in the hot season; lying, as it were, in a basin, surrounded by hills, and without a breath of cool air to absorb the heat of the cloudless days. The Arno, which sweeps along in the winter, then becomes shallow, and has sandy islands in the middle of its bed. Men breathed as in a slow fever, and panted for strength. Every morsel was valuable. The women who lived an evil life were first of all ejected from the walls. The next dismissed were those living in the country who had fled within the walls. Roofs of houses were torn off for fuel. Desperate resolves began to appear. Lorenzo Soderini, one of the most distinguished men, being convicted of connection with the camp, was hung; and the people fell almost into sedition, because they would have preferred tearing him to pieces alive. Every sickness now took the form of the plague. Matters had reached such a point, that the only success they looked to was not to be given alive by Malatesta into the power of the enemy. Ferrucci was appointed commander-in-chief of all the troops, and ordered to march towards Florence. At the smallest tokens of his approach, the citizens declared they would force their way through the gates. The Imperialists should be attacked on both sides. They would fight to the last drop of blood. If they were defeated, those who remained to guard the walls were to kill the women and children, set fire to the city, and rush against the enemy; so that — such was the end of the resolve — nothing should remain of Florence but the remembrance of the great souls of those who stood forth as an immortal example to all who were born for freedom, and would preserve it.

4.

On the 14th July, Ferrucci received the message from the Government. Two young Florentines, who stole by night disguised through the camp of the Imperialists, conveyed it to him. He resolved at once to set forth for Pisa, and from thence to reach Florence. Volterra, Pisa, and Florence form an equal-sided triangle, the southern point of which is Volterra. Each city is distant from two to three days' march from the others. To go direct to Florence from

Volterra in a north-east direction was not possible; for the mountainous and divided territory of Siena, hostile to the Florentines, had to be passed through. Ferrucci was obliged to endeavor to reach Pisa by Livorno, a city on the sea-coast, in a north-west direction, and not far from Pisa. Turning from Livorno towards the east, and marching in the valley of the Arno, he would have most quickly reached Florence. But the middle of this route was formed by the now lost Empoli. It was necessary to find another way.

Ferrucci made his way to Pisa. It was impossible to the Spaniards to stop him. But he had no sooner arrived there than he fell a victim to the sickness which had been subdued by force at Volterra; and thus fourteen precious days were lost. Money failed, and the troops rebelled. Commanding with fearful severity from his sick-bed, he extorted from the Pisans the necessary sums. Ferrucci went so far that he ordered a citizen, who had asserted he would rather starve than give the money, to be arrested and deprived of all food, until his relatives laid down the sum. With immense energy he prepared for his march to Florence, where, recovered at length from his severe sickness, he arrived on the last day of July.

With the recapture of Empoli they could not concern themselves. Ferrucci resolved to go through Lucca, Pescia, Pistoia, and Prato, which, lying in a circle, slightly arched to the north, form a chain between Pisa and Florence. He had a magnificent plan in his thoughts. He knew how miserably the soldiers of Orange were paid, and how easy it was to bring troops to revolt who receive no pay. A great part of the Imperialists consisted of so-called Bisogni, the worst sort of soldiers at that time, who were held together by no respect for their captains, but by the prospect of booty alone, and who always took the course where they hoped to satisfy their desire for spoil. Suddenly appearing before the prince's camp, he intended to make the same proposal to his army as that with which Bourbon had before diverted his men from Florence; namely, of leaving the city, and marching with them to Rome, which had long ago become again rich enough, and must at that time have fallen defenceless into their hands.

On the 1st August, Ferrucci appeared before Pescia, marching through the territory of Lucca. But supplies, as well as a free passage, were refused him. By indirect routes, adopted for the sake of misleading Maramaldo, who was following close at his heels, he moved on through the mountainous country towards Pistoia. The position of this city was peculiar. Two parties had for many years contested within her. Recently, however, that one which had been favored by Florence had been conquered and expelled. Its adherents had assembled at Pisa, and had joined Ferrucci. By taking part in his expedition they hoped to arrive again at authority. But their adversaries had also armed themselves, and formed a strong body of one thousand men, against whom Ferrucci had to defend himself. Besides this, there were Spanish troops quartered in the city, a band formed of seditious deserters from the besieging army, who wandered about the country burning and ravaging on their own account; and, after having proffered themselves previously to the Florentines themselves, were impelled to fight against them by the prospect of the approaching fall of the city.

With combined powers and common plans, the enemy would have been now superior to Ferrucci, who, hindered by his baggage and surrounded with spies, struggled with difficulty towards Florence. No one, however, ventured to attack him.

Had a man like him stood as a prince at the head of affairs in Florence, and conducted the war at his own discretion, how different would have been the course of things! When we read his reports, in which with pertinent accuracy he relates events briefly and concisely, we fancy we can see before us the severe, circumspect, unwearied man, and can hear him speak. He is ever foremost in person, doing the heaviest work. He is always of good cheer, and his mind is full of expedients for repairing losses suffered. Wearied by his last illness, and often scarcely able to keep up, he gives the most careful orders, and never for a moment loses sight of his position. Difficulties increased his elasticity. Unlimited was the confidence of the troops in his command. From his youth up, he had come forward fearlessly whenever he saw wrong committed in the streets of Florence as well as in the field. More than once, contending parties had appealed to him. Loved and honored by his friends, esteemed and feared by his foes, he now gave evidence how much he merited the reputation he enjoyed. Unhappily they recognized in Florence too late the position they ought to have given him.

The fourteen days in which he lay sick at Pisa had been fatal to the city. Had they been able boldly to advance on the day when the resolve was taken to conquer or to die, they might have exhibited the heroism of which their words gave promise, and met death with courage and calmness. Instead of this, they were obliged to wait and starve. The idea of negotiating with the pope was at length aroused even among those who had before loudly declaimed against treachery whenever it had been mentioned. Still those who were for extreme measures maintained the ascendency. Preachers animated the people for the last great contest; Malatesta's remonstrances were not listened to; he was obliged to yield, because, amid the general enthusiastic feeling, he was not certain whether his own soldiers might not forsake him, and place themselves under the immediate command of the gonfalonier. The last great review was held on the 31st July: sixteen thousand armed men, soldiers, and citizens, were drawn up in array, with twenty-one guns. The captains received the sacrament. On the 1st August, an immense procession took place. The gonfalonier and the members of the Government at the head, the people went barefoot in a body from church to church. The sacrament was universally received; wills were made; every one ordered his house as if he were taking farewell for ever. On the 2d August, while Ferrucci was coming down from the heights of Pistoia, the contest was to be undertaken. Two thousand men were to advance towards him; while the rest were to rush upon the camp of the enemy, whose destruction seemed all the more easy as Orange and his troops had left it on the same day. The prince had wished to oppose Ferrucci in person.

A decisive contest was therefore possible. The match was equal. What might have decided the contest in favor of the citizens was the fatal enthusiasm with which they longed to fight, the co-operation of Ferrucci, and, lastly, the uncertainty of the Imperialists, the greater number of whom, just on the point of revolt, would have allowed themselves to be beaten, and, had victory inclined to the Florentines, would have joined them.

On that 2d of August, however, the treachery of Malatesta was consummated. He refused to allow the sortie to take place. No one knew better than he, that the camp was as good as devoid of troops, and was easy to conquer. He had more accurate tidings on this point than either the gonfalonier or the Signiory; for these latter did not know that Orange had set out for Pistoia with the flower of his men, only because he had Malatesta's promise in his hands, to prevent an attack on the intrench- ments on this day.

For a long time, negotiations had been passing between them. At first they were of such a nature that the Government knew of them; and, when the latter would agree to nothing, they had been of late without their knowledge. But Malatesta did not treat with Orange entirely upon his own account.

A number of noble Florentines — not only such as were for the Medici, for these had long ago either left the city, or were placed in confinement, but men of all parties, united by the common conviction, that the contest could not be carried on further — joined themselves to Malatesta. No conspiracy took place; but a kind of tacit guarantee was afforded him that they would agree to any accommodation for peace which he should effect. Without this, he would not now have ventured to oppose the Signiory with the assertion that the sortie was impossible. And without this party, the importance of which the Signiory themselves felt, they had at least effected the sending of the two thousand men to Ferrucci. On that 2d of August, however, when Malatesta still showed good-will towards the Government, and only pleaded strategic reasons why there should be no fighting, he had informed the prince that his Highness should decide whether he, Malatesta, should leave the city with all his troops, or whether he should compel her to receive the Medici again of her own accord. And the prince, having decided on the former, had marched against Ferrucci.

Malatesta had not ventured to appear in the palace. He had enumerated to the Government in writing the reasons why they should not fight. This writing was a lie. They replied, that he must hold to what he had promised, and that they would fight. On the 3d of August, he answered. While the first letter contained a pertinent representation of military affairs, in the second another tone was assumed. He declared, that, as the battle was impossible, he

would send one or two plenipotentiaries to Orange.
If the prince were to make conditions incompatible
with the honor of the city, then he would be ready
to venture the final contest. But, before this, the
consiglio grande should be convoked; the Government should express its sentiments in their presence;
and he also would appear and state his views. If
the voice was then for the contest, he would undertake it, and submit to the will of the community.

The intentions of the parties, working by means
of Malatesta, appeared so clearly from the tone of
this letter, that the Government could be no longer
in doubt as to what was going on. The conclusion
of the letter especially, urging for speedy decision,
sounded like an insolent challenge. It was evident
that an insurrection against the Government was
being provoked. Malatesta and his party wished so
to obtain the ascendency, that Florence should surrender herself to the pope, and that without outward force. Every moment he expected tidings of
the destruction of Ferrucci; and this last blow was
to give the signal for decision.

The Government, however, now also understood
the position of things. The people still held firm
to the belief in their invincibility. Within the last
days, an eagle had been caught; and his head had
been carried in triumph to the palace of the gonfalonier, as a good token of the annihilation of the
imperial power. Preachers were never weary of
repeating Savonarola's prophecies. A great tumult
arose when the tidings of Malatesta's message passed
through the streets. The citizens rushed together,

with arms in their hands, to dismiss Malatesta from his office. The city was divided into two camps: in the one — in old Florence — was the Government. swearing death to the traitors; in the other — in the southern city — was the general, with his soldiers, ready to drive back the citizens. Between both was the river, the bridges of which would have furnished the battle-field, as they had done centuries before, when the last families of the old nobility awaited the citizens on the bridges.

Tidings, however, wholly different to the expectations of all, arrived. A battle had been fought; Ferrucci had conquered; Orange had fallen. The citizens were filled with immense rejoicing and renewed confidence, while Malatesta and his party suddenly became accommodating. The Government accomplished, that, without an attack, a challenging sortie against the camp should take place. They approached close to the intrenchments; but no one appeared, and they made no attack. They were awaiting Ferrucci. It was time enough to fight when he should arrive. It was time enough then to settle with Malatesta.

But Ferrucci came not. He had won the battle; Orange was killed. Both facts were true; but fortune had turned in the course of the day, and Ferrucci, like his enemy, was dead. The engagement had taken place near one of the small cities in the mountains of Pistoia. Want of provisions had compelled him to make the attack. While he was entering the place on one side, the Spaniards were advancing to meet him through the other gate. They were fighting at the same time within the streets, and without in the open field. At the point of victory, Ferrucci was repulsed by their advancing superiority. Forced into a house with a few followers, he fell into the hands of the Spaniards, who brought him before Maramaldo.

The latter had the man at length in his power who had so often confounded him by his art, and whom he had never otherwise opposed than to be conquered or avoided. On their march from Volterra, the soldiers had called "Miau, Miau!" because Maramaldo in the dialect of his birthplace, Naples, is pronounced Maramau. A trumpeter, whom he had sent to Ferrucci with a flag of truce, had been hung by the latter. We can understand that the furious Neapolitan should now take a pike, and thrust it with a curse through the breast of the defenceless and fainting general. "You kill one who is already dead," were Ferrucci's last words. He fell to the ground. The Spaniards struck him until he was completely dead.*

This took place on the 3d of August; but only on the 5th, it seems, the tidings were verified in Florence. All who heard them, says Varchi, began to feel the ground totter under them, and became pale as death. The Piagnoni alone, who believed on Ferrucci as on a second Gideon, still hoped that angels would come and defend the walls of Florence. The old prophecy had declared that all must first be lost, but that at last the city would conquer. The spirit of the citizens made one last, fearful effort. Destruc-

* See Appendix, Note XX.

tion and safety seemed alike to them; they desired
only to fight. But the number increased of those
who endeavored to snatch the city at any price from
such fatal excitement. Round the palace there gathered together those who remained firm, and the gonfalonier issued his last warning to Malatesta. The
other party now openly gathered round the latter, in
arms also, not only that they might hold their ground
within the walls, but they might resist the army without, which was now streaming back to the city greedy
for booty.

Malatesta had only been pledged to the Prince of
Orange. He at once placed himself in connection
with Ferrante Gonzaga, his successor, who sent to
him Baccio Valori, the pope's commissioner in the
camp. Three points were agreed upon with him
as the fundamental conditions of subjection, — the
return of the Medici; the freedom of the city; the
submission to the decision of the emperor, to be made
within four months, as to the ultimate arrangement
of things. Clement, we see, is ever compelled to
promise freedom, because he was obliged to make
the final concession to the emperor, to whom he stood
opposed only as one of two parties. Gonfalonier,
Government, and people had also to be won over;
for the course at least stood open to them of setting
fire to the city, and giving themselves up to death.

Malatesta simply communicated to the Government what had taken place. The nobles fell into
such fury, that they wished to whip the bearers of the
message back again, with their hands bound behind
them. Grown calmer, they resolved upon a written

reply. They declared that Malatesta should lead them to battle, — that his honor required it. Malatesta upon this petitioned for his dismissal. It was resolved to meet his demand. The written documents were dated the 8th August. The dismission desired was communicated to him in the most honorable form ; and at the same time he was ordered in the strongest terms to leave the city with the troops. Upon this he fell into a fury. He struck the messenger through his breast with the dagger, who brought to him the letter from the Government. The citizens, who were on the watch for every insignificant event, rose to avenge the outrage. The gonfalonier took up arms ; and the attack commenced on the bridges, towards which, from the other side, Malatesta directed his cannons, while he threatened to open the gates to the troops of Ferrante Gonzaga. Soldiers fought against soldiers, citizens against citizens ; for many of the soldiers had gone over to the gonfalonier within the last five days, and had pledged themselves with sacred oaths to the utmost ; while more and more of the citizens joined Malatesta, to fight with him, if necessary, against the Government. And, besides all this, there were the Imperialists without, who began to perceive that Florence was not to be given into their hands, and, like furious vultures, swarmed round the dead body which they dared not touch.

The contest was on the point of beginning in the city. It needed only that the gonfalonier should mount his horse for the signal for storming the bridges to be given ; but, at the last moment, he was persuaded by his friend to make a final attempt at peaceful negotiation.

Girolami yielded; and this turned the scale.

The citizens had been ready to die, but still to wait, to delay fighting for two days! Perhaps, had they not been so completely starved, they might have done so. But suddenly the power failed them. A citizen was dispatched to Malatesta from the palace. Night approached. The citizens were to assemble on the square under the standards, to mount guard. They came not. A loss of energy had begun, which, like sleep after many wakeful nights, fell like a leaden weight upon men; and, looking motionless on events, they stirred no longer to arrest them.

The standards remained alone on the square. The men who had just before wished to rush into death ventured not to set foot in the streets; and, so long as foreign troops were in the city, no soldier ventured by night to leave the quarter, and to show himself: and thus, without striking a blow, Malatesta was suddenly master of Florence. Such was the end of the freedom of Florence. On the evening of the 8th August, 1530, its last spark expired; and, in the night which followed, further proceedings were organized at will by the followers of the Medici.

CHAPTER ELEVENTH.

1530—1534.

Return of the Medicæan Power — Reconciliation with the Pope — Work in the Sacristy — The Aurora — Ancient Art contrasted with Modern — The Dawn, the Evening Twilight, the Night — Alessandro dei Medici, Hereditary Lord of Florence — Negotiation with the Duke of Urbino — Journey to Rome, and new contract respecting the Monument — Increased Work in the Sacristy — The Citadel of Florence — Erection of the Hercules Group of Bandinelli — Death of Clement VII.

ON the 9th August, the Government proclaimed that every one was free to lay down arms, and to attend to his affairs. On the 10th, those citizens who had joined Malatesta demanded the liberation of the political prisoners. Sixty-five noblemen regained their liberty. Malatesta ordered the Dominican to be arrested who had preached most furiously against the pope. He wished to make Clement an acceptable present of the man, who, conveyed to Rome, and placed in the Castle of St. Angelo, was slowly to starve away in dirt and misery.

The people now broke open the prisons; and whoever was within received liberty. The cry, *Palle, palle!* again resounded through the streets. The form of capitulation was discussed anew. They still persisted in this, — that liberty must be preserved,

and that the emperor should definitively decide respecting the arrangement of affairs.

A faint touch of energy seized those who had
fought for freedom, when, on the following day, the
four ambassadors, sent by the Government with
authority to settle affairs, had gone to Ferrante
Gonzaga. Armed citizens assembled in front of the
palace. Scarcely had this reached the knowledge
of those about Malatesta, who possessed a kind of
military post in the southern city, than they, too,
appeared on the square with naked weapons. Varchi is of opinion, that it would have come once more
to a general contest; but the citizens who had first
appeared, dispersed, and the others kept the field.
At evening the ambassadors returned from the business they had dispatched. On the 11th, the capitulation was accepted; on the 12th, it was signed.
The army outside received eighty thousand scudi.
Within two days, all whom he designated were to be
delivered up to Gonzaga, to the number of fifty
persons. Malatesta watched the city until further
commands arrived from the emperor. Otherwise
all was to be forgotten and forgiven. Such was the
end. Whoever possessed the least amount of experience knew that the whole capitulation might be
gathered into one sentence, — the pope treated the
city according to his own pleasure, and took revenge
on his enemies whenever he could get possession of
them. Whoever could escape, escaped, — the greater
part to Venice and France. Many also concealed
themselves in the city. In churches, monasteries,
and houses, there were hiding-places enough. Every

house had at that time a place of concealment, just
as it possessed its secret store-chambers for times of
plague and famine.

Michael Angelo also kept himself concealed. While
his house in the street of the Ghibellines was repeat
edly searched, he was living in the bell-tower of San
Nicolo oltra Arno, in the southern part of the city,
not far from the gate leading to San Miniato. He
had thus, it seems, held his post to the last.

The Medici now slowly advanced. They only
succeeded with difficulty in restraining and getting
rid of the army before the walls, who were furious
at the refusal of plunder. The Spaniards and the
German soldiery fought a regular battle between
their camps. By night, however, they mutually
attacked the city, and were obliged to be bloodily
repulsed. Out of revenge, they prevented the supplies. It was scarcely possible to procure provisions.
There was no harvest this year. The land round
about was devastated, and the small cities had been
impoverished by Florence herself. Here, after so
many citizens had been killed, or had died, or escaped, executions began, and the prisons were again
filled. Girolami was poisoned in the tower of Pisa.

The 20th August was the first day of the new
rule. Baccio Valori had the great bell sounded,
and the parliament convoked. Twelve men received
absolute power to give the city a new constitution.
This office was assigned to the most declared adherents of the Medici. On the 12th September, Malatesta left the city; a train of wagons following him,
to carry away whatever he had obtained for himself.

The artillery also was given to him as a present.
The German soldiery, who formed part of the besieging army, marched in as a papal garrison.   It is
again their humanity which is commended.   Nardi
relates how they succored Florentine women and
children, who, driven by hunger, ventured abroad,
and attacked the Italians, who wished to fall upon
them.

Thus the Medici at length were again masters.
But what they possessed was no longer the old
Florence.   The rich, proud, luxurious, haughty,
free city, surrounded by suburbs, villas, and flourishing gardens, had become a fable which would be
told to those who came subsequently into the world,
as a tale of decayed and magic glory.   As Rome
was changed in form and spirit for all ages after
1527, so was Florence after the year 1530; and
henceforth she was without the power of drawing
from her own resources, which had hitherto been
her glory, and the source of her freedom.

Michael Angelo's name was too great for them to
venture to incur the ignominy of either killing such
a man or throwing him into prison.*   Besides it
belonged to the policy of the pope to keep up the
appearance of having had all that was distinguished
on his side during the war against the city.   To this
appearance he adhered.   The war had been only an
insurrection of the noblest families of the second
rank against those who stood in the first.   And, in
conformity with this, the sentences also were carried
out.

* See Appendix, Note XXI.

Freedom, security, and the continuance of the old commissions upon the old conditions, were offered to Michael Angelo, if he would come forward. At length he came forth from his concealment, and proceeded quietly to his work for the sacristy. During the siege, the scaffolding had been broken down and used for fuel. Michael Angelo let the building rest at first, and chiselled the figures for the monuments. He exerted himself with morbid haste. He killed himself with work. With such labor did he carry on his work, that within a few months he had placed in niches in the wall the four colossal figures which lie on the stone coffins at the foot of the statues of Lorenzo and Giuliano. He had, it is true, completed none entirely; but, unfinished as they are, they have excited the admiration of men from the date of their origin up to the present time. They are the greatest things produced by Michael Angelo as a sculptor.

2.

His design was to represent time symbolically; and, in four different figures, he portrayed Morning, Evening, Day, and Night. Taken in pairs, as they are grouped on the sarcophagi, each pair gains a new signification. For, as the two figures at the foot of Lorenzo represent the perfect contrast between life and death, — in the one the utmost power of the man, Day being portrayed as a powerful human figure; in the other, defenceless powerlessness, idealized by a woman sunk in sleep, — so Evening Twilight and Early Dawn, at the foot of Giuliano, exhibit

Dawn.

MICHAEL ANGELO.

the passage of the soul from the one state to the other. The manly figure sinking into rest, his eyelids seeming to droop, is a symbol of farewell in death; the woman casting off her slumber, seeming to feel the new light almost like pain, is a symbol of the waking into immortality from the sleep of death.

. This figure, L'Aurora di MichelAgnolo, is the most beautiful of all. It is also the most finished. For whilst, in the others, the heads are only roughly designed (Michael Angelo, it seems, worked generally at the countenance last), every line of the face in this one possesses a spiritual meaning of its own.

She is lying outstretched on the gently sloping side of the lid of the sarcophagus. Not, however, resting, but as if, still in sleep, she had moved towards us; so that, while the upper part of the back is still reclining, the lower part is turned to us. She is lying on her right side; the leg next us, only feebly bent at the knee, is stretching itself out; the other is half drawn up, and with the knee bent out, as if it was stepping forward and seeking for sure footing. This leg, from the thigh to the point of the foot, is wonderfully executed. The other foot is not quite finished at the toes.

The right arm, on which the bust might have leant, seems, effortless and weary, to have been only a casual support. The shoulder is pressed forward. The face, completely turned to us, is bent gently back with the expression of the deepest despondency. The other arm is raised over the left side, with the elbow sharply bent; the hand is thrust back upwards, and the fingers rest in the folds of a veil, as if she intended to draw it over her eyes, as a protection against the brightness of day. It is strange, how, with Michael Angelo, the motives recur. In the paintings of the Sistine Chapel, where the creation of the sun and moon is represented, we see, among the child-angels surrounding the flying form of God, one drawing a fold of the far-flying mantle over his face, as a protection from the brightness of the luminary, which, touched by the hand of the Creator, flames forth for the first time.

It would be a vain effort to describe the beauty of the body, which Michael Angelo has left without drapery; for the veil surrounding the head conceals no more than the hair would cover.[*]

Vasari says that this work eclipses every thing which has been produced even by ancient art.

This is a verdict which seems somewhat on a par with the assertions of the French, by whom the tragedies of Corneille, Racine, and Voltaire, are ranked above those of the old poets. It is true, that, in Vasari's time, Greek statues were scarcely known. The majority of the works in marble found at that time belonged to the latter period of Greek-Roman art. To have surpassed these would be a more moderate praise for such a man as Michael Angelo. But, assuming that Vasari had seen all with which we are acquainted, and still expressed the same opinion, in what would he have erred? What attributes give precedence to the works of the Greeks before those of Michael Angelo?

If we heard it said of a modern artist, that he had

* See Appendix, Note XXII.

even equalled the works of the Greek masters, the
Venus of Milo would rise before us in her divine,
smiling beauty, in derision of all other statues which
we might try and place beside her. She — I speak
of her alone, because, darkened and scratched, without nose and arms, she still outshines all others
— she stands there so triumphantly, that it seems
impossible to compare a work of more modern sculpture with her. If we were to place beside her the
Aurora of Michael Angelo, the different ages in which
they were produced would be expressed by them.
Indeed, had Michael Angelo given his statue a
similar position; if they both had the same proportions, and were formed of the same stone, — still,
broken in pieces, and mixed up together, a glimpse
would be sufficient to distinguish the work. A
wonderful and unavoidable compulsion is possessed
by artists, to infuse their age into their works; and,
as we say that the Greeks felt differently to the
Italians, so in sculpture of different periods we perceive a distinction that admits of no mistake.

The human body has indeed been always the same
among the nations of Caucassian race; but the mode
of viewing things has changed, and with it the idea of
perfect representation. The ideal has no standard;
but, as the word itself implies, it is the appearance
of an object in contrast to what really exists. The
ideal varies, just as the mind of man is free or not
free, and his eye practised or unpractised. The ideal
may be compared to the picture of a woman, as it
appears before the mind of one who is fascinated by
her. That which he who loves her beholds, is a

representation of beauty apparent to *his* eye alone.
The ideal of man is that of a perfect figure unattained
and unattainable, hovering before the eyes of an
entire people, embodied as one man. In the same
way we say " the German," and mean all Germans.
Such a being is composed of infinite parts. Whatever a man feels to be most beautiful in person, and
most noble in mind, he imparts to it. Nothing im-
perfect is permitted in connection with it. Hence,
as the countless eyes of a people become more and
more practised in recognizing what they consider
perfection, just as at the present day in England
there are thousands who can decide with acuteness
even to the most minute details respecting the value
of a horse, the more difficult will it be to arrive at a
common decision respecting the different parts, and
the more strictness will be observed in ejecting that
which falls short of their demands.

An image of such corporeal perfection hovers less
distinctly before us, who live in the present day, than
before the Greeks. The distinction which we make
between man and man relates to his mental condition ; our ideal lies in the inner power, in the fixed
character of the man : among women, it lies in what
we call the womanly, the attractive, and the happy
qualities. We almost separate mind and body. We
are obliged to enter into the feeling of pictures and
statues, before we can appreciate them : at first sight
they seem to be nothing more than the veil of the
mind within.

" The first sight of beautiful statues," said Winckelmann. " is, to him who has feeling, like the first

view of the open sea, in which the eye is dazzled by its infinity; but, by repeated contemplation, the mind grows calmer, and the eye more steady, and we pass from the whole to the detail." So much composure and long consideration was required even by him, who was endowed beyond all others with the quality of perception. At the time, however, when the best statues of the Greeks were produced, numberless eyes had given long years of labor to the contemplation of the human body. To discern its perfections was a holy exercise. We might say, this perception, and the effort to realize that ideal, was the task of the Greek people.

Hence the unusual delicacy of their taste, and the almost inconceivable ability with which their artists knew how to satisfy it. If the attention of a people is once awakened, one mind is sharpened by that of another into the keenest acuteness. Like musicians at the present day, who at once so strongly perceive the character of a melody sung or played, however impossible it may seem to the unpractised ear, that, where it sounds false to them, they feel themselves jarred as if a carriage was jolting over a stone; so, in Greece, an entire people criticised the outline of the human form, and regarded the most insignificant lines in its representation as parts of the whole figure, judging from them the degree of capacity possessed by him who was fashioning it. And, because this consideration related not merely to the material frame, but to the entire man, — to language, mind, character, and all that, which, as a manifestation of human existence, is capable of higher perfection, —

they adhered constantly in the plastic art to that which was connected with all these attributes. A statue, as an object of public criticism, was to the Greeks what to a portion of our public a poem or a symphony is, in which there may not be a word nor a note unfilled with the spirit of the author, and one single empty phrase in the middle of a great work is felt and censured.

We can only surmise what an image of their own beauty presented itself to the mind of the Greek people, when they regarded themselves either in reality or in the works of art. While men and women of good society are with us always well dressed, the Greeks were accustomed to their own unclothed bodies, and felt themselves freest and best when they wore as few garments as possible. By this means, while with us only the movement of the countenance, and at times of the hands, are a mirror of the feelings, with them the whole body was the expression of the soul within. They knew how to interpret every line. Every movement had its meaning. They saw in the muscles of the naked man what we see in the present day in the wrinkles of the brow. And this knowledge was so familiar to every eye, that the artists possessed more through what they knew without learning, than they can obtain with us as the first groundwork by acute observation and labor.

And hence came the freedom with which the Greeks handled the material which they fashioned into form. As poets often, instead of expressing things, only intimate them so ingeniously in their

verses, that we imagine we understand them more
surely so, than if they stood before us in printed letters ; so we see every thing expressed by the Greek
artists plainly, yet with few touches.   They leave
out the incidental without our missing it.   Often they
give only the bare muscles, as if the skin and the
flesh under it had been torn away ; often they make
the surface appear as smoothly worked as if nothing
lay below it.   Then again their treatment of bronze
and marble is different.   And lastly, according to
the kind of marble, the conception of the forms va-
ried.   Coarser stone was treated differently to finer.
In the coarser, there were smoother surfaces, lighter
shadows, softer edges ; in the other, deeper chiselling, sharper corners, and more delicate shading of
the surface.   The same artistic feeling of just treatment was possessed by the Greeks throughout every
thing, both with regard to the material and the subject ; so that almost all works of importance, which
are preserved, exhibit some variety in the mode of
treatment.   One thing, however, is common to all ;
and this distinguishes them from the Roman works,
i.e., from the works which were produced centuries
after the prime of old Greek sculpture, by later
Greek artists in the employ of the Romans, — they
all seem to have proceeded from a direct knowledge
of nature, and from a loving contemplation of her.

What are these works compared with those of a
man who found no school to guide him at the outset, and no people to estimate him ?   What could
the solitary Michael Angelo do compared with those
masters whom every thing helped forward ?   One

thing compensated to him to a certain extent for this loss : he found a school of painting whose works afforded him much ; he found some antiques in the garden of the Medici, and at Rome, from which he studied the works of the old masters. He had, moreover, patrons who gave him employment. But, taking all together, what a pitiful dowry in comparison with that bestowed on the Greek sculptors ! He stood alone, and used his best powers, that he might but obtain firm footing. He found no rules of art, no previous works in any way available. With Michael Angelo, the study of anatomy was revived. He was obliged to discover for himself that ideal, to find which the whole of Greece had labored, and to represent it from his own resources. How the muscles of the body are to be formed ; how they move and change with years ; where individuality ceases, and universality begins, — all this he had to observe, and had no master from whom he could learn it. He alone understood, at first, the delicacy with which he fashioned his work. He studied the ancients ; but he imitated nothing. Wholly independently, Michael Angelo advanced forwards.

That by such a course he did not arrive at that to which the Greeks had attained, is natural. But since his genius was so mighty, and his power for work so inexhaustible, he knew how to create a world for himself ; and, though the solitude in which he lived deprived him of much, it nevertheless procured him some advantages.

He worked more unconcernedly than the ancient masters had done. Public opinion, exercised to

such an unlimited extent, was a check upon them.
They were obliged to conform to it on many points.
They could neither ignore, nor could they escape,
the influence of what had been done before them,
and what took place around them. Michael Angelo
was fettered by nothing. As no path lay before him
which others had cut out, he remained unbiassed in
the choice whither he would turn. He imitated
accidental positions in the naked figure with an accuracy which the Greeks never obtained. He chiselled wrinkles in the skin which would have been
impossible to an antique sculptor; he represented
protuberant, compressed muscles in the arm rigidly
and strongly, as no antique work has done, though the
same position may have been chosen, and though
nature is in accordance with Michael Angelo's con
ception. The Greeks always adhered to a certain
line, and avoided or softened, in artistic work, whatever went beyond it. Michael Angelo knew of no
restriction; and this reliance upon his own authority,
without being checked by any considerations, is the
last reason to be assigned for the difference between
his works and those of the Greeks.

Like the Greeks, we also separate the stages of life.
Childhood, boyhood, youth, manhood, and old age,
have their characteristics, — evidenced first of all in
the physical condition. Yet we judge, when we use
them, less according to the outward appearance than
to the character. The Greeks, however, had formed
an ideal scale for physical representation, according
to which certain periods of life were taken as the
centre of fixed epochs, and were adhered to by the

artists. There is in boys, at three or four years old, a time of shooting up, when they grow thin and slender. I have never found this produced by Greek sculptors. Such periods of development and growth occur again after the vigorous boyish age: this, also, they have passed over. The Greeks always produce only the prime of the human form, at least in those works which have reached us.

Michael Angelo, on the contrary, worked after his models, without caring whether the figure was the representative of a definite period of life, such as the Greeks intended. His statues have an individual character about them. His Bacchus, his earliest Roman work, lacks the slightest breath of that finished exuberance in which the Greeks fashioned their young divinities. The Cupid in the Kensington Museum in London, which belongs to the same period, seems produced in the same spirit. A description of it, sent to me, points out impartially this very thing, and furnishes thus, at the same time, a proof of the genuineness of the work. The David and the Dying Captive for the tomb of Julius are conceived in the same individual manner. They represent stages between boyhood and youth, the portrayal of which makes a strange and unwonted impression upon us, from the fact that our eye has been more schooled by the sight of antique works than by those of nature. In the David, I have often remarked this to others as well as to myself. That which appears strange to us in it, is imputed to the contradiction between the extremely youthful form and the colossal size of the statue. That this is not

Statue of Cupid. South Kensington Museum.

MICHAEL. ANGELO.

the true ground, is evinced by the still more colossal statues of Antinous, which present nothing strange to us, because we are familiar with this conception by the habit of looking at it.

But going through the works of ancient art, so far as they have reached us, from the earliest Greek works to the later imitations of Hadrian, we find none which, as in the David, combines such a strong, almost thick head with such a slim and even slender figure, and, lastly, with such large hands and feet. Nature permits such a combination of contradictions. This very union of awkwardness and agility distinguishes a certain age; and nothing could be more characteristic than Michael Angelo's David, if he was, as the Bible describes him, at once a youth and a hero, — a shepherd's boy, more dexterous than strong, like a horse which has not yet entirely lost the colt-like feeling in his limbs.

Michael Angelo's adherence to nature, when observed independently of other considerations, is still more striking in his female forms. As Homer makes Penelope or Helena always appear in blooming youth, however numerous their years may be proved to be by the calculation of events, so the Greek sculptors exhibit their women in the soft, pliant form of their early beauty. This was, perhaps, because among Greek women, after the disappearance of youthful brilliancy, the transition to age was too sudden to be at all capable of representation. Michael Angelo, however, chiselled what he saw, — the elaborate, coarser muscles of later years. He seems, indeed, to have preferred them. He knew not how to invest his figures with a maiden-like tenderness; he almost always aims at the colossal female form. His Roman models may have been to blame for this. The Roman ladies early exhibited a kind of power in their aspect, which makes its way also into Raphael's works. In his paintings he endeavors to soften this; but in his studies it appears unveiled. Michael Angelo's women are no Iphigenias, but seem more like sisters of Lady Macbeth. And thus Michael Angelo's Dawn is no Greek figure, — such as the sleeping Ariadne in the Vatican, or the Niobe, — but a Roman woman, as far removed in her form from the antique as the naked female figures of Dürer and the German school were from Michael Angelo himself.

We will take the Venus of Milo as the embodied ideal of the greatest sculptor. What does he say to us in his work? Not only does the countenance speak, but every thing speaks in her from the armless shoulders downwards; all the lines round the body and bosom are mirrored before us, as the verses of some exquisite poem linger in the ear. And what do they say? Just what Homer and Æschylus and Sophocles say, — legends, charming poems of the beauty of a people who have vanished, and of the splendor of their existence; enchanting us when we long to dream; making us increasingly happy when happiness is around us: merry, lovely, serious, thundering music, but bringing neither happiness nor love nor terror itself into our souls. No verse of Sophocles or Pindar affects us like Goethe and Shakespeare; no remembrance is awakened of the ideal in our own breast, when Antigone speaks and acts, or when we look at the Venus of Milo. Magnificent forms they are, but still shadows, which, unlike the living type of our own day, appear no longer formed of flesh and blood when we place beside them Goethe's Iphigenia or Shakespeare's Juliet, in whose words we seem to listen to the expression of love which would enchant us from the lips we loved most. From the eyes of Raphael's Madonnas, glances come to us which we understand; but who ever hoped for that in Grecian statues? The Greeks, who worked for themselves and their age, cannot fill our hearts. Since they thought and wrote and carved, new world-exciting thoughts have arisen, under the influence of which that work of art must be formed which is to lay hold of our deepest feelings.

A strange coldness is breathed forth from the history of the ancient world. The masses appear to us cold as shady woods in the hot summer; single individuals seem solitary and unconnected with the rest. In spite of the vast deeds which enthusiasm prompts them to accomplish, they infuse this feeling into me. The life that they lead has something motionless in it, like the progress of a work of art. I see characters of such a fixed stamp, that our own appear eclipsed by the contrast; but that is wanting, which is the element of our own day, which, in its extreme, becomes fanaticism, melancholy, despondency; and which, in a less degree, we call a disposition of the mind, a longing, and foreboding. They live and die without scruple; and their philosophy never frees itself from mist, to lose itself in mist again. No feeling of unsatisfactory longing makes them desire death as an admission to higher thoughts; but, taking farewell of life, they bid farewell likewise to the sun, and descend calmly into the cool twilight of the lower world. It is as if a breath of that shadowy repose, into which they then sink completely, had encircled them even in life, and had kept their thoughts uniformly fresh. They knew nothing of the restless impulse which impels us to meet uncertain events; they knew nothing of that which Goethe calls the "dulness" of his nature, the alternating up and down into distinct and misty perception, the sadness which the sight of aught completed awakens in the soul. They felt none of this, — none of this swaying hither and thither by destinies within; none of this seeking after repose, at discord with themselves, with society, and with the thoughts of the time. Their estimation of things was always clearly defined; and the thoughts of those who felt otherwise were like single clouds which never obscured the sun to the entire people, nor darkened their sky. Whatever Greek sculptor wished to fashion beauty, represented her as an immortal being with an eternal smile. He knew not that shuddering feeling of the transitoriness of the earthly, which snatches from our souls the delight we experience at the sight of beauty.

Dark clouds form with us the background to the brightest production. Our masters have a greater affinity with us than those of the ancients. Goethe and Shakespeare are indispensable to me; I would give up the ancient poets for them, if I had to choose. And so, too, I would not exchange Michael Angelo for Phidias. It would be as if I were to give up my own child for a stranger, though the strange one might appear fresher, stronger, and more brilliant. This inner affinity is of course the only thing which raises Michael Angelo above the Greeks. To me it nevertheless surpasses all other considerations. Wherever his art may be compared with that of the Greeks, it stands lower: but, wherever the comparison ceases, there is an advance; and, in the Aurora, this is stamped most purely. In the Last Judgment, Michael Angelo has represented in every stage this half-unconscious rising from sleep, and restoration to thought; while, in the Dying Slave, he has portrayed the sinking into the dream of death. In the whole range of sculpture, I know nothing finer than the countenance of this youth. In the Aurora, the feeling that fills her shines forth from every movement, wherever we look at her. We see her struggling against an intense weariness of body and mind; she has already supported herself on her arm, and is partly raised; she has placed her foot to step forward, and sinks back again. How magnificently has Michael Angelo, in the movement of the left arm, expressed the stretching-out of the limbs at waking The elbow is raised, and the hand, extended over the shoulder, lays hold of the folds of the veil. An entire symphony of Beethoven lies in this statue.*

A casual circumstance strengthens the symbolical meaning of this figure. Michael Angelo saw in this

* See Appendix, Note XXIII.

the principal difference between sculpture and painting; that the sculptor produces an effect by taking
away, and the painter by adding. He said of works
in clay, that they were rather a kind of painting.
Stone must be freely handled; the small model is
only a help to the memory. Michael Angelo considered a marble statue, not as the copy of a statue
in clay, but as something complete from the first,
which, concealed within the stone, was released by
the chisel from the covering that veiled it. "The
greatest artist," he says at the beginning of one of
his sonnets,* "can devise nothing that does not lie
within a single block of marble, concealed under the
surface which covers it with superfluous stone. And
the hand alone which is obedient to the mind, can
give it form."

But, in the statue of the Dawn, the otherwise perfectly finished limbs are in some places lost in the
rough, thick marble; and the figure seems to us to be
struggling forth from the stone. And, no one having
come to liberate it completely, the truth of the idea
is proved, — how, without the hand and without the
mind which it obeys, the marble must for ever retain
the form. This idea must have often come before
Michael Angelo in his work.

> "As when, O lady mine! with chiselled touch,
>   The stone unhewn and cold,
>   Becomes a living mould,
> The more the marble wastes, the more the statue grows;
> So, if the working in my soul be such,

---

* See Appendix, Note XXIV.

Day.

MICHAEL ANGELO.

That good is but evolved by time's dread blows,
    The vile shell, day by day,
    Falls like superfluous flesh away.
Oh! take whatever bonds my spirit knows;
And reason, virtue, power, within me lay!"

These verses were, I suppose, written to Vittoria Colonna, and belong to a later period; but the idea which they contain was peculiar to Michael Angelo from the first.*

The sarcophagi, on which the four figures lie, are oblong stone boxes, resting on two high transverse supports. The lids are placed flatly upon them, so that the figures, from the centre downwards, lie extended on both sides on the slightly inclined surface. Next to the Aurora, back to back, rests Evening Twilight, *il crepuscolo*, a male figure, according to the gender of the Italian word.

Comparing it with the antique works, the moment chosen for this figure is almost the same as that of the Farnese Hercules. The limbs are more full and round than in the Laocoon; whilst the recumbent statue of the Nile, in the Vatican, would seem smooth and devoid of muscles by the side of it.

The man lies there prostrate like a fallen oak: we should have to use a lever to move him from his place. While, in the Aurora, the bent arm on which the upper part of the body rests shows the possibility of her supporting herself and of raising her figure, the arm on which this figure lies is completely pressed down by the bust, and indicates the most profound repose. The other, stretched out to its full

* See Appendix, Note XXV.

length, reaches the upper part of the thigh of the left leg, which, raised at the knee, crosses the thigh of the other that lies below. The head is left almost unchiselled; but we fancy we can see the face buried in the beard, with the brow nodding forwards.

The contrast to this figure is that on the opposite sarcophagus,— the Day, *il Giorno*. Instead of the front, which is turned to us in the other, a part of the back is visible here. One shoulder, strong as a block of rock, is pushed forward; above it we see the face lying behind it, looking upwards with a keen glance, surrounded by a full, Jupiter-like beard; the hair of the head, however, appearing in front in thick, tangled locks. In the statue itself, the countenance is here also almost entirely lacking; but the small model is preserved, which exhibits in delicate characteristic work all that was intended on a larger scale.*

Next to Il Giorno is the last of the four figures —the famous statue of the Night, La Notte di Michelagnolo, that work known by name to all who have heard of Michael Angelo. Of none can it be asserted with so much justice, that he alone could have produced it.

She appears completely in profile, lying stretched out from right to left. What first strikes us is the immense thigh of the leg next us, which, drawn high up, is at the knee almost on a level with the head, which is inclined forwards; whilst the foot, close beside the knee of the other more extended leg, treads on a thick bundle of poppy heads. This thigh

* See Appendix, Note XXVI.

exhibits a colossal amount of flesh. But what a surface it has! Greek artists would never have omitted here some concealing drapery: Michael Angelo compensated for this by representing the muscles. There is not a particle that does not appear living; and, surprised as we feel at the first moment, we soon contemplate the work with admiration.

But yet more. By raising the thigh so high, the body is compressed on the one side, and we see four deep wrinkles running across it. These wrinkles have been often subsequently imitated; but who, before Michael Angelo produced them, would have ventured to consider them as at all representable?

The arm lying nearer to us is stretched backwards, and allows room for a piece of rock to form a support for the back below the shoulders. The other, on the contrary, rests with the point of the elbow against that colossal thigh; and the hand forms a support for the head, which we see in profile, and which is falling forward in sleep. It is not, however, the forehead which rests on it; but it is with the diadem rising above it, that the drooping head with its closed eyelids supports itself against the back of the hand. The face, unhappily, lacks more delicate finish.

It is really impossible to describe it. The position appears so complicated, that in explaining the various parts the impression of the whole cannot be retained. The attitude is not unnatural; only we are thoroughly unaccustomed to see nature fixed at such a moment. The figure has something immense in it. The chest is broad; the bosom expansive, full, and strong, but

still small in proportion ; and all the muscles on the
neck and shoulders have the stamp of power and
size. It is as if we were looking at a gigantic woman,
who, on awaking, would begin to hurl down rocks ;
before whom wild beasts would creep ; and whom
none others could subdue but the male figure of the
Day by her side. No one would think of applying
to her the word " beautiful." A Greek would have
gazed at her as at the image of a Scythian. One
could imagine a wild Bacchante, wrestling with lions,
more calm, sweet, and gentle. The Aurora, compared with this Night, appears less colossal, more
harmonious, more maiden-like. For here we see
nothing but a woman, strong in the strongest sense
of the word, without a touch of feminine tenderness ;
and this creature, that the contrast may be perfect,
is fallen into profound sleep.

In the rocks, over which she has thrown her left
arm, a mask is chiselled, with vacant eyes and whim-
sically hideous features, perhaps representing dreams.
Under the raised thigh, we see an owl in a cave.
Below the figure, a mantle with many folds is
spread.

3.

These figures engaged Michael Angelo from the
September of 1530. He also completed the statues
of the two dukes. It seems that all six pieces were
carried on equally. The pope received with satisfaction the reports of Figiovanni, the Prior of San
Lorenzo, whose duty it was to superintend the building of the sacristy ; and he was ordered to treat

Night.

Michael Angelo.

Michael Angelo with especial consideration. Whatever money was required was to be paid at once. The political past was to sink into oblivion. In one point alone they saw themselves obliged to mortify Michael Angelo: the block of marble was restored to Bandinelli. He who had never denied his adherence deserved this acknowledgment. Besides, the act of the revolutionary Government was not to be recognized. It would have been a political mistake to have made an exception here; all the more as the decree of the 22d August, 1588, had been drawn up intentionally in opposition to the decisions of the Medici.

Michael Angelo never denied his views. When the statue of Night was exhibited for the first time, the following lines were found among the verses affixed to it, according to the custom of the time: " Night, whom you see slumbering here so charmingly, has been carved by an angel in marble. She sleeps, she lives; waken her, if you will not believe it, and she will speak." Angel and Angelo, as a part of Michael Angelo's name, allow a double meaning, which in this manner has been often used in his praise. The author was Giovanbatista Strozzi, one of the most decided adherents of the Medici, who had left the city in 1529, and had occupied himself in Padua, during the war, in scientific works.[*]

Michael Angelo made the statue itself reply to these verses. The poem runs thus: " Sleep is dear to me, and still more that I am stone, so long as dishonor and shame last among us; the happiest

[*] See Appendix, Note XXVII.

fate is to see, to hear nothing; for this reason waken me not, I pray you speak gently."

> " Grato m'è 'l sonno, e piu l'esser di sasso,
> Mentre che 'l danno e la vergogna dura;
> Non veder, non sentir m' e gran ventura;
> Però non mi destar, deh ! parla basso."

It is not possible to translate this into verse. As often as I attempt it, the grand, simple train of thoughts and words suffers from it. Whoever does not understand Italian must relinquish the hope of feeling the passion of anger to which he here gives vent.

It seems to have been in the spring of 1531, that this took place; for Baccio Valori, who was soon recalled from his post in Florence, had seen the statue before he left the city. If we consider how banishment at that time hovered over any one who even ventured to grumble, we may estimate the full extent of the gloom which Michael Angelo ventured to express in these verses. He worked without rest. He was in a sad condition. Not to mention that scarcity prevailed, that the city was impoverished, that the plague broke out with renewed violence, — public affairs also were growing worse from day to day. Any watchful eye must have soon perceived whither the pope intended to carry matters. In the capitulation, the preservation of liberty had been promised; that is, of an independent Government formed of citizens, no matter of what party, but of free citizens: the details were to remain conditional on a union of the city, the pope, and the emperor. Clement thought to manage things otherwise; and the course which he took was chosen with so much cunning, that, although it was seen through, he attained his end. For who could prevent the citizens from desiring from the emperor, instead of liberty, the rule of a prince? And who could prevent the pope from making the citizens in this sense follow his will?

Clement had conquered with the help of the emperor, at the same time also, as in 1512, with the help of his party. As at that time, there were among the Palleski men of wealth, ambition, and energy, who resisted the slightest mention of the dominion of a prince. The pope used them to subdue the rebels, and ventured to do nothing which could give them offence. And thus it was soon evidenced that in reality every thing remained as of old. In the palace of the Medici, Baccio Valori dwelt as the pope's representative, just as Cortona had done three years before. He at once succeeded in making his authority decisive in affairs of State. The citizens paid him court. He was the sovereign; his opinion was obtained in the smallest matter. Michael Angelo himself did not disdain to keep him in favor with his family, by a work in marble which he intended for him. The Apollo in the Uffici, still in a rough state, and only to be known by its attitude, — a figure three-quarter size, — is said to have been begun by him at that time for the all-powerful Valori. Very soon, however, just as before, only this time more rapidly, a second centre of public affairs was organized in the palace of the Government. Men of rank, adherents of the Medici, aristocrats, men held in the same estimation in Florence as

Palmerston, Clarendon, and similar nobles are in England, demanded from Valori that he should repair to them when matters were being regulated. If he would not do this, they told him he might remain away; but the decision rested not with him, but with them. These nobles were in nowise in disgrace with the pope. Clement could not do without them, so long as they were powerful. But he wished to remove them; for his intention was, that Alessandro, his son or nephew, should become Duke of Florence.

From the manner in which he here went to work, we cannot withhold from the pope the praise of a cunning political deceiver. He took the task in hand according to all the rules of art. Alessandro, already promoted Duke of Penna, was staying with the emperor in Flanders. There was no mention of him made in Florence. Clement gave the city far rather to understand, that his design was to discover the most truly advantageous and worthiest constitution; and he begged the noblest Palleski to give in writing their ideas on the subject. But he requested each separately! This trait is admirable; for, instead of the nobles being now united, and making one common proposal, each considered himself the most influential, and a whole series of projects were sent in. One contradicted another; conferences on the matter were held in Rome; and while they were discussing, examining, remodelling, and intriguing there against each other, time and scope were obtained in Florence for advancing more powerfully in favor of the actual project.

Baccio Valori, satisfied with the Presidency of the Romagna, quitted the city; and Niccolo Schomberg, Archbishop of Capua, entered upon his post. Better acquainted with the affairs of the city than any one else, not a representative of the Medicæan party, but a ruler attached to all citizens, and considering all interests, he knew so well how to bring the minds of the people into the tone required, that, in February, 1531, Alessandro dei Medici, absent and unknown as he was, was declared by the Government capable, on account of his distinguished qualities, of being invested with all the offices of the State. Met by envoys on the frontier, he arrived at the end of June with a splendid train, within the neighborhood of Florence. On account of the plague, he did not enter the city; but he received in Prato the four deputies sent to testify the reverence of the citizens. A few days after, an envoy from the emperor appeared with sealed letters, which contained the final decision respecting the form of the Government of the city. Alessandro, splendidly escorted, entered Florence with him. On the 6th July, there was a solemn sitting in the palace of the Government, that the will of the emperor might be read aloud. With loud rejoicing, the citizens received Alessandro at the hand of the highest ruler, as their sovereign for life, with the right of legitimate succession for his children or lawful heirs. The duke received the homage of the authorities, and proceeded to Rome; while Schomberg continued to rule as if no change had taken place. Thus they advanced as quietly as possible, and the principal matter was always treated as secondary.

At this time, September, 1531, we find the first notice of Michael Angelo since the conquest of the city, in a letter addressed to Baccio Valori in Rome, from an uncle of Antonio Mini, who was in Michael Angelo's service. The object of the letter is to let the true explanation of his condition reach the pope. Michael Angelo's friends seem to have chosen for this task a man whose profession was not letter-writing, as style and orthography evidence : —

" A faithful servant," he begins, " such as I am, should not fail to communicate any thing which, I imagine, might meet with the especial disapprobation of His Holiness. And this respects Michael Angelo, His Holiness's sculptor, whom I had not seen for many months, having remained at home for fear of the plague ; but three weeks ago he came twice to my house in the evening, for amusement, with Bugiardini and Antonio, my nephew and his pupil. After much conversation upon art, I determined to go and see the two female figures, and did so ; and in truth they are something quite marvellous. Your Excellency, I know, has seen the first, — the statue of Night, — with the moon overhead, and the starry sky ; but then the other — the second — surpasses it in beauty. In every respect, it is an extremely wonderful production ; and, at the present moment, he is working at one of the two old figures, and I think nothing better could be seen.

" But, since the above-named Michael Angelo appeared very thin and emaciated, we spoke together about it very particularly, — I, Bugiardini, and Mini, for both are constantly with him ; and we arrived at last at the conviction, that Michael Angelo would soon come to an end, if nothing were done to prevent it, because he works too much, eats little and badly, and sleeps still less, and for a month has suffered much from rheumatism,* headache, and giddiness; and, to come to an end, there are two evils which torment him,—one in the head and one in the heart; and in both help might be given for his recovery, as what follows will show.

"As regards the evil in the head, he must be forbidden by His Holiness to work in the sacristy during the winter: for there is no remedy against the keen air there; and he will work there and kill himself: and he could work in the other small chamber, and finish the Madonna this winter, which is such a wonderfully beautiful work, and also the statue of the Duke Lorenzo of blessed memory. In the meanwhile, the marble wainscoting could be executed in the sacristy; and the figures already completed could be placed there, and also those partly finished; and these could be retouched on the spot: and in this manner the master might be saved, and the works forwarded; and every thing, if it is bricked up, will have a better place than crowded together under the roof. Of this we are certain,—that Michael Angelo would be pleased at it, though he can come to no resolution, which I gather from the fact that he is reproached with not concerning himself about it.† This is our opinion of what would be good for him; and His Holiness might send word to Figiovanni to speak with Michael Angelo on the matter; and we are convinced it would not be disagreeable to him.

"The evil, however, that lies at his heart, is the matter with the Duke of Urbino: this, they affirm, robs him of repose; and he wishes ardently that it could be arranged. If he were to be given ten thousand scudi, he could have no better present. His Holiness could render him no

* See Appendix, Note XXVIII.   † *Ibid*, Note XXIX.

greater favor. This they tell me, and I have heard him
say it times innumerable. His Holiness is considerate;
and I am certain, if Michael Angelo were ruined, he
would gladly ransom him with a large sum of money;
and especially now, when he works so laboriously, he
deserves to be considered. My love and devotion to our
master have made me write thus diffusely."

How closely this letter brings affairs before us!
We see the almost old man — for he now lacked
little of sixty — tormented by sorrow, sick, and wil-
fully continuing to work in the cold and freshly
walled place. He had no relish for food, and it did
him no good. He did not sleep. His head suffered.
His friends thought, with alarm, of the winter, and
contrived how they might prevent him from working
himself to death. And, in the midst of this misery,
he had just completed the wonderful figure of the
Dawn.

The Duke of Ferrara had also to suffer from
Michael Angelo's desponding state of feeling. The
Leda had progressed so far during the siege, that it
was ready to be delivered up a few weeks after.
Michael Angelo notified this to the duke, who
thanked him for it from Venice, at the end of October, in the most amiable manner, and begged him
to name the price himself, as he alone knew how
to estimate the labor he had bestowed upon it.* As
a nobleman sent to receive the statue did not, however, deport himself quite as Michael Angelo thought
fit, he broke off the transaction at once, and gave the

* See Appendix, Note XXX.

painting to Antonio Mini. It was almost the same as if he had thrown it out of the window.

Added to all this was the quarrel with the Duke of Urbino. It had already lasted for twenty years. The claim on the part of the Rovere had been proved. The matter oppressed Michael Angelo to the heart. He solicited the pope, as well as the heirs of Julius, that it should be brought to a conclusion. The reproach, however, that he had lost his time upon other works, was unjust. Even in May, 1531, he had refused a pressing offer of the Duke of Mantua; while, earlier still, he had withheld the material for the mausoleum from Leo, who wished to have it for the façade of San Lorenzo. But he had received money, and had produced no work; that was a settled thing; and his present impulse to come speedily to an agreement arose from the fear, that he should perhaps not survive the winter, and that his heirs would in that case be entangled in an unhappy lawsuit.

Mini's second letter, written a week after the first, shows that the pope had taken the communication to heart. Valori had been commissioned to take steps both as regarded Michael Angelo's health, and the settlement with Urbino. " To-morrow," writes Mini, " is a holiday. I will then visit him; for when he is at work it does not do, and I know your letter will please him.* As you said, make the attempt to negotiate with his enemies: true people and money settle every thing; and you are a man who understands how to bring about greater matters than this,

* See Appendix, Note XXXI.

and have furnished proofs of it.   Would to God that
Michael Angelo had set out at once, and all would,
long ago, have been settled!   For this affair, as it
now rests, is a nail in his coffin (*lo sotterrà un pezzo*),
so much is he depressed by it.   He lacks the courage
to carry out his own desires.   He has latterly felt a
little better."

Michael Angelo's friends were therefore of opinion,
that he had managed the affairs carelessly, and
ought to have negotiated at once, in Rome, with the
duke's agents.   The expression is significant, that
Michael Angelo was *pusillanimo a richiedere*, — faint-
hearted in demanding.   Occasional verdicts of this
kind reveal much.   We see a confirmation of his
inability to come forward boldly when his highest
intellectual interests were not involved.   There is a
tender-heartedness and modesty in him, revealing
the tenderness and sensitiveness of his mind, and
exhibiting in their true light instances in which he
was severe and repulsive.   Self-defence alone compelled him at times to appear unfeeling.

The affair of the mausoleum was settled by Sebastian del Piombo, who, at that time, shared with
Bandinelli the favor of the pope in Rome, and held
the lucrative office from which his surname takes its
origin, and which brought him in yearly five hundred scudi.*   As piombatore, he furnished the papal
bulls with the leaden seal.   The post was generally
conferred on artists.   Sebastian was engaged upon
the portraits of Baccio Valori, the pope, and the
young duchess Caterina.   Staccoli, the duke's agent,

* See Appendix, Note XXXII.

had applied to him as a man of trust; and the letter
is extant, which was written by him to Michael
Angelo about the middle of November.

Sebastian begins with informing him of his position. "If you were to see me," he writes, "as an
honorable lord, you would laugh at me. I am the
finest ecclesiastic in all Rome. Such a thing had
never come into my mind. But God be praised in
eternity! He seemed especially to have thus decreed
it. And, therefore, so be it." Then follows in
detail what Staccoli had told him respecting the
matter of the mausoleum. The duke would have
preferred if Michael Angelo had completed the mausoleum, as had been stipulated anew after Julius's
death. As, however, in this something yet remained
to be paid on the part of the duke, which His Excellency could not afford, he wished that Michael
Angelo should make a new design, for the execution
of which the money already received would be sufficient. He, Sebastian, had replied to this, that
Michael Angelo was not the man to engage in drawings, models, and such like. There were only two
ways of bringing the matter to an end, — either to
break up the contract concluded anew after the
death of Pope Julius, and simply to leave it to
Michael Angelo's free will how and when he would
himself work for the monument, for the money
already paid to him; or to bring about a new contract, by which Michael Angelo should pledge himself to have the monument completed by others
within three years, at the cost of two thousand scudi,
— a sum which could be raised upon his house in

Rome. He had now to declare which of the two proposals he preferred. He concluded with the promise of visiting him in Florence in the following summer. The letter is long, and badly written : *—

"My dear Sebastiano," — replied Michael Angelo, — "I cause you too much trouble. Bear it calmly, and remember it is always more glorious to raise the dead to life† than to create forms which only seem to live (*i.e.*, than to paint). Respecting the mausoleum, I have reflected much. There are two ways for me, just as you say, to fulfil my obligations, — either to do the work myself, or to give money, and let others work on my own account. I must, of course, adopt that of the two ways which pleases the pope. He will, I imagine, not wish that I should finish the work, because then I could not work for him; it must therefore be brought to this, — that he who has the matter in hand, should take the money, and have the work executed. I would furnish drawings and models, and whatever is required; and I think with what is already completed, and the two thousand ducats which I would add, a beautiful monument might be made. We have workmen here who would do it better than I should myself. If, therefore, they consent to this, — to take the money, and to continue the work on their own account, — I could pay one thousand ducats at once, and the remainder subsequently. Yet let them resolve on whatever suits the pope. If they are for the last proposal, I will write respecting the other thousand ducats, how they shall be procured, and that in a manner which I think will be agreeable to them.

"With regard to myself, I have nothing particular to say: only this much, — that three thousand ducats, which I took with me to Venice, became, when I returned to

* See Appendix, Note XXXIII.   † *Ibid.*, Note XXXIV.

Florence, fifteen hundred;* for the Government claimed
fifteen hundred.   More, therefore, I cannot give.   Still,
ways will be found, I hope, especially when what the pope
has promised me is taken into consideration.   These,
Sebastiano, my dear godson, are my proposals; and to
these I must adhere.   Have the kindness to take cognizance of them."

Clement decided as Michael Angelo had supposed;
and the way in which he gave him to understand
this, was by issuing a brief, which forbade him, on
pain of excommunication, to touch any other work
than that on which he was now engaged for the
pope.   The document, which was full of choice and
flattering expressions, speaks of his merits, his weakened health, and the pope's love for him.   We feel,
that, in drawing it up, he intended to say things that
were agreeable to him.   To the Envoy of Urbino,
Clement represented himself as inclined to give
gladly a helping hand to any advantageous accommodation, and promised that Michael Angelo would
himself bring the matter to a conclusion in Rome.
The pope had not at first wished to permit this journey; but Michael Angelo, who saw its necessity,
begged urgently for permission to be allowed to
come.   "As Michael Angelo wished it," Staccoli
informed the duke, "nothing was left to the pope
but to agree."   Michael Angelo was known as one
to whom nothing could be refused.   Pope Clement
did not even venture to sit down when he spoke with
Michael Angelo, for fear that the latter, unasked,
would do the same.   And, if he ordered Michael An-

* See Appendix, Note XXXV.

gelo to put on his hat in his presence, it was probably only because Michael Angelo would not long have waited for the invitation to do so.

Michael Angelo's wish now to leave Florence was very natural. At the beginning of the winter, the duke had returned there. Like his father and grandfather, Alessandro belonged not to those who, as had been usual with the Medici, went to work with secrecy and hypocrisy. As little as these had done, did he conceal that he intended to become absolute sovereign of Florence. Opposition was indifferent to him; hatred did not frighten him; he even allowed it plainly to be observed upon whom he vented his dislike.

What the origin of his aversion to Michael Angelo was, we know not. No especial grounds were, however, required. We may well believe that Alessandro would not have allowed Michael Angelo so much liberty, had the favor depended on him. The "mule square" into which Michael Angelo had wished to transform the palace of the Medici, had been aimed at him. The journey to Rome now presented a good opportunity for avoiding the new sovereign. It is not accurately said when Michael Angelo left Florence. He probably only arrived in Rome at the beginning of March, when he at once placed himself in communication with Staccoli, and endeavored to give such a turn to his negotiations with Urbino, that his work at the monument might prevent his returning to Florence.

The letters we have quoted show the state of affairs. Julius II. had decided upon ten thousand ducats for the whole thing. After his death, in the second contract, the price was raised to sixteen thousand ducats. This sum, the Rovere now asserted, Michael Angelo had received, had applied to his own advantage, and had given nothing for it. This was the reproach which stung him, and took away his rest.

Upon the production of the receipts, however, it now became apparent that he had received no more than five thousand ducats at the most. If they wished to add the necessary sum, he declared he was ready to complete the monument as agreed in the second contract. The pope, however, told him to his face, that it was pure madness to imagine that Urbino would pay more money. Two ways now remained, — either to deliver up the marble works that were completed, to add two thousand ducats, and to leave the duke to have a monument completed from this by other workmen ; or himself to make the monument as good as he could for the five thousand ducats he had received. The former plan would have been most agreeable to Clement ; the second, to Michael Angelo. A kind of middle course was chosen. He proposed having only a single front wall on a reduced scale. The pieces already finished he purposed applying to this. Six of the statues he would execute with his own hand, among them the Moses and the two captives (the bronze parts were to be omitted). Within three years the whole was to be completed ; and, in each of these three years, he would come to Rome for two months,* that during

* See Appendix, Note XXXVI.

this time he might devote himself entirely to the work. The question of its position, in which church it was to be, was to be decided within four months. The Church of St. Peter was given up; but they still hesitated whether Santa Maria del Popolo, or San Pietro in Vincola, was to be preferred.

The contract was concluded on the 29th April; and, on the next day, Michael Angelo returned to Florence by order of the pope, to continue his work at the sacristy. For the first time, he was now obliged to depart from his principle of not allowing himself to be helped. He brought with him from Rome a sculptor named Montorsoli, who under his direction had made a statue of St. Cosmo, the model for which Michael Angelo overlooked, adding head and arms entirely from his own work. Montorsoli helped also in the ornaments of the ducal statues; Tribolo, too,* to whom the two naked figures were assigned, which were to be placed in the niches to the right and left of Lorenzo.† One figure, that of "Earth," with extended arms, and with bent, cypress-crowned head, mourning the death of the duke; the other, "Heaven," with upraised hands, and a smiling, beaming countenance, greeting his admission among the blessed. Montelupo, a third sculptor, was to execute St. Damian, as a corresponding piece to St. Cosmo, — the two tutelar saints of the Medici. Acknowledged, as they are, as works of merit, they yet appear stiff in attitude, and heavy in marble, by the side of those of Michael Angelo.

Besides these three, a number of stone-masons

* See Appendix, Note XXXVII.   † Ibid., Note XXXVIII.

were employed on the architectural parts of the marble ornament. Giovanni da Udine was called upon to paint the ceiling. Carvers in wood made, under Michael Angelo's direction, the shelves for the manuscripts of the library; the completion of which, however, like that of the whole, belonged to the following decade. For, quickly as they worked, nothing was hurried. It did not belong to the spirit of the time; and therefore, when the work was afterwards suspended, nothing was finished.

We ought to have the interior of the sacristy accurately before our view, to understand the artistic care expended on it, which extended to the smallest detail. We ought, at the same time, — and, for one acquainted with Italy, this is scarcely possible, — to forget every thing which in succeeding centuries arose from imitation of this architecture, that we may thoroughly feel the originality of its creation. Vasari says that the sacristy of San Lorenzo is the beginning of a new style of architecture. It contains the elements from which endless works have subsequently emanated. It was the beginning of that wonderful mixture of antique regularity with the capricious bizarrerie of modern times, the last barren fruit of which was the rococo; and, at the same time, it was the conclusion of the more tender manner of Bramante, Raphael, San Gallo, and Peruzzi, who adhered closer to the antique. It is difficult to bring the works of these four masters, and their followers and imitators, into a system; for their buildings are too much like each other, and are yet again too different in many points

to be classed according to fixed relations. We are
obliged to take hold of their characteristics. And
then it becomes apparent, that, whilst we see in them
a free, but ever true, imitation of the antique, the
source from which Michael Angelo drew his creations is a boundless, self-supplying fancy. Regardless how it came into his mind, he made use of all
that an unusual experience had amassed within him
for new combinations, and added to what he imitated
so much of his own, that, whilst he appears as the
master of a new creation, the hands of his imitators
fail in producing from it any thing good. For the
sacristy of San Lorenzo soon became to sculptors
what the Brancacci and the Sistine Chapel were to
painters, — what the Pantheon and Colosseum were
to architects, and the Belvedere at the Vatican to
statuaries. Here they sat and copied, and fancied
they were receiving more than nature and the antique could offer them.*

The interior of the sacristy is a quadrangular
space, giving the impression of circumscribed size.
The wall opposite the narrow and insignificant entrance, which is placed in one corner, widens into
a large niche, containing an altar fashioned after
the antique, with candlesticks on each side, both
after designs of Michael Angelo. The wall with the
door is ornamented by the saints executed by Montorsoli and Montelupo, with the Madonna between
them; all three, if we may use the expression,
only put down in their several places. The principal things are the two other walls, also unfinished,

* See Appendix, Note XXXIX.

but fully calculated to let us feel how Michael Angelo would have carried out the whole.*

The sarcophagi, with the figures lying on them, occupy so much space in breadth, that the feet of the figures almost touch the strong pillars of dark marble forming the corners of the sacristy. Behind the sarcophagi, which from their high pedestal stand light and slender, the lower part of the wall is inlaid with marble. At a height easily reached by extending the hand, a bold projecting frieze intersects the wall, and forms the beginning of the upper architecture. The heads of the recumbent figures rise above it; the statues of the dukes, on the contrary, rest their feet on it; each sits above his sarcophagus, and the figures lie at his feet to the right and left. The union of the three figures into one group which thus arises, and the opposite position of the two groups on the two walls, affords a magnificent sight, the real ground of which seems not so much the marble figures in themselves, as their perfect harmony with the architecture of which they form a part. Throughout, we see Michael Angelo acted upon by this one true idea,—that architecture, painting, and sculpture are not to be considered as any thing separate, but are only to be fully estimated in their true value when they can be employed at the same time in the same place. Had the sacristy of San Lorenzo been completed, it would probably be the finest example of the truth of this maxim.

The niches with the dukes are bordered by double fluted pilasters, two on each side, forming the archi-

* See Appendix, Note XL.

tectural element which occupies the centre of the wall. The space from these pilasters to the pillars projecting in the corners of the sacristy is again used for two corresponding and shallower niches, placed like windows; and for those on the one wall those statues of Tribolo's, Heaven and Earth, which were never executed, were designed. What was intended for the other, we do not know. The capitals of the pilasters in the centre are far higher than the side niches with their cornice. Above these capitals a balustrade-like ornament crosses the wall; and above this a large projecting cornice of dark marble, like the corner pillars, upon which it rests at the corners, and with which it forms a frame for the wall, which is thus closed round like a picture executed in sculpture and architecture. The only thing which in this arrangement appears a little bare and unfinished, is that balustrade-like ornament. Michael Angelo, however, must not be charged with this. His intention was to place a trophy in the middle of it, over each of the two dukes. These were already begun by Silvio Corsini, the same sculptor who had worked also at the capitals of the pillars: but they were afterwards left with the rest; so that, beyond Vasari's notice, nothing but a corbel-like projection, over which the trophies could have been placed, notifies this last touch of the architecture.

Above the cornice, forming a square round the top of the wall, the vaulted ceiling begins. Giovanni da Udine had begun to execute it in stucco and gold, with arabesques of masks, birds, and leaves, to be painted in gay colors; he himself, and many others under him, were engaged in it. The work had advanced so far when it was left, that it would only have required fourteen days to finish it. At the present day, nothing of it is to be seen. If we add to this the unfinished state of the figures on the sarcophagi, and the empty condition of the four niches of which we spoke, we have in the sacristy of San Lorenzo no completed work of Michael Angelo's, but an undertaking only half carried out, and which must be judged as such.

4.

In April, 1532, there was certainly the best will to complete it speedily. In June, the pope doubled the number of workmen at the request of Michael Angelo. At the beginning of September, Michael Angelo went to Rome, and sketched his third design for Julius's mausoleum, the drawing according to which it was at length finished. He could only now prepare these plans, because he was obliged first to take the measure of the blocks of marble conveyed to Florence in 1515, and because the high tides of the Tiber, which occurred in November, 1531, had placed the works, which were left in Rome, and which were intended for the monument, so much under water, that he had no time, during his short residence there in the spring of the year, to examine whether they were available for the new plans.

In the beginning of 1533, he returned to Florence. We have nothing belonging to this year, but the notice, that he borrowed a horse, in September, of

Sebastian del Piombo (who, every summer, it seems, was accustomed regularly to visit Florence), to ride to San Miniato del Tedesco to see the pope, who was on his way towards Genoa. Caterina dei Medici was to be married there to the eldest son of Francis I. Clement went by Livorno, where he embarked. He did not come near Florence. Since the siege, he was either afraid or ashamed of setting foot again within the city. For this reason he turned off from Siena, westward towards Pisa. San Miniato del Tedesco lies where the road from Siena opens into that between Florence and Pisa.

It was perhaps at this time that Michael Angelo prepared the small chapel in the Church of San Lorenzo which was to receive the relics given by the pope, and which Moreni, in his history of this church, cites as a work of Michael Angelo's, occurring at the beginning of the third decade of the century. It seems to be only an unimportant piece of architecture, for which Michael Angelo made the design at his leisure. I know nothing of it when I was at Florence.

An anecdote related by Vasari might be placed at this time. Bugiardini, whom Michael Angelo calls a good, simple being, and who seems to have run after him everywhere like a faithful dog, was at times in a state of embarrassment, not merely on account of lacking orders, but, even when they had at length reached him, with regard to their execution. In both cases, Michael Angelo was wont to help him. Bugiardini was harassed at one time with a Martyrdom of St. Catherine: the moment chosen was that when the lightning shatters the instruments of torture, and scatters asunder the executioner's servants. He requested Michael Angelo's assistance in this, and asked him to sketch in the foreground some soldiers struck by lightning. Michael Angelo placed himself before the picture, took a piece of charcoal, and drew a number of naked figures, rushing here and there in the boldest fore-shortenings. Bugiardini thanked him heartily. But they were only outlines. Tribolo the sculptor was now called upon to help. Michael Angelo's figures were modelled by him in clay, and light and shade were thus produced. Bugiardini himself then worked so long at the picture, that no one would any longer perceive that Michael Angelo's hand had touched it. This picture also, which is still in Florence, I have not seen.

We lack further information of the year 1533. Equally so of the following one, up to September. On the 25th of that month, Clement died, and Michael Angelo at once discontinued his work at the sacristy and library of San Lorenzo, — this time never again to resume it.

He was in Rome. Condivi says, that it was ordained by heaven that Michael Angelo should not be in Florence at the pope's death. Alessandro, freed from the control which had hitherto restrained him, would have made him feel his hatred. For, besides the general grounds from which the duke's aversion to him sprung, an especial motive had recently been added.

In that same spring of the year 1532, when Michael Angelo's contract with the Duke of Urbino had been brought about in Rome by the pope, Clement had obtained something far greater in another quarter.

Alessandro's appointment to be hereditary ruler of the city was, in his eyes, only a transition step. Not a Duke of Penna, but a *Duca di Firenze* was to rule in Florence. Clement, however, knew human nature. It was better that the citizens should solicit this themselves, than that the emperor should ordain it. Under various pretexts, he called those men to Rome whose opposition was most to be feared. Negotiations again began in the Vatican respecting that which they regarded as the ultimate formation of the Florentine constitution. But the nobles were now aware what the pope wished; and they yielded this time, that by their readiness they might save as much for themselves as was to be saved. And thus it was, that the twelve men invested with dictatorial power by the parliament of 1530 now elected anew twelve citizens, called reformers; and by these Alessandro was raised to be hereditary Duke of Florence.

This was followed at the same time by a total change of the civil organization. There was no longer a gonfalonier and Signiory. The division of the city into quarters, on which the old constitution had absolutely depended, was abolished. The offices resulting from this division were done away with. The guilds were at an end. In one word, the independent citizens, organized according to ancient usage, were transformed into an equal mass of dependent subjects; and, as a still greater step, all legitimate change of this new condition was cut off for all future time. Michael Angelo must have arrived again at Florence on the 2d or 3d May, 1532: on the 1st, Alessandro had been appointed duke in the palace of the Government, and had passed through the streets amid the extravagant rejoicing of the people.

The possibility of such a change in the views of the Florentines seems scarcely conceivable. At the least, a gloomy silence might have been expected as a reply to this act of violence. Instead of this, there was delight and enthusiasm. As regarded the Palleski of rank, the pope had certainly made concessions to them. He had explained to them, that it was not his intention to exclude the nobles from the Government of the city; that this only he desired, and must desire, that, if a revolution should again occur, the Medici should not be again alone compelled to withdraw, while their party came to an understanding with the revolutionists. His family had been hitherto the scape-goat; that there must be an end to it, and Alessandro's elevation was the only security for this. The Florentine nobles were to occupy from henceforth the position of peers. In this sense, the new duke made his appearance. He was the most amiable of companions with the sons of the first families. They were with him in the palace: hunting, games, festivities of every kind, followed each other; and Alessandro, who surpassed the best in physical activity, allowed the appearance of a distinction of rank to be so little evident, that the pope himself was displeased. Schomberg still conducted the higher matters of Government. He, as well as the duke, showed himself mild and accessible; decided quickly and justly in matters of justice; and, in affairs of importance, never acted without taking counsel of the heads of the great houses. These, consequently, liked the change of the Republic into a monarchical duchy. And no less so the multitude, who, politically beyond the pale of the law, had gained a noble, youthful, and mild tyrant.

The city was ripe for being tyrannized over. While Alessandro restored to the Pisans the privilege of bearing arms, the order of the Florentines to deliver up their weapons was carried out on pain of death. While the Florentines had formerly sent their citizens into the subject cities to maintain the authority of the Government, troops were now brought from thence to Florence, to keep watch over the citizens, and to guarantee public tranquillity. There was, however, no stir. Those with whom a rebellion might have originated against such an humiliation of their native city, sat at home either silent or humble, or went far away into exile, from whence to utter unavailing curses.

We should have these facts before us, in estimating Macchiavelli's book on princes. Such things had never come into his mind. When he showed Alessandro's father the way to make himself master of the city, he only thought of the ruling leader of a party. Lorenzo was to raise himself and the citizens of Florence into a power governing the whole of Italy. Macchiavelli perceived that Tuscany was too small a territory for Florence; she required the whole peninsula. Alessandro set about the matter more practically. He wished for no citizens with him, with whom he should share the authority, and who would at times have probably ruled him, just as much as he ruled them. And thus, while Macchiavelli argued that it was disadvantageous to fortify a capital, the new duke perceived the pressing necessity for building a citadel. In order to hold the Florentines with perfect security under foot, he must have his Castle of St. Angelo.

Michael Angelo might be of use to him here. Alessandro sent to him Vitelli, the general of his mercenary troops, and invited him to ride with him round the city, and select the most suitable place for the fortress. Michael Angelo replied that he was in the pope's service, and was not commissioned to do this. Respect for Clement restrained the duke from manifesting his displeasure at this answer; but, after the 24th September, 1534, he would have taken his revenge. And for this reason it was well that Michael Angelo was in Rome at that time; and, of course, upon no condition did he return to Florence.

Two things he saw take place there, which might be considered as symbols of the complete shipwreck of all his hopes for Florence. The first, the laying of the foundation of that citadel in July, 1534 the building of which was completed in a marvellously short time by Antonio di San Gallo, the nephew of the two San Galli, to whom Michael Angelo was indebted for so much in his youth.[*] The

---

[*] See Appendix, Note XLI.

second was the setting-up of Bandinelli's group, which was conveyed to its pedestal opposite the David, on the 1st May, 1534.

Just thirty years had elapsed, since Michael Angelo's first great work had filled his native city with amazement. It was also in May that it had been carried through the streets. It was in May, when, in Florence at the feast of the spring, they danced in the public squares, singing songs which the old Lorenzo had himself written for the citizens. And what a work now occupied as an equal the other side of the gateway! How stiff and lifeless the Hercules of Bandinelli stood there with his club! how miserable did it appear, by the side of the living work of the man, over whom the bungling of an intriguer had gained the victory! There are works of Bandinelli's, drawings for example, the skill of which, at any rate, is not to be denied; but what is there for any one to admire in this group, even when predisposed in its favor? Bandinelli had played his cards so well with the Medici, that he carried his point in every thing. He lived in the ducal palace. He allowed no post-day to pass by without sending ample details to the pope in Rome. He wrote about every thing: his letters are full of the gossip of the city, of calumnies, of barefaced requests for himself. When Alessandro came to Florence, the citizens demanded Bandinelli's removal. He hastened, however, to Rome, and knew how to represent to the pope so impressively his own fidelity and devotion, and the baseness of his enemies, that the duke received orders to take especial interest in this much-

tried man. Under these circumstances, he finished
his work. To effect its erection, however, he was
obliged to go to Rome again; for the duke, to whom
popularity was of consequence, and who well knew
that nothing does a ruler greater injury than to
manifest want of taste in matters of art, would give
no order for the erection of the group. The pope,
however, wrote, and commanded it. There was now
no longer an opposing will. Antonio di San Gallo
and Baccio d'Agnolo built the scaffolding for its
transport. Scarcely was it there, than a torrent of
deriding sonnets and bad witticism was poured forth
upon it. The scandal became so bad, that the duke
ordered some of the poets, whose verses surpassed
all bounds, to be arrested. Bandinelli had no cause
for complaint. Besides the stipulated payment, he
received an estate as a present from the pope.

Among the reasons why Michael Angelo avoided
returning to Florence, even in later years, when
Duke Alessandro had long been dead, Bandinelli's
activity there is alleged as one. Indifferent what
master he served, the influence of this man increased
more and more. The Medici did every thing for
him. When, after the death of Clement VII., Alfonso Ferrarese, one of the younger sculptors of that
period, had designed a monument for the popes of
the house of Medici, from a sketch of Michael Angelo's, and was on the point of setting out to Carrara
for the marble, Bandinelli managed, by an intrigue
of the Mediçæan ladies, to effect that the order
should be taken from Alfonso, and transferred to
him; a task which he executed badly enough, and

which at the present day, standing as it does in the Minerva, tends to his own dispraise. But his envy of Michael Angelo reached its highest point under the government of Duke Cosmo. The latter required marble for a monument of his father, and asked Michael Angelo's permission to use some of the blocks lying in his Florentine atelier. Michael Angelo granted it; and Bandinelli, authorized to select the blocks suitable, committed the crime of ordering some sculptures of Michael Angelo's, which stood there already begun, to be cut up as blocks.

From 1534, there was no more Florence for Michael Angelo. The unfinished figures for the monuments could not entice him back again. The façade of San Lorenzo, which was to take its turn after the completion of the sacristy, was given up for ever. Hitherto, though he had often been detained for years in Rome, he had always felt himself a stranger there, and at home at Florence. From henceforth he looked upon Rome as his home.

CHAPTER TWELFTH.

1584—1541.

Progress of Italian Painting from the beginning to the middle of the Sixteenth Century — Leonardo da Vinci's Influence — The Venetians — Correggio — Paul III. — The Last Judgment in the Sistine Chapel.

THE thirty years between the erection of the David and Bandinelli's Hercules, contain the rise, the progress, and the early decline of Italian art. The painting of 1504 and that of 1534 are so different, that in the latter scarcely a trace is to be found of the mind which filled the former. In the year 1504, Raphael was scarcely beyond boyhood; and, devoted to the imitation of Perugino, he never thought of out-stepping that master's range of ideas. Since then, he had become the first painter of the world; he had allowed himself to be influenced by the boldness of Michael Angelo, the purity of the antique, the coloring of the Venetian school, and the variety of Roman life; he had drawn round him a troop of younger artists, and had instructed them in his taste: and what was left of all this in the year 1534? Not a single man in Rome who could be designated as his successor. Giulio Romano had left, and had passed over to Michael Angelo's style;

the rest, after having completed that which their early lost master had bequeathed to them as a last charge, undertook only insignificant tasks. Raphael had been too simple to furnish material for imitators.

It is only given to the greatest to adhere purely to nature: the less gifted, even when they think to study nature, use the eyes of others to look at her. The study of the Buonarroti figures became habitual in Florence and Rome. Luini in Milan copied Leonardo. Every artist who now appeared, sought out the master by whom he wished to be guided. Puntormo in Florence painted even for a time after Dürer conceptions, before he devoted himself to Michael Angelo. Vasari seems never to have had any thing to do with nature. There was no longer that calm pertinacity with which masters had before pursued their own ways, but a seeking for knowledge which was obtained by copying works of art as far as they could be procured. And this production, increased, as it was, by more rapid work, corresponded with the greater extent of the market for works of art. At Raphael's beginning, painters were confined usually to their own city, or to the places which they visited in their wanderings: their works now travelled in increasing numbers to Spain, France, and the Netherlands. The fashion of having canvas instead of wood for pictures facilitated this transmission.

As another result of this, we see a change in the personal appearance of the Italian artists. They had before only exceptionally worked for royal mas-

ters; the greater part of their productions arose
from orders given by the middle class of wealthy
citizens and ecclesiastics, who adorned their houses,
monasteries, and favorite churches, with paintings
and monuments. Art was no luxury, and a moderate price was usually given for paintings. If they
worked for courts, the artists still remained what
they were, — artisans, living in the circle of their
families and friends, and not as an appendage to
the princely household. Raphael under Leo X.
was the first exception to this, and the influence of
Roman life appeared in him. He worked more quickly, and looked more to the effect of the whole than
to the completion of the detail. By degrees this way
of proceeding became usual: artists began to appear
who must do much, and must do it quickly, to be
successful. There were energetic, talented men,
who had seen every thing, and knew how to make
use of every thing, but who lacked time and inner
repose to watch nature, and to represent faithfully
and laboriously the beauty that shone forth in her;
and whose highest ambition was to satisfy as much
as possible the eagerness of the public to see something new. To contrive a grand arrangement of
their subject; to devise unknown tricks of art; to
make an impression for the moment; to produce
something *inestimabile, stupendo, terribile,* — was now
the far more natural aim of their wishes than the
hope to surpass Raphael or Michael Angelo, whose
works had been esteemed from the first higher than
nature herself.

For this is the reason why the appearance of great

masters is followed by decline: the public, accustomed to the effect of works of importance, make the same demand upon every thing produced. Their successors endeavor to fathom this effect as something peculiar in itself, that they may imitate it. They discover indeed some outward marks. These they copy; and, that they may not appear as mere copyists, they do so in an extravagant manner. Condemned thus, *a priori*, to disregard their own peculiarities, they devote themselves with a kind of passion to their great models; they believe themselves also on the same path; and, after having first deceived themselves, they persuade others that their works, with all their imitation, still possess intellectual merit. It is marvellous that this merit should in some cases really exist.

As poets might write in the language of Shakespeare or Schiller, without being themselves devoid of mind, — so painters have appeared, who, incapable of apprehending nature otherwise than as Raphael and Michael Angelo have done, still produced original and important works. So that even in this way the beautiful truth seems confirmed, that great minds enrich and elevate all that comes in contact with them. Let us take a painter like Parmegianino. Arriving in Rome as a young man, after Raphael's death, at a time in which Michael Angelo also was no longer there, he allowed the works of both to influence him. We feel, that, without this school, he would not have produced the works to which we cannot refuse even our admiration. It is as if the mind of the men had lived within him, and had given extent and depth to his own mind. He was in Rome in 1527, when the troops of Bourbon stormed it. They broke into his atelier; and, petrified by the sight of a Madonna which he was just painting, they spared him, and bid him continue it. Vasari tells this anecdote. The painting, now in the National Gallery in London, does not give it the lie. A wonderful majesty surrounds the mother of God: there is something gigantic in her which reminds of Michael Angelo, — something living, tender, and graceful which speaks to one of Raphael. And, as with this figure, so is it with the entire composition, — there is a mixture of the two elements, uniting, as it were, into a new mind in Parmegianino. For his works are at the same time sufficiently peculiar to be known as his own. It is the same with Giulio Romano; with Rosso, who likewise experienced the storming of Rome in 1527, and fled to France; with Perruzzi also, who by the same misfortune was banished from Rome, and reached his native city, Siena, plundered of every thing. In all these, there is a certain majesty of conception, which, although we know its origin, does not lose its effect.

Nevertheless, though the superiority of Raphael and Michael Angelo had thus indicated a fixed course to Roman and Florentine art, a path was still found beyond the limits within which they held themselves and their successors. Progress was sought for and found independently of them; and a new element was introduced into art, the influence of which was so victorious, that all the great productions of modern painting seem traceable to it.

2.

At all times in the history of an art, when the superiority of a master or of a school is rebelled against, it is owing to a return to the study of nature.

Thus Cimabue's want of freedom was broken through by Giotto: thus Masaccio overcame the influence of Giotto, and Perugino that of Masaccio: thus, lastly, Michael Angelo surpassed Perugino; and Raphael, Michael Angelo. Cimabue was the representative of the old Byzantine style: Giotto examined nature, and relieved his figures from the golden background to which they had stuck like colored patterns. Giotto's figures, however, were set in too hard an outline, and they wanted shading: Masaccio, in returning to nature, removed this want. But his paintings lacked roundness: Perugino and Leonardo bestowed this upon their figures. Michael Angelo then appeared; he divested his figures of impeding garments, and gave them freedom of attitude in the boldest fore-shortenings. Raphael, taking nature to help, softened these positions, and blended color and outline into perfect harmony. Only one thing yet remained to do: more thoroughly to effect, in the separate colors, that contrast of light and shade, which had hitherto been only treated generally; and this was done by Leonardo's successors in Upper Italy.

We perceive in Raphael's compositions a symmetrical and architectural arrangement of figures. He generally spreads them out, arranging them rather

Madonna, Infant Christ, and Angels.

GIOTTO.

evidently side by side. When he crowds figures together, each retains its separate position and a certain quantity of space round it. He likes best to divide the whole into two parts, — one more distant, which, drawn straight across the picture, covers the background; and one nearer, which, again divided, occupies the foreground to the right and left, and joins at the edge of the picture the figures of the background. By this means, a free centre is left, surrounded by figures in a half-circle. Thus the Disputa, the School of Athens, the Mass of Bolsena, Heliodorus, Parnassus, and other compositions, are arranged. Such also, to mention the last as well as the early ones, is the case with the Ascension of Christ. When Raphael does not carry out this most perfect mode of arrangement, he either makes two groups from both sides, meeting in the centre, in the foreground alone, — as in the Expulsion of Attica, or the Incendio di Borgo, — or he places them in a row next each other, but always so that the picture has a distinguishable centre, from which the figures are arranged to the right and left in equally proportioned masses. The ground-line of the picture generally runs parallel with that of the frame in which the picture is inclosed.

By chiaro-oscuro, he understood at the same time how to separate the groups, and the figures they contain. We have sketches of his, which were only made to obtain the just distribution of masses of light and shade. The outlines of the groups, however, never lose their architectural symmetry; and

the coloring seems only to be added afterwards as an
embellishment.

In smaller paintings, Raphael has produced works
which are thoroughly equal to the most brilliant
paintings of the Venetians: the utmost extent, however, of the assistance which color affords composition, he left for them and their adherents to derive.
By them the groups were no longer arranged according to the lines which form the outline of the figures;
but, while they placed masses of color in just relation
to each other, and endeavored to obtain the effect of
the whole from the harmony arising from this, they
gained a freedom in the movement of their figures,
which was unattainable by the Romans and Florentines.

The principles for the proportion of the naked form
to the drapery, for the purity of the limbs, and for
the most graceful folds of the garments, which had
been gained with so much labor by Raphael and
Michael Angelo, were again given up in this conception of art as something unnecessary and even
hindering. In the paintings of the masters of the
fifteenth century, especially of the Florentines, we
see portraits and the newest costume introduced.
But, the higher painting rose, the purer became the
figures and the drapery. In Venice, on the contrary,
they fell back into the old style with confidence as
soon as the peculiar painting of Giorgione had given
the tone; and the larger scale on which figures were
now painted here, increased the strangeness of this
mode of art. For while, from the similar proportions
of the old masters, a kind of ideal distance between

the picture and the spectator was produced, the scale of the Venetian pictures brought their figures into immediate proximity. They acquired something intentionally portrait-like. We stand before them as if we could give our hand to them; we bend forward to hear them breathe. And in order to excite this feeling as strongly as possible, and to satisfy it, they often introduce figures only from the girdle, standing out in the composition; they place the frames close against the figures, and understand how, by ingeniously distributed light, to represent on the limited space an abundance of action, such as would never have been so closely brought together by the Roman school. And, on the other side, while landscape or architectural work is brought into that general harmony of color on which the whole composition depends, the figures and groups, separated far from each other, form a unity together, which is equally unattainable to the Romans and Florentines.

Whether the freedom obtained in this manner was an advance to higher things, is a point respecting which many would probably be inclined to dispute. I think we cannot decide at all with regard to the manner in itself: we can only speak of the works which thus or thus originated. We cannot imagine but that Raphael, had he seen what was produced after his time in Venice and elsewhere, would have appropriated the advantages which this style of painting afforded. On the other hand, weighing what really happened, and not what might have happened, there can be no doubt that the victory does not belong to the adherents of color, and that the Roman-Florentine school is far superior to the Venetian.

No one would imagine, with regard to the Sistine Madonna, that Raphael had wished to awaken the feeling in the spectator of a real form coming down through the frame out of real clouds. What we feel before that work is something higher. Perfectly certain that we have painted canvas before us, a dream nevertheless fills the soul; and we feel carried upwards and transformed, just as when we listen to a verse of Goethe's, or to the music of Beethoven. It is otherwise with the works of the Venetians and their followers. We fancy we may touch what we see: the real nature seems to break in upon us. It would have been a triumph to them, if the birds had picked the painted fruit. When Titian painted Paul III., in later years, and the painting was placed in the open air to dry, the Romans who passed by believed they saw the pope himself, and saluted him. This would never come into the mind of any one in the portrait of Leo X., which Raphael painted; but let us think of them together to feel which of the two is the more genuine work of art.

Raphael endeavored to raise the actual above itself. The limbs which he painted, and the folds in which he enveloped them, have a grace and an elevation which at once reveals the nobler view of nature which he fostered. As the Greeks in their statues sought to transform their model to a measure of higher beauty, he perceived the ideal in forms; and, without obtruding it, he makes it shine forth. The Venetians, on the other hand, adhered to human incidents. These often furnish that which is most useful for the striking effect of the painting. They represented it, however, not out of love of truth, as Raphael had often done in his earliest works, but because a sharp, striking characteristic seemed by this means attainable. The eye was attracted more quickly, just as short sentences, with pregnant, cutting words, seem at first sight to give the sense of an author more forcibly than an artistically finished mode of writing. Raphael can paint no face without secretly adding a particle of pure beauty. He makes, as it were, a poem upon it, in which we see the figure truly, but elevated. He did this in portraits as well as in historical pictures; and the longer he painted, the more consciously. Let us call to mind his Ascension of Christ. Like the work of a poet, who, stringing thought to thought, never brings one profane word into his verse, this composition stands before us, stone above stone, hewn in noble proportion, and built up into a perfect temple; while Titian's famous Ascension of the Virgin presents, as to its design, nothing, as it were, but a mass of rocks, which, without color and light, would appear roughly heaped up over each other.

3.

It was not with the Venetians, however, although their art corresponds so thoroughly with the nature of their country, that the sway of this new element in art originated. The first impetus proceeded from Leonardo da Vinci, who made a study of color with

changing light, and pointed out its advantages.
The clear light of the bright, open air, he writes, is
good for nothing.   We ought to paint as if the sun
was shining through a mist.   To see the naked
body beautifully, the walls of the atelier should be
hung with crimson, and clouds should obscure the
sun.   Bad weather is the best light for faces.   An
atelier should be twenty feet high, the same in
breadth, and double in length; the walls should
be black, and fine linen should be stretched over it.
He gives the same directions in a pamphlet upon
painting.   In this course, the school of northern
Italy followed him.

In one direction alone, however, did the Venetians take advantage of what Leonardo had set
forth; another school was founded through him;
a master was formed upon the principles which he
had given out, who — just as Parma, where he
painted, lies in the middle between Milan, Florence,
and Venice — seems thus to stand in the middle
between the three cities and their art.   This man
was Correggio.   Greater than all who came after
Leonardo, Raphael, and Michael Angelo, he has in
many respects even surpassed these three.   Correggio, unlike the Venetians, did not remain behind
in design; he embraced the whole art, and carried
it forward.

If we were to imagine streams issuing from the
mind of Raphael, Michael Angelo, Leonardo, and
Titian, meeting together to form a new mind, Correggio would be produced.   He has the dreamy,
smiling manner of Leonardo; and, to add an out-

ward characteristic, he was, like him, a stranger to troubles within or without. He has the cheerful, beaming, inexhaustible qualities of Raphael; and again, to mention an external likeness, he was cut short in the prime of life, while he, too, contentedly clung to a circle of limited extent. He has the boldness of Michael Angelo, the desire for unheard-of positions, and the knowledge of fore-shortening. The humid brightness of his coloring, and the talent of representing the trembling naked flesh, as if the pulse were beating in it, seem to ally him with Titian.

Correggio died at forty years of age, in 1534. He had met with none of the great masters, so far as we know: he had neither seen Rome nor Florence. We have, except a few dates concerning him, nothing of him but his works, — no letters, no words, not even his portrait. We neither know what books he had read, or with whom he was intimate. All sorts of fictitious adventures are associated with his name: none of them are capa-ble of being authenticated. From a misunderstood word of Vasari's, *misero*, meaning " poor and miserable," and, at the same time, " frugal and avaricious," — a word which was applied to him in its first signification, while it was supposed to have been the second, — a tragical story has been formed of his death. Vasari relates that Correggio had had a numerous family; that he was obliged to be sparing, and for that reason had carried a picture himself to the place of its destination; that he was overcome by the heat, and by this means had brought on his fatal illness. Correggio, however, was not poor; he left property behind him. Oelenschläger's tragedy is without foundation, and is just as little true as the meeting of Correggio with Michael Angelo, which occurs in it. When Michael Angelo returned from Venice in 1530, the route ordered in the pass was, as has been related, through Modena. It is not quite impossible that he may have met Correggio there; but nothing is mentioned of it anywhere, and the scene between the two in Oelenschläger's poem is an invention.

We can imagine Correggio as a man who led a quiet life, made happy by his art. For he finished his paintings with an unwearied care, such as quiet and ease alone permit. And he worked into them the light of that sun which had brightened Leonardo before. A kind of earthly rapture is expressed in them, — a feeling far surpassing, it seems to us, the acknowledged beauty of the production.

Any one of his pictures may be cited in proof of this: The Adoration of Christ, famous under the name of "the Night of Correggio," where the child casts rays of light around on the mother and the shepherds, like a star fallen from heaven, from which a magic light emanates. Or the Glorification of Mary, who sits on her throne surrounded by saints, whose forms are filled with the brightness of inspiration. Lastly, his Ecce Homo in the Berlin Museum, a painting in which pain and sadness and beauty are united into the most touching spectacle. Like the veiled moon in the nightly heaven, the face of Christ lies on the delicate canvas on which

The Adoration or " Night."

CORREGGIO.

it is impressed. We feel that Correggio painted it. Leonardo alone, besides him, could have painted it.

What most distinguishes Correggio's painting, however, from those of other painters, is a peculiarity in his conceptions, which seems to stand in connection with the quiet, retired life which he led. There is a difference between the poet, who, filled with religious enthusiasm, writes a hymn upon the Virgin Mary ; and another, who, struck by the charming legends that surround her life, writes sweet verses, in which her beauty is extolled. Raphael, and those others with whom we have before compared Correggio, worked as it were like dramatic or epic poets, in whose soul the enthusiasm of the people, to whom they had regard in their labors, involuntarily co-operated with their own. Correggio, contrasted with them, seems like a lyric poet, who writes wonderful verses in solitude, and only for the sake of delighting himself. For this reason, it is all one to him what he handles, if it is only beautiful, and capable of that mysterious lustre which he spreads over all his figures. He paints scenes of heathen antiquity and Christian legend in the same spirit, and endows them with the same capacity of having an almost intoxicating effect upon the beholder. In his solitude, he seems to have formed a world for himself, which he places in the magic gardens of Armida. Leonardo was the first to transport the Virgin into strange, fabulous regions. Correggio took up this idea, as he had done Leonardo's smiles, and the tender, pale tint of his coloring, in which none of the burning colors of the Venetians are to be found. Leonardo was every thing to him in Milan, possibly because his earliest studies were made under him. But what Leonardo always treated as a charming accessory, became with Correggio the chief meaning of the painting. If, in his "Night," we imagine the light away, which is the centre of the picture, all must have been differently arranged. It is not the beauty of the child which touches us in its examination; it is not even the smiling face of the mother bent down over him, but the mystical glow of light which affects us, just as children are affected by the sudden brilliancy of the lighted Christmas-tree. It was this he desired to obtain. Color and figures, and accidents of place, he interwove into an inseparable whole, and made effect his principal matter. We could not, as in a picture of Raphael's, separate this or that from a group, and consider it alone as the single act of a drama or a soliloquy in this act. Correggio's paintings are poems, which we must take at once as a whole from the first to the last word.

In his representations from ancient mythology, we feel what has been said before of the Venetians,— the absence of the influence, not only of antique statues, but of sculpture in general. Raphael's and still more Michael Angelo's figures have something abiding in them, just as the positions of a good actress, however passionately she is playing, and passing from one movement to another, have in them a steadfastness which impresses them upon us. The statues with which Rome is filled may be to blame for this. Correggio's figures seem to tremble. In his Io, who sinks down in rapture as into a sea of bliss, the cloud in which Jupiter embraces her seems to become now thicker, and now clearer; and through it Io's limbs gleam out, as if she were moving, and altering her position. Or his Leda. With Michael Angelo she is a gigantic figure; with Correggio, a trembling, youthful woman, to whom the swan rises from the water. It is as if he had just shaken off the last drop, while the rushing of the stream penetrates into Leda's heart, like a divine song. She is leaning with her back against the moss-grown roots of a tree, while over the point of her foot the shallow tide flows from the woody ground, where her companions were attacked by other swans. One is moving about in the shallow water, playing timidly with one of the birds; a second looks with a doubting smile after another which is flying away: she looks for him as she ascends the bank, where an old attendant is waiting to throw a garment over her. On the left side of the picture, on the other hand, where the landscape opens, a slender, boyish Cupid is lying in the shady grass, and touching the strings of a golden lyre: he seems playing no melody, but only now and then to touch the strings. These would be nothing but different groups, unconnected, but for the landscape, and the feeling that all is worked one into the other. No painter at that time would have understood how thus to separate his figures, and yet to connect them, as Correggio has done.

But what made it possible for him to exercise an

important influence even upon the schools of Raphael and Michael Angelo in later times was his superiority in design. If his productions in this branch may be designated more as trick than art, he always achieved it; and, by the imitation which he called forth, he created a new style of ceiling painting. We find the germs of it in Raphael and Michael Angelo; but the fundamental appropriation of these elements belongs to Correggio, and only an uncommon talent like his could have succeeded in doing what he achieved.

Michael Angelo, in his historical pictures, had never fallen into Raphael's architectural arrangement, — perhaps because he ceased painting just when Raphael began, and thus a re-action could not take place; perhaps also because, in his opposition to Perugino, with whom the lighter arrangement of composition originated, the natural even here prevailed over the artificial. When he gives a greater number of figures, — as in the cartoon of the Bathing Soldiers, or in the Deluge on the ceiling of the Sistine Chapel, — he makes his figures fill the breadth of the space, without a central point: where there are only a few figures, he arranges them in groups as if they were copies of statues. He endeavors, by fore-shortenings, to separate them from the background, and ignores, as it were, the level on which they are painted; but he never exaggerates. Although in the Sistina he creates an apparent architecture by the art of perspective, he applies this artifical means only sparingly to his principal figures. Among the prophets, he painted Jonah alone so: he seems to be leaning back, while the surface of the arch on which he is painted is inclined forward. He felt, that, in the non-essential part alone, this might be attempted.

Raphael thought so also. On the ceiling of the Farnesina, he has painted in different places, where the blue sky is seen through the winding wreaths, groups of Cupids, who exhibit themselves in the strangest fore-shortenings, as if they were fluttering like butterflies in the open air. This is so managed, that, if the pictures were taken down and placed against the wall, they would all be standing on their feet. Raphael went still farther in the ceiling paintings of the Chigi funeral chapel in Santa Maria del Popolo. But this work, a secondary thing which he never finished himself, cannot be regarded as a proof of especial predilection for such things. Correggio carried it much farther. He developed the idea with unheard-of boldness. He was not satisfied with the illusion of a second architecture on his ceilings, with which he could bring the position of his figures throughout into perspective harmony; but he transformed the ceiling entirely into the open sky, filled with fore-shortened colossal figures. This idea has been used by the Italians to an immense extent. The vast interior of the dome of the Cathedral of Florence is painted as if one was looking into the infinite heaven, the clouds of which are peopled. Vasari, little as he knows of Correggio, praises him exceedingly. It appears to me, without a doubt, that, had the field been now left to Correggio alone, —had the Venetian painting gained a footing in

Rome through Titian, as it almost did, — Raphael's and Michael Angelo's school would soon have been driven from its absolute position there, and the new style would have had a brilliant entry.

It was under these circumstances that Michael Angelo, who had almost ceased to be reckoned among living painters, took up his brush again, after thirty years' rest, to paint the Last Judgment on the altar-wall of the Sistine Chapel; and produced a work which so far surpasses every thing that had been hitherto done in painting, that every influence in Rome from without was destroyed, and his own was again confirmed as triumphant.

4.

The interior of the Sistina is, as we have before said, a quadrangular space, three times as long as it is broad. Under the windows, placed high up on the two longer walls, a belt of fresco paintings runs round the interior, so that the two smaller walls are intersected by it. These were to be filled with painting; and Michael Angelo was to cover the two immense surfaces with two works, one of which represented the Fall of the Angels, the other the Last Judgment. The one, the beginning of sin after the revolt of Lucifer; the other, the final consequence of this act, — the unalterable separation of mankind in eternity into the blessed and the condemned.

For an artist like Michael Angelo, no higher theme could have been devised. Every feeling that moves the human heart, from the tenderest emotions to the outburst of the utmost passion, must be exhibited here, and that in its most ideal form. As Dante embraces in his poem the destiny of all men, an artist who would represent the Last Judgment must make all mankind appear. A genius who felt himself capable of such a task, could, when it was placed before him, have had no other feeling than to seize it with avidity. Michael Angelo, placed before the two walls assigned to him, must have experienced what, in the noblest sense, a warlike prince must feel, who, instead of having ten thousand men under him, suddenly sees himself before a field on which he is to lead half a million to battle. Michael Angelo evaded the task, when Pope Clement first came to him on the subject. It is said, and it is credible, that he declined from conscientious motives. He had promised his utmost energy to the monument. But he readily, however, I imagine, gave his consent to the efforts made by the pope to set him free, as regarded the Duke of Urbino, in favor of the new project.

As early as the winter of 1533, when he returned to Rome from Florence for the first time on account of the mausoleum, Clement proposed the new work to him, and refused, when he met with opposition, to confirm the contract by which Michael Angelo was pledged to continue the mausoleum. Michael Angelo upon this began to make designs. The matter had gone so far, that, under the direction of Sebastian del Piombo, one wall of the chapel was freed from all ornament, and was prepared for painting. It had even already given rise to disputes. Sebastian was in favor of having the Last Judgment painted in

oils.   Oil-painting on lime and stone was his especial
delight, a penchant which was just as disadvantageous to his works as it became to those of Leonardo.
Michael Angelo declared himself against it.   Oil-
painting was for women : men ought to paint in
fresco.   And when Sebastian, in spite of this, had
the wall prepared according to his method, it was
for this reason that Michael Angelo delayed beginning the work in the chapel.   He is said never to
have forgiven Sebastian, his best friend, for this; so
that from this time a coldness set in between them.
Sebastian's lime cement was again scraped off, and
the wall was prepared according to Michael Angelo's
plan.   It is not known whether this took place under
Clement, and whether the painting was begun during
his life.   If this were the case, it was of course left
off again at once on the pope's death, and Michael
Angelo returned to the mausoleum.

It may be considered as a piece of rare good fortune, that now again a pope succeeded who knew
how to estimate Michael Angelo to the full extent
of his merit.   Paul III., whose family name was
Farnese, had been made a cardinal by Alexander
Borgia.   His sister had fixed this reward as a proof
of her favor.   Sickly, and full of years, Farnese's
weakness seemed increasing to such an extent, especially at the time of the election, that the cardinals
gave him their vote because his speedy death was to
be expected.   Scarcely, however, was he pope, than
the mask was thrown aside.   He ruled for fifteen
years, and understood, as well as his predecessors
had done, how to turn this period to the advantage

of his family. His son was to be Duke of Milan;
his grandson, still but a child, was made a cardinal.

Paul III. appears before us with a certain degree
of innocence. He possessed the base qualities of
Borgia, but without his cruelty. He did not fall
upon his prey with the same open brutality as the
others. He possessed Leo's taste and classical culture, without his foolishness. The foreign relations
of the Vatican were more worthily carried on under
him. He possessed Clement VII.'s cunning in de
ceiving, but without his nervous timidity. It was
of more importance to Paul to stand there free from
reproach, than to others; and he succeeded. His
secret private life, however, the manner in which he
suffered, overlooked, and denied the base conduct
of his son, compared with whom Cæsar Borgia appears heroically great, allows of no doubt as to his
true nature : and yet, as is possible among Romanic
nations, that in one and the same man immense
depravity in morals and politics may be united with
taste, amiability in intercourse, ay, even with generosity and qualities of the heart, which, separately
considered, cast a dazzling light upon the character :
so it was with him. Respecting the noblest mental
efforts of his time, he appears as a considerate and
kindly master ; and his intercourse with Michael
Angelo exhibits him in the best light.

With regard to an earlier connection between
Farnese and Michael Angelo, we only know, that, in
the year 1531, he had made designs for two can-
delabra for the cardinal, which still at the present
day stand in the sacristy of St. Peter's. He was

now sent for to the Vatican, and told that he was to consider himself as in the employ of His Holiness. He excused himself with reference to the Duke of Urbino. "It is now thirty years," cried Farnese, with vehemence, "that I have had this desire; and, now that I am pope, shall I not be able to effect it? Where is the contract, that I may tear it?"

Michael Angelo remained firm. He even thought of withdrawing to Aleria on the Genoese territory, the bishop of which owed his position to Julius II., and was on terms of friendship with himself. He would there complete the mausoleum. Carrara lay conveniently near. Another time the thought occurred to him of going to Urbino itself. He had already sent one of his men there to purchase a house with some land, when the pope induced him to meet his wish. He appeared one day in his atelier with eight cardinals, and asked to see the sketches of the Last Judgment. Michael Angelo was just then working at the Moses. "This one statue is sufficient to be a worthy monument to Pope Julius," cried the Cardinal of Mantua. Paul examined the designs. He could arrange, he said, that Urbino should be satisfied if only three of the statues were executed by Michael Angelo himself. The end of the matter was, that the contract was not ratified by Paul III.; that he took upon himself all that arose in consequence; and that Michael Angelo began to paint in the chapel.

5.

Many fresco paintings belonging to the sixteenth century are at the present day in a sad state; few, however, have been more cruelly trifled with than the Last Judgment of Michael Angelo.

He had endeavored to protect it against the dust by giving the surface of the wall a trifling inclination forwards. Vasari considers it about a foot, which is scarcely perceptible in so great a height. It did not strike me. Moreover, as soon as the work was finished, Michael conferred upon his servant Urbino the office of taking care of the paintings in the Sistina. This office was a permanent one. But the smoke of the altar-candles has had a fatal effect in the course of centuries. The lower part of the painting is most damaged. Irons have been placed here for the occasional strengthening of the papal throne. In the unusual number of naked figures, almost without drapery, of which the composition consists, Michael Angelo had avoided all monotony by the delicate shades of the skin (a print in the Berlin Museum, colored at the time, shows, in my opinion, how happily the groups and figures are separated by this distinction of color); but, at the present day, this has disappeared in the uniform darkness that covers the whole. Cornelius is of opinion, that a mere washing with water or wine would have a splendid result. Much has become too dirty to be discerned. The greatest evil has, however, been intentionally done to the work: the nakedness of the figures has been considered offensive; and they have been covered with painted, and often glaringly bright, drapery. The harmony of the colors, as well as of the tints, must have suffered from this. There is scarcely a single figure in it at the present day utterly devoid of all garment. From all this, the work appears in such a condition, that only after long study is it possible to form an idea of what it was in the year 1541. Early copies in oil, as well as engravings, sketches of many groups by Michael Angelo himself, which have reached us, make it possible to perceive, step by step, what was formerly there. The impression of the whole, however, and its overpowering effect at first sight, is lost.

For now, when the power of the color has almost disappeared, the immense composition cannot at first be taken in. The space is too great, and the connecting element is wanting. The Last Judgment, when we first look at it, appears like an endless throng, — like a stormy sky with clouds shifting together, gathering restlessly and unequally from all sides. The composition only slowly arranges itself before us. We learn how to follow and apprehend the multitudinous train. We see the angry frown of Christ as the upper centre of the painting; and around him, as a broad, cloudy halo encompasses the shining moon, we see crowds of countless forms; and around these, other multitudes, like a second broader ring, which below, however, instead of closing, makes a curve, and again turns outwards, meeting thus the lower edge of the painting, from whence on both sides the train of figures rise into the air.

For the idea of the composition is this: the whole wall is regarded as the infinite open space of heaven, into which we are looking. Christ forms the centre, with Mary, who is sitting, clinging to his knee; and from this centre beaming rays emanate on all sides. An immense circle of saints, each with the insignia of his dignity in his hand, surround Him as the chief in heaven. Below this circle, Christ's foot-stool as it were, is the angel of judgment, with trumpets directed into the depths below; and from these depths on the left side arise those awakened from the dead, while on the right the condemned are striving upwards, and are thrust down by struggling angels and devils. (Right and left as regards the spectator; so that, as seen from the picture, the condemned, as they ought, come on the left side.) Quite above, however, high above the circle of the elect, are the blessed with the instruments of the death and sufferings of Christ, which they bear, hovering about in triumph. Such are the contents of the painting, which not only differs from the earlier representations of the Last Judgment, but also, as regards the artistic work, is such an astonishing production, that nothing which has been executed by any painter, before or after, can be compared with it.

Groups of figures seem completely to rise from the surface on which they are painted. The foreshortenings are so bold, and are at the same time executed in so masterly a manner, that the idea of the difficulty overcome is lost sight of, — an idea which generally at once rises. As Shakespeare could say every thing, he could draw every thing. At the left, where those set free from the long captivity of death rise from their graves into light, and

gradually ascend, we can imagine we feel the breath
of ether wafting them upwards, carrying them gently
up like rising air-bladders; whilst, on the right, the
heavy falling of the condemned, as they strive to
rise, is expressed with the same power. Everywhere the feeling which fills and animates the figures is brought powerfully before the mind, and
excites our sympathy as in the suffering characters
of an affecting tragedy.

6.

The figurative representation of the Last Judgment is as old as Italian art. In all ages, we meet
in sculpture and painting with the dead rising from
their graves, the multitudes of the condemned driven
into the abyss, the blessed rising to dance with the
heavenly bands; and in the midst, above them all,
Christ in judgment, surrounded by his saints. The
arrangement, too, was according to the old custom,—
the good on the left, the bad on the right: in the
midst, between them, at the feet of Christ, the angel
of judgment; and above, the instruments of suffering, borne like trophies through the air. The religious worship of Italy in the past century, gathering
together, as it had done, every thing that could
strengthen its influence, required the representation
of the last fearful day as one chief means for affecting the mind. The dim moment, lying in remote
futurity, respecting which the saints themselves know
not when it will begin, was a fruitful soil for the
imagination of artists. All these representations,
however, appear formal and rude in comparison with

that which Michael Angelo produced. In this he proved himself even here as a genuine artist, that he exhibited not the judgment itself, but only the path to it. The tragic lies not in the fearful deed, but in its inevitable approach; not in the enjoyment of happiness, but in the attaining of that enjoyment. We see not, therefore, the delight of the blessed, but the trembling expectation of speedily obtaining it; and, on the other side, we see not the suffering of the condemned, but the last horrible moments before sinking into eternal torment. Every figure bears in itself the tenor of its destiny. Whatever we suffer on earth, — whether overwhelming joy or destroying grief, — no single, unmixed feeling ever prevails in us: remembrance and expectation always weaken the force of the moment, however powerfully it takes possession of us. But here, as the garments have fallen from their bodies, and earth has vanished under their feet, the man is fettered no longer; penetrated by the one thought, as a bell vibrates with the one tone which the stroke of a strong hand has produced, he is filled with the experience of the moment. And the degrees of these feelings — from the first faint recognition of light, through happiness and misery, up to the destroying knowledge of everlasting condemnation — we find represented in this painting.

The wall is half as high again as it is broad. Hence the necessity of a higher and lower centre. The judging God rules the upper half; the troop of angels sounding to the judgment, the lower. Both centres are, however, so well united, that not a

figure could be found which may appear superfluous
or unnecessary to the whole train. The unity of
the picture, and at the same time the separateness
of the different groups, is marvellous. The angels
strike the trumpets as if the whole world must quake
at the sound, and, as St. Matthew says, as if all the
tribes of the earth must mourn. Unceasingly, while
they blow, men awake to be judged. The trumpets
are extended in all directions, except to the right,
where close beside them the condemned are hurled
down. One of the two angels, who ought to be
blowing the trumpets there, has placed the trumpet
over his shoulder, and looks with frightened curiosity
at the ruin of the guilty; while the other, with the
trumpet at his lips, turns away his head inquiringly,
as if he had just received orders to hold his breath.
Two other figures of this group, which, surrounded
by clouds, seems itself like a single heavy cloud,
hold open books, — that of condemnation directed to
the one side, that of life to the other; while below
them, in the deep rocky ground, the awakened dead
are disengaging themselves. Skeletons, bodies still
veiled with palls, naked figures rising, some still
half in the ground, from the holes of which they
crawl, others already so far advanced, that, kneeling
and supporting themselves with their arms, they
attempt to stand until they begin to soar; and the
higher, the lighter grows the movement, up to
the highest of those who, completely freed from the
sleep of centuries, fly towards the great circle, which
in wide circumference joins the first circle, surrounding the form of Christ.

In the contrast of these rising figures to the ruined ones on the other side of the painting, Michael Angelo has displayed his greatest art. It is as if we saw masses of clouds covering the sky, and gigantic figures suddenly climbing up them, or starting from their projections, and hovering aimlessly towards the sun; and opposite, on the other side, as if leaden, devilish powers hung to those pressing upwards to the same light, and drew them down into the abyss. We see it not; but an endless profundity seems to open, over which they desperately contend to the utmost. This contest between the condemned and the devil is world-famed. Things are represented here which are not to be described. And, equally awfully below, we see Charon emptying his crowded boat. As if he was emptying a sack of mice, he makes the crowds of the guilty spring down into the flames and smoke. He is standing on the edge of the vessel. With his foot upon the fore part, he brings it to the brink; and, with uplifted oar, he strikes among the throng, who are seeking to cling to it, and tremble at the leap into the abyss. Dante describes how Charon drives them to the boat: we have here the continuation of his poem, — the arrival. They excite still greater pity than those wrestling with the devils in the air above. For above, the decision is yet delayed; a possibility of disengaging themselves remains: here, however, all is lost. And the anxiety of mind with which the wretched beings perceive this, is represented by Michael Angelo as if Dante had stood by him, and inspired him with his spirit.

7.

Yet this was Michael Angelo's perfect art. To him who knows Dante, his works must appear like the second revelation of the same genius. Dante created a new world for the Romanic nations, by remodelling the forms of heathen antiquity for his Christian mythology. What before floated in mysticism, he endowed with more tangible life. He built up anew heaven and earth. But still he did this only to meet the imagination, until Michael Angelo came, and congealed the flowing stream of verse into form. Now, for the first time, it possessed complete reality. Raphael trod in Michael Angelo's footsteps; and all succeeding masters yielded to him. From henceforth there were fixed pictures of God the Father, of Christ, Mary, and of the countless saints, with which, even at the present day, we see the heaven of the Romanic nations filled. The multitude, who look up devoutly to these figures in the churches, imagine not that these were thus created by a few artists only a few centuries ago, and that the statues of the ancient heathen contributed just as much as nature did to their creation. It was this Last Judgment that gave the final stamp to this new generation of divine forms. The idea of immensity was introduced into figures; of the strong muscular frame, which was subsequently countlessly imitated. It is astonishing how Michael Angelo attained so much, in spite of this clumsiness of the corporeal, which often seems to fall into awkwardness. For we find no trace of that ethereal tenderness, which, according to our feeling, should never be absent from the form of a departed spirit, if such a form is at all events to be represented.

It is repulsive to the German mind to see things, which cannot even be arrived at in imagination, represented in a fixed figurative form. All that can be obtained are but surmisings, which are for ever changing their hue, like the heaven above us, according to the position of the sun. These outlined colored forms fail to suggest an idea of aught surpassing the limits of human life, because we know too accurately the changing ideas of different epochs, until the conviction is forced upon us, that every thing figurative is but the product of a definite period, whose conceptions, even if they were to last hundreds of years, would still one day lose their faith-awakening power. What was the form of Christ? A picture rises before us, mild and gentle in expression, with oval countenance, high brows, parted beard, majestic walk, beauty and calm dignity in every movement. Whence, however, comes this picture? There were times belonging to the earliest ages of the church, when the opinion prevailed that he was insignificant and poor in appearance. The early Christians seem to have thought of him thus in contrast to the beauty of the heathen deities. The Greeks asserted that the greatness of God had been thus most fully manifested, by his having revealed himself imbodied in the weakest mortality; while the Latins maintained that the outward beauty must have corresponded with that of the soul. This opinion at first only slowly made its way. Pictures

next appeared of the Byzantine type.* But, at the
time in which modern painting developed itself, individual features were chosen at will, — sometimes
with a Byzantine feeling, sometimes without a trace
of improvement. It was under Michael Angelo and
Raphael that our present representation first arose.
But still, as many paintings show, there was no type
to which it was necessary to adhere. And thus,
while Michael Angelo chiselled his first great work,
the dead Christ on the lap of Mary, more in harmony
with the Byzantine style; in his Christ in the Minerva, he introduced the elements of the antique into
the features. Indescribably superior, however, is the
aspect which the Christ in the Last Judgment presents. An unclothed, broad-shouldered hero, with
arms upraised that could strike down a Hercules,
distributing blessings and curses, his hair fluttering
in the wind like flames which the storm blows back,
and his angry countenance looking down on the
condemned with frightful eyes, as if he wished to
hasten forward the destruction in which his word had
plunged them. The form of the head strangely calls
to mind the Apollo Belvidere, — there is the same
triumphant majesty in the features, — but at the
same time the whole figure recalls the words of
Dante, in which he calls Christ *Sommo Giove*, — the
most high Jupiter. This he is here; not the suffering Son of man, gentle as the moon, silent rather
than speaking, with the foreboding of his fate written
on his sad eyes. Yet, if a Last Judgment were
to be painted, with everlasting condemnation, and

* See Appendix, Note XLII.

Figure of Christ, from the Last Judgment.

MICHAEL ANGELO.

Christ as the judge who pronounces it, how could he appear otherwise than in such terribleness?

And around him is the immense double circle, with every eye fixed upon him. Each is expecting the decisive word from him. Those nearest to him are the calmest: the more distant from him are the more passionate in their movements. Their heads are stretched forward to hear the verdict better; they beckon to the more distant to come nearer, or they notify what is taking place; there is a throng streaming from all sides towards Christ, to whose raised right hand belong salvation and misery. The movement is represented when the universal decision is just taking place.

Such is Michael Angelo's Last Judgment. While we cherish a feeling that at that day, whenever it occurs, the love of God will remit all sins as earthly error, the Roman sees alone anger and revenge as proceeding from the Supreme Being, when He comes in contact with humanity for the last time. For the sinner is for ever, from henceforth, to be condemned. It is an echo of the old idea, often enough recurring in the Old Testament, that the Divine Being is an angry and fearful power, which must be appeased, instead of the source of good alone, abolishing at last all evil as an influence that has beguiled mankind.

It is difficult, if not impossible, to speak of such things. Our feeling respecting them is too profound to succeed in obtaining clear light upon it. Still we venture not to pronounce as shadows those material images which have been transmitted to us as sacred bequests; but, in the course of spiritual development, it appears to me that these ideas must become paler and paler, and others must take their place, as the symbol of eternal things. For without symbols, whether tangible images or ideas, we are never satisfied, however plain it may be to us that every thing symbolic is but a similitude, — empty to him who does not fill up its meaning from his own soul. As we look, however, at the Last Judgment on the wall of the Sistine Chapel, it is no longer a similitude to us, but a monument of the imaginative spirit of a past age and of a strange people, whose ideas are no longer ours.*

* See Appendix, Note XLIII.

CHAPTER THIRTEENTH.

1536—1542.

Plans against the Duke of Ferrara — The Brutus — Ippolito dei Medici — Alessandro dei Medici — The Emperor in Rome and Florence — The Reformation in Germany — The Great Council — The Pope's Change of Views regarding the Lutherans — Religious Movement in Italy — Death of the old Lodovico Buonarroti — Occhino's Party in Rome — The Oratorium of Divine Love — Caraffa — Overthrow of the Liberal Party in the Vatican — Inquisition in Rome.

MICHAEL ANGELO began the Last Judgment about the year 1533; at the end of 1541, he put the last touch to it. He worked without assistance. During these six years, events of importance had taken place around him.

Scarcely was Clement VII. dead, than the attempt was made in Rome to overthrow the Government of the Duke of Florence, and to restore liberty.

Alessandro's conduct daily exasperated the nobles more and more. Fear of the tyranny of the middle and lower classes was set aside; the existence of the ducal power became an insufferable oppression; all who had been banished or frightened away from Florence by exile or discontent, gathered together in Rome after the death of the pope, and labored for Alessandro's ruin. They met together, and debated how liberty was to be restored.

The central point of those efforts was Cardinal Ippolito dei Medici. On his side stood the cardinals Salviati and Ridolfi, his near relatives; they formed the head of the cardinals to whom Leo X. and Clement had owed their elevation, and who had only given their votes to the election of Farnese, because they had been deceived by the miserable appearance which he exhibited. Ippolito lived magnificently. His palace was the meeting-place for his countrymen in Rome. He employed Florentine artists: he was the friend and patron of Michael Angelo.

We know not whether the latter worked definitely for the cardinal; but he accepted a present from him, — a thing he refused from any other. Ippolito had a magnificent Turkish horse in his stables. Michael Angelo admired the animal. One day it appeared before his house with a groom, and ten mules laden with provender. Michael Angelo consented to accept it. Ippolito dei Medici appears, from the beginning to the end of his short life, as one of the few characters which lose nothing of their lustre upon closer examination.

He had been made cardinal in the year 1529, when his uncle was at Orvieto, sick, moneyless, without allies, without prospects of regaining Florence, and in the greatest distress. He was a beautiful, passionate youth. The ecclesiastical dignity which was awarded to him altered nothing in his conduct. When matters became more favorable for the pope, Ippolito soon stood at the head of Roman society. He hated Alessandro, and Clement had difficulty in keeping them apart. When Alessandro

was to be established in Florence, and was on his
way there, Ippolito suddenly appeared. He loved
Caterina, and wished as her consort to govern the
city. Up to the misfortune of 1527, he had been
the one there who, though only in name, had decided
in affairs of State, and who bore the title Magnifico,
while Alessandro was treated more as a child. With
difficulty he was induced by Schomberg to give up
his plans and return to Rome. " He is mad," cried
the pope; " he will be no cardinal!" He then
marched to Hungary against the Turks, as commander of the Italian auxiliaries. On the way back,
his men rebelled, and Charles had him arrested as
instigator of the movement, of course only to set
him free again; but he gave him credit for it. Ippolito's portrait, painted at that time by Titian, is still
to be seen in Florence; it is a knee-piece as large
as life. He stands there in a smooth, close-fitting,
dark red-velvet coat, a band of gold buttons across
his breast, dark cap, and white plume. A pale Italian countenance with black hair; large dark eyes,
bold and noble features; a dog by his side: no one
would suppose a cardinal in that proud, youthful
figure. Richly as money flowed in upon him, he
always gave more than he had to give. At the same
time, condescending as he was towards his friends,
he was proud in his behavior towards princes. When
he accompanied his uncle to France on the marriage
of Caterina, he refused all Francis I.'s presents; he
would only accept of a tame lion, which the king
offered him. This was in the year 1533. At that
time he was in love with the beautiful Giulia Gon-

zaga, the most beautiful woman in Italy, who held her court at Fondi, on the Neapolitan frontier. He sent Sebastian del Piombo there, accompanied by an armed force, that he might paint her; and this portrait, completed within a month, is said to have been the most marvellous that Sebastian has painted. Giulia was so beautiful, that the Sultan, who had heard of her, wished to seize her for himself. A vessel landed secretly on the coast, and the Turks surprised the palace by night, while Giulia, throwing herself on a horse as she was, fortunately escaped. When we hear of such adventures as these; when we see Ippolito not only surrounded by the outward enjoyments of life, but at the same time a poet, a translator of a song of the Æneid into Italian verse, a statesman and head of a powerful party, in the midst of the perpetual vicissitude of events large and small, — when we remember all this, we understand such an existence too justly to expect from him that strictness of conduct and seclusion of life, which alone could fit him for all that Christendom demanded of a cardinal of the Church of Rome. He was eighteen years old when he became cardinal, and twenty-four when he died by poison.

The Duke of Florence had sent an embassy, on the elevation of Paul III., to congratulate him. Filippo Strozzi and Baccio Valori took part in it. These, it seems, gave the final ratification to the combination against Alessandro, by whom they were declared rebels. Both had lived a past, which nothing could palliate. By their co-operation, for the most part, the freedom of the city had been destroyed.

Portrait of an Unknown.

SEBASTIAN DEL PIOMBO.

Strozzi had eagerly promoted the building of the citadel, and had been mentioned as the principal participator, indeed originator, of Alessandro's excesses. In spite of this, when he refused to allow them that share in the Government which they claimed, but treated them as subjects, making them feel bitterly the power which he owed most of all to themselves, they turned against him, and the freedom of Florence was again their motto. By the magic of this word, friends and foes were once more united. The old exiled democrats of 1530 gathered together in Rome from all quarters of their banishment, and made common cause with them. Ippolito's influence completed the feeling of mistrust. Jacopo Nardi, the historian, who had lived as an exile in Venice, came at that time to Rome. He relates how Ippolito persuaded him. By night, one of Strozzi's sons conducted him — the stern old democrat — into the palace of the Medici. He went up the gloomy steps, and they left him there alone. Then a form entered the apartment, with a noble, military bearing, his shaggy hat drawn over his face, and a mantle over his shoulders. "I am the cardinal," he said. And then, sitting down together, Ippolito began to speak so eloquently of Florence, of the freedom of his poor country, that they both burst into tears. Nardi now induced his companions to trust in the cardinal, and the union of all against Alessandro was brought about.

We have no indication that Michael Angelo took part in this. He was painting at his Last Judgment from morning till night. It was in winter of 1534 and 1535, and the following spring, that these things were carried on. But it is scarcely to be supposed, that one who was so intimate with men whom he now saw again for the first time after the sad events in Florence, was not among them and a sharer of their designs. The entire Florentine community in Rome joined the cardinal. Cardinal Ridolfi was Michael Angelo's friend and patron. He was executing for him the unfinished bust of Brutus. He was intimate with the Strozzi, especially with a son of Filippo's, named Ruberto. Moreover, he hated Alessandro, and was enthusiastic about the freedom of the city, with which even the Farnese seemed to be inspired. Paul III. believed no better means could be found for the elevation of his family, than the humiliation of the Medici, whose internal discord he endeavored to foster. He appeared animated by the best wishes to help the famed and noble city to regain her freedom, and he stood on the side of Ippolito and the exiles.

The latter now arranged themselves in due form. On the 25th March, an embassy was dispatched to Spain to the emperor, charged with complaints against Alessandro, and imploring the re-establishment of the consiglio grande, or of a constitution not less democratic in its character. If the emperor granted neither, they were commissioned to demand that the cardinal should rule in the way that things had been, prior to 1527. Nobles and democracy, who, in spite of their union, differed on many points in their conferences in Rome, had declared themselves agreed as to the substance of these demands.

The emperor was on the point of sailing for Tunis when the nobles reached him. The policy of Spain had made this expedition appear necessary. Proof must be given that they were a match for the Turkish powers in the Mediterranean. One of the most famous corsairs had seized upon Tunis, with the help of the Sultan Soliman; had made the coasts insecure; and had threatened to take Sicily and Sardinia. The moment was favorable for striking a blow, as the sultan was engaged in other wars.

The emperor was also in alliance with Alessandro. All depended on the offers made by the duke and the cardinal. Ippolito offered more; and this obtained for the embassy the expressions of good-will with which they were received. Charles dismissed them upon this for a time. In Naples, he added, whither he would repair on the termination of the war, he hoped to see them again. All should then be decided on.

Ippolito was dissatisfied. Something ought to have taken place at once. He thought of going direct to Florence, and of bringing about a division there. Then he resolved to follow the emperor to Africa, to take part in the war, and to paralyze Alessandro's influence. Arms had always been his favorite profession: in Rome he always maintained a number of military leaders who were devoted to him; and so, accompanied by a splendid train, he set out in July for Naples, to proceed from thence by ship. But he did not complete the journey. At Itri, he suddenly took sick, and died. That he was poisoned is certain; it is uncertain whether the pope or Ales-

sandro ordered the murder to be committed.   It lay
in the interests of both, that Ippolito's career should
be put an end to.   Paul gave his revenues to Cardinal Farnese, his grandson, a youth of fourteen.
Ippolito had indeed played a false game with the
Florentines when he spoke of liberty.   He wished
to rule as Alessandro ruled.   He is said even to
have secretly negotiated with the latter, to effect a
friendly division of power; still it excites pity to see
such young and blooming vigor suddenly destroyed
in so sad a manner.

The Florentines in Rome did not give up their
cause on this account.   After a glorious termination
to the expedition, the emperor came to Naples in
November; and here, where he spent the winter,
the two parties sought to obtain his decision.   Em-
bassies arrived from Rome and Florence.   Alessandro appeared with princely pomp.   In the streets
of Naples, it sometimes happened that members of
the same family — some exiles, and others adherents
of the duke — would meet, spring from their horses,
overcome with rage, and fall upon each other with
daggers.   The Cardinals Salviati and Ridolfi, who
had come forward in Ippolito's stead, were not in
disfavor with Charles.   We have long documents
and records, in which the parties asserted their
claims.   Guicciardini was Alessandro's counsellor.
The emperor seemed doubtful: for the sake of com-
pelling the duke to do what was agreeable to him,
he supported the hopes of the cardinals for a time.
He offered Alessandro such hard conditions, that he
was on the point of leaving Naples in anger.   Guic-

ciardini restrained him. Baccio Valori, the old
intriguer, again played on both sides. The end was,
that the duke united with the emperor; that the
old and almost relinquished project of the marriage
between Alessandro and Margherita, the natural
daughter of Charles, was taken up, and the betrothal
was celebrated in February, 1536. While the cardinals and their party returned sadly to Rome, the
future son-in-law of the emperor set out joyfully on
his way to Florence, to make every thing ready there
for the emperor's reception.

At the beginning of April, Charles set out for the
north, with seven thousand men, the remainder of
the African army, the other half of which went by
sea to Genoa. His plan was a war with France.
Francis I. was again making preparations against
Milan. It was this, too, which had given the turn
to the decision in favor of Alessandro. The duke
had bound himself to pay important sums; he had
promised to consign the citadel of Florence to a
Spanish garrison, and to undertake a command in
the war itself. If the emperor had declared against
him, Florence would have gone over to France.
Even at the time when the exiles were negotiating
with Ippolito in Rome, this question had been
broached.

The pope was so alarmed at the impending march
of the emperor through his dominions, that he
thought of escaping to Perugia. Then, changing
his mind, he armed the Romans, assembled a body-
guard of three thousand men, and received his noble
guest in the most magnificent manner. It was long

since a Roman emperor had been received by a pope
at the foot of the stairs leading to St. Peters. Four
days Charles remained in Rome. Simply dressed,
he roamed through the city, that he might accurately
examine its magnificence. I know of no more de-
tailed account of these days, from which we may
gather whether Michael Angelo was introduced to
him. That he did *not*, however, meet him is scarcely to be supposed. Michael Angelo was the first
artist in the world: he had been just appointed by
Paul to be chief architect, sculptor, and painter of
the apostolic palace; and he was admitted among the
number of the peculiar *protégés* of the Vatican.
Charles, who had distinguished Benvenuto Cellini
in the most condescending manner, could not have
passed by Michael Angelo. Even for the sake of
his own honor, the pope must have produced him.
The only thing that we know on the matter rests on
Vasari's statement, that the emperor also wished to
get Michael Angelo into his service. This can only
have happened at that time.

Charles does not appear in history as a prince
who had especial predilection for art. Compared
with Francis I., he is inferior in this. Our slight
acquaintance with Spanish buildings may be in fault,
and he may not be known in this respect so well as
he deserved. Titian was the master he preferred,
and he received splendid proofs of his good-will. But
that which here, as everywhere, spoils the impression
of Charles's character, is the pedantic coolness of
his nature, and the oppressive etiquette that he required. It is possible, that his experience proved

the necessity of the artificial halo with which he surrounded himself. Yet it belonged to the tendencies of his family generally to keep themselves separated, by golden barriers, from other mortals. Charles possessed nothing attractive, nothing inviting confidence: he appears so bold and calculating, that one involuntarily takes the side of his adversaries, even when they are evidently in the wrong. But it belongs to our nature to have greater sympathy even for crimes, which proceed from passion, than for virtues, the source of which is a cold reserve.

The emperor availed himself of his sojourn in Rome to give out a programme of all that the world might expect from him in the time to come. In a solemn assembly, at which the cardinals stood, and the pope alone was seated, he made known his views respecting France. He spoke Spanish, as if Rome were to be shown in what idiom from henceforth the history of the world was to be carried on. He pointed out what he had done for Rome; he referred to the danger threatening from the Lutherans; and addressing, in conclusion, the French ambassadors present, he condemned the behavior of their king, whom he was now compelled to remind of his duties by force. The nobles desired to reply; but they were cut short.

From Rome, Charles proceeded to Florence, which was transformed by Alessandro in all haste into a pompous theatre. These were the days which Vasari, as supreme leader of all the arrangements, celebrated as his greatest triumphs, and which he extols as the paradisaical age of Florentine art.

The whole troop of architects, sculptors, and painters, were desperately busy under him. He scarcely
permitted himself rest at night. And what delight
was it when the duke touched him on the shoulder,
and spoke a gracious word! Triumphal arches, statues of gypsum, painted ceilings, standards, all on
a colossal scale, and sufficient to fill almost every
street, were produced in the shortest time. The excellence with which these works were accomplished,
as well as the rapidity with which they were done,
show the course which Florentine art had taken.
Quickness was genius; size was grandeur; the cor-
rupt was beautiful. That influence of Michael Angelo's upon art, which must, without indeed any
fault on his part, be designated as fatal, was here
glaringly evidenced. It was not his doing, that they
imitated the colossal size and the positions of his figures. Nature was no longer talked of; effect was
desired; and thus, with unusual power of imitation
and readiness of hand, they created things which
they designated works of art, and which many in our
own day would also so designate; clumsy productions, the intellectual value of which was nought.
And, as the opportunity often returned, similar de-
corative undertakings became so frequent among the
artists in Florence, that every studio soon aimed at
disputing for fame; and the successes obtained in
them were regarded almost as the highest sought
for. The old Florentine art had rendered service to
freedom; that which followed it rendered homage
to the dukes.

The last visit of the emperor in Florence was to

the sacristy of San Lorenzo. Coming out of the church, he mounted his horse, and left the city. This visit was the first of three scenes, which Michael Angelo's work was now to witness in quick succession. The second was the marriage of Alessandro and Margherita. The duchess was married to him almost as a child, rather as a pledge of the obligations mutually entered upon, than for the sake of being his wife already. Festivities were repeated, as at the entry of her father. Vasari was again at the head of all. We understand how, at the loss of the duke, he almost fell into despair, and depicted his master as the essence of virtues, the existence of which his enemies alone denied. He lost him soon enough. This was the third scene acted in the sacristy of San Lorenzo. Alessandro's own cousin, a gloomy, silent character, whom he had continually with him as his most intimate friend, allured him into a place of concealment, and had him assassinated. The death was kept secret, to avoid an uproar in favor of freedom. They carried the body by night, wrapped up in carpets, to the sacristy, and placed it in one of the sarcophagi. Michael Angelo had little anticipated this when he chiselled it. But liberty returned not. A grandson of one of those Medici who had returned into the city under Savonarola,—a young man sixteen years old, named Cosmo,—was sent for by those who had placed themselves at the head of affairs after Alessandro's murder; and, amid many promises, all of which he willingly made and broke, he was elected duke. Guicciardini was again one of those who assisted most. It was Cosmo who founded the dynasty of the succeeding rulers of Tuscany, and who completely set aside the little relic of the old citizen-like independence which had remained under Alessandro.

2.

All this took place in 1536, the second year of Michael Angelo's work at the Last Judgment. Other things, too, were happening at that time. We have said nothing at present of the Reformation. It was like a great war, by which hitherto the Italian frontier had been scarcely affected; but it now began to be carried into the land itself.

Riformare is to remodel. *Riformare lo stato* signified, for Florence, to overthrow the constitution, and to establish a new one. The reformation of the Church was an old necessity, acknowledged by the popes themselves. At first, however, a remodelling in the outward life of the clergy was understood by it. The state of things was acknowledged to be intolerable. And, as when any thing is sick and diseased, the most evident consequences are generally regarded as the cause of the evil, so now the universal watchword was " Reformation," — the removal of this disorder.

The popes had already shown themselves favorable to such a change, because, with the introduction of a stricter morality, greater dependence upon Rome was to be looked for. Rome was the capital of the world; every thing appeared beneficial which strengthened her in this capacity. The renewed

obedience of the clergy would have caused a renewal
of the dependence of all Christians. But Rome had
to take the lead in setting a good example; and this
was the great step upon which neither popes nor
cardinals could resolve. And any one who is well
acquainted with the Romish affairs will perceive
that this was not to be done. We might as well
demand of Paris at the present day, that she should
renounce the study of fashion; that all dissolute men
there should become moral, all thieves honest, all
women quiet maidens. Whoever knows Paris will
say that this cannot be. And so, too, it could not be
the case in Rome, that pope and prelates should conform to a simple Christian walk. But that this could
not be, was the reason why half Germany apostatized
from the Romish Church.

The word Reformation was, at the beginning of the
sixteenth century, the watchword, somewhat as Constitution is in the beginning of our own. They felt
the wretched state of things; and this word implied
to them a remedy for every evil. Connected with it
was the idea of a general council, at which the people might independently establish their faith anew,
and the Church might be thoroughly remodelled,—a
council which should be a union of the noblest mental powers of all nations, and the decisions of which,
pope, princes, and people would have to submit to.
They knew not rightly how, and where, and when;.
but they urged it. And this idea, which was too
high and too general for any one to work at its real-
ization because this or that advantage was to accrue
from it, but which every one saw only in the distance

as a kind of earthly tribunal, effecting a universal return to purer forms of life, — this idea suddenly kindled in Germany, and brought about that change, and those contests and results, which, at the present day, comprising it all as one event, we call the Reformation. To us, Reformation signifies a historical act; to the sixteenth century, the word contained a multitude of ideal wishes and expectations.

After having long studied the history of the Romanic nations, we become unavoidably habituated to regard moral things under an artificial aspect. We see how the beautiful, and often even the good and great, may spring up amid the most criminal circumstances and people; and we at last cease to condemn: we merely contemplate. Justice forbids more. We come even so far as to regard men like Savonarola, who did nothing but call the actions of the world by their right name, and this from the noblest motives, and who endeavored even until death to bring about a change, — we come so far as to regard these as disturbers of the peace, as men who touched with rough hands the harmony of existing things. Goethe thus condemns him in contrast to Lorenzo dei Medici, who scarcely deserves to be mentioned in comparison with Savonarola's noble purity. It was Savonarola whom Luther declared to be his champion. But, as different as Luther is from Savonarola, so different is Germany from Italy. Savonarola was like a drop of water, which fell in vain on a burning stone: Luther was fruit-bearing seed, which was sown at the right time in a susceptible soil.

The internal condition of Germany appeared, at the beginning of the sixteenth century, of such a nature, that almost from time immemorial it had exercised no influence abroad. Germany furnished armies for the war-waging princes of the rest of Europe; but they fought not for their own country. The soldiery might be led for money against any foe. There was no power to express a will as a German nation. So closely and so strangely linked were the shackles which bound land and people, that, attacked from without, they could not even have defended themselves. But no one attacked them. The wars which the Emperor Maximilian waged against France were paid for by Burgundy; his Italian campaigns by Milan. What he received from Germany was small. The country, which in a united state would have been stronger than any nation in the world, lay there at that time inactive, split into infinite pieces, filled with the continual feuds of all these small States with each other. It was a matter of course that the emperor could not interpose. Albert Dürer wrote home, how in Venice the German emperor was ridiculed as powerless; but at home things were no better. There was nothing aggressive in the German nature. They only desired to defend themselves. And thus each kept his place, — citizen, knight, prince, and ecclesiastic; each endeavoring to secure himself, each with his thoughts turned within. And, as no outer impulse jarred, the state of things was rich and luxurious. Macchiavelli, when he came upon the German frontier, in one of his diplomatic journeys, wrote a book on Germany, in which he depicted it to the Italians, as Tacitus had once done to the Romans, as a prosperous and model land, enviable from its excellence.

Into this retirement flowed the current of thought that had been newly awakened in Italy. No people is more capable of giving themselves up to the influence of mind than the German. They eagerly seized upon all that came across the Alps, and worked it into a possession of their own. An involuntary union arose among those who had obtained the new mental treasures, or who wished to acquire them, — a kind of free fellowship, which spread over the land without regard to dwelling-place and birth. They held together; without object, without aim, without mystery, but united by the one feeling, that Germany was in an unworthy condition, and that it must be otherwise. Formerly the emperor had ruled the whole world; now he was despised. Immense sums were sent by the country yearly to Rome to be expended uselessly. A numerous body of clergy in Germany itself possessed the best land as permanent property. Full of shame, the only man who felt all this, and would gladly have changed it, saw himself powerless as regarded the state of things, even though he had belonged to the mightiest of the land.

This discontent, however, never condensed itself into practical ideas, such as we require at the present day in every social or political movement. Hutten, who wrote most vehemently and plainly, nowhere says any thing which presents itself as obviously feasible, and which could have brought about a reformation of things. No one would attack law, order, and custom. Nothing, moreover, urged to instant movement. In those times, when the intercourse was so slight, that what was taking place in the south of the country only reached the knowledge of the north after tedious months, when tidings for the most part were current only as vague reports, political desires were weak incitements. But classical culture and freedom of thought increased more and more; and the soil which received them most easily was the clergy themselves, who, accustomed to reflect, and endowed with the capability of expressing thought, readily accepted the new ideas, and digested them.

It is difficult at the present day to form an idea of the power and extent of the clergy at that time. In Catholic Germany, at the present day, there is nothing to be remotely compared with it. Even Italy, which seems to be filled with monks and abbots, would appear empty compared with the state of things at that period. It is scarcely exaggeration to say that half Germany belonged to the clergy, just as we should now say that the army of the country absorbs half the revenue. Indeed, our standing army gives the best idea of the position of the clergy in the sixteenth century. We have only to imagine these thousands of soldiers, from the peasant's son in the lowest position, to the greatest noble in the highest, changed into religious functionaries. They were nothing but a band of men, who, organized among themselves, and dwelling in the midst of the country, were yet freed from its laws, and occupying the most favorable places. We may imagine the barracks as monasteries, the fortresses as bishops' palaces, and the whole mass, not perhaps as maintained directly by the State, but each barrack, each fortification, so richly endowed with land and working subjects, that not only was the daily maintenance supplied by them, but enough was left to send to Rome, or to lay up for personal superfluities; and, lastly, this profession was protected like none other in the land, and was daily increasing by gifts of every kind. The men were rich. They had leisure to employ themselves with spiritual things. They gained recruits from all families. They were implicated in the affairs of all. It was no small matter to command such power from Rome; for upon it the authority of the Church throughout the country depended. And these are the ecclesiastics, whom, subject to no outward power, we have now to imagine suddenly of themselves receiving the new ideas, and desiring a reformation of the Romish sway in the national mind. The divided condition, the sovereignty of almost every city and every estate, which stood so hinderingly in the way of Germany as a political power in its influence abroad, was of advantage to it in this intellectual movement. There was no central will by which they could have been oppressed. Had the emperor wished to rule otherwise than by entreaties and remonstrances, he must first have conquered Germany. Setting aside its helplessness as a whole, it was so free in its individual members, and so perfectly united, and there could be no mention of carrying general measures without the good-will of the people. Such was the character of the soil on which Luther appeared. The impetus which he gave was so vast and so resistless, that, within the ten years between 1520 and 1530, a change of affairs took place in Germany, no less radical than that which occurred between 1806 and 1815.

Wholly different was it with the rest of Europe. In France the king dwelt in the midst of a mighty, and often refractory, people ; so sensitive, however, when the honor of the country was at stake, that neither nobles nor citizens ventured to refuse obedience. The clergy were in his power. At Bologna, in the year 1515, Leo X. had been obliged to resign to Francis I. the right of patronage in ecclesiastical posts. The king was thus enabled to reward services rendered, with rich abbeys and bishops' sees. The French cardinals in Rome formed a division, fighting for the king. Francis I. was lord of his land : only small sums flowed into Rome from France. He could not prevent the movement of minds, free as they yet were ; but he could take precautions that nothing should take place to curtail his power. For this reason, when things had so far prospered in Germany, that the ecclesiastical possessions had become a sort of unprotected booty, which every one endeavored to lay hands upon, no authority being interposed to check it ; for cities, princes, and ecclesiastical lords themselves transformed the possessions of the Church into private property, — while matters were thus in Germany, Francis considered the Reformation in his States as rebellion, and treated

those accordingly whom he thought proper to apprehend as guilty. The first heretics were burnt in
France by his order.

Yet if, in spite of this, the movement met with
hearing and diffusion in France, the most marvellous
contrast to Germany was formed by Spain. While
the Germans were impelled slowly towards reformation by their historical progress and their national
character, the fate of the country, as well as the
peculiarities of thought among the Spaniards, produced just the opposite. One of the most splendid
paragraphs in Buckle's History of Civilization shows
how fanatical adherence to princes and religion is
the distinguishing feature of the character, and the
source of the greatness and the decline of this people. Not only did the Spaniards from the first repel
the new doctrine: it was they alone, who, by their
help in later times, rendered possible the immense
efforts of the Hapsburg dynasty to force Germany
back to Roman Catholicism.

For many years before it arose in Germany, the
Inquisition had been in active force in Spain. When
Ferdinand and Isabella, towards the end of the fifteenth century, had completely driven the Moors
back to Africa, the kingdom was so inundated with
Mohammedans, Moors, and Jews, who by their industry not only often raised themselves above the
Spaniards, but also often connected themselves with
them by marriage, that the nation required a purifi-
cation of the land. These Moors and Jews had often,
of course, become Christians. Numerous conversions
had taken place; but this just rendered them all the

more intolerable. And when, added to this, their wealth began to attract the king, spiritual tribunals were established at his desire, with the object of deciding whether those who called themselves Christians were indeed Christians. The pope himself, when he issued the bull by which the Inquisition was established, did it with reluctance, and warned against its abuse.

It was soon no longer Jews and heathens who were among the victims of this tribunal. The enthusiasm for pure doctrine became a morbid passion. For centuries they had fought against the unbelieving; the present excitement was but a continuation of this contest. The Inquisition was popular in Spain; they longed for funeral piles, as they had before desired bull-fights. Between the years 1480 and 1517, thirteen thousand heretics were actually burned in Spain, and eight thousand seven hundred in effigy; one hundred and seventy thousand met with spiritual punishment; and, within forty years, in Seville alone, forty-five thousand were put to death by fire. Every form of persecution was resorted to against aught that could damage the pure doctrine. Six thousand books were burnt to ashes in Salamanca, in one batch, during the last ten years of the century.* Reading and writing were restricted to the utmost extent; Greek and Hebrew Bibles were entirely forbidden. Such were the clergy against whom Columbus had to contend; such was the state of things before Luther was even thought of. As his appearance, however, carried away many,

* See Appendix, Note XLIV.

and the danger of contagion awaited all, the Inquisition rose as a counteracting power with such energy,
that the history of the Spanish Reformation can tell
only of individual martyrs, but nowhere of a popular
movement.

Italy alone, politically and mentally, possessed the
conditions which allowed of a liberty similar to that
of Germany. The popes, too, were hated enough
there ; and countless opportunities would have prosented themselves for subverting their authority.
But men were accustomed to it. To kindle such a
fire as broke out in Germany, all the mental growth
of centuries must have been transformed into fuel,
as in the formation of a turf-moor. In Italy, however, it had already burned for ages unceasingly.
There was no store there of material ; an agitated
political life filled the daily thoughts of the people ;
no calm, brooding atmosphere prevailed there as in
Germany. They were daily ready for fanatical outbreaks, such as had taken place in Florence, and
enthusiasm had been preserved even freshly for
some years ; but at length they had fallen back into
ironical indifference towards the disorders of the
priests. At the same time, the political condition
of things was too closely connected with the existing
state of Romish affairs for a change to be wished for.
Venice, Florence, Naples, liked to have their cardinals
in Rome, and regarded their splendid appearance as
a means conducive to the maintenance of their influence. Besides, no one in Italy had a desire for the
property of the Church. Every thing was arranged
too fixedly, and was regulated according to the gen-

eral advantage. This was the case especially in
Rome, the welfare of which entirely depended on
the worldly prosperity of the prelates, and where the
money supplied by the nobles prevented the necessity
for having recourse to her own resources. The
grievances only concerned single points. These
were things which they denounced; but they desired
no fundamental change. Indeed, the possibility of
such a change was not conceivable to the people; their
hatred expended itself on certain individuals. They
wished not to destroy the wild wood, but only to
prune it. The popes made an effort to this effect,
but never arrived at success. So externally did
they regard things in Rome, that they imputed the
lowest grounds to the conduct of Martin Luther;
not from hatred, but because they judged him by
themselves. Luther had beat an alarm, they thought,
because the collecting of indulgences had been withdrawn from his order. Leo had committed the raising of this money to a Genoese house, as payment
on account for sums advanced in earlier times. It
was known in Genoa, that the Augustines, who had
possessed the old privilege of collecting indulgences
(and to whom Luther belonged), were accustomed
to retain a considerable percentage; and the business
was therefore committed to the Dominicans. Luther now came forward respecting the indulgences.
It would have been a matter of commercial dishon-
esty on the part of the pope — thus they regarded
the matter in Italy — not to come to the help of the
Genoese in any way, and to facilitate their exaction
of the money. The house had paid for it; and they

were, besides this, Leo's relatives. The pope, too, had no money to cover the deficiency himself. Hence there was no hesitation in the Vatican: Martin Luther must be put down; he had revolted against the Church. The application of the most powerful means was decreed. Leo acted from Rome towards Germany much as the Emperor Nicholas would have acted towards a remote province, which, on account of over-burdens and other injustice suffered, might have protested against the constitution. Obedience first, then examination. No one, however, in Rome and Italy, had any remote idea, when the Lutheran movement began, that this could be the commencement of a reformation. And thus, while in Germany all were doing their utmost, and the general state of things had become in a short time so much changed that a restoration of the old condition was no longer possible, in Italy no feeling of acquiescence or imitation was excited.

In Germany, the mind of Luther filled all classes of society. He, too, was at first mistaken by those, who, as advocates of progress, placed themselves at the head of the movement. They knew nothing of him, and suspicions were excited; but soon the splendid character of the man prevailed. Luther attacked the matter in hand in a genuinely German manner. Savonarola had wished to train the Florentines to a better life: he had preached practical morality, and not the peculiar theology of his creed. Luther did just the reverse. What has a Romish pope to do with us Germans? he asked. What have the cardinals to do with us? Who has given these people at all the right to stand where they stand? What does the Bible know of a pope? There is no innate mental dependence on Rome. The Church has no authority without the Bible. It alone contains religion. Every free man is permitted to seek in it what profits him. That which Savonarola only uttered under the utmost pressure, more in his own defence than for the instruction of the people,—that the convictions of his own breast were to be esteemed higher than the pope,—this was what Luther began with; and not only for himself, but for all men, he claimed the liberty of appealing in matters of conscience to God alone. Rome, pope, cardinals, hierarchy,—all were at once set aside as false. Beginning afresh with the words of Christ himself, as the Bible contains them, it was no new though proscribed doctrine with which he came; but he desired a return to the early state of things, when every man with the words of Christ in his heart formed his own creed. There was to be no distinction between clergy and laity. Each man was a priest who felt himself filled with the spirit. And while this doctrine flowed from the lips of a man, who like a magician carried away all minds, from the German princes to the peasants who understood his tongue, it rushed on like a fire amid dry wood, exciting the storm, which suddenly appeared as a revolt against the pope and Romish influence, such as never had been experienced since the existence of the Catholic Church.

It is striking, how, even then, when the importance of the German affairs had been perceived, the Italian

11*

politicians of that day only paid regard to the political changes, which outwardly appeared as the first consequences of the movement. Princes and towns, they reasoned, were covetous of the wealthy possessions of the Church; the lower clergy were allured by the liberty of being able with impunity to pass into civil life; the spiritual lords would be glad to change their temporal authority into a dynastic: but no one in Italy mentioned the strongest of the powers at work; namely, universal conviction.

It is not to be denied, that the political aspect of things was often favorable to the Germans, whose cause preponderated. The opportunity was very convenient for cities and nobles to seize the possessions of the Church in their zeal for the new belief. They would not and could not again give up the increase of liberty, both in heart and life, which they owed to the new doctrine. Probably, had Francis I. been emperor, affairs might have come to an unhappy end; as he was defeated, his support was of advantage to the German reformers. Those whom, had they been his subjects, he would have endeavored to destroy, he furthered in their refractory conduct towards the emperor. And Charles, to whom the helpful power of the German princes was indispensable, saw himself compelled to give promises to his rebellious subjects, instead of recalling them by force to the authority of the Church. It is often said, in the tone of reproach, that Charles was no German emperor, but a Spanish king, who neither spoke German nor lived in Germany; but the Germans themselves forced him to rely on his non-

German subjects. When they elected him, his greatest recommendation was, that they might expect him to be as little burdensome to the land as possible. Charles was not to blame, when in future he aimed at showing the Germans that he was their master; but the Germans had better right on their side, when they repudiated the rule of the Romish priesthood, together with the temporal power of an emperor, which, in its too close alliance with that spiritual authority, was now more than ever obnoxious to their minds. For the service demanded from the people was evidently not to be applied to the good of the country in the spirit of the true empire.

This was perhaps felt in Italy; but no active steps were taken. Upon this they built their plans. As concerned the dogma which really divides Catholics and Protestants at the present day, it was regarded as a point upon which they would undoubtedly come to an understanding, if only an agreement upon other things could be obtained. For the Protestants (to use a name already, which arose subsequently) appeared only fixed and agreed in the political part of their demands; whilst, with respect to their new belief, various opinions were soon expressed and contended for with a vehemence which made a return to the old ecclesiastical dominion appear a necessary termination.

For this reason, much as this state of affairs in Germany lay at the heart of Leo X., we have no doubt, that, at this time, the expulsion of the French from Lombardy, and the elevation of his family, was an affair a thousand times more important to him;

and that even Pope Clement's sleepless nights, and
the vexation from which he at last sunk, were not
caused by the German heretics. If Clement VII
was affected by a loss inflicted on the Catholic
Church, it was the fall of Rhodes, which fell into
the hands of the Turks. That was an irreparable,
shameful loss. To give up Germany as lost would
never have come into his mind. What filled him
with fear respecting Germany and Luther was the
urging for a council. Nothing in the interests of
the Romish Church could perhaps at that time have
inflicted a heavier blow upon Luther than a general
assembly, to which every one must have yielded.
The Germans, I believe, would at last have remained
in the minority; for the matter would soon enough
have so turned, that, setting aside all amendments
of the Church, the Romans would have made no
concessions to the Germans. But Clement, for private reasons, did not wish for the council. He
trembled at the idea, that the question of his illegitimate birth might be discussed there. He could
not wipe away this stain. He had even beheaded a
Florentine citizen who had ventured to touch upon it,
and had had it sworn to by credible witnesses, that
his mother had been secretly married to Giuliano
dei Medici.

Besides this, since Germany possessed no central
point, and only isolated facts were reported of what
was going on, the movement appeared in Italy less
than it really was. They perceived not the importance of the translation of the Bible, and the sudden
use of the German language in religious matters, in

which hitherto the Latin had prevailed. All classes felt themselves newly allied in national feeling; for Luther handled the language with such power and beauty, that his Bible was not merely a work of learning, but, like a poem, it irresistibly forced its way into the hearts of men. Highly as the Germans honor this work, they are at the present day scarcely able to feel in themselves the effect which Luther's work exercised at its appearance. At the present day, the language in which it is written has become a cold theological style: at that time, it was the choice of that which was the current tongue of all classes.

How should this have been perceived in Rome, or by the cardinals, who, like physicians in an infected land, came to Germany to acquaint themselves with the malady on the spot, and appeared with suitable proposals? The delusion to which they resigned themselves in the Vatican was fostered, — that it would be possible, if force did not avail, to effect a re-union possibly by compliance, from the readiness of the Germans to negotiate. They contested and disputed; they perceived at times, on both sides, that the only concession with which the Reformers would have been satisfied, was the annihilation of the Romish authority: and thus the matter was put off. And, while in Germany the reformed state of things began to be strengthened by years into a legitimate condition, the minds of men in Rome grew more and more irresolute and uncertain.

There had been doubts, even under Leo X. Luther's assertion, that the popes had no right to remit sins for money, was a surprise; they began in Rome

itself seriously to study the question, and came to
no sure result. They were, moreover, not agreed
whether Luther ought to be condemned without
hesitation before being heard. Leo cut short this
doubt by the bull in which Luther was condemned;
and the cardinal sent by him to Germany went so
far as to insult Luther publicly, and to desire that
the safe-conduct guaranteed him in his journey to
Worms should not be respected.

Adrian VI. undertook this dispute with the fixed
intention of coming to a just decision. The main
substance of the dispute was the question, whether
eternal happiness depended on the belief in the forgiveness of sins obtained by the death of Christ, or
whether good works were also necessary. Good
works, however, might be compensated for by money;
and, for money, Leo had settled arbitrarily that the
pope could remit the punishment of sins. Adrian,
a strict ecclesiastic of German blood, grown old in
the scientific treatment of things, attempted to establish his own conviction instead of the decision
lightly given by his predecessor. That man was
forgiven, he asserted, who did a good work. If this
was done in a perfect manner, perfect forgiveness
took place; if any thing were lacking in it, forgiveness could only be vouchsafed in the same proportion. This just decision, he thought, must put an
end to all dispute. And perhaps, had the revolt of
the Germans against the Church not been based
upon the desire to shake off dependence upon Rome,
as well as on the theological question of free-will, an
agreement might have been come to with respect to

this point; for even Luther did not go so far as
to wish to carry the principle of personal investiga-
tion of the Bible to its utmost extent. Free and
independent as he made the community, he yet
subordinated them to ecclesiastics, to whom he gave
a certain power over the spiritual welfare of their
flocks. Adrian's attempt at reconciliation was the
only one honestly meant which ever emanated from
Rome. For the sake alone of truth and of the honor
of God, this pope sought the true good of Christendom, losing sight of all the outward losses which
might thus accrue to the Church.

But the cardinals, among whom he took counsel,
understood him not. They reproached him with
setting the papacy thus too much aside. The popes
were not to give out of their hands the right they
possessed, that by them alone the way to happiness
was opened. If Leo had issued his bull in over-
hastiness, as was acknowledged, he was, in spite of
his error, infallible as pope; and what he had said
could not be annulled. Whence would they take
the money to repay the Genoese? Adrian was over-
persuaded. Indeed, Soderini, who was at that time
in his favor, asserted plainly, that it was against his
own interest to interfere with the State, the prosperity, and the morals of the Romish court, since it
would appear as if Luther had effected this by his discussions. Deeply cast down, the pope at length acknowledged to his nearest friends that he was grieved
at it, but that he saw well that with the best will it
lay beyond the power of the popes to effect the good.

Clement VII. of course upheld Leo's decision.

Other things, however, hindered him from interfering rigorously against the Lutherans: those disputes between Rome and the emperor broke out, which turned so much to the advantage of the Germans, so that, when, ten years afterwards, a new pope was to be elected, the Lutherans formed no longer an unsettled, undefined multitude, but an organized whole, possessing both the power and courage to resist all attacks.

Under Clement the new doctrines had become known in Italy. In 1524, at the diet at Nürnberg, the pope's legate complained that Luther's writings were eagerly read throughout Venetia. In the following year, an order was issued at Lucca, that all Lutheran books were to be delivered up or burnt. The word Lutheran obtained in Italy the meaning with which we have applied at different times the designation demagogic, democratic, and the like. The fearful misfortunes of Rome had been brought about by Lutheran soldiery. For this reason, when Florence rose against the pope, they endeavored with anxious severity to keep aloof from the suspicion of cherishing heretical ideas. All disputes on matters of faith were forbidden. Bruccioli, who was suspected of fostering Lutheran ideas, scarcely escaped with his life. The most zealous against him were the Piagnoni and the brothers of San Marco. They declared that Savonarola had desired, not apostasy from the Catholic doctrines, but their elevation alone. It is wonderful, that, even afterwards, when the new doctrines emerged everywhere, the Florentines never showed the least inclination for them.

An important testimony, however, is preserved of the secret opinions regarding Luther entertained by men of cultivated minds and high position in Florence. Guicciardini, when he mentions the name in his historical work, expresses the feeling in Rome about him, and condemns the mischief arising through him. But private records from his hand have come to light, papers in which he wrote down his thoughts during 1527 and 1528; and there he speaks differently. One desire alone lives within him; namely, the ceasing of this cursed priestcraft in his country. He openly confesses, that his personal interests compel him to keep these thoughts secret. " I have," he says in one of his ejaculations, " ever wished in my innermost soul the destruction of the ecclesiastical State; but fate has willed it, that I should myself labor under two popes, not only for the extension of their power, but that I should be obliged to make this even the object of my wishes. Had not this consideration existed, I should have loved Martin Luther as myself; for I should have been permitted to hope that his adherents would have destroyed the accursed despotism of the clergy, or at least have clipped their wings." *

The contempt for Romish matters was so great, that similar expressions — the love for Martin Luther, perhaps, excepted — were not necessarily secret. Clement gave Macchiavelli an order to write a Florentine history. Macchiavelli speaks in it of the nephews of the popes, and of the efforts of the highest priests of Christendom to elevate, not the Church,

* See Appendix, Note XLV.

but their own families. These nephews, he says, have now even grown into sons; and it only remains for the popes, as they have taken care to leave behind princely descendants, to contrive also to make the papacy an hereditary dignity. And such assertions as these, Clement allowed to be applied to himself; for Alessandro dei Medici was designated his son by the people. The pope cared little about such historical animadversions; he suffered Filippo Strozzi to ridicule religion at the papal table itself, and to show himself, by his wicked conversation, as worse than unbelieving.* In the writings poured forth from the Vatican, the want of piety, of discipline, and the like, was at the same time lamented in the most tragic expressions that the Latin tongue afforded; and a manner was assumed with respect to the Lutherans, as if there were an assembly in Rome of holy men completely absorbed in the duties of their high vocation, against whom the German rebels had risen as a wicked and criminal faction.

Clement died. Farnese, whom we might call a white fox, if Julius II. was called a white lion, came to the helm at a time when the germs slumbering in the soil began to be evident throughout Italy, and the policy pursued hitherto, of occasional interference, was necessarily exchanged for more energetic treatment. Through the German soldiery under Bourbon, the Lutheran views must have been first carried to Naples. At any rate, the incapacity of the pope to exercise the slightest influence as ruling head of the Church, which continued for a year after

* See Appendix, Note XLVI.

the conquest of Rome, must have contributed to prove to the Italians, that the idea that they could live without such popes, was practically possible. About this time, the first societies formed themselves in Italy, and this in all parts of the land ; and, as their object was not the plundering of the Church, nor the abolishing of monasteries, nor the obtaining rights, the possession of which might have attracted princes and cities to take part in the religious revolution, but as their sole interest lay in the spiritual purport of the questions pending, those who felt themselves influenced by them could only be such as were entirely devoted to these objects, and took an earnest and deep interest in them. They thought not of opposition to the Church: they wished only to purify her. They shared the opinion, fostered in the Vatican itself, that the German Reformers were not to be regarded as separate from the pale of the Church. The Catholic doctrines were at that time so inconsistent and ambiguous, so little established on so many points, their re-modelling was felt in Rome, for the most part, as such an urgent necessity, that those who occupied themselves deeply with such questions, even if they gained convictions of their own, contrary to those established by custom, appeared in nowise as enemies of the Catholic doctrines. Inclination to Luther's doctrines, to a certain point, was no heresy. Intercourse took place between conspicuous reformers and Italian laymen and ecclesiastics. They endeavored to enlighten each other, and to weigh the conditions on which they could again be agreed. Study was required for this.

The disputed points were discussed historically, philosophically, and politically; and thus there arose a movement in Italy, gentle in its progress, and without an idea of force, the advocates of which closely surrounded the pope, and had the greatest influence upon the way in which the German matter was treated at the Vatican. Nothing seemed to lie nearer to the heart of Paul III. than a settlement brought about by the gentlest means. Cardinals, whose conciliatory sentiments were well known, went to and fro between Rome and Germany; and although, in returning, they rather carried the fire into their own territory than extinguished it abroad, the pope seemed to take pleasure himself in the eagerness with which the more important powers in Italy occupied themselves with the solution of the great questions. The heads of the Catholics and Reformers discussed the points with friendliness; the brutal, imperious manner, with which the legates under Leo had come forward, was given up; there was no mention made of yielding at discretion. The most attentive consideration was bestowed in Rome on the proposals of the Lutherans. Counter-proposals were made; the best will was shown; and they seemed mutually to have but the one aim before them, — to discover forms which, presenting a kind of just medium, would allow of re-union in word, without insisting upon the more exact expression of that which on both sides would be silently maintained at the same time. The necessity for a speedy reform was officially acknowledged in Rome. They exposed unsparingly their own evils. A committee of car-

dinals, appointed by the pope for the settlement of
these evils, drew up the result of their conferences
in a series of propositions, in which they were most
plain-spoken. I will only quote one,—it was a
scandal that cardinals should be seen in the bright
noon in worldly garb, in the society of women of bad
fame. It was not the women that were objected to,
but their quality. When, at the present day, we
blame the celibacy of the Catholic clergy, pitying the
recluses who are condemned to the want of family,
we are taking a point of view certainly entertained
by few in those times. The question was at that
time only how to change into marriages the usual
intercourse of the clergy with women, out of regard
for common moral security. It was a point especially
urged in Germany, because it seemed necessary to
the citizens on account of their own wives and
daughters; for no one thought of wishing to pro-
hibit the spiritual lords from making alliances, or
of considering it scandalous if they had children.

Paul III., however, took these active steps in religious matters chiefly on political grounds, which
would certainly have biassed Clement VII., had he
not felt himself far too dependent on the emperor.
Paul could again, with better powers, resume the
old policy of operating with France against Spain,
or with Spain against France. Under pretext of
reconciling the two foes, Francis and Charles, he
used their disputes for his own advantage. His
interest demanded, that, as far as possible, they
should be kept equal in power. And, as France had
gradually fallen into an increasingly disadvantageous

position, Charles must be kept from too considerable
an augmentation of power. This would have been
awarded him, had Germany yielded to him. Clement had therefore, before this, considered a certain
sympathy with the Lutheran princes as giving him
political power. Paul, however, went further. His
endeavor was to enter into an alliance with the Germans, and to bring about a direct understanding
with them. But to this the emperor presented an
obstacle, by endeavoring, on his side, to satisfy the
German princes without the pope's mediation. They
were not to go to him through Rome, but to be
brought back to Rome by him; he wished to make
them, not only good Catholics, but, above all, his
subjects. And thus, while pope and emperor were
counteracting each other, neither being in the position to use force, the Lutherans gained an advantage they never could have obtained, had they been
left to their own energy.

This state of things lasted as long, both in Germany and Italy, as was satisfactory to the pope's
desires. For the intellectual life of Rome, these
were prosperous times; and their repose and hope-
ful industry appear in all the more agreeable light
from the sad state of things under Clement which
had preceded them. In the years from 1535 to
1540, the careless liberty of the days of Leo X.
seemed to have returned, when every thing was permitted, and nothing proscribed. Paul III. was a
man of taste, who loved splendor and magnificence
of life. Better than Leo X., who often at random
elevated the mob, and left important powers disre-

garded, he drew a circle of distinguished men to
Rome, and made them cardinals. Among these
were Contarini, a Venetian nobleman, who enjoyed
the highest consideration as a diplomatist and a
scholar; Pole, a relative of the English royal family,
who had given up his country when Henry VIII.
made himself the head of the English Church;
Bembo, one of the first men in Italy as a scholar;
Morone, Sadolet, Ghiberti, and others, — all classi-
cally cultivated and experienced, and full of a spirit
of true human moderation. These formed the society which gave the tone to the Vatican. Their
presence bestowed that lustre upon Paul III. which
Raphael had given to Leo X. Their endeavor was
to bring about the great reconciliation, by means of
which the Lutherans might be won back to the
Romish Church, and might influence its life by their
presence.

Among these men was Michael Angelo. Not that
he had daily intercourse with them, or was actually
drawn into the interest which agitated their minds;
but the distinguishing feature of their efforts was
the same. He knew what they hoped; and he cherished in his soul those thoughts for the establishment
of which they were contesting.

Yet Michael Angelo's position with regard to them
allows us to perceive how far removed they were
in the South from wishing to identify themselves with
the transactions in the North. They bore no relation to Germany in a theological respect, just as in
political things, at the present day, a State would
probably, when casting off a monarchical govern-

ment, attach herself to a neighboring Republic, and make its forms her own. There may have been many in Italy who thought thus; but the liberal party, considered as a whole, shared not these views. Independent as we find Michael Angelo, nothing betrays sentiments in his mind hostile to the pope and the Romish Church. Conciliatory as Contarini, Pole, and their companions appear, they were subsequently accused of Lutheran machinations; yet they little thought of sacrificing the slightest portion of the pope's authority, and of substituting German ideas in the place of Italian ones.

What, moreover, could the doctrines of Luther have afforded these highly cultivated Italians, which they did not already possess? The Bible was opened to the Germans, for the first time, like a gift from heaven. They plunged into religious questions as into a mine of gold, of which no one had before rightly known, and which suddenly lay open there, for young and old to investigate. It was otherwise in Italy. They needed no increase of material. They had long known the Bible; they possessed Dante or Petrarca, if they wished to absorb their imagination with ideas of immortality; they had the same subject brought before them in another form in works of art. Michael Angelo often reverts to death and immortality in his sonnets. In philosophical calmness, however, he writes down his thoughts, so alien to the sentiments of the Bible, without the aid of which we should not have ventured to touch upon such subjects in Germany, that he would be considered rather a scholar of Plato's than a Christian, if the stinging unrest which fills him with regard to his own unworthiness, did not show how much he is so nevertheless.

3.

One event, occurring at that time, brings to light Michael Angelo's deepest thoughts on these subjects. His brother Buonarroto died, and he soon after was followed by his father at an extreme old age. We cannot state the time very accurately; but, as we know that Buonarroto died before his father, and that the latter attained his ninety-second year, and, as the year of his birth is known, the year 1537 or 1538 may be given as that of his death. It is recorded, that one of his brothers died of the plague, in Michael Angelo's arms. As this may have been Buonarroto, his death must have been, of course, somewhat earlier than 1536. The Florentine papers will probably furnish information respecting it.

Little is known about Buonarroto. Michael Angelo's letters to him in earlier years afford, with all their detail, but little information with regard to his character. In the year 1515, he was among those who carried the canopy under which Leo X. entered Florence. He was rewarded for this with the rank of count, and the right of adding the Medicæan balls to his arms. We know nothing further of him. He alone, of all Michael Angelo's brothers, left children behind him.

We hear more of the father. Lodovico seems to have been a good-natured, unpretending man, but at the same time too easily persuaded and pas-

sionate. The brothers made use of him when they
wished to effect any thing with Michael Angelo. At
times, the latter broke out into anger about it.
At such moments, he cast before them how he had
constantly sacrificed himself for them, but that they
had never acknowledged it. Soon, however, he
would return to his natural position : that, namely,
of working for them ; and they to theirs, — that of
consenting to it.

We have two letters of Michael Angelo's, written
between 1520 and 1530,* which show what discord
existed within the domestic circle. Both are written from Florence : —

"DEAREST FATHER," — says the first, — "I was much
astonished when I did not find you at home yesterday ; and
now, as I hear that you have complained about me and said
that I had driven you from home, I am still more astonished. For this I know as certain, — that, from the day
of my birth to the present, it has never come into my mind.
either as regards trivial things or more important ones,
to do any thing that would be opposed to you. I have
burdened myself with all my labor and work only for your
sake ; and you know well, since I have come back to Florence from Rome, that I have remained in Florence for
your sake alone, and that I consider all that belongs to me
as your property. A short time ago, when you were ill,
I promised you never willingly to leave you ; and now I
cannot but feel astonished that you have so quickly forgotten all. Thirty years you have known me now for
what I am ; and you know how I have done and intended
good for you wherever I could.

* See Appendix, Note XLVII.

"How could you now say that I had thrust you out of the house? This alone was wanting to all the sorrow I have had about other things, and all for your sake. And this is my thanks for it!

"But now, be it so. Let it be I who drove you from the house: be ashamed of me, and consider you have suffered injury through me. It shall be so. Then let me beg for forgiveness: forgive your son; and, if he has never been good for any thing, and has brought you into all imaginable harm, yet once more, I pray, forgive me, criminal as I am, and don't let the shame remain with me, of having driven you out of the house; for it signifies more to me than you believe, and I am still your son!

"The bearer of this is Raphael of Gagliano. For the sake of God, and not for my own sake, I beg you to return to Florence; for I must start on my journey, and I have important things to communicate to you, and I cannot come to you. My servant, Pietro, has not behaved himself to me as he ought. I shall send him to-morrow morning to Pistoja, where he shall remain; I will not have mischief arise through him in our house. Had you all spoken to me sooner about it, knowing what a man he was, — nothing of which I was acquainted with, — this scandal would not then have happened.

"I am urged to set out, and I cannot do so without having spoken to you. You must not remain at Settignano. I beg you, let all the sad things rest, and come.

"Your MICHELANGELO."

It seems as if Pietro were to blame for the quarrel. As Antonio Mini is first mentioned in the year 1525, Michael Angelo may at that time have changed his servant, and the date of the letter may be thus determined.* Previous, therefore, to the Romish journey of 1525, or that to Carrara, this flight of the old Buonarroti took place. How beautiful is the term with which Michael Angelo, half in irony, half in sadness, confesses to all with which he is reproached, and asks pardon like a child who has been really guilty of the offence imputed to him!

The second letter, however, shows the progress of the matter. Lodovico had not returned, but had sent a written reply. Michael Angelo could now endure it no longer. He was a man almost fifty years old; and he would not be so trifled with by those who were thus instigating his father to act, while unseen themselves. He wrote that he would only briefly reply to what was absolutely necessary. Lodovico, he says, had written that he had received no money, because he, Michael Angelo, had prohibited it. But his father was deceived by those in whom he placed his confidence. All had been thus arranged only for Lodovico's comfort: he knew no longer what he wished. But, if he had caused sorrow to his father, the latter had found means to revenge himself for it.

" The whole of Florence knows," — he continued with ironical bitterness, — " that you are a rich man, and that I have given my life for you, and gain only punishment for it: you, however, gain great praise for it. Tell people what you will, but write to me no more; for it would hinder me at my work, if I were now to tell you what you have received from me through twenty-five years.]

* See Appendix, Note XLVIII.

should like better if I need not say this to you; but I cannot change the necessity for doing so. Beware of those of whom you have to beware. We only once die; and we return not back again to make amends for that which we have done amiss. Have you therefore lived so long to act thus? God be with you!

"MICHELANGELO."

We feel that the letter was not written only for Lodovico. Unfortunately, all information as to the particulars is missing. Among those of whom the father is to beware, Gismondo and Giovansimone are intended, as they more than once had worked through him against Michael Angelo. Severe provocation must have occurred, to have given rise to such bitter expressions. Still it is possible that he also was not without blame. For we have often seen that he allowed himself to be hurried into words for which he had to make amends, and for which, indeed, he always did make amends. We frequently observe, that those who act most tenderly, most self-sacrificingly, when they feel themselves misunderstood, are often carried away into a severity of expression, which, had they weighed their words, would have seemed insufferable even to themselves.

Lodovico died from old age. His death, says Condivi, was so easy, and his color after his departure was so natural, that he seemed to slumber. The sorrow that shook Michael Angelo's heart when he, himself crossing the threshold of old age, had lost those to whom all his work had been hitherto consecrated, is shown by the following poem, in which he endeavored to soothe his grief: —

'On the Death of his Father Lodovico, after the Death
of his Brother Buonarroto.

"Already had I wept and sighed so much,
  I thought all grief for ever at an end,
  Exhaled in sighs, shed forth in bitter tears.

But death comes digging at the fount of woe,
  The very roots and veins, invidiously;
  Filling with grief the soul, with pain the heart.

Therefore from one sole point two sorrows spring,
  Distinct, and full of bitterness, — twofold, —
  Subjects for separate tongue and pen and tears.

For thee, my brother, and for him who was
  Of thee and me the parent, love inspires
  A grief unspeakable to vex and sting.

One is first painted by fond memory's strokes;
  The other, sculptured deeply in my heart,
  As though the life were scarcely lacking yet.

But these, though bitter things, yet had at last
  Their consolation; for, worn out with age,
  Thy days, O father! closed in unconsciousness.

Death is less hard to him who wearily
  Bears back to God a harvest fully ripe,
  Than 'tis to him in full and freshest mind.

But cruel were the heart that did not weep,
  That he should see no more upon this earth
  Him who gave being first, and then support.

Our grief's intensity, our weight of woe,
  Are less or more, according as each feels;
  And all my utter weakness, Lord, thou knowest.

And if my soul to reason's teaching yields,
And hides its pain, so galling is the rein
That greater torment springs from the restraint.

And did I not look inward, O my soul!
And see at last that thou shalt one day smile
At death, which now thou fearest over much,

My pain would grow; but these, my crying griefs,
Are tempered by firm faith, that Heaven affords,
At death, safe shelter to the godly man.

Our intellect, o'erloaded by the weight
Of the weak flesh, is more in fear of death
The more the false persuasion is declared.

Full ninety times the sun had bathed his face
In the wet ocean, ending his annual round,
Ere thou attainedst to the Peace Divine.

But now that Heaven has taken thee away
From wretchedness like ours, still sorrowest thou
At Heaven's decree that I should spring from thee?

Thou art to dying, dead, and made divine;
Thou neither wishest nor dost fear a change:
I cannot choose but envy thee for this.

Fortune and time no longer now shall strive
To cross thy threshold, bringing in their train
Uncertain cheerfulness and certain pain.

There are no clouds to darken thy bright day,
No portioned hours to bind thee 'gainst thy will,
Nor chance nor need to force thee here and there.

Night cannot hide thy glory, nor can day
Increase its brightness; e'en meridian sun,
With all its heat, fails to enhance thy light.

From thy calm death, I learn to meet my end,
O happy father! and in thought I see
My passage upwards into heavenly spheres.

Death is not, as some think, the worst of ills
To him whose latest day outshines the first
Through grace divine, close to the seat of God;

There where (to Him be thanks!) I think thee now,
And hope to see again, if my cold heart
Be raised from earthly mire to where thou art

And if 'twixt sire and son the noblest love
Still grows in heaven, where every virtue grows,
While giving glory to my heavenly Lord,
I shall rejoice with thee, in heaven's bliss."

"In Morte di Lodovico Padre, dopo la Morte di Buonarroto Fratello.

" Già piansi e sospirai pur tanto e tanto
    Ch' io mi credei per sempre ogni dolore
    Coi sospiri esalar, versar col pianto.
Ma morte al fonte di cotal umore
    Le radici e le vene invida impingua,
    E duol rinnova all' alma e pena al core.
Dunque in un punto sol parta e distingua
    Due querele amarissime per voi,
    Altro pianto, altra penna, e altra lingua.
Di te fratel, di te che d' ambi noi
    Genitor fosti, amor mi sprona e stringe,
    Nè so qual doglia più mi stringa e annol.
La memoria l' uno prima mi dipinge,
    L' altro vivo scolpisce in mezzo al seno
    Nuova pietà che di pallor mi tinge.

Ma quei pur cose acerbe all' ultim' ore :
  Stanco dagli anni il giorno estremo oscuro
  Traesti, o Padre, ond' ho vìe men dolore.
Poco all' increscitor già 'l morir duro,
  Di chi riporta a Dio la propria messe
  Allor che 'l ver del senso è più sicuro.
Ma qual cuore è crudel, che non piangesse,
  Non dovendo veder di quà più mai.
  Chi gli diè l' esser pria, nutrillo, e resse.
Nostri intensi dolori, e nostri guai
  Son come più o men ciascun gli sente,
  E quanto io debil sia, Signor, tu 'l sai.
E l' alma mia, s' alla ragion consente,
  Si duro è 'l fren per cui l' affanno ascondo,
  Che' n farle forza più mi fo dolente.
E se 'l pensier nel qual io mi profondo,
  Non mi mostrasse al fin, ch' oggi tu ridi
  Del morir che temesti in questo mondo,
Crescerè 'l duol, ma i dolori stridi
  Temprati son d' una credenza ferma,
  Ch' uom ben vissuto a morte in ciel s' annidi.
Nostro intelletto dalla carne inferma
  E tanto oppresso, che 'l morir più spiace
  Quanto più 'l falso persuaso afferma.
Novanta volte l' annua sua face
  Ha 'l sol nell' ocean bagnata, e molle,
  Pria che sii giunto alla divina pace.
Or ch' a nostra miseria il ciel ti tolle,
  Increscati di me che morto vivo,
  Se 'l ciel per te quaggiù nascer mi volle.
Tu se' del morir morto, e fatto divo,
  Nè temi or più cangiar vita, nè voglia,
  Che quasi senza invidia non lo scrivo.
Fortuna e tempo dentro a vostra soglia
  Non tenta trapassar per cui s' adduce
  Infra dubbia letizia certa doglia.
Nube non è ch' oscuri vostra luce,
  L' ore distinte a voi non fanno forza,
  Caso, o necessità non vi conduce.

Vostro splendor per notte non s' ammorza,
 Nè cresce mai per giorno, benchè chiaro,
 Nè quando 'l sol più suo calor rinforza.
Nel tuo morire il mio morire imparo,
 Padre felice, e nel pensier ti veggio
 Dove 'l mondo passar ne fa di raro.
Non è, com 'alcun crede, morte il peggio
 A chi l'ultimo dì trascende al primo
 Per grazia eterna, appresso al divin seggio.
Dove, la Dio mercè, te credo e stimo,
 E spero di veder, se 'l freddo cuore
 Mia raggion tragge dal terrestre limo.
E se tra 'l padre e 'l figlio ottimo amore
 Cresce nel ciel, crescendo ogni virtute,
 Rendendo gloria al mio divin fattore
Goderò con la mia la tua salute." *

The train of thought in this poem is of the greatest beauty. From his own grief, Michael Angelo slowly rises to the glory of his father, and concludes by placing himself at his side. How clearly he recognized here the union of earthly sects. Yet, in a Christian feeling similar to Dante's, he holds himself aloof from the dispute which is agitating the world around him. There is no trace of purgatory in Michael Angelo's verses. The idea never occurred to him. From the first, he entertains a certainty of the old Lodovico's perfect happiness; and, in evidence of this, he urges the grace of God, *la grazia divina*, which is pre-supposed as something which cannot fail him who surely expects it. This was the purport of the proposition about which

---

* From the MS. In the British Museum, which in some passages varies considerably. I insert the Italian text here, and afterwards very frequently ; as my translation, aiming more at the spirit than the words, cannot take the place of the original verses.

Rome and Germany were disputing: Michael Angelo expresses it here as if no one doubted it. How little he adhered to outward ecclesiastical rule, is shown by the letter which he wrote to Florence on the death of his brother Giovansimone.* "Although," he there writes, "all those sacraments which the Church enjoins were not administered to him, yet if he showed true repentance and resignation to the will of God (*buona contritione*), that is sufficient for his eternal blessedness." In the same correspondence, we discover also his views of good works. He commissions Leonardo again and again to inquire secretly whether there is not some poor citizen to be raised from distress, and assisted perhaps with a dowry for his daughter. He was to write to him about it; for he wished to do something for the welfare of his own soul. But he was to do so quite in secret, that no one might hear of it. The doctrine could not be more nobly understood. But, to any man who thought thus, the German idea that nothing depended on good works must have been scarcely intelligible.

It was not the Bible alone, though he studied it sufficiently, which was the source of Michael Angelo's convictions. Dante must be also included. Michael Angelo's poems plainly evidence to what a great extent Dante's thoughts had passed into his mind. In the verses on the death of his father, there is the half-antique Dante conception of the heaven above the clouds, of the sea of light; there is the personifying of Time and Fate, who venture

* See Appendix, Note XLIX.

not to pass beyond its gates. Michael Angelo would
have painted them as voracious, idle beings, looking
helplessly through the barrier they might not pass.
The principal distinction between the Germanic and
Romanic mind consists in this,— that, with the Germans, forms lose themselves again in ideas; while,
with the Romans, the most uncertain idea fashions
itself into form. The Germans were aiming at that
time to free themselves from this Olympus of formed
beings, so foreign to their notions; but, in doing so,
they must have appeared to the Romans as sacrile-
gious destroyers. For, even among those who understood the doctrine of Luther the most clearly, the
greater part were unable to conceive the invisible
without the visible. Hence the reason why worldly
thoughts were again and again imputed to the Lutherans; why it was imagined that Luther could be
made a cardinal; why Protestantism was received as
merely negative, without a belief of its own, and the
possibility of its endurance was not allowed. And
therefore in Michael Angelo, though in his thoughts
he approached the doctrines, and though his whole
nature inclined to speculations on this subject, there
is no trace of his taking cognizance of Luther and
his doings. We may even infer the healthiness of
Michael Angelo's nature from this; for, wherever
the religious movement now asserted itself in Italy,
it appears more frequently the result of something
which I will call neither sentimentality nor over-
straining; but which was at any rate not the strong,
citizen-like spirit which animated it in Germany,
and which gave to it vigor and continuance.

4.

Between 1530 and 1540, Rome received free ideas from three different quarters.

She received them from Venice, where freedom of thought was most permitted, and where the closest intercourse with Germany prevailed. Here dwelt the Florentine exile Bruccioli, and translated the Bible. From hence also an address was sent to Luther, and an answer received.

She received them from Geneva, where, under the direction of Calvin, a spiritual authority had been formed, such as Savonarola had vainly endeavored to raise in Florence, and which was situated as an unassailable theological fortress between France, Germany, and Italy. Thither the glances of Savoy were directed, — for Margaret, sister of Francis I., and the friend of Calvin, dwelt there; and those of Ferrara also, — for Renata, the consort of the young Duke Ercole, likewise a French princess, and still more associated with Calvin than Margaret, had almost publicly confessed the new doctrines. Many ties connected Ferrara with almost all the more important cities of Northern Italy.

The third attack, however, proceeded from Naples; and from hence, to use the technical expression, the breach was opened.

Whilst in the North the matter was openly carried on, and the heretical writings were poured freely into the country across the Alps, in Naples, independent of such impetus from without, there arose, among the highest aristocracy, a fanatical enthusiasm for the pure doctrine, which, not appearing at first in its true colors, avoided the counter-exertions of those who endeavored to oppose it. The movement was controlled in the north, and was soon restrained by prohibition; in Naples this was not possible, because it was never admitted that heretical ideas were tolerated.

Fra Occhino, a Capuchin monk from Venice, was the soul of the Neapolitan movement. He was learned, highly esteemed, and animated by such ardor when he spoke, that, as the memoirs of a Neapolitan living at that time inform us, he could have melted the very stones to tears.* In Lent, 1536, when Charles V. was in Naples, Occhino was preaching there. At the same time, when the emperor was issuing an edict, by which not only all heretics, but even those who came in contact with heretics, were threatened with loss of life and property, he attended the preaching of Occhino, and acknowledged the power of his glowing eloquence. And so skilfully did Occhino conceal his innermost thoughts, that the pope himself appointed him his confessor, and summoned him to Rome.

Here he now appeared at the head of the party who were laboring to bring about a peaceable agreement with the Lutherans; and who, although the attempts of the pope to negotiate with Luther, and to induce the Germans to attend a council in Italy under the auspices of the Romish Church, remained fruitless, did not, however, support the influence of those who were in favor of the application of authoritative force to the Lutherans.

* See Appendix, Note L.

For that the Lutherans would not come to terms was clear at last to many. The Germans desired a council endowed with sovereign power to remodel every thing thoroughly. The more courteous, the more considerate, were the advances from Rome, the more rude were Luther's replies. Paul III. had selected a man to negotiate with him, who, by his subsequent apostasy to the German cause, exercised the greatest influence upon events. This man, Vergerio, a high ecclesiastic, had already gone to Germany on a similar mission under Clement VII. He declared, when, after having failed in his object, he arrived in Rome, that war was the only means of accomplishing any thing.

In spite of this, they adhered strongly in the Vatican to the idea of a peaceable solution of things, and submitted patiently to the progress of the reformers in their own land.

This moderation, however, and the endeavor purposely exhibited by Paul III. to draw free-minded, unbiassed men to the Vatican, did not spring simply from the motives to which it was assigned.

Besides the party in Italy of those who wished for reform in a liberal sense, Luther's appearance had aroused another, at whose heart lay no less the renovation of the Church, but who saw the means for making Rome again what she ought to be, — not by a remodelling of her principles, but by a return to the old strictness, by the maintenance of her privileges, and by the restoration of her authoritative position with regard to secular rule. A new spirit was needed; but it was the old, the lost one. There was no occasion to treat with heretics, but regardlessly to correct the evil in themselves. They must feel what they were, and live and act accordingly. The Church had to be renovated; but, under any circumstances, the people had to be silent and obey.

Men had met together, even under Leo X., who saw in this the only safety of the Church, — that, by fasting, prayer, and self-discipline, the beginning of a better life might be entered upon at once. They felt that Heaven would prosper these germs, and thus, at last, excellence would be restored. They began to form themselves into a community. Prayer, meditation, and mutual strengthening in a self-denying, holy course of life, were their aims. The union was called, "The Oratory of Divine Love." Not only ecclesiastics, but men of all positions in life, took part in it. They really desired to form a contrast to the disorderly condition into which Romish life had fallen.

During the first twenty years of the century, this union had produced the order of the Theatines, so called from Pietro Caraffa, Bishop of Theate, who stood at his head, and who, by his exemplary life, was a pattern to others. Deprivations, and complete abstraction in spiritual thoughts, which ought truly to form the basis of all orders, but which at that time were exchanged for wealth, luxuriousness, and worldly employments, often of the most objectionable character, were indeed possessed by the Theatines; and a spirit of zeal and unyielding severity was fostered by them, which made them act on the offensive towards all those, who, according to their opinion, injured the Catholic doctrines.

The order had afterwards removed to Venice, and from thence to Naples, just at the time that Occhino was preaching there. The Theatines soon perceived the heresy of his doctrines, and accused him. Occhino, however, knew how to defend himself, and came off victorious from their accusations. Caraffa, their founder, however, was too powerful a person for the pope to dispense with. Three times he summoned Caraffa, before he accepted the call to Rome. At length he appeared, and was appointed member of the committee which had to state and consider the evils of the Church. As all the different views were to be represented in Rome, Caraffa's appointment appeared to be an act of justice. His mere presence, however, was sufficient to exhibit the hostility of his party to Occhino's; and soon nothing was required but to wait so long as the Liberals were at the helm of affairs.

It seems as if the pope, from the first, had been filled with a certain fear of being obliged some day to rely on Caraffa's party; and that, therefore, his wish to be on good terms with the Lutherans had arisen from the feeling, that, if ever compulsion and severity were of necessity employed, he should have to yield to those who would in that case be at the helm.

Caraffa declared himself in the committee in favor of immediate reform in the outward life of the clergy. It would be sinning greatly against God to delay this, he said, even for a moment. This could,

of course, be of no service to the pope. It would
have been a noble spectacle, if the young Cardinal
Farnese, who owed his outward position to the possessions of the murdered Ippolito, could have been
compelled suddenly to become a worthy and abstemi-
ous priest. Paul deferred the proposed praiseworthy
measures to better times. He still hoped to effect a
compromise with the Germans.

The prospects of the emperor had assumed an
increasingly sorry aspect, ever since the campaign
against Francis I., so pompously announced in Rome,
had taken an unsuccessful turn. He could no longer
think of driving back the Lutherans to the pope by
force. The political position of the Lutheran princes
was most favorable. France and England, who had
now revolted from the pope, were their allies. The
emperor and pope vied with each other in obsequiousness. Each hoped in this way to turn things to
his own advantage.

In the year 1539, it was clearly shown how both
stood with regard to the Germans. Paul had called
a council: it was to meet at Vicenza. Charles, on
the other hand, had come to an agreement with
the German princes, that Reformers and Catholics
should hold a religious conference in Nürnberg,
and should decide the questions pending, without the
pope's participation. This was an imperial council
against a popish one. A high ecclesiastic was at
once dispatched to Madrid, charged with complaints.
The disorders in the Netherlands afforded the emperor a pretext for deferring the matter for the
present; in the following year, however, he again

resumed the plan. His brother Ferdinand, King of Rome, and special Regent of Germany, met him in the Netherlands; and it was decided between them in what way they would manage the Lutherans. Cardinal Farnese, who was at the imperial court, used every means to prevent these resolutions, but in vain. The imperial diet, at which matters were to be decided, was agreed upon behind his back. Farnese left the court at once; and, travelling back through Paris, he obtained an edict against heretics, which was carried out with ostensible severity.

In Caraffa's mind, this was a step onwards. Still, however, the milder view of things prevailed in Rome.

The pope showed himself ready to send a legate to the diet appointed at Ratisbon in March, 1541. The Lutherans had declared their consent to this. Up to the last moment, before the pope took this step, they had endeavored to induce the emperor to refer the religious question to the Council of Vicenza, as the only tribunal of authority. This was refused, and the pope yielded. Contarini, the mildest of the liberal cardinals, the tried friend of the emperor, who had personally desired him to be sent, went to Ratisbon; and the negotiations began.

During Contarini's absence, however, the decisive step took place in Rome.

The young Cardinal Farnese stood at the head of those who urged for violent measures. It is true, not from Caraffa's motives. The Farnese desired an alliance with France, and war against Lombardy. If, however, a reconciliation between Germany and the emperor were now effected, the latter would acquire an increase of power, which not only would be a direct advantage to him, but would limit the ravages of France in North Germany, from whence she drew her best soldiers. It suddenly occurred to the liberal cardinals, that they might be conspiring with the emperor. The council, the deposition of the pope, the elevation of Contarini, or of one of his friends, appeared possible. All the free-minded Italians, whose number increased daily, had become allies of the new power. Contarini was on the point of coming to an understanding with the Lutherans, all secondary considerations having been set aside, and the one most important question respecting justification by faith being alone treated of; and, on this point, Melancthon had shown himself inclined to come to an accommodation, to which Contarini had promised the pope's consent. Suddenly orders arrived from Rome, calling him back.

Under the reproach of having outstepped his instructions, and charged with the suspicion of having assented to the plans of the emperor against the pope, although it was well enough known in Rome that one charge was as groundless as the other, he was sent as legate to Bologna; Cardinal Pole was dispatched in the same capacity to Viterbo; and Caraffa, who obtained the glory of having opened the pope's eyes, was the one left behind.

In confirmation of the new ideas, the Inquisition was established in Rome, in the summer of the year following, by Caraffa, and Loyola, who had arrived there.

A panic spread through Italy. Whoever could, escaped. This was the period at which Michael Angelo's Last Judgment was completed. At the Christmas festival of 1541, the Sistine Chapel was re-opened. When Biagio da Cesena, the master of the ceremonies, saw himself furiously portrayed in the form of the infernal judge Minos, the pope could still venture the jest, that he could do nothing, as even the popes themselves could release no one from eternal condemnation. Soon, however, the painting was abused from the pulpit.

All was now silent respecting the Fall of the Angels, which was to have occupied the opposite wall. Michael Angelo had already made designs for it, none of which, however, are now to be found. A Sicilian painter, who was in Michael Angelo's service as color-grinder, is said to have used them in painting the Church of the Trinity in Rome. Vasari describes the picture; but I have not seen it there, and I have never found it mentioned elsewhere.

CHAPTER FOURTEENTH.

1536—1546.

VITTORIA COLONNA.

IN spite of the sorrow into which Michael Angelo
was plunged by the loss of his father and brother,
I may call the period from 1536 to 1541 an especially
happy one.

Whenever we contemplate the life of great men,
the most beautiful part of their existence is, that,
when meeting with a power equal to their own, they
find one worthy of measuring the depth of their
mind. I do not say, worthy of their art, or of that
which, with those who are not artists, takes the place
of art: for it is enough for them to have found a
being, by whom they are understood to their utmost
desire; one to whom they can speak without being
obliged to explain their words; one who, even when
they express only the disjointed part of a thought,
supplies the deficiency without difficulty from his
own mind. There is no deeper desire than that of
meeting such a mind; no greater happiness than
having found it; no greater sorrow than to resign
this happiness, whether it be, that it has never been
enjoyed, or that it has been lost.

Vittoria Colonna.

MICHAEL ANGELO.

Goethe certainly never felt himself happier than in interchange of thought with Schiller, — never more solitary than when death took away his friend. All the early friendships, so ardently entered into, which had always ended either in coldness or flight, had been vain attempts to discover men whose understanding could fathom his mind. Goethe had long given up the hope of finding any but, at the best, kindly pliable souls, who at least did not oppose where they did not understand, when he met with Schiller. Few beside him are known to whom fate was so beneficent. We know of no equal-minded friend vouchsafed to Dante, Shakespeare, or Beethoven. Byron found Shelley. But, if to the greater number that is denied which might be considered in its perfection as the lively echo of their own mind, it is at least awarded almost to all to be allowed to delude themselves with the feeling that they have found what they needed, if it be only the eyes of a girl, in the depth of which they imagined they could read the understanding of their mysteries.

Michael Angelo, however, had become old in solitude. "I have no friends: I need none, and wish to have none," he wrote home in his early years from Rome. In Florence, when artists met for conversation here and there, or for festivities, Michael Angelo was rarely with them. This was increasingly the case, the older he became. We have no intimation that any other spirits approached him than those of the great dead of his country. He seemed to have suffered the living who formed his society to gather so closely round him, because they never burdened his thoughts with their own. He had blockheads sometimes in his house, who entertained no thoughts at all, and whom he endured as children to whom he condescended. He loved children. A boy is said to have once told him in the street, that he should like him to draw something; and Michael Angelo took the sheet offered, and granted his request at once. That he loved women is shown by his poems. There is, however, no single one which expresses any other feeling than that of resignation or sorrow at unrequited passion. Like Beethoven, he seems never to have won her for whom he longed.

One poem among many we will quote here, in which he says what conflicts he has endured : —

> " Oh for the time, when, with a lightsome heart,
>   To my blind hopes I gave unbridled play !
> Oh for the cheerful brow, serenely gay,
>   From which all beauty must for aye depart ;
> And the slow steps, laboriously ta'en,
>   That grow so tardy as we grow in years !
> Oh for a flame of love, a fount of tears,
>   That I might satisfy thee once again !
> And if thou livest but to awaken love,
>   And call forth mortals' sweet and bitter tears,
> Weary and old I meet not thy desire ;
>   Because my soul, nearing the land above,
> Too poor an aim for thy bright rays appears,
>   And the burnt wood but feebly feeds the fire."

> ' Tornami al tempo allor che lieta e sciolta
>   Al cieco ardor m'era la briglia, e 'l freno,
>   Rendimi 'l volto angelico, e sereno
>   Ond 'oggi è seco ogni virtù sepolta.

E i passi sparsi, e con fatica molta
Che son si lenti a chi è d' anni pieno,
Tornami l'acqua, e 'l fuoco in mezzo 'l seno,
Se vuoi di me saziarsi un' altra volta.
E s'egli è pur amor che tu sol viva
De' dolci amari pianti de' mortali;
D'un vecchio stanco omai puoi goder poco.
Chè l' alma quasi giunta all' altra riva
Fa scudo ai tuoi di più pietosi strali,
E d'un legni 'arso fa vil pruova il fuoco."

He had thus grown old, — sixty years old; a time when men cease to believe in the fulfilment of their hopes, as well as on a requital of fate. And yet he was even now vouchsafed what he longed for. He met at last <u>Vittoria Colonna.</u>

The friendship between Michael Angelo and Vittoria Colonna is well known. Whoever has heard his name knows hers also. In the year when expectation was aroused in Rome by the freer intellectual life in Italy, Vittoria appeared there, in close connection with the men who were laboring for the promulgation of the new ideas; and, next to Occhino, she was, as it were, the second intellectual centre around whom the followers of the doctrine taught by this man united.

She came from Naples, where she had become acquainted with Occhino. She had probably effected his summons to Rome. As the daughter of Fabrizio Colonna, and the widow of the Marchese di Pescara, the two highest nobles and generals of her time, she stood on a par with the first nobles in Europe. Pescara had thought of becoming King of Naples. Pompeo Colonna, Clement VII.'s rival, was more powerful in Rome than the pope. In the palace of Vittoria and the beautiful Giulia Gonzaga, there met a society formed in the highest circles of Naples, the soul of which was Valdez, a Spaniard, whose duty for many years had been to keep the emperor currently acquainted with the German movement, and in whose heart the truth, thus involuntarily imbibed, burst into flame on coming in contact with Occhino. He remained in Naples; began to preach; and, so long as his short life lasted, he kept alive the thoughts with which Occhino and Vittoria Colonna now entered Rome itself.*

Vittoria was received by the pope as became a princess of her rank. The emperor, while in Rome, visited her in her palace. The Cardinals Pole and Contarini, the heads of Occhino's party, were her intimate friends; and those not linked with her by the interests of religious reform were attracted by her beauty and amiability, and that which is styled by her contemporaries, her learning. People were proud of being able to reckon themselves as her friends, adorers, or *protégés*. For her connection, and the high consideration of her family, permitted her to take many under her protection.

We know not how she became acquainted with Michael Angelo. She was not in Rome for the first time in 1536. She had been there as a young married woman with Pescara, her sun, as she calls him, to whom she had been betrothed in her cradle, and who, it was decreed, was to die far from her. He was severely wounded in the battle of Pavia.

On the way to him, she heard of his death, and returned back to Rome, where Clement VII. had to prevent her by force from taking the veil. He forbade the nuns to attire her for the ceremony. But she lived like a nun. She would hear nothing of splendid proposals of marriage, nor could it be expected of her. Then came the evils in Rome which her family brought upon the city; she offered her whole property to make amends for the losses. Then she went back to Ischia, where she had once lived so happily with Pescara. She was childless. From thenceforth till 1536, she divided her time between Ischia and Naples. It seems that in this year she first became the friend of Michael Angelo.

We should not have known so much as this, had not that wonderful Providence, which will allow nothing to be for ever concealed which may increase our knowledge of great natures, brought to light a document which exhibits Michael Angelo and Vittoria in the most life-like manner in the spring of the year 1537.

A miniature-painter, Francesco d'Ollanda by name, was sent to Italy, between 1530 and 1540, by the King of Portugal, in whose service he was; and, on his return, he furnished an account of his experiences. His manuscript, dated 1549, was found in one of the Lisbon libraries; and Count Raczynsky published some parts of it, translated into French, in his work upon art in Portugal. We see Francesco in the midst of Romish life, and, as we have no cause to doubt his truthfulness,* in such close

* See Appendix, Note LII.

intercourse with Vittoria and Michael Angelo, that
we can scarcely wish for any thing more favorable
or full of detail.   He describes two Sundays which
he spent with them, and he gives the conversation
which took place.   The little Church of San Silvestro on Monte Cavallo, opposite the Quirinal Palace,
where they met, still stands.   No longer, indeed, as
at that time; for it is full of the ornaments of a later
date.   The small comfortable sacristy behind the altar
is painted with Domenichino's frescos;   the carved
choir-stools are no longer the old ones, — at that
time the monastery to which the church belonged
was a nunnery, at the present day it is tenanted by
monks, — but the small dim space is as it was then;
the convent-yard, which I found filled with flourishing lemon-trees;   and, behind it, the Colonna gardens, rising from the palaces, standing at the foot
of the hill, up the Quirinal and through the paths of
which Vittoria ascended to the convent, which was
not situated then, as now, on a square surrounded
by palaces, but lay alone on the height, amid gardens and small houses.

What, however, makes the meetings which Francesco describes of still greater importance, are some
mistakes, which have crept into the statement, either
from an error of memory (for he wrote almost
twelve years afterwards, and expressly says that the
names had begun to vanish from his mind), or from
the confusion of the copier; for I suppose the Messer
Lattantio Tolomei, introduced as a friend of Vittoria's, is far more probably Claudio Tolomei, known
as belonging to the circle of the Marchesa and Mi-

chael Angelo, and one of the noblest and most
distinguished literary men at that time in Rome.
Farther, I should imagine that Fra Ambrosio of
Siena, the famous pulpit orator, was more probably
Fra Bernardino of Siena; that is, Occhino himself,
who appears in Vittoria's letters under this name.
If we add Michael Angelo to these two, the first
minds in Rome are presented to us by Francesco
d'Ollanda, and his record becomes increasingly valuable.

He begins with an explanation, intended for his
king and master, respecting the object of his residence in Rome. He says that he had had only art
in view : —

"I was not seen," he says, "in the suite of the great
Cardinal Farnese, or of the high ecclesiastics, courting
their notice. I was in quest of others, — of men such as
Don Giulio di Macedonia, the famous miniature-painter
(a master, we may observe by the way, who, though he
labored in a different style to Michael Angelo's, still, on
the whole, imitated him so much that he was called the little Michael Angelo); Baccio, the noble sculptor (he means
Bandinelli, who at that time was executing the monuments of Leo and Clement VII.); Pierino del Vaga,
Sebastiano del Piombo, Valerio of Vicenza, Jacopo Meli-
chino (an architect in the employ of Paul III.), and Lattantio Tolomei: men whose friendship was of higher value
to me than the favor of nobles, even though these might
belong to the highest rank of earthly grandeur. Michael
Angelo, however, awakened such a feeling of faithful love
in me, that, if I met him in the papal palace or in the
street, the stars would often come out in the sky before I

let him go again. Don Pedro Mascaranhas, our ambassador, may be my witness how difficult it was to get so far with him. Don Pedro was there one evening, and heard how Michael Angelo jested with me over my work, when, at his order, I had undertaken to make a series of the remarkable things in Rome and Italy, which were wished for by the Cardinal Santi Quattro. My highest model was the venerable Pantheon, the most insignificant columns of which I drew; or the monuments of Agrippa and Augustus, the Coliseum, the baths of Caracalla and Diocletian, the triumphal arches, the Capitol, and whatever the city contained besides in remarkable buildings, the names of which have unfortunately already begun to escape my memory. No other thought, however, impressed me in the splendid apartments of the pope, but admiration for Raphael d'Urbino, who has adorned it with his noble work.

"While I was thus sparing of my time in Rome, I went one Sunday to Messer Tolomei, to visit him as my habit was. He had helped me to become acquainted with Michael Angelo through Blasio, the pope's secretary, a man of importance, whose noble views, high birth (he was a relative of the pope's), great age, and irreproachable conduct, had rendered honorable. I did not meet him; but he had left word that I should find him on Monte Cavallo, in the Church of San Silvestro, where, with the Marchesa di Pescara, he was hearing the exposition of the Epistles of St. Paul. And so I started off for San Silvestro.

"Vittoria Colonna, however, the Marchesa di Pescara, and sister of Ascanio Colonna, is one of the noblest and most famous women in Italy, and in the whole world. She is beautiful, pure in conduct, and acquainted with the Latin tongue; in short, she is adorned with every grace which can redound to a woman's praise. Weary of the brilliant life which she formerly led, she has quite devoted herself, since the death of her husband, to thoughts on Christ and to study; she supports the needy of her sex, and stands forth as a model of genuine Catholic piety. She was the intimate friend of Tolomei, and I owe her acquaintance to him.

"I entered: they asked me to take a place, and the reading and exposition of the Epistles was continued. When it was ended, the marchesa spoke; and, looking at me and Tolomei, she said, 'I am not quite wrong, if I imagine that Messer Francesco would rather listen to Michael Angelo upon painting than Fra Ambrosio upon the Pauline Epistles.'

"'Madam,' I replied, 'Your Excellence seems to entertain the belief that every thing which is not painting and art is foreign and unintelligible to me. It will be certainly very agreeable to me to hear Michael Angelo speak; but I prefer Fra Ambrosio's expositions of the Epistles of St. Paul.'

"I had spoken somewhat with pique. 'You need not take it so seriously,' interrupted Tolomei; 'the marchesa certainly did not mean that a man who is a good painter is not good for any thing else. We Italians rank art too high for that. Perhaps the words of the marchesa were intended to intimate, that, besides the enjoyment we have had, the other, of hearing Michael Angelo speak to-day, is still in store for us.'

"'If it be so,' I replied, 'it would, after all, be nothing extraordinary; for Your Excellency would be only following your usual habit, of granting a thousand times more than one ventured to desire.'

"The marchesa smiled. 'We ought to know how to give,' she said, 'when a grateful mind is concerned; and here, especially, when giving and receiving afford equal enjoyment.' One of her retinue had approached at her call. 'Do you know Michael Angelo's dwelling? Go, and tell him that I and Messer Tolomei are here in the chapel, where it is beautifully cool, — the church, too, is private and agreeable; and that I beg to ask him whether he is inclined to lose a few hours here in our society, and to turn them into gain for us. But not a word that the gentleman from Spain is here.'

"I could not refrain from remarking, in a low tone, to Tolomei, with what art the marchesa knew how to treat the slightest thing. She inquired what we were saying. 'Oh! answered Tolomei, 'he said with what wisdom Your Excellency went to work even in so trifling a message. For as Michael Angelo knows, that, when he once meets Messer Francesco, there is no possibility of separating: he avoids him wherever he can.'

" 'I have remarked it,' said the marchesa; 'I know Michael Angelo. But it will be difficult to bring him to speak upon painting.'

" Fra Ambrosio of Siena, one of the pope's most famous preachers, had hitherto not uttered a syllable. 'As the gentleman from Spain,' he now began, 'is himself a painter, Michael Angelo will be cautious of speaking of painting. The gentleman ought to conceal himself, if he wishes to hear him speak about it.'

" 'It would perhaps be more difficult than you imagine, to keep the gentleman from Spain concealed from Michael Angelo,' I replied, with some severity, to the reverend gentleman; 'even if I were concealed, he would observe my presence sooner perhaps than your reverence would were I not concealed, though you took spectacles to help you. Only let him come, whether he remarks that I am here or no.'

"The marchesa and Tolomei laughed. After some moments, in which neither of them spoke, we heard knocking at the door. Every one feared that it could not be Michael Angelo, who lived down below on Monte Cavallo.* Fortunately, however, the servant met him close by San Silvestro, as he was just on the point of going to the Thermæ. He was coming up the Esquiline Way, in conversation with his color-grinder, Urbino: he fell at once into the snare, and it was he who knocked at the door.

"The marchesa rose to receive him, and remained standing some time until she had made him take a place between herself and Tolomei. I now also seated myself at a little distance from them. At first they were silent; then, however, the marchesa, who could never speak without elevating those with whom she conversed and even the place where she was, began to lead the conversation with the greatest art upon all possible things, without, however, touching even remotely upon painting. She wished to give Michael Angelo assurance. She proceeded as if approaching an unassailable fortress, so long as he was on his guard. But at last he yielded. 'It is an old experience,' she said, 'that no one can rise against Michael Angelo, who would contend against him with his own weapons; that is, with mind and art. And so you will see there is only one means of having the last word with him; and that is to speak of lawsuits or painting, and he will say not a word more.'

"'Or rather,' I now remarked from my corner, 'the very best means of wearying Michael Angelo out, would be simply to let him know that I am here; for he has not seen me up to this moment. Of course, the surest means of concealing from him any thing as unimportant as I am, was to come close under his eyes.'

* See Appendix, Note LIII.
13*

"'Pardon, Messer Francesco,' he called out, turning with astonishment towards me, 'it was impossible to see you. I saw no one here but the marchesa. But, since you are providentially there, come as a colleague to my help.'

"'The marchesa,' I replied, 'seems, like the sun, to show things to one, but to dazzle another, who looks at her. With you, she is to blame that you have not seen me; and, with me, she is the cause of my seeing you at all to-day. Who, moreover,' I added. 'in discussion with Her Excellency, would have any thoughts left for his neighbor? He needs them truly for himself. And for this reason alone,' I concluded, turning to Fra Ambrosio, 'it before seemed to me superfluous to follow the good counsel of a certain reverend gentleman.'

"All laughed. Fra Ambrosio rose, took his leave of the marchesa, greeted us, and left. He has been subsequently among my best friends.

"'His Holiness,' said the marchesa, again renewing the conversation, 'has had the goodness to grant me permission to build a new convent in this immediate neighborhood, half-way up Monte Cavallo, where the tower stands from which Nero looked down on the burning city. The footsteps of pious women are to efface the traces of the wicked. I don't know, Michael Angelo, how I shall have the building erected, — how large, and facing which side. The old wall, perhaps, might be still employed.'

"'Certainly,' he replied: 'the old tower might hold the bells. I see no difficulty in this building. We would, if Your Excellency likes, take a view of the place on the way home.'

"'I had not ventured to ask this,' answered she; 'but I see the words of our Lord, "Every one that exalteth himself shall be abased, and he that humbleth himself shall be exalted," are true under all circumstances. But

you understand how to give conscientiously where others
only lavish at random, and therefore your friends rank
yourself so much higher than your works; and those who
only know your works, and not yourself, value that in you
which can only be called perfect on a lower scale. I cannot but admire the manner in which you withdraw yourself from the world, from useless conversation, and from
all the offers of princes, who desire paintings from your
hand, — how you avoid it all, and how you have disposed
the labor of your whole life as one single great work.'

" ' Gracious lady,' replied Michael Angelo, ' these are
undeserved praises; but, as the conversation has taken
this turn, I must here complain of the public. A thousand
silly reproaches are brought against artists of importance.
They say that they are strange people, that they are not
to be approached, that there is no bearing with them.
No one, on the contrary, can be so natural and human as
great artists. But they persist in saying (I am not speaking of the few people who think rationally) that they are
whimsical and strange. This charge, however, is least
consistent with the nature of a painter. It is true, painters
have certain peculiarities, especially here in Italy, where
the painting is better than anywhere else in the world;
but how should an artist, absorbed in his work, take from
it time and thought to drive away other people's ennui?
There are few enough who do what they have to do with
perfect conscientiousness. But he who belongs to these
few will understand why it is not easy to deal sometimes
with great artists. Their arrogance, certainly, is not to
blame for this. But how rarely do they meet with a
mind capable of understanding ideas, if they enter into
commonplace conversation which diverts them from their
own deep thoughts? I can assure you, His Holiness himself often perplexes me, when he asks me why I do not

oftener show myself. I believe I can be more useful to him, and can serve him more conscientiously, by remaining at home, than by appearing in the palace for every trifle. I generally reply to such questions from His Holiness, by saying that I prefer to work for him after my own fashion, instead of parading before him like others all day, and not stirring a hand.'

"'Happy Michael Angelo!' I cried, 'there is only one prince among all the princes of the world, and that is the pope, who would forgive such a sin.'

"'It is just in this that princes should be most forbearing,' he said. 'As regards the pope,' he continued, after a time, 'the importance of the work which he has commissioned me to complete, has given me such a freedom towards him, that in conversation, sometimes, I put my felt hat here on my head, without thinking,* and speak openly. And it never occurs to him to have my head cut off for this; on the contrary, he lets me live as I like, and it is just at such moments that I serve him most zealously. Of course, if any blockhead were to fancy being quite alone, not having a human being near, and call this the true enjoyment of life, his friends would justly let him go; and the world, with good reason, would condemn him: but not to let an artist indulge in quiet, who lives solitarily, because his object in life obliges it, or because he will utter no false expressions, and who, besides, demands nothing from any one, is the greatest injustice. Why wish to make him, by force, take part in killing time? He needs quiet. There is mental work which demands the whole man, and leaves not the smallest part of his soul free to give up to any. Had he so much leisure time as you have, he would be driven to death if he did not fill it up exactly as you do,—with obeisances and other usages

* See Appendix, Note LIV.

of courtesy. If, however, you break in upon him, and praise him only for the sake of honoring yourself, and seek his company because you are proud of it, he must please you as he is. If pope and emperor speak with him, be satisfied. I say, an artist, who, instead of satisfying the highest demands of his art, tries to suit himself to the great public; who has nothing strange or peculiar in his personal exterior, or rather what the world calls so, — will never become an extraordinary mind. It is true, as regards the ordinary race of artists, we need take no lantern to look for them: they stand at the corner of every street throughout the world, ready for all who seek for them.'

"Michael Angelo paused a little here, and the marchesa continued : —

" ' If only those good friends who beset great artists resembled those of ancient times! Archesilas once visited Apelles, who was sick; and, whilst arranging the pillows. he secretly placed under them a handful of gold. When the old servant afterwards discovered the treasure, Apelles quieted her, saying, "She need not be at all surprised: Archesilas had been there." '

" ' Great artists,' began Tolomei, ' would exchange with no other mortals. For the most part they are satisfied with that which they gain from their work: often little enough. They do not envy the rich, for they consider themselves richer than the richest. A mind schooled by art perceives the emptiness of the life of those who consider themselves as the mighty of the earth, and whose glory is all laid in the coffin with them. What is called happiness, in the common sense, can no longer allure him who is striving after a fame which has indeed no attraction for the multitude. An artist is prouder of a successful piece of work, than a prince is of a conquered province. "I can make earls and dukes," said the Emperor Maximilian, when he had pardoned an artist who was sentenced to death; "but God alone can make a great artist."'

"'Messer Tolomei,' said the marchesa, 'give me your advice. Shall I now venture to request Michael Angelo to enlighten me a little upon painting? or would the act enable him to show at once, that great men, in spite of every thing, really listen to no reason, and are humorsome after all?'

"'My lady,' replied Tolomei, 'Messer Michael Angelo must make an exception here, and communicate his thoughts, though he may hold them concealed from the world.'

"'Your Excellency has only to command, and I obey,' said Michael Angelo.

"The marchesa smiled. 'Since we have come so far as that, I should like to know what you think of the Netherland painting. It seems to me more religious in its character than the Italian.'

"'The Netherland painting,' replied the master slowly, 'will suit in general all who call themselves religious, more than the Italian will do.* The Netherland works will bring tears to their eyes, when ours leave them cold. The cause, however, does not lie in the power of those paintings, but in the weakly sensibilities of those who allow themselves to be thus affected. The Netherland painting suits old women and young girls, ecclesiastics, nuns, and people of quality, who have no feeling for the true harmony of a work of art. The Netherlanders endeavor to attract the eye. They represent favorite and agreeable subjects, — saints and prophets, of whom no ill can be said. They use drapery, wood-work, landscapes with trees and figures, whatever strikes as pretty, but

---

* Netherland painting (*peinture flamande*) was the name given in Italy, not only to Netherland art, but to German generally.

which possesses in truth nothing of genuine art in itself, and where neither inward symmetry nor careful selection and true greatness is involved. In short, it is a painting without meaning and power. But I will not say that they paint worse than elsewhere. What I blame in the Netherland painting is, that in one picture a multitude of things are brought together, one of which would be important enough to fill an entire picture. None, however, can thus be completed in a satisfactory manner. The works that come from Italy can alone be called genuine works of art. Italian art, therefore, is the true art. If they painted thus elsewhere, the art might equally well be denominated after any land where it is thus executed. True art is made noble and religious by the mind producing it. For, for those who feel it, nothing makes the soul so religious and pure as the endeavor to create something perfect; for God is perfection, and whoever strives after it, is striving after something divine. True painting is only an image of the perfection of God, a shadow of the pencil with which He paints, a melody, a striving after harmony. A lively intelligence, however, can alone feel wherein the difficulty lies. And therefore is this art so rare, and so few are there who attain to it.

"'But that in Italy alone any thing good can be accomplished, is not an assertion without basis. Let a painter work elsewhere, a master using every effort, and take any pupil who has learned among us, and let both draw and paint, each after his own fashion, and compare; and you will find that he who was only a pupil in Italy has produced more with regard to genuine art than the master who is not from Italy. So true is this, that even Albert Dürer, a master who works with such skill and delicacy of feeling, when he wished to paint something which should deceive us as to its having been executed in Italy, whether the work he produced were good or bad, could still paint nothing in which I could not observe at once that it neither came from Italy nor from an Italian artist; and, therefore, no other people, one or two Spanish masters excepted, can paint as we paint. We feel at once the difference.

"'Our art is that of ancient Greece; not because it is somewhat Italian, but because it is good and correct. We say, That is painted as if an Italian had done it; and whoever attained to this without having painted in Italy, would still be called so. Art belongs to no land: it comes from heaven. We, however, possess it: for nowhere has the old empire left behind such distinct traces of its glory as with us; and with us, I believe, true art will set.'

"He was silent. I encouraged him to continue. 'Then you maintain that painting is peculiar to the Italians?' I said. 'Is that, however, a matter of astonishment? Have you not in Italy just as much reason for painting well as other people have for painting badly? You are industrious by nature: you come forward with will, taste, and talent. No one is satisfied in your land to remain an artisan: you work to rise. Mediocrity is hateful to you. All is in your favor: you have the great models; they obtrude upon you at every step. The land is full of masters, who instruct you; of princes, who protect you; of minds, that understand you. Every thing with you revolves round art; all honor is bestowed upon it. Among so many princes and nobles, one alone, however, has gained the surname of the divine, — one painter only, and that is Michael Angelo!'

"'You speak like a good Italian, and as if you had been born among us,' said the marchioness, as I finished. And then she began a eulogium upon painting: she spoke of its ennobling influence upon a people, — how it led them to piety, to glory, to greatness, until the tears came into her eyes from the emotion within. Thus passed the time. It had become late. Michael Angelo first rose. The marchesa stood up. I begged her to grant me the happiness of being allowed to appear at this re-union again on the following Sunday. She acceded to my request, and Michael Angelo promised to come. We accompanied them to the gates. Tolomei went with Michael Angelo, and I with the marchesa, from San Silvestro up to the monastery where the head of John the Baptist is preserved, and where she lived. From thence I set out on the way home."

Such is the description of the first meeting. On the following Sunday, Francesco again appeared at San Silvestro. He had roamed through the city, filled as it was with the festive crowd in honor of the Duchess Margherita, Alessandro dei Medici's widow, whom Paul III. had obtained from the emperor as the consort of the young Ottavio Farnese. In her honor, the carnival of 1537 surpassed in splendor any that had before been celebrated in Rome. Francesco saw the magnificently attired horsemen and the triumphal carriages descending from the Capitol. He admired the standards, the golden equipments, the splendidly accoutred horses. Then ascending Monte Cavallo, where all was solitary, he found Tolomei and Michael Angelo, with Fra Ambrosio. It was afternoon. They went into the garden behind the monastery, where they sat down under the shadow of the laurel-trees, with the distant city at their feet. Vittoria was this time not present. On the third Monday, the marchesa expressly invited Francesco. The meeting is not described in the records of Francesco communicated by Count Raczynsky. It probably did not seem important enough to the count; for the conversation that passed on the second Sunday is not of sufficient consequence to find a place here. The works of the Italian masters throughout Italy were discussed; but that personal coloring is lacking which appears so important and so striking in the beginning of this conversation.

Let me expressly state, that I do not consider Francesco's record sufficiently authentic to regard it simply as the leaves of his journal. He evidently arranged things. The form into which he has brought his communications was one common at that time, and may have received from him the artistic finish which Plato gave to the meetings in which Socrates and Alcibiades appeared. In a similar manner, Macchiavelli makes Fabricio Colonna converse with his friends upon Italian strategy under a tree in the garden of the Rucellai. Still, what Francesco relates is true.* We feel he could not have invented it, he stood in such close intercourse with Vittoria, Tolomei, Ambrosio, and Michael Angelo; and he gave the characters faithfully and without addition. That of Vittoria especially, who belonged to that class of women, who, apparently with no will of their own, never seek to extort any thing by force, and yet obtain every thing which is placed before them. In an equally

* See Appendix, Note LV.

gentle manner, she may have accomplished her first essay in Naples, in transforming her husband's nephew, the young d'Avalos, the same who fought against Ferruccio before Volterra, from a wild, unrestrained youth into a man who loved art and science. She was proud of having done this. And how tenderly she exercised her authority over Michael Angelo, who had never before been approached; whom she now for the first time inspired with the happiness of yielding to a woman, and for whom the years which she passed at that time in Rome, she made a period of happiness, which he had never before known!

A woman needs not extreme youth to captivate the mind of a man who discovers in her the highest intelligence. Vittoria was, at that time, still beautiful and cheerful. She stood at the head of the party to whom the future seemed to belong. Had her friends been successful, Vittoria's name would have been surrounded at the present day with still greater lustre. She, Renata of Ferrara, and Margaret of Navarre — all three united by friendship and constant intercourse — formed the triumvirate of women, under whose direction the whole of cultivated Italy at that time entered the lists. Pole or Contarini had only to obtain the highest dignity after Paul' death, — an end both had in prospect, — and the victory would have been gained.

These hopes excited and animated Vittoria. After long years of mourning and solitude, a new and prosperous time seemed beginning for her. In 1538, her poems were published for the first time. In

Ferrara, she received the homage of a court which was bent on the acknowledgment of intellectual merit. Ariosto immortalized this period by his verses upon Vittoria. And, returning to Rome, her friends there received her with envious joy. For five years this lasted, undoubtedly the happiest granted to Michael Angelo during his whole life.[*]

Then came the revolution in the year 1541, and with one blow a sorrowful change took place.

Vittoria left Rome, where Caraffa ruled. Following Cardinal Pole to Viterbo, she gathered around her there a few of her old friends; no longer, however, in intercourse with them as of old, — that had passed, — but now only endeavoring to secure herself from the hostility of those whose attacks were a matter of course. In the following year, Contarini died in Bologna. It might be said that grief had killed him. To the last, he denied not his opinions. When Cardinal Morone, one of the most faithful adherents of the party, came to him from Modena to ask his advice, because his city was entirely infected with the "new opinions," he recommended the greatest mildness. By instruction alone, he would have the erring brought back. Neither of the two foreboded that soon the mere discussion of the new opinions would be punished with infamous death. Contarini died before matters came to such a point. We have Vittoria's consolatory letter to his sister. She had herself lost scarcely less than his relative. Pole, she says in it, is now the only one left to her. We have also a sonnet from her upon Contarini's

* See Appendix, Note LVI.

death. He ought to have been pope, she says, at its close, to have made the age happy.

The death of Contarini had been sad for his friends; but that which completely subdued them was the flight of Occhino. Cited by the Inquisition to defend himself, he was already on the way to Rome, confident of his cause, when suddenly, close by the city, he changed his mind, and fled. His friends were struck with fear. We still possess Tolomei's letter, calling upon him urgently to return. But he went further: openly going over to the cause of the Lutherans, Occhino began to turn against the pope. All his Romish adherents now left him; but, in spite of this, Occhino's act fell upon them, and mostly upon Vittoria, who had hitherto defended him to the utmost. She herself belonged from henceforth to those held in suspicion by the Inquisition. She and Pole were now obliged to submit entirely to the new authority. When Occhino sent the apology for his escape to her at Viterbo, as to an old friend, she delivered up the letter and pamphlets to Rome, and declared that she only wished to write an answer, if she was ordered to do so. No doubt Caraffa's spies watched her in every thing which she did and wrote and said. How dangerous she appeared to the Inquisition is shown alone by the fact, that when, twenty years after her death, a noble Florentine was condemned to be burnt to death in Rome, one of his principal crimes was that of having once belonged to the circle of Vittoria and Giulia Gonzaga.

To this period — namely, 1541-1543 — belong the

letters forming the correspondence between Vittoria and Michael Angelo, and the poems which he sent her. She is said to have written many letters to him; but we only know of one, in the possession of the British Museum. Eight others are still kept back at Florence. Of Michael Angelo's letters to her, I am only acquainted with the sheet which is contained in the Vatican manuscript of his poems. Of the poems which he addressed to her, only four can be pointed out as certain. He is said to have sent many, and written so often that Vittoria asked him to restrict himself a little. She herself, she said to him, was hindered by them from being of an evening with the sisters of the Convent of St. Caterina, in which she lived; while he, by writing so much, could not go to work of a morning at the proper time. This is just as she would have spoken to him at San Silvestro.

And it is just that tact which Francesco d'Ollanda designates as inimitable and indescribable, and which is really nothing but the art acquired by experience, of basing every request upon the greatest consideration, which appears especially to belong to women of high position, who, for the sake of intellectual advantage, are obliged sometimes to seek in regions below them what their equals do not afford, —it is just this tact, I say, which we find in the single letter of Vittoria which we possess. Michael Angelo had sent her the design for a crucifix. Vittoria was to approve of it, and send it back, upon which the crucifix was to be begun. But the drawing pleased her so well, that she would not give it back under any circumstances, and she wrote respecting it, —

"Unique Master Michael Angelo and my most especial friend (*Un co maestro Michelagnolo e mio singularissimo amico*), — I have received your letter and have looked at the crucifix, a work which truly effaces the remembrance of all the other representations I know. For nothing more lively and more perfect is possible than this image of Christ, with such inconceivable tenderness and wonderful power is it executed. But now, whether it be the work of any one else but yourself, I will not have any one else execute it. Let me know whether really any one but yourself has designed it. Forgive me the question. If it is your work, you must, under any circumstances, give it to me. If, however, it is not your work, and you have wished to have it executed by one of your workmen, we must first talk it over; for I know how difficult it will be to work a second time over such a drawing. I would rather that he who did it, should execute for me something else. If, however, the drawing is yours, pardon me if I do not return it. I have examined it narrowly, both with glass and mirror; and nothing more perfect has ever presented itself to your sincere   MARCHESA DI PESCARA." *

With what tact she says, "I would rather that he who did the drawing should execute something else for me." She does not rely on Michael Angelo himself, that even he, if he wished to execute the crucifix after the design, could achieve something equally perfect; and she found a way of expressing this without offending him.

Condivi says of this work, that, contrary to the

* See Appendix, Note LVII.

ordinary idea, Christ is represented not with drooping head, as already dead, but with his countenance
joyfully raised heavenward, as if he wished to breathe
out his last. A wonderfully beautiful design in the
possession of the Oxford collection, may, perhaps,
from this circumstance, be decided on as the sheet
sent by Michael Angelo to Viterbo.

Michael Angelo's letter seems to be connected
with this one letter of Vittoria's. I cannot help supposing that perhaps Vittoria had long begged him
for the drawing, and that he had neither sent it nor
answered her by letter. The marchesa now applied
to a third person, who was to remind Michael Angelo
of his promise; and he wrote in consequence, —

"SIGNORA MARCHESA, — As I was myself in Rome, you
need not have commissioned Messer Tommaso with regard
to the crucifix, and have placed him between Your Ladyship
and me, your servant, to demand my services in this way.
I would have done more for Your Ladyship than for any
one else whom I could name in the world, had not the work
which burdens me made it impossible for me to show this in
deed to Your Ladyship. I know Your Ladyship is familiar
with the saying, 'Amore non vuol maestro,' — 'A loving
heart need not be urged;' and also, 'Chi ama, non dorme,'
— 'He who loves, sleeps not.' It was unnecessary to make
inquiries through others. For, although it seemed as if I
had forgotten it, I wished to give no hint about it only
because I had a surprise in my mind. I am now deprived
of this pleasure.

> "Mal fa chi tanta fè si tosto obblia.
> He errs who so soon forgets so much fidelity.

"Your Ladyship's Servant"

No name is below: this first appears under the poem on the second page: —

> "Now on the one foot, on the other now,
> 'Twixt vice and virtue balancing below,
> Wearied and anxious in my troubled mind,
> Seeking where'er I may salvation find.
> Like one to whom the stars by clouds are crossed;
> Who, turn which way he will, errs, and is lost.
> Therefore take thou my heart's unwritten page,
> And write thou on it what is wanted there;
> And hold before it, in life's daily stage,
> The line of action which it craves in prayer.
> So that, amid the errors of my youth,
> My own shortcomings may not hide the truth :
> If humble sinners lower in heaven stood,
> Than the proud doers of superfluous good.

> "MICHELANGELO BUONAROTTI in Rome."*

> "Ora in sul uno, ora in sul altro piede †
> Variando cerco della mia salute
> Fra'l vitio e la virtute;
> L'alma confusa mi travaglia e stanca,
> Come, chi 'l ciel non vede
> Chè per ogni sentier si perde e manca.
> Ond 'io la carta bianca
> Convien ch 'a pietà mostri
> Che, qual di me si voglia, tal ne scriva;
> Ch 'a ogni muover d'anca
> Infra grandi error nostri
> Mie picciol resto più quaggiù non viva,
> Chè 'l vero di se mi priva:
> Nè so, se minore grado in ciel si tiene
> L'umil peccato che'l soperchio bene."

We see how the great question of justification through faith was pending between them both. Who Messer Tommaso was, I know not; perhaps Tom-

* See Appendix, Note LVIII.
† Above *uno* is written *destro*; above *altro*, *manco*, by the same hand

maso da Prato, Michael Angelo's agent in the lawsuit
with the Duke of Urbino ; or Tommaso Cavalieri, a
young Roman, who was his especial favorite. The
work which hindered his working for Vittoria, was
the painting of the new chapel, built by Paul III.,
which the pope had urged upon him after the completion of the Last Judgment.

The second poem which we know for certain was
addressed to Vittoria, and which was the first perhaps which he sent her to Viterbo, seems to refer
to the present which she gave him at parting, and
which was a collection of her poems : —

> " Not all unworthy of the boundless grace
>   Which thou, most noble lady, hast bestowed,
>   I fain at first would pay the debt I owed,
>   And some small gift for thy acceptance place.
>   But soon I felt, 'tis not alone desire
>   That opes the way to reach an aim so high ;
>   My rash pretensions their success deny,
>   And I grow wise while failing to aspire.
>   And well I see how false it were to think
>   That any work, faded and frail, of mine,
>   Could emulate the perfect grace of thine.
>   Genius and art and daring backward shrink ;
>   A thousand works from mortals like to me
>   Can ne'er repay what Heaven has given thee ! "

> " Per esser manco, alta Signora, indegno
>   Del don di vostra immensa cortesia,
>   Con alcun merto ebbe desire in pria
>   Precorrer lei mio troppo umile ingegno
>   Ma scorto poi ch' ascender a quel segno
>   Proprio valor non è ch 'apra la via,
>   Vien men la temeraria voglia mia,
>   E dal fallir più saggio al fin divegno.

E veggio ben, com 'erra s'alcun crede
La grazia che da voi divina piove
Pareggiar l' opra mia cadusa e frale.
L 'ingegno, e l 'arte, e l' ardimento cede ;
Chè non può con mill' opre, e chiare, e nuove
Pager celeste don virtù mortale."

The most beautiful testimony, however, to the influence which Vittoria exercised over Michael Angelo, is contained in the third poem. He here speaks most openly. Just as philosophically calm as is the beginning of the sonnet, is its close passionate; and this here also, only in the form we find it in his own manuscript: for, like most of his verses, they appear spoiled and devoid of power in the published edition of his poems : *—

* "When godlike art has, with superior thought,
    The limbs and motions in idea conceived,
    A simple form, in humble clay achieved,
Is the first offering into being brought :
Then stroke on stroke from out the living rock,
    Its promised work the practised chisel brings,
    And into life a form so graceful springs,
That none can fear for it time's rudest shock.
Such was my birth : in humble mold I lay
At first ; to be by thee, O lady high !
Renewed, and to a work more perfect brought ;
Thou giv'st what lacking is, and filest away
All roughness : yet what tortures lie,
Ere my wild heart can be restrained and taught !"

"Da che concetto ha l' arte intera e diva
    Le membra e gli atti d' alcun, poi di quello
    D' umil materia un semplice modello
E 'l primo parto che da quel deriva.

* See Appendix, Note LIX.

Poi nel secondo in pietra alpestra e viva
S' arrogie le promesse del martello,
E si rinasce tal concetto bello
Ch' el suo eterno non è ch' il prescriva.
Tal di me stesso nacqui e venni prima
Umil model, per opra più perfetta
Rinascer poi di voi, donna alta e degna.
S' el manco adempie, e 'l mio soperchio lima
Vostra pietà, qual penitenzia aspetta
Mie fiero ardor se mi gastiga e insegna ? "

Mie fiero ardor, he says, which even here is too
mildly translated. Taken literally, the last idea is
this, — What torture may my wild and glowing
nature expect, if you begin to curb and to tame it?
— as it were the last thing she would attempt. He
spoke not, indeed, of his passion for her, but of that
to which Vittoria had alluded at San Silvestro, when
she expressed the fear that he might suddenly be
disinclined to do something, just when she wished
to induce him. He was proud and passionate. He
was sensitive and suspicious, and had grown old in
his ways. What a man would Michael Angelo have
become, had fate led him into connection with Vittoria in his younger years, and had she met with
him then, when she was herself less wearied by years
and experience! Such as they now found each
other, she could give him nothing but that kindly
gentleness with which she softened him; and he
ventured to desire nothing but what she could bestow.

There is one of his poems, a sonnet, in which he
confesses this, and gives language to his feelings so
beautifully, that we can bring forward no happier

expression of his thoughts: " That thy beauty may tarry upon earth, but in possession of a woman more gracious and less severe than thou art, I believe that nature is asking back thy charms, and commanding them gradually to leave thee. And she takes them. With thy divine countenance, she is adorning a lovely form in the sky; and the God of love endeavors to give her a compassionate heart; and he receives all my sighs, and he gathers up my tears, and gives them to him who will love her as I love thee. And, happier than I am, he will touch her heart perhaps with my torments; and she will afford him the favor which is denied to me."

How touchingly are the present and future here contrasted! It is the most beautiful exhibition of resignation which I have met with in the works of a poet. It is charming, how he changes despair into expectation, and turns the disappearance of youth and beauty into something almost joyful.

It is probable, that Michael Angelo, as he was influenced by Vittoria to cultivate poetry at all again, received from her also the impetus to those views; for the subject of all these verses is glorification of the past, resignation for the present, and expectation of the future compensation for all sorrows. Longing for her husband, who, almost always in the field, left her alone at Ischia, suggested to her her first verses. Sorrow for his loss; a natural inclination to intellectual thoughts; a complete abstraction at length in religious feelings, after all her hopes in this world had been shipwrecked, — formed the natural steps by which she rose to be a poet. Nothing was more different, however, than Michael Angelo's poems and her own. He, often even severe in his language, with a fixed tangible idea always in his mind, which he endeavored to give as strongly and simply as possible; she, on the contrary, aiming at the gentle expression of her feelings, reflecting them in images, which did not penetrate deeply like Michael Angelo's, though the euphony of her verse, however, is so great, that even he who is not an Italian feels it, and there is sometimes an enchanting truthfulness in her ideas.

> "And, as the light streams gently from above,
>   Sin's gloomy mantle bursts its bonds in twain;
>   And, robed in white, I seem to feel again
> The first sweet sense of innocence and love."

Thus ends one of her sonnets, in which she speaks of the divine influence to which she owes consolation. And this is the feeling of most of her poems, — seeking to be self-reconciled in the spirit of Contarini and his friends. Her poems were read with avidity in Italy. The first edition was prepared without her knowledge; five editions followed during the next ten years, and the demand for new publications was not quieted by these. She was accustomed to send to Michael Angelo any new thing she wrote. He thus received forty sonnets, which he had bound up in the same book with the first he received from her. In later years, he sent it to an ecclesiastic at Florence, an old acquaintance with whom he was in correspondence, and who had begged him to let him see the relics he possessed of Vittoria.

But when was that sonnet written by Michael Angelo, which I have translated into prose because I can find no verse for it? I only expressed a supposition, when I assumed that it was addressed to Vittoria at all; and I now do no more, when I say that it seems to have been written by him after 1542, after Vittoria's return to Rome in the autumn of this year, when she again left Viterbo, perhaps because Cardinal Pole was from henceforth absent from there in the service of the Church.

It must have been a melancholy meeting again between Vittoria and Michael Angelo. She had gone through a severe sickness (we know this from Tolomei's anxious letters); she came with shattered health; and, as the last storm that could now befall her, the ruin of her family had broken over her, and her powers were utterly weakened. However great and true was Vittoria's humility before God and the Church, she ever remained a Colonna, — a royal daughter of the first and proudest family in Italy. We need only read her poems on the death of Pompeo, or on the captivity of her husband after the battle of Ravenna, and on the wounds with which he returned, to feel the pride that filled her heart. She made much of her family, and believed in their greatness, as royal houses still believe in the superiority which Nature and Providence have awarded to their family; a belief which may appear justifiable to them, as results and general acquiescence have confirmed it for centuries.

The Colonna had been too powerful for the popes of the House of Medici: the Farnese, however, re-

solved upon their ruin, and it came. The blow
struck her family about the time that Vittoria went
to Viterbo. She had employed all her influence to
prevent it, but in vain. The castles of the Colonna
were seized, and Vittoria found none of her family
in Rome when she returned. She withdrew into
the Benedictine Convent of St. Anna dei Funari
(now Dei Falegnami), and there spent in ill-health
the few years that yet remained of life.

To this time her portrait may belong: it is a large
oil-painting which was ascribed to Michael Angelo,
until the mark of Marcello Venusti was discovered
upon it. We know, however, that Michael Angelo
sketched her; and nothing prevents our supposing,
that Venusti, as was often the case, only colored in
this instance his master's work. I am only acquainted with the picture, which is in England, from the
lithograph which is added to Campanari's work, who
wished to prove Michael Angelo as the executor of
it; but even in this sheet we can perceive the mind
of him with whom the work originated. I believe
none other but Michael Angelo could thus have
represented Vittoria. We have before us an aged
woman. There is no longer the fair hair, which
once invested her with such a charm: a white,
widow's veil, brought low down upon her brow,
envelops her head, and falls over her bosom and
shoulders. A tall figure, dressed in black velvet,
upright, and sitting without support on a chair, the
circular, simply formed back of which is grasped in
front by her right hand, while the other is lying on
an open book in her lap. There is a grand repose

in her features, a slightly painful compression about the eyes and mouth. She appears aged, but not decrepit; and the deep lines which fate had drawn are noble and energetic.

It is possible, that, during the drawing for this painting, that sonnet of Michael Angelo's was written. She had spoken, I imagine, of how sorrow and sickness had suddenly taken from her what years had so long spared; how she had become an old woman, and hourly felt almost the decay of life: and, to console her, he showed her herself as young and immortal in her own earthly beauty.

At the beginning of 1547, Vittoria's last strength failed. Dangerously ill, she was conveyed from her convent to the palace of Giuliano Cesarini, the husband of that Giulia Colonna who was the only one of the family present in Rome. Cardinal Pole had not yet arrived. He belonged to those to whom Vittoria intrusted the execution of her will. Sadolet and Morone, almost the only remnants left of Occhino's party, were the two others. Michael Angelo saw Vittoria up to the last. He was so affected by her death, that, as Condivi relates, he almost lost his senses. He once said to Condivi, years afterwards, that he repented nothing so much as having only kissed her hand, and not her forehead and cheeks also, when he went to her at her last hour.

The last thing he had drawn for her was a Madonna sitting at the foot of the cross. Her eyes and arms are raised to heaven; in her lap, the corpse of her son has fallen between her knees upon the ground, so that his arms are laid across her knees, as it were upon crutches. Two angels, on both sides, have placed their hands under the arms of Christ, as if they would ease his position and lighten his burden. On the cross, however, which is of a strange form, like a great Latin Upsilon, the two arms of which are connected above by a cross-piece of wood, so that the beams assume the mystical form of the triangle denoting the Trinity,* those words of Dante's are written, —

"Non vi si pensa quanto sangue costa!
No one reflects how much blood it has cost!" —

a verse which comprises, in few words, the great lamentation of the age. Dante speaks thus in the twenty-ninth canto of the "Paradiso," of the Holy Scriptures: "No one reflects how much blood it has cost to disseminate them in the world, and how much favor he finds before God, who penetrates with humility into their depth. For they are only now read for the sake of outward appearance; and every one carries into them his own devices; and preachers discourse about them, and the gospel itself they keep secret." This was now the secret lamentation of those who, from the greater violence of the measures used, saw before them the increasing suppression of free belief in Italy. With whom, however, was Michael Angelo to talk over such things, since he had lost Vittoria? How great the loss was which he sustained, can only be realized by him who has himself felt the void which the loss of a superior intellect irretrievably leaves behind it. It must have been to him as if a long-used, magnificent book, in

* See Appendix, Note LX.

which he found words suiting every mood, had been suddenly closed, never to be re-opened. Nothing can compensate for the loss of a friend who has journeyed on with us for many years, sharing our experiences. Vittoria had been the only one who had ever fully opened her soul to him. What profit could he draw from the reverence of those who would have ceased to understand him had he exhibited himself such as he was in truth? The only thing that consoled him was the thought that his own career was near its close. In the same degree, as he saw the remnant of life, which he believed still before him, grow less and less, his thoughts, roving beyond it, must have become absorbed in that which awaited him after death. He was seventy years old. His strong nature began to shake. He may at this time have written many of the poems in which, surveying the past years of his life, he discovered not a single day in which he had been happy, and regarded all his thoughts as lost which he had not turned to the consideration of divine things.

Vittoria died in the end of February, in the fifty-seventh year of her age. I can nowhere discover the place of her burial. We will attempt to give here a translation of one of the sonnets in which Michael Angelo gave vent to his sorrow:—

> "When she, the aim of every hope and prayer,
> Was called by death to yon celestial spheres,
> Nature, who ne'er had fashioned aught so fair,
> Stood there ashamed, and all who saw shed tears.
> O cruel fate, quenching the dreams of love!
> O empty hopes! O spirit rare and blest!
> Where art thou now? On earth thy fair limbs rest:
> Thy holy thoughts have found their home above.

Yet let us think not cruel death could e'er
Have stilled the sound of all thy virtuous ways :
Lethe's oblivion could extinguish nought ;
For, robbed of thee, a thousand records fair
Speak of thee yet ; and death from heaven conveys
Thy powers divine, and thy immortal thought "

" Quando il principio dei sospir miei tanti
Fu per morte dal cielo al mondo tolto,
Natura che non fe' mai si bel volto,
Restò in vergogna, e chi lo vide in pianti.
O sorte rea dei miei desiri amanti,
O fallaci speranze, o spirto sciolto,
Dove se' or ? La terra ha pur raccolto
Tue belle membra, e 'l ciel tuoi pensier santi.
Mal si credette morte acerba e rea
Fermare il suon di tue virtuti sparte,
Ch' obblio di Lete estinguer non potea ;
Che spogliato da lei, ben mille carte
Parlan di te ; ne per te 'l cielo avea
Lassù, se non per morte, albergo o parte."

CHAPTER FIFTEENTH.

1542—1547.

Julius's Mausoleum — The Paintings in the Capella Paolina — Aretino — Titian in Rome — Death of Giovansimone Buonarroti — Death of Francis I. — Cosmo's Proposals — Leonardo Buonarroti — Antonio di San Gallo — The Church of St. Peter — Italian Architecture — Roman Architecture — the Capitol — The Farnese Palace — Della Porta — Vignola — Ammanati — Vasari — Da Volterra — Cavalieri — Marcello Venusti — Pierino da Vinci — Last Work in Marble.

IMMEDIATELY after the completion of the Last Judgment, Michael Angelo had wished to rid his mind of the work, the tardy progress of which Condivi not unjustly styles the Tragedy of the Mausoleum. Scarcely, however, had he manifested this desire, than the pope even now refused to yield to it. Paul III. had added a new chapel to the Vatican, called, after himself, the Capella Paolina; and Michael Angelo was selected to adorn it with frescos.

Negotiations of a painful character now took place respecting it between him and the Duke of Urbino. The duke had a right to demand the completion of the work so long ago paid for. He hated the Farnese, and would not be neglected just for their sake. That no means might be overlooked, the matter was brought by his side before the public. Michael Angelo was called in Italy a deceiver, who had from the first entertained the intention of taking money and doing nothing for it; and he was obliged to tell the pope that it was impossible for him to execute the paintings in the chapel. We paint not only with our hands, he said, but with our heads. He who has not a free mind, is ruined. He was overwhelmed, he added, with accusations, as if he had helped to stone Christ. By the drawing-up of the last contract, he had been induced to use evasions which he had not at all liked, and to own to concessions which he had never made. If they now compelled him to paint, nothing but trash could be produced.

However much Michael Angelo declared himself injured by the contract drawn up under Clement, he was himself not without blame in it. It is just such natures as in ordinary life are honesty and unselfishness itself, and would be too proud to serve their own advantage with one false word, which allow themselves, in matters of business, for the furtherance of that which they consider the best, to give vent sometimes to expressions, in which they have respect rather to their pure conscience than to objective truth. Clement had not wished to allow the works for the mausoleum of Julius to be carried on at the same time as those in San Lorenzo; yet, to extort the pope's consent, Michael Angelo had agreed to avow the receipt of larger sums on the part of the Rovere than he had in truth received (only that he might appear pledged to a greater extent), and to consent to the admission of these sums in the new contract. This was now taken advantage of by the

Rovere. They appealed to Michael Angelo's signature, and tried to assume that the feigned sums had been actually received.

The second thing of which he had to complain was the circumstance, that the copy of the contract laid before him for signature had not agreed with the document which had been drawn up in his presence at the negotiations. His house at the Macello dei Corvi was mentioned in it as a guarantee for the money issued by him for the completion of the mausoleum. But he asserted that it would never have occurred to him to agree to this.

This now became a matter of discussion. The end of the negotiations was, that Michael Angelo was vindicated; and Urbino declared that he would be satisfied with the monument, if nothing but the Moses should be executed by Michael Angelo's own hand. The house on the Macello dei Corvi was declared free of all molestation.*

Michael Angelo could thus more quietly set about the paintings in the Paolina; and he completed them within eight or nine years, — two large, extensive compositions, representing the Crucifixion of Peter, and the Conversion of Paul. At the present day, after having been obscured for a long time by the accumulated dust of centuries, they have been cleaned and restored; but they have been handled at the same time so coarsely, that probably not a single stroke of Michael Angelo's is any longer to be perceived. Old engravings show the two paintings just as well as these misused originals. They are

* See Appendix, Note LXI.

extensive compositions, striking from the fact that many groups, widely separated, admit of no true unity. The figures are very numerous; they are not wanting even in the clouds. Of the effect probably produced by these works long ago, nothing is left but the affecting sight of Peter nailed to the cross, with his head downwards. The movement of the neck, when he fruitlessly endeavors to turn his head round and to raise it, has something in it affectingly true. We feel the powerless effort and the suffering. What the colors were, we know not. These paintings, unlike Michael Angelo's former works, do not seem to have excited any noise at their exhibition.

It is this Crucifixion of Peter, which Vittoria meant in her letters, when she cuts short Michael Angelo's too passionate correspondence, with the observation that he could not go to his work at the right time in the morning, and must therefore be untrue to the vicegerent of Christ upon earth. The work, indeed, gave him trouble. He required, he said himself, more vigorous physical power for fresco-painting, in which he had to do with wet lime, and had a large surface before him, which must be reached by climbing up scaffolding. Even in working at the Last Judgment, he had injured his leg in falling at a considerable height from the scaffolding. Furious at this, and tortured with pain, he kept himself shut up in his house, and would admit no surgeon until a Florentine doctor, Baccio Rontini, a very clever man, and a great admirer of Michael Angelo's, got into the house through the window, penetrated from room to room, and thus at last reached the old master, whom he found in a state of despair. Baccio remained with him until he was well, without leaving him alone for a moment. This had taken place in 1541. In the year 1544, Michael Angelo lay seriously ill in the house of his friend Luigi del Riccio, where the pope sent daily to inquire for him, and the cardinals themselves came to visit him. These pictures are the last paintings he produced.

2.

The affair with the Duke of Urbino, however, although an agreement had been come to, was not at rest. Reports against Michael Angelo continued, and terminated in a mortification, which, from the quarter whence it came, and from the way in which the blow was inflicted, must have touched him painfully.

There lived and wrote at that time, in Italy, a man who belongs to the most remarkable characters of his nation. This was Aretino; his name has been already mentioned. In characterizing him briefly, it might seem sufficient to declare him to be one of the most clever and at the same time one of the most contemptible of men. But, true as this is, such characteristics would have little meaning without a statement of the circumstances amid which the man worked. Aretino stands out as a character, loathsome even to him who makes the weakest demands of a moral kind upon men. This was the opinion of him in Italy in his own time. At the same time, however, his writings were allowed to exercise an influence on public opinion, such as is possessed in our own day by no journal in France, England, or America; for even the most powerful paper is not without its opposition, as sole possessor of public opinion. Aretino's writings, however, influenced without competition, when he sent them forth to the world from Venice, where he dwelt, like a poisonous toad in an isolated, unapproachable swamp.

He is the father of the modern men of letters. He wrote upon every thing and for every one. He wrote in prose and verse, on worldly and religious matters, on things edifying and seductive. By order of a woman like Vittoria Colonna, to whom he at times even ventured to address letters, he wrote a religious book. For Marcanton, the engraver, he wrote the text for a series of representations of so repulsive a character, that they brought the artist himself to prison, in spite of the protection of high cardinals. Aretino, however, effected his release through Clement VII. So striking was his wit, and so cutting his satire, that almost all the princes and higher nobles of Italy, including the emperor, were afraid of him. Many endeavored to gain his goodwill by presents. None could appear against him unpunished; he sent forth his arrows on all sides, and never failed in his aim. Titian, when he was in Rome in 1548, wrote home to him, "Every one here asks me about you; all wish to know your opinion: you give the tone to every thing." Aretino even called himself the "Scourge of Princes," and was proud of this surname. When the nobles did not pay, he threatened; and, if money then failed, he struck. Woe to him who was his victim then! But he was generally soon appeased. From many princes he received regular pensions.

It was natural that Aretino's paramount influence should affect artists also. He recommended those who were his friends. But he required gratitude. Titian found in him an unwearied eulogist. Aretino was the friend of his house; we know much of Titian's work only from his letters. Sansovino, who at that time somewhat played the part of a Michael Angelo in Venice, and had large orders, was his friend, and enjoyed his assistance in difficult emergencies. Vasari was his friend. These connections brought him in, from every quarter, statues, sketches, or drawings, which he again presented to princes who were his informers, though, as a matter of course, not without receiving gifts in return. Among his correspondence, there is a letter of the utmost coarseness which he wrote to Bandinelli, when the latter neglected to transmit his tribute. He reminds him first of the good service he had rendered him of old, when they both belonged to the Medicæan Court; then he reproaches him with his ingratitude; and in conclusion he derides his insolent assumption in wishing to surpass Michael Angelo. The letter must have wounded the vain man at every word. Such letters Aretino was accustomed to forward not only to those to whom they were addressed, but to send transcripts of them throughout Italy. This was his method. And his writing was so piquant, that they were read with eagerness. His

style is not what is called clever, in a nobler sense;
but he knew how to make the most of things, to
bring his language into rare combinations, and, suddenly leaving his distorted sentences, to display
double power in the most ordinary words. He was
an artist in his own line. Worthless and heavy as
the greater part of his writings appear to us now,
they influenced the period for which they were
intended by their cutting severity.

Aretino, therefore, feeling it a necessity to be connected with all the prominent men in the world,
addressed himself at last to Michael Angelo. It does
not seem that he was acquainted with him during his
earlier sojourn in Rome. Raphael, indeed, he himself boasts, had not disdained to listen to his advice;
he had met him at the court of Leo X., and Sebastian del Piombo belonged to his most intimate friends.
In 1527, Sebastian requested him, in the name of the
pope, to represent to the emperor the sad state of
Rome;* and the promises, upon which Aretino
hoped subsequently to become cardinal, date their
beginning to that time. Michael Angelo, on the
contrary, I do not find mentioned by him till the
year 1535. Vasari, probably for the sake of varying
the tokens of esteem with which Duke Alessandro
held the powerful writer in favor, sent him at that
time two drawings and a modelled head of Michael
Angelo's work; and Aretino thanked him for them in
a manner as if the greatest works of art in the world
had arrived in Venice.† What head it was, and
what has become of the two drawings, — the one a

St. Catherine, which Michael Angelo had sketched as
a boy, the other an ear,—I have not been able to
discover. Aretino writes about them as if the whole
town had burst forth in astonishing admiration.

Though this may be an exaggeration, still it shows
us how highly Michael Angelo ranked in Venice.
Aretino knew on what this depended. He never
thought of even comparing Titian or Sansovino with
Michael Angelo. He understood the difference between color and drawing. "Fine colors without
drawing," he says in one of his letters in the year
1537, * "with which all sorts of gay trash is produced with no true outline,—what honors do they
gain? The true glory of color lies in pencil strokes,
such as Michael Angelo can make, who is such a
complete master of nature and art that it is impossible to know whether nature learns from him, or he
from her. A good painter must understand more
than how to imitate well a velvet cloak or a belt-
buckle." We see how even at that time the contest
was at its height, which has since continued uninterruptedly among artists. Aretino knew on which
side to station himself; and in the very year in which
he thus gave his opinion upon Michael Angelo, and
exhibited to the world his unqualified adherence to
him (for it is a matter of course that such a letter
was duly disseminated), he addressed himself at
length to the great master himself.

He first expressed his boundless reverence for
him. Then followed the reason for this,—his chief
merit, namely, his capability of expressing so much

* See Appendix, Note LXIV.

by outline alone. Then, after having stated this in plain words, as preliminary, he proceeded to the principal point in the following manner: "And therefore I, who can do so much by praise and blame, that almost all the acknowledgment or contempt of others has been bestowed by me, — I who am still so little, and, so to speak, nothing, salute you. I would not venture to do so, had my name not lost much of its unworthiness by the esteem which its mention excites among princes. And yet, in addressing you, I feel nothing but reverence! There are kings enough in the world; but there is only one Michael Angelo! What a wonder, that nature, who can produce nothing so sublime that you have not attained to, cannot imprint upon her own works that stamp of lofty majesty which the mighty power of your pencil carries with it! Phidias, Apelles, Vitruvius, stand in shadow beside you." And thus he continues for many sentences, until at last he makes mention of the Last Judgment; and, with a profusion of allegorical and poetical ideas, — half thoughts, half images, — he explains how he himself would have conceived this great event as a painting. In conclusion, he asserts that he had taken an oath never again to go to Rome, but that Michael Angelo's work would make him break his faith. Besides, he wished to satisfy his burning desire to publish his praise to the world. In style and detail, this letter belongs to one of the most shameless productions which has ever come before me. How great the power of the writer must have been, is shown by the manner in which it was answered.

Nothing was more insufferable to Michael Angelo than assumption. Whenever he met with it, it stirred him up to regardless contradiction. He would tell people to their faces, that they understood nothing of things. Had he had before him in Aretino a man of less power, dictating to him how the Last Judgment should be painted, he would have either been silent with contempt, or he would have so repelled him in few words, that he would never again have had to fear good advice from this quarter. But Aretino was mighty indeed. And so Michael Angelo, in his reply, avails himself of the means which were equally ready to him, — of that subtle persiflage, which was no less feared by his foes than his unconquerable openness.

"HONORED SIR AND BROTHER," — he writes, — "Your letter has filled me with both sadness and joy. It has rejoiced me because it comes from you, who are unique in your way; it has saddened me, because so great a part of my painting is already completed, that I cannot avail myself of your ideas in it; for, had you been an eye-witness of the Last Judgment, you could not have described it better than you have done in your letter.

"With regard to your offer of writing about me, it not only gives me pleasure, but, as emperors and kings deem it the highest favor to be mentioned by your pen, I solicit it. If, with regard to this, any thing in my possession should be desired by you, or be agreeable to you, I offer it with the greatest readiness. And, in conclusion, concerning your resolution of not again coming to Rome, do not break it for the sake of seeing my paintings. That would be indeed too much. Adieu."

Michael Angelo must have dispatched this letter more than a quarter of a year after receiving Aretino's epistle; for the latter only replies to it on the 20th January, 1538. Instead of perceiving that he was, as it were, called to account for his promise, he took Michael Angelo at his word, and begged him for a small sketch, "such as he would have thrown into the fire," — his usual method of setting to work with artists. No answer was returned; and Michael Angelo was left in peace for five years by the man who dispensed disgrace and fame. In 1544, Aretino began again. He announced that the emperor had made him reckon on his privileges; that he had shown him *stupendi onori*. Cellini had written to him, that his salutation had been well received by Michael Angelo. This was worth more to him than all. He honored him. He had wept, he said, when he had seen his Last Judgment, and he thanked God that he had been born in his age. Titian honored him, and delivered flowing speeches in praise of his superhuman art. Titian had himself written to Michael Angelo with due reverence; for he was the idol of them both.

No answer followed. Two months later, Aretino requested a friend at Rome to remind Michael Angelo of the promised sketch. The request came at an unfavorable moment. Michael Angelo lay at that time sick in Riccio's house.

Aretino again allowed a year to elapse. Benvenuto Cellini was this time the channel through whom he sent the repeated request to Michael Angelo for the fulfilment of the old promise. At last, something

The Last Judgment, Sistine Chapel.

MICHAEL ANGELO.

was sent. But what? It is not expressly said what
Aretino received; but the drawing must have been
of such a kind as to induce him at the close of his
letter of thanks, with all its sweet flatteries, to give
it to be understood, that he could not consider
Michael Angelo's promise fulfilled by such a gift.
Again no answer followed this. The Venetian now,
at last, lost his patience. He probably had received
some old ends of drawings, which were rather a
mockery than a gift. He wrote a threatening letter
to Cellini. Buonarroti, he said, ought to be ashamed
of himself: he desired to be told whether he was to
have any thing or no; he insisted on an explanation,
or his love would be turned into hatred.

This was in April, 1545. Again nothing came.
In the autumn of the year, however, Titian came to
Rome; and through him, it seems, the matter was set
to rights. He came, at the invitation of Paul III.,
to paint his portrait. Dwelling and atelier were
assigned him in the Vatican. He brought various
letters of recommendation from Aretino, and they
wrote to each other during the period of their separation.

In Aretino's first letter, art was the only topic.
He awaited his return, he said, with longing to hear
from him about the antiques, — in what Buonarroti
surpassed them, in what they excelled him, and
whether Raphael was equal or superior to Michael
Angelo in painting. What enjoyment to talk with
him about the building of St. Peter's Church, which
Aretino, from the period of his own sojourn in Rome,
calls Bramante's building! Then he asked after

Perin del Vaga, and Sebastian del Piombo; the former at that time the most important master in Rome, as Sebastian, since he had held a rich position, had done nothing more. Del Vaga painted, after Michael Angelo's designs, the ornaments in the Sistina, — which fill up the wall below the Last Judgment to the ground, — and the ceiling in the Paolina. Here, however, Michael Angelo was himself at that time fully occupied. The letter concluded with the warning not to be too much absorbed in the contemplation of the Last Judgment, so as to make him and Sansovino wait for him in vain throughout the winter.

Titian and Michael Angelo met. Michael Angelo did not become acquainted with the Venetian in his most favorable works. The picture of the pope, from Farnese's terrible ugliness, — his small aged face, with its old pinched-up features, looking like that of an evil spirit, — could exhibit nothing but Titian's skill; and the other things that he painted at that time in Rome do not belong, as Vasari says, to his best works. I do not myself remember having seen any of these paintings. Michael Angelo openly expressed, that Titian would have done better if he had learned to draw, and had had better models in his atelier. There was a lack of these in Venice. His coloring, however, pleased him exceedingly; and he considered his conceptions so true and life-like, that, had Titian understood how to draw, as he knew how to paint, he would have produced things not to be surpassed. Thus did Michael Angelo express himself to Vasari, who was at that time in Rome, serving as guide to Titian; and he gives this verdict with the observation, that all Roman artists were of the same opinion.

But not only was Titian coolly received in Rome: he was even hated by the artists. They feared he would remain. Perin del Vaga was of opinion, that he was speculating upon works impending at that time in the Vatican, which was always being rebuilt and painted, and that he was relying on having these works himself. Del Vaga was so furious against him, that he studiously avoided him; and, as Del Vaga was a *protégé* of Michael Angelo's, and the latter, as architect of the Vatican, had a voice where orders were concerned, it is not impossible that he greatly assisted his pupil even here. What happened between Michael Angelo and Titian we know not; but, in Aretino's following letters to Rome, we find no allusion to Michael Angelo. Perhaps Titian had also mentioned the promised drawing, and had now received an answer, which had informed Aretino more plainly than his vanity had hitherto allowed him to perceive, of Michael Angelo's opinion of him. In a scene of this kind, it seems to me, communicated by Titian to Aretino, we may look for the most natural explanation of his apparently sudden conduct; for he determined seriously to requite Michael Angelo's rejection of his many years' request.

Aretino had hitherto only heard of Michael Angelo's Last Judgment. All that he had seen were some groups brought as studies by a young artist. At length, the engraver, Enea Vico, came to Venice,

having with him the preparations for the great engraving, probably the same as that which affords us
at the present day the best idea of the painting, free
from subsequent additions.* In connection with
this work, Aretino, in the November of 1545, dispatched the following letter to Michael Angelo : —

"SIR, — Having now seen the whole composition of
your Last Judgment, I perceive in it, as regards the beauty
of the composition, all the famous grace of Raphael ; but
as a Christian, who has received holy baptism. I am
ashamed of the unrestrained freedom with which your mind
has ventured to represent that which is the final aim of all
our devout feelings.

" This Michael Angelo, therefore, so mighty from his
fame, this Michael Angelo whom we all admire, has wished
to show men that he lacks piety and religion in the same
proportion as he professes perfection in his art. Is it possible that you, who condescend not, on account of your
divinity, to have intercourse with ordinary men, should
have introduced them into the highest temple of God,
above the highest altar of Christ, in the first chapel of the
world, where the greatest cardinals of the Church, the reverend priests, and the vicegerent of Christ himself, in holy
ceremonies and in divine words acknowledge his body, his
blood, and his flesh, and behold them with adoration ?

" If it were not almost a crime to draw the comparison,
I would here boast of that which I have succeeded in doing
in my Nanna, where, instead of exposing things in the insufferable way you have done, I have, with wise caution,
handled the most unchaste and wanton material in delicate
and moral language. And you, in such a sublime subject,
allow the angels to appear without heavenly pomp, and

* See Appendix, Note LXV.

the saints without a trace of earthly modesty! Have not
the heathen themselves veiled the Diana in drapery; and,
when they chiselled a naked Venus, made her appear
almost clothed, from her attitude and from the position of
her hand? And you, who are a Christian, — you so subordinate belief to art, that you have made the violation of
modesty among martyrs and virgins into a spectacle, such
as we should only venture to contemplate with half-averted
faces, even in houses of evil report. Such things might be
painted in a luxurious bath-room, but not in the choir of
the highest chapel. Truly, it would have been better had
you belonged to the unbelieving, than in this way, belonging to the faithful, to have attacked the faith of others.
But Providence will not go so far as to leave the extraordinary boldness of your marvellous work unpunished. The
more wonderful it is, the more surely will it prove the
ruin of your fame."

After having thus gone on preaching in a lofty
manner, Aretino reverts to himself. He is not, he
says, writing in this tone from vexation about the
things he had asked for in vain: —

"It would certainly have been well if you had fulfilled
your promise with due care, had it been only to silence the
evil tongues who assert that only a Gherardo or a Tommaso know how to allure favors from you! But truly, if
the heaps of gold which Pope Julius bequeathed you, in
order that his earthly remains might rest in a sarcophagus
executed by you, — if so much money could not induce you
to keep your promises, upon what could such a man as I
rely? Yet, O great painter! it is neither your avarice nor
your ingratitude that is to blame, that Julius's bones sleep
in a single coffin; but it is Julius's own merits. God would
rather that such a pope should stand on his own merit,

than that he should seem to become great through a mighty edifice executed by you. But, in spite of this, you have not done what you ought; and that is robbery.

"Our souls are benefited little by art, but by piety. May God enlighten Pope Paul as he once enlightened Gregory, of blessed memory, who preferred rather to see Rome poorer in statues of heathen deities, than that her inhabitants should lose their reverence for the humble images of the saints!

"Had you, in the composition of your picture, wished to adhere to the scientific instruction concerning heaven, hell, and paradise, which my letter, familiar to the whole world, contained, then, I venture to say, nature would not now be compelled to feel ashamed of having invested you with such great talent, that you stand forth yourself as an idol in the world of art. On the contrary, Providence would have protected your work as long as the world stands.

"SERVITORE ARETINO."

With what skill has Aretino combined things in this letter! Michael Angelo's mighty mind is throughout acknowledged: but to his old friend, Pope Julius, he is represented as an ungrateful man and a thief; and this at a time when the history of the mausoleum had become a perfect scandal through the Rovere. To be called an unusual artist, but a foe to Christianity! And this again now, when the Inquisition was stretching out its feelers farther and farther, and a slight charge could bring about the destruction of a man. I have only given extracts from the letter, as the whole amount of the infamy with which it is written cannot be exhibited. I am acquainted with a number of base attacks upon great men and great undertakings; none, however, seems carried out with such art and so much calculation upon public opinion. Aretino was not wrong when he threatened before, that he could revenge himself; and he had done so. For that he succeeded, is evident from the words of Condivi, who complains bitterly that the false opinion, that Michael Angelo had acted deceitfully in the matter of the mausoleum, had taken firm root in men's minds. Aretino sharpened the sting, which pierced the soul of the solitary old man.

The next step, too, was entirely in character with Aretino. He had a copy of the letter sent to Michael Angelo; but, as a postscript to it, he added in his own handwriting, "Now, as my rage against the outrageous manner in which you requited my respectful submission has a little cooled, and as I have afforded you a proof, as it seems to me, that, if you are *divino* (*di vino*, wine), I am not water (*dell aqua*), tear up this letter, as I have done, and acknowledge that I am in a position to receive answers to my letters from kings and emperors."

That the whole thing, however, was nothing but a literary trick, appears from the fact, that Aretino, in a letter addressed a few months later to Enea Vico, extols him for having made the Last Judgment accessible to the whole world by an engraving. "That no copies should exist of this painting," he writes, "were an injury to the religion for whose glory it was painted. As it represents the last day appointed by God, it is a good work to make the world share in this spectacle of fear and triumph.

The Son of God and the Duke of Florence will immortalize you, and grant you temporal reward for it. Go forward, therefore, in your praiseworthy undertaking. The scandal which Michael Angelo's artistic liberties will excite among the Lutherans takes no honor from your merit. It is you only who make the work accessible to all."

Here, therefore, we find the complete contrary to the reproaches he had written to Michael Angelo. But what was done, was done; and, great as Michael Angelo was, the vengeance of Aretino had cast a stain upon him which clung to him to the last.

3.

Titian left Rome, and never returned. Had he only arrived a year later, he would not have found there either Perin del Vaga or Sebastian del Piombo: they died in 1547, as did also Giulio Romano in Mantua. Sebastian is said to have thoroughly fallen out with Michael Angelo on account of the Last Judgment. In spite of this dispute occurring in the very times in which Vasari lived, from reasons which Vasari himself furnishes, I am inclined to doubt it. He relates how Guglielmo della Porta, a Milanese sculptor, was recommended by Sebastian to Michael Angelo, and how the latter received him with warmth; but he alleges nothing which actually proves the estrangement of the two old friends. Sebastian led an easy life, and painted but little: he and Michael Angelo perhaps rarely appeared together in Rome, and met seldom. Yet he who was not himself an eye-witness of the events of the time, feels called to no decision upon such matters; and therefore it remains uncertain how great was the void left in Michael Angelo's life by the death of Sebastian. It seemed as if the year 1547 was to be especially fatal to those whose life was precious to him. His own brother Giovansimone died in it. He stood aloof from Michael Angelo; but the way in which he spoke of him in his letters to Leonardo, shows that the loss was deeply felt.

The saddest thing, however, which befell Michael Angelo in the year following Vittoria's death, was the annihilation of his last hopes of the restoration of his country's independence.

The belief in the Heaven-decreed liberty of Florence was too firmly established in his heart for even the election of Cosmo after the murder of Alessandro, and the loyal tranquillity of the people at this event, to have been able to shake it. He reckoned on the King of France. As long as Francis I. lived, the day might still come, in which the tyrant should be expelled, and the exiles return. In the year 1544, when Michael Angelo was in Strozzi's house, — for Luigi del Riccio was their agent in Rome, — he sent a message to Roberto Strozzi at Paris, that he should tell the king, that, if he would come and free the city, he would erect an equestrian statue to him on the Piazza in Florence at his own expense.

In the year 1546, it seemed as if such a thing were once again possible. Francis I. and the pope had resolved on war against the duke, and the forces which were to burst against Tuscany were assembled in Rome. Then suddenly the king died, and these dreams also came to an end for Michael Angelo; for from henceforth he cast off all idea of what seemed no longer possible. Cosmo dwelt in safety in his palace, and held his faithful subjects so surely in check by a policy, the craftiness, wariness, and boldness of which astonished even the Venetian ambassadors, that, except some unfortunate conspiracies, the people never again ventured to stir. Even if the duke himself had possessed less talent in making the inhabitants of Florence understand how much more advantageous it was, instead of indulging the old ideas of liberty, to become distinguished for devotion and fidelity, he would have been supported by the emperor; who now, after the death of his formidable adversary, had applied himself with more success than formerly against the Lutherans in Germany, and had even here transformed a number of rebellious princes into good subjects. Besides this, the most stirring men among the Florentines were no more. Baccio Valori, who had brought about Cosmo's elevation, and then again had joined the Strozzi, had been beheaded on the Piazza; Guicciardini had been poisoned; and Filippo Strozzi, the friend of the emperor, the king, and the pope, — the richest, most amiable, most dissolute, and most cultivated noble in Italy, on whose behalf even Vittoria Colonna had written imploring letters, — had been strangled under the name of suicide in the same citadel, the building of which he had effected.

His sons alone remained. Holding important positions at the court of their cousin Catherine in France, even after the death of Francis I., they did not give up their hopes. But they aimed at much more than liberty, as had been the case with Ippolito. Had they with French troops robbed Cosmo of his land, they would have attempted to keep it in obedience to themselves by the same means. They must have taken Cosmo's spies into pay; and, like him, must have joined the Jesuits, who, forcing their way into every family, rendered extraordinary services to the State.

Cosmo felt himself so secure in his power, that he even ventured to take no cognizance of Michael Angelo's opinions, and endeavored to induce him to return upon splendid conditions. Alessandro, when he abolished the old constitution, had established, instead of the upper assembly of citizens, a sort of high chamber of forty-eight appointed members, to which a second chamber was attached of two hundred members, from among whom the forty-eight were elected. It was these who had confirmed Cosmo, and whom he in his turn supported. To belong to the forty-eight was from henceforth the highest thing a Florentine could attain to. Cosmo offered Michael Angelo this honor. Letters as well as verbal messages were sent to him on the subject. Benvenuto Cellini went to him by the duke's order into his atelier, and extolled Florentine life, and Cosmo's clemency and love of art. Michael Angelo excused himself: partly with reason, urging the impossibility of his leaving Rome, and partly with culpable indifference to the offers made him, he evaded the summons so graciously given. It would have been an insufferable change: in the place where he had once been a part of the ruling power, to receive orders now in common with Bandinelli, as a paid servant of the duke; ay, even to be obliged perhaps to draw back before the miserable pliability of his colleague, while in Rome he was an independent man, as regarded the pope.

4.

He might have replied to Cosmo's proposal with even less courtesy, but for consideration for the children of his brother Buonarroto, whom he would not have wished to injure with the duke in Florence.

The corespondence with his nephew Leonardo, in the possession of the British Museum, begins with the year 1540. These papers, extant in a long series, touch upon scarcely any thing else than domestic affairs. Mention is never made of art or of intellectual things. This alone becomes evident from them, that Michael Angelo continued to maintain and rule the family; and they afford information as to his health. Leonardo's sister was a nun. Growing old and sickly, she complains to Michael Angelo of her sufferings, and he consoles her with his own weakness. At Giovansimone's death, he writes how much he had wished to see his brother once more before his end. When Leonardo, who had only briefly informed him of the death, and probably because he too stood on bad terms with the deceased, sent no more accurate account afterwards, Michael Angelo wrote to him, " Remember, Giovansimone was my brother! Whatever he was, I mourn for him and

desire that something may be done for his soul, as
has been done for that of your father. Take care
not to be ungrateful for that which has been done
for yourself; for you possessed nothing in the world.
I am astonished that Gismondo has not written to
me; for the death concerns him as closely as it
does me."

And when Leonardo's letters now tardily arrived,
and he offered excuses for their not having been
sent before, Michael Angelo still replied with dis-
satisfaction. "In spite of all," he writes, "you
might have apprised me soon enough, so that I
should not have heard of the death from the lips of
a third person sooner than from your letters." Gismondo, he says, is the heir, as no will existed. In
spite of this, he begs Leonardo to take care that
something is done for Giovansimone's soul, and
that no money is spared. His brother Gismondo,
in whose favor Michael Angelo seems to have resigned his own portion, he therefore certainly did
not trust to take these duties upon himself.

He had interest in all that was going on in the
family. An old servant died, and he spoke of her
with the greatest love, and regretted that he had
outlived her, because he had intended to leave her
something in his will. He entered into full correspondence with the widow of another servant, and
treated the sensitive woman with touching kindness,
entering into all her complaints, and having an eye
upon the future of her children.

"I had observed, that you had somewhat against me,"
he writes to her (her name was Cornelia); "but I could

not discover the cause. From your last letter, I think I have now perceived what it is. When you sent me the cheese, you wrote at the same time that you had wished to send me other things, but that the pocket-handkerchiefs were not ready; and I, that you should not be at expense for my sake, answered you, that you must now send me nothing more, but rather ask things of me, and in this way give me the greatest pleasure: for you must have known, or rather you possessed proofs of how much I still love the blessed Urbino, although he is dead, and how close to my heart are all connected with him.

" You wish to come here, or to send me the little Michael Angelo: as regards both these wishes, I must tell you how matters are with me at home. I cannot advise you to bring Michael Angelo here, as I have no woman in the house, nor any household at all; and the child is still of too tender an age, and vexation and unhappiness might arise from it. Added to this, for about a month, His Grace the Duke of Florence has been using all his authority to make me return to Florence, holding out the greatest inducements. I have now begged for a little respite, that I may bring all things here into order, and may leave the building of St. Peter's in a fair condition; so I shall remain here through the summer to bring all my matters to a conclusion, as well as yours also respecting the money at the pawnbroker's. In the autumn, I shall remove permanently to Florence, as I am old, and have no time to return to Rome. I shall see you on my journey; and, if you give me Michael Angelo to take with me, I will nurture him in Florence with greater love than the son of my nephew Leonardo, and will have him taught all that his father, I well know, would have taught him. I received your last letter yesterday, the 27th March.

" MICHAEL ANGELO. Rome."

This letter belongs, as to time, to a subsequent period, — to a time in which Michael Angelo actually seems to have thought for a moment of returning to Florence.

He cared for Leonardo as if he were his own son; but, on the other hand, he required due attention, and was severe when he thought himself neglected.

"Leonardo,"— he writes in the spring of 1547, — "I have not been able to read your last letter, and have thrown it into the fire; I cannot therefore answer its contents. I have written this to you more than once: every time a letter arrives from you, I get a fever before I can decipher it. Therefore, from this time, if you have any thing to communicate to me, apply to some one who can write; for I have other things to do than to fall into despair over your letters."

Michael Angelo had reason to complain; for Leonardo's handwriting was very bad, as we see from some remarks on his letters, while Michael Angelo's even, clear handwriting is the same in every letter.

"Messer Giovanfrancesco," the letter goes on to say, "tells me that you wish to come to Rome for a few days. I am astonished how you should be able to get away from Florence, after having entered upon the partnership of which you tell me. Take care not to throw away the money I sent. Gismondo, too, should think of this: for he who has not earned it, knows not the value of money; and it is an old experience, that he who grows up in wealth often ends badly as a spendthrift. Keep, therefore, your eyes open; and do not forget amid what troubles and privations I, an old man, spend my life.

" A Florentine citizen came to me to-day, and spoke of a girl, one of the Ginori, in connection with whom you are mentioned as admiring her. I do not believe it is true. I can, however, give you no advice in the matter, as I do not know the circumstances; but I do not like you to choose as a wife one whom her father would not give to you, if he could establish her better. My wish would be, that whoever desired to have you as a son-in-law should think of you, and not of what you possess. It seems to me, that you should not care about a great dowry, but that you should look to a healthy mind, a healthy body, good blood, and good education, and what sort of family it is. This only is necessary. I have nothing to say further. Remember me to Messer Giovanfrancesco." *

When Michael Angelo insists upon noble blood, he does so not so much for the sake of allying Leonardo with a family of rank, but, as Condivi specially says, because, after the fashion of the ancients, he considered good birth as an important guarantee for noble sentiments, — a belief which has endured through all ages, and will endure.

Nothing came of the match. Leonardo's plans of marriage spread over years of correspondence, as those of his father, Buonarroto, had done before him. Michael Angelo ever returns to the principles expressed above, — good family, and no regard to wealth. This very fact proves how advantageously he had placed his nephew. Reading Michael Angelo's letters during this and the following years, he appears as a quiet, steady man, taking things practically and cautiously, without sentimentality, and

* See Appendix, Note LXVI.

expressing his opinion without verbosity. But we must remember his poems, if we would bring before us the other side of his character, — how increasing sadness filled him; how he was utterly solitary in that sphere in which his true life first began; and how Vittoria's picture hovered before him, wherever he turned his thoughts. It was during the long days, and soon also during the nights, which he passed, as his illness increased, in sleepless solitude, when his sense of abandonment found expression in those verses which alone consoled him, and which he wrote down with no idea of publicity, and revised again and again, — poems which were first found among his remains after his death.

5.

Michael Angelo had grown old, and had worked sufficiently, even had he now died, to leave a name behind him, the greatness of which no later artist could have rivalled. He had produced the mightiest things as painter and sculptor. And, as if nature were to show her inexhaustibility in this single man, a position had been allotted him by the juncture of events, which at once placed before him, when as a young man he was just beginning to work for himself and the world, the highest task of all, and made him enter, in the twenty years which he had still before him, upon that work, by which he stands, in architecture also, as the greatest of modern masters. At the end of 1546, Antonio di San Gallo, the director of the building of St. Peter's, died, and his office was conferred upon Michael Angelo.

Antonio di San Gallo was the last who had kept alive Bramante's old hatred of Michael Angelo, as the possessor, as it were, of an old and sacred heritage. The times of Julius II. had almost grown mythical. But, for long years, the passions had smouldered, which had, at that time, burst forth into flame.

San Gallo's nature suited well with Bramante's, in whose service he had entered while young. He worked resolutely, quickly, and with taste. He executed countless things. He owed his subsequent good fortune to Farnese, through whom he received a position with Raphael, when, after Bramante's death, Giuliano di San Gallo and Fra Giocondo, who had been coadjutors with Raphael in the building of St. Peter's Church, retired on account of sickness and old age. When Raphael also died, and Peruzzi took his place, he worked with the latter; and, when Peruzzi at last retired also, he alone was left. After Farnese's election to the papal chair, he became the man in Rome who stood foremost in architectural works.

It was San Gallo who had undertaken San Miniato when Michael Angelo fled to Venice, and who built the citadel in Florence, which Michael Angelo disdained to erect. He executed it with astonishing rapidity. For the third time, he came in contact with Michael Angelo at the building of the Farnese palace, which the pope had consigned to him. They had advanced as far as the cornice of the building, when Paul, instead of intrusting it to Michael Angelo alone, opened a competition. Perin del Vaga,

Vasari, and Sebastian del Piombo, sent in designs for it. Michael Angelo also made a drawing. But he did not come himself to the conference. He alleged illness as an excuse: it seems, however, that he did not wish to meet San Gallo. The pope gave preference to his drawing, and ordered a piece of the cornice he had designed to be executed in wood, in its natural size; and this, placed on the roof, was admired by the whole of Rome.

This could not have been agreeable to San Gallo. Still less so, when, in the fortification of the Vatican quarter of the city, which had been carried out by him up to a certain point, Michael Angelo was again brought forward by the pope, and, without ceremony, declared that the matter must be set about differently. San Gallo urged against him, that, as a painter and sculptor, he could understand nothing of fortification; to which Michael Angelo replied, that he was certainly not utterly inexperienced in painting and sculpture, but that he, nevertheless, knew more of fortification than San Gallo and all who preceded him.[*] When he began upon this to point out the errors in detail, such a clamor arose that the pope himself was obliged to order silence. Michael Angelo, upon this, prepared sketches of his own for the works, which were, indeed, not executed, but so much was effected that San Gallo's plans were left untouched.

When San Gallo's death occurred, Giulio Romano was talked of first; but he declined on account of illness. After long entreaties, Michael Angelo now

* See Appendix, Note LXVII.

showed himself willing to occupy the post. He was still engaged upon the frescos of the Paolina, which were only completed in 1549; and his sickness made the undertaking of such an important post appear doubtful. At last he accepted it, but on the condition that he should give his services without any pay.

We are accustomed to consider architecture as that art which is most nearly allied to mechanical skill. Leonardo da Vinci laid down this rule: The less resistance afforded by the material which is worked, the higher the art. According to this, therefore, the painter stands higher than the sculptor, the sculptor is better than the architect, the poet is superior to the painter. In the middle of the century, the Florentine literati, who were in search of innocent matter about which they might grow warm without exciting suspicion, started the doubtful question whether painting or sculpture was the nobler art. We possess many letters written on this subject. They applied to Michael Angelo for an opinion. In his youth, he might have perhaps answered with irony; in his old age he preferred, as Vasari says, so to express things that they could be variously interpreted.* He gave the gentlemen to understand that it was better to leave off such disputes, out of which nothing came; while he had answered Vasari, when the latter had one day asked his decision upon the same question, that sculpture and painting had one and the same end in view, — an end reached, however, by both only in very rare instances.

* See Appendix, Note LXVIII.

In the present day, no one would enter upon such discussions. There is no difference of rank between the arts. Only among those who practise them is a difference perceived in the depth of their feeling. Music, poetry, painting, sculpture, architecture,—all alike are offered as a medium to him whose mind is filled with a longing to impart that sense of beauty which lives within his soul to those who can appreciate, though they cannot create.

All art has its origin in the desire of a people to see that embodied which they consider beautiful or sacred. The symbols which thus arise form the vehicle for their best thoughts. We cannot speak of any thing as a work of art, unless a people can recognize in it the mystery of their own idea of beauty ; and when what in this sense we call a work of art chances to be placed beside that produced by skill, the difference is so forcible, that we may say it is impossible for any thing mechanical to rise into art without the aspiring thoughts of a people, and the genius of a master. Ideas must form the substance of a work of art : without them none can be produced.

Architecture furnishes the simplest proof of the truth of this view. It seems more than any to satisfy practical necessities, and yet it has least to do with them. It has nothing to do originally with human dwellings. It is utterly lacking to some nations. It is found only among those who possess that wonderful enthusiasm for the soil on which they dwell, which others are without. In our historical experience, the Germanic and Roman nations form a strong contrast even here. The German feels his country is wherever his companions are around him; the Roman clings to the land on which he has been reared. Wherever his city is, he is at home, though all the inhabitants should have died or been carried away. And this was the case with the Greek, the Roman, the Egyptian. They felt so linked with their plains and mountains, that every rock, every tree, every spring, became, as the dwelling-place of a deity, a part of their existence; while, with the old Germans, the gods hovered in the clouds, and marched with them wherever the people turned their steps. Therefore, among the people who possessed this inward relation to the soil of their home, there arose a longing to confirm by visible means this union between man and his land, and hence the beginning of architecture: efforts to make that their own to the utmost, which they held most dear; to sanctify the beloved soil to the eye by visible monuments. And thus the pyramids, the obelisks, and temples of the Egyptians were living tokens of the people who desired to strengthen their power by them: the land was theirs, and they raised these buildings to prove it! And the temples of the Acropolis and the Capitol were, as it were, jewels which the people set in the golden soil of their home, crowns and golden chains which they placed upon it. The rocks with which the fate of the cities was allied, were to be adorned just as they would be defended. And, therefore, the first origin of architecture was not the impulse to build dwelling-places, even for the gods, but the instinct to raise tower on tower, and to give a noble form to the work, to polish rocks within and without, and to erect columns. It was the belief that the protecting deity of the land abided with them, while, as it were, they adorned the land itself, and invested it with attractive beauty. Where, on the whole terrestrial globe, could Pallas Athene have felt a dwelling more worthy of her than the Acropolis? and where could the whole assembly of gods have lived but in Greece? The temples were their abodes. Slowly, as civilization advanced, the idea sprang up in these at first planless sacred buildings, that, as the gods had human forms, the form of human habitations for them might be a guide to thought. And thus, out of the idea of the inaccessible in itself, arising from that of the untrodden space in which the most Holy One dwelt, and to which the temple formed but the entrance, the sacred architecture of the ancient nations flourished : while the Germans, dwelling scattered through the land, had no Acropolis to leave when they changed their habitations, and, making retired woods the abodes of their gods; they only began to cultivate an architecture when it was brought into their land with a foreign religion, as something already complete.

Hence architecture is the first and the earliest of the arts, — the source of painting and sculpture from the adorning of the temple walls; the source of music and poetry from the solemn processions. Every thing secular in the arts is a foreign element that has been subsequently acquired. But, singular to say, it is only with the admission of this secular element that art has flourished in all its richness.

For only when men appear, who begin to express their own thoughts in addition to this universal feeling, is that freedom possible which gives the highest development to an art. The antique images of the gods remained stiff and lifeless till artists came forward who mingled their own especial views of human beauty with that demanded by religious necessity. The Egyptians, therefore, whose sculpture reached such a height, were yet really without an art in this respect. Not one of their statues exhibits individual ideas as their buildings do. Hence the statues of the Christian Madonna only became works of art, capable of piercing the heart, when the painter, secretly at first, gave to the divine countenance the features of some well-loved woman.

The decline of painting and sculpture, however, began when the sacred element wholly disappeared, and when the artist's single aim was to satisfy the purchaser of the work.

Michael Angelo, both in painting and sculpture, stood at the point where decline began. In architecture, other causes are at work. Architectural art declines with the common power of the people. Architecture is the least individual of the arts. It is rather the symbol of the physical power of nations than of their mental power. It expresses the extent and might of their political greatness; the oppression rather that they exercise over others, than the freedom by which they become great in themselves. Nations, who are the slaves of their princes, can produce an architecture which is beautiful and magnificent, while other arts languish. Thus it was in the sixteenth century. The apostasy of Germany from Rome brought about in Europe an intellectual advancement and a gathering together, not of the German, but of the Roman people, who, united by the renewed power of Catholicism and by common political views, maintained themselves for almost two centuries above the Protestant lands, until their breaking-up at length took place. Michael Angelo's architecture represents this period of excitement; and the gigantic building of St. Peter's Church might be compared with the immense efforts with which the reformed Romish Church endeavored to assert herself. For, to the Romans, the Church itself is a sacred place; to the Germans, the assembly of the faithful is the Church. The Germans care little about the soil on which their convictions prevail; while the subjects of the Papal Church are divided into provinces, the limits of which are kept under the eye of Rome, and which they endeavor to enlarge by new churches as by defensive forts. The model for these religious fortifications was formed by the Church of St. Peter, in the style of which they continued to build through the seventeenth century.

The union of the visible with spiritual power was peculiar from the first to the Roman-Catholic Church. As the old Romans had made their Capitol the flower, as it were, of their city, around which, as an ideal centre, Rome unfolded her luxuriant growth on all sides; so, after the city had become the seat of the popes as her sole masters, the aim of the spiritual princes was to place a new ecclesiastical

Capitol by the side of the old one, to which the inhabitants, even after every trace of secular rule in the old sense had been lost, might cling with superstitious reverence. The popes founded a new city by the side of the old, to the north, on the opposite side of the Tiber, where St. Peter's Church with the Vatican palaces formed the centre of Christian Rome; and all the riches of Christendom were poured forth to establish in its splendor this object of universal longing. The church which Michael Angelo was to rebuild, was the first and the most sacred. At the period of its rebuilding, the territory of the Catholic world was transformed from an unconnected feudal State into an absolute monarchy: the new St. Peter's witnessed a mightier worship than the old one out of whose walls it rose (for, for a time, both churches were standing at once, as they went forward step by step, breaking down and building up); and as, centuries before, the Gothic style had passed over Europe, remoulding every thing, until scarcely a building was exempt from the touch of this mighty fashion, so now the architecture of St. Peter's began its victorious march through the world, and new façades, if not domes, were added to every building.

No form of art is so fettered as that to which architects belong. Their work depends on the soil on which it is to stand; on the materials with which it is created; on the time which the money allows; on the whim of the commissioners, who often bring forward other masters with other plans. But, when all this is favorable, the strongest influence is unavoid-

ably exercised over the new edifice by the adjacent
buildings already finished. Architects stand in a
relation to each other, as regards imitation, more
than any other artists. Hence the development of
a style can be nowhere more clearly followed out
than in architecture; and it may be safely assumed,
that, when sudden transitions appear, these are either
to be ascribed to the effect of more remote models,
or to the loss of the intermediate process. The
transitions from the Egyptian architecture to the
Greek would lie undoubtedly clearly before us, if
too much belonging to those ages had not been destroyed. From the Greek, however, to our own day,
the line may be shown in an almost unbroken course;
how one century has used the works of the preceding;
how the Greek style has produced the Roman, the
Roman the Romanic, the Romanic the Gothic.

Sculpture and painting keep equal pace with the
æsthetic culture of nations, as architecture does with
their political progress. Therefore, as the former
began to decline under the Roman emperors, architecture advanced; and, as heathenism passed into
Christianity, the Romish temple was changed at the
same time into the Christian basilica. The division
of the empire caused the different development of
the same style in the East and West. From the
imitations of the Byzantine forms under the Moham-
medan rule in Asia and Egypt, there arose that
which made its way, as the Gothic, across the sea
into Venice, Sicily, Naples, Spain, and through
Southern France, into Germany. The flourishing
condition of the cities in Germany at the time of the

appearance of the Gothic, and the consequent desire
for splendid buildings, allowed this style to attain to
the perfection it reached in Germany; while with its
upward-soaring lines, dividing the building in height,
it was never able to overcome the length of the
Italian style of building, and was speedily given up
again in places where the influence of antique
models existed.

I do not doubt, that, if at the time when the Gothic
forests sprung up throughout Europe, there had
been popes in Rome possessing the money and power
of subsequent ones, all would have been Gothicized
there as elsewhere. As it was, however, little was
built there in this style, and the old basilicas and
the remains of antique works were left untouched;
the former unchanged, the latter used to a slight
extent, for the sake of the material. For what has
been pulled down in Rome and elsewhere seems to
amount to more than conquest and plunder ever
destroyed; and the pulling-down was carried on
everywhere unceasingly.

After the return of the popes from Avignon, however, that mental movement began which turned
with eagerness to ancient literature. The reverence
even for old buildings was revived. Florence looked
to Rome. While in Germany, Spain, and France,
the Gothic gained ground, in Rome the remains of
the old buildings stood in new romantic splendor.
By a mighty step backwards over a whole succession
of centuries full of natural progress and development, the remains of antique creations in architecture, as well as in poetry and philosophy, were

brought forward as models. From the vault of the
Pantheon rose the dome of Santa Maria del Fiore;
from that, that of St. Peter's; and from this, all the
churches in all countries, which arose either in direct
imitation of Michael Angelo, or after the form pre-
scribed by him.

How this was done; how the outward forms of
antique buildings effected an influence at first;
how the constructive power then came into play;
how different masters drew direct from this common
source; and how, at the same time, that which was
built in this manner led to a distinct understanding
of the antique, — all this would be possible to show,
but would be of no use here. There are studies
which cannot be pursued without devoting one's self
wholly to them. The essentials in architecture are
proportion, due relation between height and breadth:
that which the public care for most, the ornamental
part, holds a second place. He who would understand any thing of this, must endeavor to see for himself. We can only write for him who has already
gathered his own experiences.

Michael Angelo began late to come forward as an
architect on a large scale. The art was not foreign
to him from the first. I find, indeed, no authentic
proof that he made the plans for the fortifications of
Civita Vecchia for Julius II. The first time that he
appeared as an architect, was in the façade of San
Lorenzo. This was followed by the sacristy and the
library: these established his reputation and his
school.

But what had raised Michael Angelo at a much

earlier period, in the highest sense, above all other architects, is that, even in the ceiling-painting of the Sistine Chapel, he brought to view a grand whole, such as none besides him could have devised. Michael Angelo was the first able to imagine the colossal in a colossal manner. And in this way he devised the dome of St. Peter's. We need only compare Antonio di San Gallo's model with his, to feel where the difference lies. San Gallo raised tower above tower, increased, added one thing to another, and thus brought together a great but divisible mass. The small, however, does not become colossal by making it double or threefold: magnitude must belong to the form when it is devised. In this spirit, Michael Angelo made his plan. He arranged every proportion according to the extent of the whole work. So colossal is his St. Peter's, that, while all that Bramante and his like executed appears as the amplification of ideas originally small and even petty, the very imitations of St. Peter's, on a reduced scale, have always a colossal effect. Just as the melodies of Handel and Beethoven, even when executed in the most modest manner, make us feel the extent of grandeur of which they would be capable ; while melodies of other masters, even when produced by the largest orchestra, with all the accompaniments of drums and trumpets, never lose their true character of being only petty and trifling. Bramante, Peruzzi, and the San Galli, were besides most successful in their smaller buildings. In these they often exhibit an enchanting elegance. Bramante has executed many things of this sort in

Rome. Peruzzi truly beautified Siena by them; and
the San Galli built exquisite churches in Tuscany.
of a medium size, in elegant antique forms. But
none of them understood how to work on a larger
scale. Michael Angelo's only predecessor, who, had
he lived longer, would have equalled him, is Raphael.
The façade of the palace in Rome, the only work of
his which remains, and the house which was built in
Florence after his design, are executed with perfect
taste. Had death not removed him so soon, he
would have exhibited his power on St. Peter's itself;
for, with increasing years, he applied himself more
and more to architecture, and his last work shows
him to have been completely devoted to this study.

It is strange that his nature urged him so early to
take the same course which Michael Angelo adopted
in later life. He must have felt that painting is
only the handmaid of architecture, and he turned
to her as mistress. Architecture makes men feel
commanding. This is why princes build so readily:
they prefer this art to all others. The feeling of
creating is most satisfied in large buildings. Architecture approaches most closely to the work of nature. The expression that we use in speaking of
churches and palaces, that they seem to have grown
out of the soil, contains a touch of that transport
with which a man would regard himself, were he the
creator of a range of mountains, which had arisen in
obedience to his work and mind, where before lay a
level plain, or a formless rock. The ambition which
increases in men with years seems to rise beyond
the satisfaction of creating only the beautiful and the

enchanting. Something imposing, something overwhelming, they long to produce; and this architecture alone can effect.

It is with reverential awe that we first behold, and
then enter, a large and beautifully finished building.
The comparison, that architecture is frozen music,
has been much disputed; yet it arose in the mind of
a man who found no other image by which to designate the mute and sublime melody with which the
animated mass filled his soul. Such moments are
not to be forgotten. It will never vanish from my
mind, how at night, after the complete illumination
of St. Peter's, while the lamps were still burning,
but the throngs of people had long disappeared, I
stood alone at the foot of the obelisk on that square
before St. Peter's, which takes in the splendid colonnade in its full extent. Before me was the church,
separated by lines of light from the dark sky, like a
vision of fancy; and at the same time the feeling rose
within me, that it was no dream, but a work raised
by human hands, and that I myself belonged to the
race of human beings who had built it. The façade
stood before me in its grand lines, free from all those
non-essential ornaments with which Michael Angelo's
successors had overloaded it; the dome rose up as
if built of ice, illuminated with the glow of evening,
and the point seemed to lose itself in the night, like
the summit of a mountain which is a long way off.
It was perfectly still all around me, and the two
fountains alone roared unceasingly.

Such a view shows the artist's design. In his
mind those lines stood out just as clearly, when the

idea of the work rose before him for the first time, undestroyed by weather, unencumbered with subsequent ornament, undisturbed by the bustle of the world, — alone, as though there were only that one building on the earth, and all others stood in the shadow of its majesty.

How thoroughly that peculiarity which appears so striking in Michael Angelo's architecture, — of *working* from a whole, and having the idea of the complete structure ever in view from the first, making it the aim of all subsequent effort, — was at work in him, is shown by the two other arts in which he excelled. His first sketches were only general confused outlines, which he gradually formed into the most delicate lines. From the first they were there: he only brought them out by subsequent work. And this was the case with his statues also; his bust of Brutus, still completely covered over with marks of the chisel, seems, in spite of all, to conjure up the man before our view. And with his buildings also, the general expression is the most powerful. It surpasses all the detail. Michael Angelo had laws before him, of which we hear no more at the present day. He repeated it after Vitruvius perhaps, but certainly not without having himself tested it as true, that he only who is acquainted with human anatomy is able to form an idea of the necessity of an architectural plan. Every part increasingly necessitates the next, and nothing may be done without having the whole in mind. And hence, so much the more, none of Michael Angelo's works, which were left uncompleted, ought to be judged by the aspect they present in their unfinished state. He would not have acknowledged them as his own creations.

It may therefore be supposed, that the alterations which he undertook in the building of St. Peter's Church were of the most decided character.

Bramante laid the foundation-stone in 1506. What was commenced by him were the four immense pillars, on the top of which the dome rests, the height of which was as great as if the foundation of the Pantheon had been laid upon them, to be raised a second time. Bramante did not get beyond the erection of the pillars, their connection with each other, and the arch over the tribune; and, as all this occupied the lower end of the old St. Peter's, it was only necessary to pull down the half of it. A wall was drawn across; and, during the building, they used the front part of the long basilica, the façade and steps of which remained untouched long after the time of Michael Angelo.

After Bramante's death, when Raphael, Fra Giocondo, and Giuliano di San Gallo undertook the building, it was evident, that, before they could proceed further, the foundations must be strengthened. Vasari describes the proceeding adopted by San Gallo and Fra Giocondo. Raphael prepared the new ground-plan. Bramante had designed the dome as the centre of four divisions, equally large, and meeting together in the form of a cross. Raphael lengthened the front division, so that the Greek cross became a Latin one, one beam of which stretches out farther than the others.

Peruzzi, who after Raphael was appointed to direct the building, prepared a new plan again, to which Vasari awards the highest praise, and which limited the proportions of the preceding to a more reduced form. There was little money to expend under Clement VII. Julius and Leo had built with real zeal: the undertaking suited their ambitious ideas. Clement seems to have had no predilection for the work. After the conquest of the city, the building was discontinued. Paul III. took it up; and Peruzzi, having returned from his flight, again assumed the direction of the building, which he held until his death.

Now came Antonio di San Gallo's turn, who had worked with Peruzzi for a time; and with him, again, a new plan appeared. Peruzzi's design was rejected as too trifling; and the old size was decided on as the only worthy one. The pillars were again to be strengthened at the foundations. For ten years they continued to work thus, and much money was expended; and, at San Gallo's death, not much more was accomplished than that the four pillars were erected, and formed into a quadrangle by arches that connected them with each other. These arches are round, and so large in dimension that the height of their concavity amounts to more than half the height of the pillars on which they stand. A great deal of work had been executed in these forty years; for there are no pillars and arches like these in the world, and in addition to them there was the work under ground. Still, when Michael Angelo undertook the work, he could give the building itself any form he pleased; and as, from henceforth, his plans, for the dome, at any rate, were carried out, he stands as the real founder of the church. Only in one point was his plan subsequently departed from: for while he had returned to the original plan of Bramante, upon which he lavished the greatest praise, the form of the Latin cross was at length again adopted; and a long nave was built in front, by the projecting façade of which the view of the dome is hidden from the spectator who is not looking upon it from a height or distance. This façade, too, is not Michael Angelo's work. His own was simple and grand.

Michael Angelo's criticism of what had been done up to the time of his entering upon office, and of what was now to be done, is contained in a letter, which he must have written at the period of the first negotiations respecting his appointment as chief architect. "Bramante," he writes, " was, if any one deserves the name, one of the most able architects since the days of the ancients. He made the first design for St. Peter. Without confusion, clear and compact, well lighted and open on all sides, he wished so to place the church, that it should in nowise interfere with the Vatican palace. And, as is evident now, whatever the standard of beauty, whoever departs from his idea as San Gallo did, departs from the very rules of art. Whoever examines the model impartially must see this. San Gallo's circular building takes away the lightness of Bramante's plan, which of itself in this respect is so deficient, from its many angles and recesses above and beneath

the choirs, affording places of retreat for false coin-
ers, lurking-places for fugitives, and opportunity for
all possible knaveries.　For, when it is shut up at
night, it would at least take five and twenty persons
to find out whether any one is concealed there; and
even then there would be some difficulty in hunting
him from his lurking-place.　It would be necessary,
besides, in carrying out the building projected by
San Gallo, to pull down the Paolina Chapel and a
part of the palace; indeed, even the Sistine Chapel
would not remain untouched.

"When, however, that which has already been
completed of this circular building is said to have
cost a hundred thousand crowns, it is an untruth:
for it might have been done with sixteen thousand;
and, if it is now taken down, the loss can be but
slight.　For the hewn stones and foundations come
very opportunely just now; and two hundred thousand crowns would be spared in the building itself,
while it would acquire three hundred years of additional durability.　This is my impartial opinion.
For, if I carry it out, it will be to my own great
disadvantage.　I shall be glad if you will communicate all this to the pope.　I do not feel myself well
enough."

Thus he writes to some one whom he calls Bartolomeo.*　By the disadvantage, he meant the possibility of his proposals being accepted, and of his
being obliged to undertake the building, which was
contrary to his wish.　But the pope agreed to them.
With regard to the circular building condemned by

* See Appendix, Note LXIX.

Michael Angelo, he alluded to the extended colonnade three stories high, which, evidently in imitation of the Coliseum, encircles the heart of the building, and gives it a round form. San Gallo's model, which, still in good preservation, stands in a chamber belonging to St. Peter's Church, and is so large that one can walk about its interior, accurately shows what was intended. According to this, the whole appears as a mass of infinitely small pieces of architecture, small also in their conception; whilst the interior, simple and grand, bears its present appearance, except that the dome is dark and paltry. When Michael Angelo one day appeared at the building to inspect San Gallo's model, he found his whole party there, — *la setta Sangallesca*, as Vasari calls them, — and they gave vent to their vexation. They were glad, they said, that Michael Angelo would take the trouble: San Gallo's plan was a good field for him to feed on. "You are quite right there," was his reply. Unintelligible enough, indeed, to those whom he intended to hit; for his meaning was, as he explained to others, that they were right in calling the plan a field, as they had judged as beasts.

At the present day, but small penetration is required to perceive the difference between the two masters. Not far from San Gallo's model, in an adjoining room, there stands Michael Angelo's plan for the dome, executed in wood, in which every thing is given, up to the smallest stone and beam, so that after his death it could be carried out with accuracy. Michael prepared it for twenty-five crowns, while

San Gallo reckoned upon one thousand crowns for his. Still, Michael Angelo's is by far more simple, and smaller in extent. But what both desired is evident. Michael Angelo had in his mind a new style of architecture, grandly designed and self-dependent; while San Gallo only borrowed from others, and, without starting with a perfect idea of his own, combined as well as he could all the treasures of his memory.

Michael Angelo's first work was to strengthen the four pillars still more, so that they might bear the dome more securely; then he placed on the arches the circular tower-like building called the drum; and it was not till after his death that the double dome was completely raised upon this. Many views of Rome in the sixteenth century exhibit the church in its unfinished condition: in front, the old façade, — a great smooth surface of wall, the doors and windows simply cut in it; and between these the wall was covered with paintings. Towering far, behind it, upon the still irregular and rude substructure, was the drum, like an immense temple surrounded with pillars, rising in the sky, open and roofless, and wonderful to look at. As at the present day, standing in the square before the church, the front façade, which is not Michael Angelo's work, covers the drum as far as the dome, which was also only built after his death, we may say that Michael Angelo never really saw during his life aught of that which St. Peter's ordinarily presents to view. He did not at all design the colonnades surrounding the square; and the obelisk and fountains were also placed in the centre of the square by subsequent architects.

The columns surrounding the drum, with the windows between, and the position of the dome above them, is a triumph of architectural beauty. All appears as light and symmetrical as if it had grown there. And yet we must not forget that even here Michael Angelo's model was not perfectly carried out; for these pillars, which, placed in pairs, do not touch the wall, but standing apart from it form a kind of corridor round the drum, were intended to have their capitals, which now project baldly, adorned with pedestals surmounted with statues, which were to surround the dome like tapers. Many think to discover a fault here, because they do not know Michael Angelo's design. It is just in this, however, that he shows himself so great as an architect, that he did not regard sculpture-work as an ornament to be introduced or omitted at will; but regarded it as an architectural element, necessary to the harmony of the whole.

Considered also from within, when, throwing the head back, we look up into the dome, it presents a marvellous view. Below the windows of the drum there is a circle of figures, appearing on a white ground in delicate gray shadow, and with golden lights. The ornaments below, including those of the arches, the facing of the columns, the statues, and the paintings, belong to later times, and have little to do with Michael Angelo.

This endless ornament, with which the entire church is filled, and which, without regard to archi-

Interior of St. Peter's, Rome.

MICHAEL ANGELO.

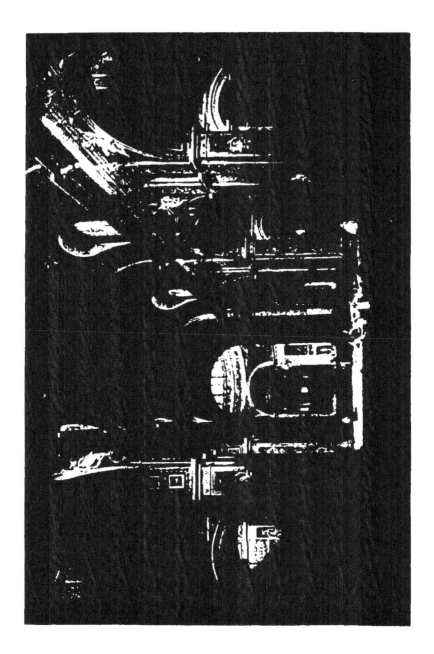

tecture, is placed wherever there is room for it, is to blame for the fact that the building does not appear in its true grandeur at first sight. The eye, that would like to wander freely over the mass, is confused and diverted by countless things. By frequent visits to the church, we become accustomed to this; we overlook the unimportant, and allow the proportions to have their true effect. We then perceive the grand power of the pillars and arches; and the distances, which could at first be scarcely estimated, become conceivable. I remember entering one afternoon. In front of where I stood, a great stream of sunlight came through the side window, casting a broad light between the arches across the ground, while, behind, it grew gradually more dusky up to the furthermost recesses where darkness reigned; and over the vault containing the bones of St. Peter, in the very centre of the dome, a corona of golden lamps was burning. This appeared in infinite distance. The shadowy arches rose gigantically above it; and the organ, which accompanied the holy service they were celebrating, only reached me as a soft murmur. It seemed as if the church had increased twofold since I last entered it.

Walking round the roof, between the roofs of the side chapels, which, towering above the flat surface, stand out by themselves as little temples, but which appear unimportant by the side of the drum supporting the centre dome, and which now rises mightily like the Pantheon, one might imagine one's self on an island in the air, which, forming a city in itself, makes every thing below appear small and

distant. We look down into the long Vatican palace
as into an empty chest; and all around our gaze is
limited by the pure blue mountains, and the glim-
mering streak of sea to the west, stretching out between the gentle slope of the mountain range. And
as we see the sea from this height, so from the sea
itself we see the first sign of Rome hovering over the
distant horizon. Or, approaching the city by land,
we catch suddenly a glimpse of it in the remote distance through rock and tree, and we feel that the
city is near. Rome is not conceivable in the present
day without Michael Angelo's St. Peter's, which in
Michael Angelo's day no eye saw but his own, when
the work that he intended to build rose before his
mind. Mighty as it appeared to him, it has appeared
to none beside; for that which floated before his
mental eye was never completed.

But without the Capitol also, as it now stands,
Rome would not be Rome; and that, too, he alone
saw in his day. The palaces upon it were built after
his plans, and in their centre stands the statue of Marcus Aurelius. He executed only the flight of steps
on both sides leading up to the old senatorial palace,
as a background to the statue of Marcus Aurelius.
It was built under Paul III. An especial love for
architecture had at that time awakened in Rome.
Under the protection of Cardinal Farnese, a society
of artists was formed, consisting of scholars and
noblemen of the highest rank, who made Vitruvius
their study.* Claudio Tolomei was the true moving
spring in this society. Vasari, too, was admitted, and

* See Appendix, Note LXX.

he here received his impulse to write biographies of the artists. Forcibly diverted by events from ecclesiastical matters, the active spirit of men of cultivated minds seems to have sought for some channel for its energies, and to have found it in architecture. The remodelling of the city was never more zealously carried on: palaces were built, rebuilt, completed; antiquities were collected with greater zeal than ever before; excavations were made, and the ideal form restored of ancient buildings which had been destroyed. Michael Angelo joined together for Farnese, the tablets on which a plan of a part of old Rome was engraved, and which, coming to light again, were placed in one of the Capitoline palaces. To this impulse to build and to beautify, those palaces seem to owe their origin, which give at least an intimation of its old glory to that summit of the Capitoline rock which had been left desolate for centuries.

The restoration of the Capitol began with the erection of the flight of steps ascending to Ara Cœli, on both sides of which, at the foot of the ascent, lie the black granite lions discharging water from their jaws; whilst above, as they open upon the square, stand the colossal Dioscuri with their horses. There had before only been steep rock here, and the ascent had only been from the forum lying on the other side; at the entrance of Charles V., the design for the new steps first originated, perhaps with Antonio di San Gallo, while the present flight of steps was not even begun at the time of Michael Angelo's death. But the erection of the statue of Marcus

Aurelius in the centre of the square took place under his own eye.   The square where it stands, the palaces round, the atmosphere of Rome, — it may be all these which lead me to regard this as the most beautiful equestrian statue in the world.   In dignity of bearing, and in harmony of composition, it seems to satisfy every demand.   It is the same statue as was kept from destruction by the popes under the name of that of Constantine, which for a long time it falsely bore.   It stood in front of the Lateran, before it was brought to the Capitol.   From the nostrils of the horse there flowed red and white wine on Rienzi's election as a tribune.*   Now, however, it has stood again for centuries on the rocky soil, which has witnessed more perhaps than any spot on the earth, since it became the dwelling-place of man.

Michael Angelo showed in its erection how such things ought to be placed, — and this as low as possible, according to the principles of the ancients. Not only did he make the pedestal of the most moderate height, but he lowered some degrees the centre of the square on which it stands; so that, from the gate of the palaces on both sides, the bronze horse appears almost on a level with the spectator. By this means, Michael Angelo produced the right effect, — that appearance of reality which is the result of true art.   The equestrian emperor appears like the occupant of the palace: the steps before him seem worthy the hoofs of such a horse; the steps to which his back is turned, worthy of being trodden by his own feet.   And thus, while all had vanished

* See Appendix, Note LXXI.

from the height of the Capitol which called the old
times to mind, Michael Angelo consecrated the place
afresh; and, as in the new Rome of the popes he
built a temple to the apostle, he here raised a
dwelling-place under the open sky, to the only one
left of the old rulers of Rome who had governed the
world.* In both works, he was not merely a great
architect in all that is truly architectural, — in
dimensions, in internal structure and ornament, —
but he was greater still in that he beautified that
spot of earth to which he directed his thoughts, in
the spirit of the old masters. Michael Angelo loved
Rome; he had known her for many years, and by his
buildings the city rose to almost greater importance.
To him most of all she owes that aspect by which
she now lives indelibly in the memory of all those
whom a fortunate star may ever lead to her gates.

Yet another of the Roman buildings received its
completion at the hands of Michael Angelo: the
Farnese palace was awarded to him on the death of
San Gallo; and although the cornice alone, as regards the exterior architecture, is his work, the
splendid court in the interior, enclosed in three rows
of colonnades, originated with him alone. His intention was to throw a bridge across the Tiber in
the direction of the great gateway intersecting the
palace, which should be contiguous with the back of
the building, and to carry a long road from hence
far into Trastevere. The plan was never put into
execution, like many others designed by him. But
here, too, we see him not merely building, but re-

* See Appendix, Note LXXII.

modelling on a large scale. He would have transformed the whole of Rome, had he possessed the
power to do so; indeed the aspect of the city would
now be very different, had that alone been executed
which was actually projected by Michael Angelo.
And thus, in the later years of his life, he fulfilled
the longing which he had cherished in the early
years of his career, and which he expressed in his
scheme for transforming the rocky mountain rising
on the shore at Carrara into a statue which might
be seen by sailors far out to sea. For this is the
spirit of architecture, — to give form to the vast,
and to compel an entire people into admiring astonishment, when all other arts only satisfy a part of
the people, however wide-spreading be the fame and
influence of the works.

Michael Angelo gained among his contemporaries
the name of Great (*il gran Michel Angelo*), a designation of which posterity has not deprived him.
Those men who, *par excellence*, are called great, form
an especial race among those universally designated
in history with the appellation "great;" they are
natures possessing a mighty soul-compelling power;
tyrants in the highest sense; men who not only rule
the world, but, when it opposes, will compel it to
accept their authority, and who forcibly impress the
stamp of their mind upon the uncertain fabric of
humanity. Frederic the Great, Peter the Great,
Alexander, Napoleon, were nothing but human con-
querors, who, just as armed battering-rams attack
the wooden colossus that seemed invincible hitherto,
vanquished the enemy, and annihilated entire forces.

Corneille is called the Great by the French, because he depicted in his tragedies those violent passions upon which the fate of States depended in his time. He had that in him which induced Napoleon to say that he would have made him a prince had he lived. This royal commanding power gained for Michael Angelo also the appellation of Great. He belonged to those minds who perceive a higher order of things, and who are not satisfied with knowing how it ought to be, but who begin to hurl the rocks aside that lie in the way, and to pile them up again where they are to form a fortress. He would have assigned another bed to rivers; he would have pierced through mountains and thrown bridges across the sea. That which is done now-a-days because the times have gradually led to it, his genius at once pointed out to him; and thus Vittoria Colonna's words might be applied even to the gigantic buildings which he raised, — that he who only admired his works, valued the smallest part in him. For his works are insignificant, if we think of those he would have been capable of producing: and even that which he did accomplish must appear unfinished when we compare with it his original designs. He was not even allowed to complete his painting in the Sistina as he intended, but was obliged suddenly to break down the scaffolding at the command of the pope.

6.

To these buildings are attached the few names of the artists, who, either as pupils or assistants, now indeed of the third generation, surrounded and survived Michael Angelo.

In the Farnese palace, Guglielmo della Porta went hand in hand with him. Michael Angelo ordered the Hercules to be placed there,—that which is now known in Naples as the Farnese Hercules, and which at that time had lost the legs from the knee to the ankle. Della Porta replaced them. Michael Angelo was so satisfied with his work, that, when he found the old legs again, he threw them aside. Goethe saw the statue before it had been conveyed from Rome to Naples. When he first saw it, he thought there was nothing to object to in the restoration; but, when the genuine feet were brought forward, he writes, it was inconceivable to him how Della Porta's work could have been thought good so long. Michael Angelo must certainly have perceived the important difference, and his conduct proves the great respect he had for Della Porta, perhaps from kindness; for the superiority of the antique work, to which at the present day anybody would yield without taking offence, was at that time not so universally acknowledged. We have only one single instance of restoration made by Michael Angelo himself; and this is imputed to him only because it could have been done by no other. The right arm of the Dying Gladiator, that on which he is resting, is an extraordinary work. All other restorations, such as many of those in Rome which are regarded as Michael Angelo's, appear to me neither warranted, nor are they worthy of him.

Guglielmo della Porta seems to have been of a

vain and suspicious nature. Because Michael Angelo did not admit his claims on another occasion,
he turned his back upon the man to whom he owed
so many thanks. The matter related to the Church
of St. Peter. Cardinal Farnese wished to have a
monument erected to Paul III., which was committed to Della Porta, who, after the death of Sebastian
del Piombo, had been appointed, at Michael Angelo'
intercession, as Frate del Piombo. The work was
to stand by itself, and this under the centre arch of
the four pillars supporting the dome, — the best
place certainly in the whole church, and which had
once been destined for Julius's monument. Michael
Angelo, however, would not give up this place, but
removed the monument to the back of one of the
four pillars. Della Porta never forgave this. He
maintained, that envy had induced Michael Angelo
to make this alteration.

The work itself, which stands there as one of the
most excellent of the monuments to the pope, shows
how slowly in Rome, in spite of the complete revolution in religious questions, and the new inclination
to decency in art, the change of theory was practically carried out. We see on the sarcophagus a
colossal female form lying naked, like a Venus of
Titian's; and the youthful figure is so thoroughly
in contradiction to the sacred place it is intended to
adorn, that Aretino might a second time have extolled the modesty of heathen sculptors. The
arrangement of the monument corresponds with
those in the Chapel of San Lorenzo. As there, two
figures are lying on both sides, on the gently sloping

surface of the sarcophagus; and, between them, in a
niche behind the wall, there is a sitting statue of the
pope. Both figures are female. The one, an old
woman veiled in drapery, the mother of the pope;
the other, the beautiful Giulia Farnese, — I know
not whether Paul's sister, to whose charms he indeed
owed enough to let them thus share a little bit
of immortality. Thick plaits of hair artistically
arranged are twisted round the head. In its work,
the monument is far inferior to those of Michael
Angelo. The marble is smooth and cold: we never
think in this statue that every line is studied from
nature; but as a decoration it stands very high.
The statue of Paul III. is in bronze. This monument also fell a victim in time to the fate of being
reduced one-half; for when, in the course of the
seventeenth century, it obtained its present position,
two other figures belonging to it were left out, and
were taken to the Farnese palace, where they still
stand.

Michael Angelo's successors, reckoning by the surface covered, have executed more extensive works
than were ever committed to him. Thus Vignola,
who built the Porta del Popolo after his designs,
assisted also in carrying on the building of St.
Peter's, and was engaged in the completion of the
Capitol: Vasari also, to whom Michael Angelo gave
work in Rome, and who displayed unusual industry
in Florence: Ammanati, too, who placed the colossal
Neptune on the Piazza in Florence. They were all
merely clever people in their line, who knew how to
work together boldly, quickly, and with great effect.

The Descent from the Cross.

DANIELE DA VOLTERRA.

The only true artist among those in connection with Michael Angelo at this time is Daniele da Volterra, whose Descent from the Cross, in Trinità dei Monti, may be called the most remarkable composition which appeared in Rome after the Last Judgment. So excellent is it, that the assertion that a drawing of Michael Angelo's formed the foundation of the picture, although expressed by Vasari himself rather as a conjecture, has been repeated almost as a certainty, and without further proof is received as such. I must confess that all would indicate Michael Angelo's hand, his helpful interference in such cases being very usual, if other works of Da Volterra's did not prove that such help was by no means necessary. He was an artist of the first rank. The chapel in the same church, opposite the above-mentioned picture, was also painted by him. We have before us here a Murder of the Innocents, the figures of which we should be compelled, in the former case, likewise to ascribe to Michael Angelo; and it appears an injustice, from the similar conception and the superior art which distinguish these paintings, to take them from him who is their author.

Daniele da Volterra's career was similar to that of Della Porta. Like him he worked under Perin del Vaga, was recommended by Del Piombo and Michael Angelo to the Farnese, and was employed in the building of the Farnese palace. In 1547, after Del Vaga's death, he found access, by means of Michael Angelo, into the Vatican. These were times, in which Michael Angelo, like Goethe and Humboldt in their old age, exercised a patronage which extended to all who wished to work, and who possessed talent. The entire training of these young men rested with Michael Angelo. He no longer met with opposition ; but his verdict was at once received in silence as decisive. He had no longer a rival. He was the man whose advice was universally sought : it was a matter of course, that, when any thing was to be undertaken, — paintings, monuments, churches, or palaces, — his opinion was required. He had only to cast a glance upon the designs, and to say that they seemed suitable. And this fame increased to such an extent, that, if Vasari said of Raphael that he had gone like a prince to the Vatican followed by a train of all the artists under him, Michael Angelo in his old age sat there like a pope, whose blessing was sufficient to call forth the greatest works.

Even his laconic habits, his inclination to solitude, and his melancholy views of life, had now become characteristic, known and respected for years as a part of his strange nature. The unusual mixture in his character of severity and tender-hearted amiability wounded no longer. They knew well, that none ever appealed in vain to his true goodness of heart. His correspondence with his nephew Leonardo shows this plainly. Severely as he expressed himself for the most part, probably because he considered it necessary, he could not wholly restrain himself, and his natural kindliness breaks through. He gives him presents; he has an eye to his welfare; and he remembers his old Florentine friends. It was a matter of course, that all which he gained by his works in Rome devolved at last on his family in Florence.

His household at Rome was of the simplest kind. His factotum was his servant Urbino: he was married, and gained much lucrative employment through his master. A stone-mason by trade, he worked at Julius's monument, in San Pietro in Vincula, respecting the final completion of which at that time letters and accounts still exist. Besides him, Michael Angelo had a maid. Here, too, we still possess one of the contracts upon he which engaged Vincenzia, the daughter of a small shopkeeper named Michele, at Macello dei Corvi, and therefore his neighbor; the condition being, that, if she behaved irreproachably for four years, she should be allowed to marry with a portion. Michael Angelo dined alone at noon, and lived moderately. When he was painting, he was satisfied with a little bread and wine for the whole day. Indeed, so busy was he at times, that he took this slight meal without discontinuing his work. He had always, however, young men in his house who were working with him. Ascanio Condivi was one of these favored ones. He relates how once a famous physician of that day, Realdo Colombo, who was very intimate with Michael Angelo, gave the latter, as an especial rarity, the corpse of a young negro, which was conveyed to his (Condivi's) retired dwelling, and there anatomically dissected; in doing which, Michael Angelo pointed out to him many secrets. Anatomy was his passion. He even dissected animals of every kind. He intended to put down his views thus obtained in a book, as Da Vinci and Dürer had done, whose writings he knew without especially admiring them; but he afterwards gave it up, because, with advancing age, writing became not only troublesome, but the dissecting made him ill, so that he was obliged to relinquish it.

Old age is like childhood even in this respect, — that it brings men more easily into relation with each other. A child says " Good-day " to every one, and offers its mouth readily to be kissed. But this confidence forms no permanent relations. The more years increase, the more important does it become whom we meet and to whom we give ourselves: beyond a certain limit, however, the first condition begins to return. An old man may come forward more freely; the world is more accessible to him, and respects his whims. But, at the same time, it is again the case that no permanent relations spring from these meetings. He receives no longer any thing mental from those who surround him; he remains the same in his ideas. It matters little to his mental preception to know those intimately with whom he comes in contact. And thus it was with Michael Angelo. It would not be worth the trouble to follow up the intimacies which he now made. They were numerous. His advice was much sought, and his answers were many; but it is almost indifferent to know the questions to which they relate.

Vasari's degree of intimacy with Michael Angelo is difficult to determine. They corresponded, and the language in their letters is often very familiar. Michael Angelo thanked him for his biography in a

flattering sonnet; but it is scarcely to be supposed,
that he did not see through the indelicate, obtruding,
tasteless nature, and that he showed Vasari greater
friendship than their intercourse rendered necessary.
Vasari possessed by far more experience in business
than the other younger artists of the time; but he
also worked most cursorily. He was avowedly proud
of completing quickly. As an architect, he stood in
the most advantageous position. He had that eye
for the requirements of a definite locality which so
much distinguished Michael Angelo. Like him, he
knew how to help himself quickly and surprisingly
in technical embarrassments. He decorated with
taste and without paltriness. And even his fault of
disregarding structure, and appearing more singular
than beautiful, reminds us of a peculiarity of Michael
Angelo's, especially evident in his later designs. We
must, however, say here that the bizarre, flourishing,
colossal intermingling of all forms, which prevailed
in Rome in the seventeenth century, and at length
set itself up as the main element of the Jesuit style,
had nothing to do with Michael Angelo. What is
laid to Michael Angelo's account in this respect
arises from ignorance. Much is imputed to him
which originated entirely without him. With regard
to the Porta Pia in Rome, for which his drawing is
said to have furnished the design, and which was
built after his death, we have not the slightest guarantee that he intended it as it stands. The dome of
St. Peter's must be seen: there lies his glory.
Every thing else, without exception, was either left
unfinished, or, where it was executed after his plans,

it received so many alterations, that it seems to furnish no just standard for estimating Michael Angelo as an architect.

The man who was dearest to him of all the young people frequenting his house seems to have been Tommaso dei Cavalieri, with whom he became acquainted about 1541, and to whom the completion of the Capitoline buildings was assigned after his death. Cavalieri was young, rich, of noble birth, and great beauty. Vasari says he could have obtained any thing from Michael Angelo. For him he drew the design with the two heads of Cleopatra, splendid faces of Roman women, with the hair twisted tastefully in plaits. The designs are in the Uffici, and photographic copies of them are abundant. For him, too, the Rape of Ganymede was done: an eagle is rising with him, while his shepherd's dog is left behind, howling pitifully after him. Giulio Clovio copied this design in miniature for Cavalieri. The composition is intended as a bas-relief; and how charming its effect is as such, is evidenced by a modern work in the Academy of San Luca in Rome, the name of the author of which no one could tell me. Cavalieri also obtained a strange drawing, full of figures, a children's bacchanal, the centre of which is occupied by a troop of naked children, who are dragging a skinned boar to a caldron, under which others have lighted a fire. This young Roman is said to have been so highly educated and so agreeable, that Varchi, the Florentine professor and court scholar of that day, in a lecture which he delivered in the Florentine Academy upon one of Michael An-

Head of Cleopatra.

MICHAEL ANGELO.

gelo's sonnets, declared him, from personal experience, to be the most attractive young man he had ever known. He then recited the verses which Michael Angelo had addressed to Cavalieri, and which express the prettiest flattery that youth could receive from age. Through him, he says, he feels anew all the freshness, ardor, and hope which in days of old had been bestowed upon his own youth : *—

" Through thee I catch a gleam of tender glow,
   Which with my own eyes I had failed to see ;
   And walking onward, step by step with thee,
   The once-oppressing burdens lighter grow.
   With thee, my grovelling thoughts I heavenward raise,
   Borne upward by thy bold, aspiring wing ;
   I follow where thou wilt, — a helpless thing,
   Cold in the sun and warm in winter days.
   My will, my friend, rests only upon thine ;
   Thy heart must every thought of mine supply ;
   My mind expression finds in thee alone.
   Thus like the moonlight's silver ray I shine :
   We only see her beams on the far sky,
   When the sun's fiery rays are o'er her thrown."

To understand this poem thoroughly, we must bear in mind what was mentioned at the very beginning of this work, — that the transition from youth to maturity is different in the South. The mind develops itself there more brilliantly and quickly. As in Plato we see the young Alcibiades sitting, as the favorite of Socrates, among mature men, and discussing philosophy with them ; so in Rome, at that time, we see temporal and spiritual princes and nobles enjoying consideration almost as boys. Thus

* See Appendix, Note LXXIII.
17*

Leo X. had come forward as a cardinal while very young; after him Ippolito, and now Farnese: thus had it been with Pico di Mirandula and Raphael himself, both so young and so enchanting. This bright splendor of early bloom must have been possessed by Cavalieri; and I must be allowed to refer to another sonnet upon him, which enlarges upon the subject of the former: —

> "He who from nothing, and ere all things were,
>   Did time create, divided it in twain:
>   To one, he made the lofty sun a share;
>   And to the other, moonlight's dusky train.
>   Then in a moment came, in dread array.
>   Chance, fortune, fate; by which, alas! I see,
>   Predestined when I in the cradle lay,
>   The time of darkness was assigned to me.
>   So, struggling with my own more darkened doom,
>   Since where most night is, there is greatest gloom,
>   My labors dark are pain and grief to me:
>   Yet I console myself; for this my night
>   Aids by its contrast to set forth thy light, —
>   That sun which, at thy birth, was given to thee."

> "Colui che fece, e non di cosa alcuna,
>   Il tempo che non era anzi a nessuno,
>   In due 'l divise, e diè 'l sol alto all 'uno,
>   All 'altro, assai più bassa, diè la luna.
>   Onde 'l caso, la sorte, e la fortuna
>   In un momento nacquer di ciascuno,
>   Ed a me destinaro il tempo bruno
>   Dal dì che prima io giacqui entro la cuna.
>   E come quel che contraffo me stesso,
>   S' ove è più notte più buio esser suole,
>   Del mio oscuro operar m 'affliggo, e lagno.
>   Pur mi consola assai l' esser concesso
>   Far chiaro di mia scura notte el sole
>   Ch' a voi fu dato al nascer per compagno."

Pietà, Florence.

MICHAEL ANGELO.

How beautiful and satisfying the conclusion! All Michael Angelo's poems, even when they express the bitterest thoughts, close with conciliatory feelings.

Michael Angelo drew a portrait of Cavalieri, life-size, — the only one he executed except Vittoria Colonna's.

7.

Although Michael Angelo did nothing more in painting and sculpture after the paintings in the Paolina, it is not to be supposed that he broke off with both arts suddenly. It had become far too great a necessity with him to chisel and to draw; and he drew till his hands could no longer hold the pencil. Yet this weakness did not come on till late. His handwriting evidences this; for it only began to shake in his last few years, and even then he formed his letters steadily and perfectly.

There was in his atelier, at Macello dei Corvi, a marble group, — Christ lying dead on his mother's lap, and Joseph of Arimathea standing by her side, — which he had begun about 1545,* and continued working at slowly for himself. He only undertook it, that he might have something at hand for his leisure hours. Vasari relates how he had once been sent by the pope to Michael Angelo, on account of some drawing, somewhere about 1550, and had found him at this work. It was dark: Michael Angelo, however, who knew Vasari by his manner of knocking, came out with a lantern to see what he wanted. Urbino was thereupon sent to the upper story to

* See Appendix, Note LXXIV.

fetch the desired sheet: but Vasari tried, while he was waiting, to catch a glimpse of the group by the limited light; and he looked at the leg of Christ, at which Michael Angelo was then working. Scarcely, however, had the latter observed where Vasari was looking, than he let the lantern fall, so that it went out, leaving both in darkness. He then called to Urbino to bring a light; and, as he and Vasari left the partition in which the group stood, he said, "I am so old that death often pulls me by the coat to come with him; and some day I shall fall down like this lantern, and my last spark of life will be extinguished."

Often, in the middle of the night, if he could not sleep, he would get up and work at this last task. That he might have good light for doing so, and yet not be himself hindered by it, he had a kind of pasteboard cap made, on the top of which he fixed a tallow candle, which would not drop like wax, and which was not in his way. He left the group, however, unfinished, because he discovered a flaw in the marble. He intended to break it to pieces; but he gave it afterwards to one of his young men. It is now in Florence under the dome of Santa Maria del Fiore, with the inscription beneath it that it is Michael Angelo's last work. The place is not unfavorable. The dim light that prevails there suits the group, which is only finished in its general mass.

Among those who in this year painted from Michael Angelo's designs, the most remarkable is Marcello Venusti. Cavalieri had him execute in oil, on a large scale, Michael Angelo's sketch of the

Annunciation: it hangs, at the present day, in the sacristy of the Lateran, and is an excellent painting. We see Michael Angelo in every line of it; and the grand idea peculiar to his compositions, joined to the most delicate coloring, gives the picture a peculiarity of its own which is not to be described. We could almost have said, that some ancient Greek painter, who had undertaken to represent a Christian subject, had been at work on it.

Marcello Venusti painted the portrait of Vittoria Colonna. Under Michael Angelo's direction, he copied the Last Judgment on a small scale, in gray. The picture is now in Naples. From a sketch of his, he painted Christ on the Mount of Olives. If I were to decide among the many galleries which imagine they possess the original, I should say the Berlin collection deserved the preference. And, lastly, instead of enumerating others, to mention the most charming of all produced by this double authorship, we may name the Madonna with the Sleeping Child; a painting which we find constantly repeated, and which is one of the sweetest representations. Mary is sitting quite in front with her knees crossed, the upper part of her body leaning back, her head inclined to one side, and her eyes cast down, contemplating the child lying asleep on her knee. He has stretched out one arm to lean his little head on it; the other hangs feebly down over his little breast. On the left side of the background, which is completely cut off by the transverse back of the seat on which Mary is sitting, the little St. John is approaching, bending attentively over the child with his finger on his lips; on the other side we see the holy Joseph, awaiting calmly the awaking of the child, his head supported on his hand, which is lost in the thick beard round his mouth. Each figure thus in a different manner indicates watchful love.

In the painting, one thing only is omitted which the sketch possesses, and which gives it a strange appearance; the skin thrown according to the fashion of the antique over the little St. John, making him almost look like a little Hercules. Mary's face in Venusti's painting has the most innocent beauty. In the holy Joseph, we are reminded of Michael Angelo's own portrait, of which there are many belonging to his later years, while there are none of his youth. The one most known, although the least advantageous, is Bonasone's profile, drawn and engraved at the time when Michael Angelo entered upon his new office at St. Peter's. The brow projecting heavily over the nose; the mighty, angular skull; the deep and frequent wrinkles about the mouth and eyes, as firmly drawn as if the muscles which they cover were as hard as the bones themselves, — all this presents a physiognomy to us, which, slightly caricatured as it appears here, portrays the nature of the man all the more distinctly from its extraordinary firmness. In the oil-paintings in Rome and Florence, the features appear less hard, and the brow handsomer. The portrait in the possession of the gallery of the Capitol is ascribed to Michael Angelo's own hand. It is not only the position of the head which justifies this supposition; for the expression is so deep, the glance so penetrating, the brow so beautifully painted, that Michael Angelo alone, it might be said, would have been able thus to conceive himself. Still it remains doubtful, as Vasari says nothing of the work, which he really would not have left unnoticed had it been executed by Michael Angelo himself.

One more must yet be mentioned of those who worked after Michael Angelo; and this was a young sculptor who studied with Tribolo, and who, had he not died young, would, according to Vasari's opinion, have attained to great perfection. His name was Pierino da Vinci, a nephew of Leonardo da Vinci's, the son of his youngest brother. I do not remember having seen any thing by him. He is said to have produced things which were regarded as works of Michael Angelo's, whose method of handling marble he had made his own. Vasari mentions a group ten feet high, — Sampson killing a Philistine, — which was begun by Da Vinci, a sketch of Michael Angelo's having furnished the first idea for it. Yet he does not say that he completed it, nor what has become of it. Equally little do we know of the fate of the little chest made by Pierino da Vinci for Duke Cosmo after a design by Michael Angelo. He died young, in 1554, when he was but twenty-three years old, according to Vasari. Yet it is supposed, and, we think, justly, that probably thirty-three was intended.

Pierino da Vinci can, however, scarcely be named as a pupil of Michael Angelo's. Michael Angelo, indeed, had no pupils. He worked alone, or, when he required help, artisans, simple stone-masons, suited

him best; and these he know how to employ so skilfully, that, to their own surprise, they produced works
which could not have been better chiselled by artists.

8.

Vasari makes this latter observation with respect
to the works of the mausoleum, which, having been
distributed among sculptors and stone-masons, were
completed before 1550.

The Church of San Pietro in Vincula, in which
the monument was placed, lies on the height of the
Esquiline Hill, with the façade turned to the west.
It is, therefore, well to visit it towards evening, when
the light of the declining day penetrates strongly
within its few and insignificant windows. Touching
the antique pillars, on which the roof of the old
basilica rests, the light strikes upon the monument
which is placed against the north wall at the end of
the church, and from which the statue of the Moses
projects. The struggle between the yellow evening
glow and the dusky light makes it appear almost
lifelike. It occupies the centre of the monument.
High above it, crossing it like a bridge, is the long
niche which divides the whole into two halves, and
here the marble form of Julius II. lies stretched in
an open sarcophagus, against the head of which he
supports his head. From the back of the niche,
behind him, there gleams out a slender Madonna,
whose child is playing with a small bird; thus representing the soul of man flying back after death
into the hands of Christ. Besides this, the monument has four other figures: in the niches, on both

sides of the recumbent figure of the pope, there are
two sitting figures ; in the niches below, on the right
and left of Moses, there are two standing females, —
Active and Contemplative Life, after Dante's idea
None of the four are the work of Michael Angelo,
neither are the pope and the Madonna. The Moses
alone is his; he chiselled at it for forty years, — forty
years in the wilderness, we might call them ; and,
from its lifeless marble, his spirit beams as mightily
upon us, as does the sunny brightness of ancient
Greece, with its mysterious charm, from the old
statues of Athens. If the spirit of Julius can ever
be affected by earthly things, with such a monument
he would not feel that too little had been done to his
memory.

No one will think so in the present day, though
neither Michael Angelo himself nor the Duke of
Urbino were satisfied with the work, which certainly,
compared with what was at first intended, must have
appeared small and poor, but which still in itself
contains enough to rank it among the most magnificent monuments which ever protected the memory
of a man from oblivion. The more we examine it, the
more majestic does it become. And then, going out
into the open air again, we pass from the quiet within
into the quiet without; and the palm-tree, on the de-
clivity of the hill before us (one of the few that thrive
in Rome), divides the landscape : on the left, the
long, slightly wooded, ruined height of the Palatine ;
on the right, the Capitol, rising with church, convent,
and palace towers, above the confused roofs of the
houses below.

The chance, and perhaps also the ill-will, which removed the mausoleum to this place, instead of St. Peter's Church, which for its sake alone had been erected anew, appears now to have been a beautiful decree of fate. The spot, measured by the ordinary standard, is less honorable; yet none worthier and more honorable could have been found throughout Rome. Least of all within St. Peter's itself, where, from the superabundance of light on all sides, from the vast architecture, and the endless ornament, any single work would appear crowded and out of place. San Pietro in Vincula, however, is the church, the title of which Julius bore as cardinal. It has been untouched within by the modern alterations which most of the old churches have seen. And around it the city still lies tolerably retired, and covered with gardens and ruins, as in the days in which Julius lived. And thus the place remained a kind of sanctuary for his memory; while the interior of St. Peter's Church reminds us neither of him nor of Michael Angelo, nor of any of the other popes, whose long train of monuments follow each other in succession along its walls.

CHAPTER SIXTEENTH.

1547—1564.

Death of Paul III. — Julius III. — Cervini — Caraffa — Intrigues in Rome — War against Tuscany — Cosmo's Proposals — War of Spain against Rome — Flight to Spoleto — Death of Urbino — New Intrigues — Nanni Bigio — Pius IV. — Last Works — Honorary Director of the Academy of Painting in Florence — Benvenuto Cellini — Sickness — Last Will — Death — Transmission of the Coffin to Florence — Funeral — Monument in Santa Croce.

CONCLUSION.

The Progress of Art up to our Own Day — Rubens — Caravaggio — Rembrandt — Winckelmann — Carsten — Cornelius.

THE appointment of head architect of St. Peter's allowed Michael Angelo full power over every thing relating to the building. He had no one to interfere with him. He could employ and dismiss whom he thought advisable; and the energy with which he now came forward, may be regarded as the power which fashioned the fate still awaiting him, and in meeting which his innate firmness never forsook him.

Long before Michael Angelo died, his death was expected. In the feeling of being soon obliged to lose him, they crowded kindly round him, and yielded to his demands. As, however, he lived, and lived, and got far beyond eighty, showing still the old character, many who felt themselves growing older, and who would gladly have stood where he stood, grew impatient.

Under Paul III. these pretensions were suppressed. The storm first appeared under his successor. We may suppose that Michael Angelo spent these years very quietly, and that the confusion of Roman life only penetrated his solitude like a distant murmur. Yet this seclusion was not that of a weak old man, who separates himself so that the small torch of his life may not flare away too rapidly; but joined to the necessity for solitude, which he constantly felt, was the sense that his mind had so little sympathy with other men, that he was compelled to be satisfied with himself.

Had he been in the least of a worldly turn, he might have dwelt in a palace as Raphael had done, and have moved about with a train of artists. He might have let works come forth as his own without touching them, and he might have sold them at a high price. What every sculptor in the present day considers as a matter of course, Michael Angelo had never done. And in Rome there was greater splendor than ever under the Medici. The ambition of the Farnese was to fill the gaps left by the Medici. Artists and scholars found in Cardinal Farnese an intelligent patron. There had never been in Rome so much building, painting, and chiselling. In spite of Jesuits and Inquisition, the old unrestraint apparently prevailed in religious matters, — a fruit of the pope's indifference at heart. He was not able to

sce in religion more than a political means bestowed
especially on the popes for the attainment of political
ends. All the violence with which the cardinal
would have raged against heretics, sprang from this
source. Not a vestige of real piety, or even of pious
emotion, was at work in it. Heretics were a sort of
political criminals of the worst sort. When Busini,
in 1548, writes as a postscript to one of his letters to
Varchi, " Some sound Lutherans have been put in
prison here in Rome," it has the same meaning as
when, three hundred years later, it was written from
St. Petersburg, that many revolutionists were arrested. For the employment of the torture and the
stake at that time in Rome, was as little a newly devised barbarity as the knout in Russia; it was the
ordinary mode in criminal cases, only that in matters
of religion, fire was chosen, because people had been
before either strangled, poisoned, or beheaded.

The renewed severity against the machinations of
the Lutherans in the latter years of Paul III. was the
result of his unsuccessful policy with regard to
the emperor, who, after the simultaneous death of
Francis I., and Henry VIII. of England, saw himself
no longer opposed by any prince of intellectual consequence in Europe, and had Rome so completely in
his hands, that the blinding power of the vast ambition that filled the Farnese could alone prevent
their perceiving it. The pope was obliged to grant
money and auxiliaries for the campaign in Germany.
The avowed cause of the war was the refusal of the
Protestants to attend the council summoned at Trent.
After the defeat of the Landgrave of Hesse, the Far-

nese became uneasy. Never had the common interest of the Lutherans and the pope, with regard to
the emperor, come so plainly to light. Paul did not
wish that Charles should become master of the whole
of Germany, and he suddenly withdrew both troops
and money. Charles, however, without regarding it,
crossed the Elbe, and defeated the Germans. Hasty
negotiations now took place between Rome and
France. The pope aspired after Lombardy for his
son Pierluigi; Genoa and the fleet in the harbor
were to be taken from the emperor at a blow. The
conspiracy, however, failed, and Pierluigi lost his
life. The emperor was satisfied with sharply observing the pope. Paul had called the council in Bologna; Charles, on the other hand, had concluded an
agreement with the Germans, by which they received
a comfortable position as his subjects. He saw that
it was impossible to bring back by force the old state
of things; he therefore accepted the position of
affairs generally, and only claimed for himself a
succession of advantages which were more incon-
venient than oppressive to the Lutherans.

That, under these circumstances, there should
have been violent proceedings in Italy against the
Lutherans, was natural. Upon the matter of attend-
ing the council, which had shortly before been a
thing of compulsion, the Catholics were now the
first to withdraw. They could not discuss religious
affairs with heretics. In Germany the vehemence
of the theologians against Rome increased. Luther
was dead. Vergerio, now a German college tutor,
wrote with Italian vehemence against the state of

things from which he had freed himself, and with which he was thoroughly acquainted : with such ardor did he speak, that his writings, which, written in Italian, were smuggled into Italy, remind us of Luther. It was now necessary for Rome to employ a keener and greater precaution ; and they began to hew down where before they had only struck superficially.*

Michael Angelo had nothing to do with the Lutherans ; nothing therefore that happened to them affected him. But the general uneasy state of things touched him in other ways. A letter to his nephew,† dated the 22d October, 1547, affords us a glimpse into the state of things under Cosmo, whose first proposals were at that time answered negatively by Michael Angelo. The duke seems not to have taken these excuses well. He had, not merely in Florence, but throughout Italy, spies, whose duty it was to watch his subjects in foreign countries. And thus Leonardo was at that time obliged to warn his uncle of bad company.

"I am glad, Leonardo," replies Michael Angelo, "that you have reminded me of the laws of banishment; for however cautious I have been up to the present time in speaking with the exiles, and in having intercourse with them, I shall in future be still more on my guard. With regard to my having lain ill in the Strozzi's house (this matter, that had happened three years ago, was therefore now brought forward against him), I was not in their house, but in the dwelling of Luigi del Riccio, my intimate friend: for, since the death of Bartolomeo Angelini, no man had

* See Appendix, Note LXXV. † *Ibid.* Note LXXVI.

better or more faithfully cared for my affairs; and after his death, as all Rome can testify, I have had nothing more to do with the house. How I live here, every one knows, I am always alone and solitary, speaking with no one, and least of all with Florentines. When I am, indeed, greeted in the street, I return a friendly bow, and go my way; but, if I knew who the exiles referred to are, I would not even give this sign of recognition. In future I will be on my guard, especially as I have so many other things in my mind that might render my intercourse with them dangerous."

This letter was indeed written that it might be read publicly in Florence. Michael Angelo knew well in whose house he had been ill, and what message he had sent to the King of France through Strozzi. When Ruberto Strozzi was in Rome, in the spring of 1546, it would have been a wonder if he had not inquired after Michael Angelo. The Strozzi always remained in connection with Rome, and with the Florentines residing there. Through them, in later years, the order for the bronze equestrian statue for Henry II. of France had been settled. Ruberto came himself to consult with Michael Angelo about it, upon which the work was consigned to Daniele da Volterra, who also cast the horse for it; the last work of importance of this kind entered upon under Michael Angelo's direction. In Florence, however, such connections had to be denied, because they might have been injurious to the family. How much more tolerable must life have been in Rome, where the danger of losing life and liberty was removed by the manifold protection of those in power; while in Florence, one single inflexible tyrant kept his net outspread, and let none go forth again who had once fallen into its meshes.

2.

In the autumn of 1549, Paul III. died.

Michael Angelo had had a severe illness in the spring. He suffered from the stone. He lay groaning all night, and could get no sleep. The physicians held out hope to him; but he brought forward, on the other hand, his age and his harrowing sorrows, and believed that his end was approaching. The baths of Viterbo were ordered for him, he writes; * but it was in March, and they could not be visited before the beginning of May. Time might perhaps bring alleviation. Leonardo, he says, must beg Francesca to pray for him. For the rest, he adds, with regard to his condition physically, he was just as he had been for thirty years past. The illness owed its origin to his not having taken care of himself, and his having regarded his life too little. If it went worse with him, he would send him word, that he might come and receive his last directions; but without such a summons he was not to come.

At length, in the summer, the illness relaxed a little. He drank some waters brought forty miles from Rome, which did him good; he was obliged to have all his food cooked with them, and to change his entire mode of life.† It seems that only a painful uneasiness was left behind, and that he devoted himself to his new office with eagerness. For the

* See Appendix, Note LXXVII. † *Ibid*, Note LXXVIII.

injury caused him by the loss of Piacenza, — the half of his pension being paid from the revenues of the ferry leading from thence across the Po, — the pope had indemnified him by a cancelleria in Rimini, which brought in also six hundred crowns. He stood well with Paul III. When Leonardo sent wine, the pope was glad to receive many bottles of it as a present.* And thus it could not be but that the loss of Farnese should affect him.

"LEONARDO," — he writes to his nephew in November, 1549, — "It is true, the death of the pope has done me much harm, and has been a great loss to me; for I stood well with His Holiness, and hoped to do better. God has so willed it, and we must submit to his will. The pope had a beautiful death; he was in possession of his senses up to the last: may God have mercy on his soul! I have nothing further to write about it. With you, I believe, all is going on well. As regards my state of health, my malady goes on as well as can be; and, when I look at other people of my age, I dare not complain of my lot. We are expecting the new pope from hour to hour. God knows what Christendom needs." †

Farnese was more than eighty years old. His last illness arose from the rage with which the conduct of his family filled him: behind his back they had entered into negotiations with the emperor respecting the recovery of Parma and Piacenza.

Whole systems seemed personified in the men who, at that time, might arrive at the highest dignity.

* See Appendix, Note LXXIX. † Ibid., Note LXXX.

All eyes were directed to Cardinal Pole. The emperor, who desired a mild and placable nature, was on his side. Contarini would have stood in Pole's place, had he still lived. Pole was still young, and would have perhaps possessed sufficient pliability to accommodate himself to both sides. He was favored also by Cardinal Farnese, who had quite gone over to the emperor, from the conviction that the interests of his family were thus most surely promoted. Caraffa, however, came forward against Pole, and called him a Lutheran. Still he would have been elected, in spite of every thing, had he not been abandoned at the last moment by the only voice upon which the election depended, and which had been already promised.

Opposed to Pole and the emperor and Farnese, stood the French party, led by the Cardinals Salviati and Ridolfi; behind whom Catherine dei Medici and the Strozzi were at work. It might be supposed what would happen, if one of these two, who considered themselves as the most genuine heirs of the old Lorenzo Medici, were to ascend the papal chair. French troops under the Strozzi would at once unite with the papal, and march against Tuscany. What for a time placed an obstacle in the way of both Salviati and Ridolfi was, that each of them desired to be pope. Ridolfi, on the point of being elected, was taken ill. On his recovery, he appeared again in the conclave; he suddenly broke down there. The opinion was, that poison had been the last means employed by the Farnese to rid themselves of this man.

Both elections would have been of the utmost importance to Michael Angelo, as he was on good terms with Pole as well as with Ridolfi, and each would have acted in a different manner in accordance with his wishes. Nevertheless, the man who was at length elevated to the papal dignity, Cardinal del Monte, upon whom they agreed because there was least to urge against him, could be scarcely less favorable to Michael Angelo. He was a member of Tolomei's academy, where Vitruvius was studied, and he loved art and artists. Michael Angelo was treated by him with a reverence which exceeded all the kindness that even Paul III. had shown him, and the most favorable position was given him during the few years of the new Government.

In political things, Monte, as was expected, did nothing. Vergerio spoke of him, in allusion to his name, as "this immovable mass which is a burden to Christendom." Julius III. — as the new pope styled himself — allowed Lutherans to be Lutherans, and endeavored before every thing to elevate his family. A youth of seventeen, whom a beggar-woman had borne to him at Bologna, and whom he loved madly, was made a cardinal; and a splendid villa was begun to be built on Monte Mario, which from henceforth, with good eating and drinking, engaged all the pope's interest, and made him a god in the opinion of the artists. Painters, sculptors, architects, had abundance to do. Michael Angelo was required everywhere. Ammanati, Della Porta, and Vasari, found themselves most in favor. Michael Angelo himself undertook no commission; yet, from his design, a flight of steps was built for the Belvedere, instead of the old ones which Bramante had erected. He drew also the plan for a fountain which Julius intended to have erected in the same place, — a Moses striking the rock. The pope, however, did not like it, because it would have required too much time. At last he designed the façade of a palace for Julius, which, however, also was never executed. The pope had him sit down by his side when he desired an audience. That the authority for continuing the building of St. Peter's was confirmed, needs scarcely be said.

With respect to this work, a new storm now burst over Michael Angelo. Under San Gallo, the building had been a source of wealth to many who were either dismissed or were cut short in their wages by Michael Angelo, who was parsimony itself. He could afford to appear all the more regardless here, as he himself accepted not the slightest pay. Paul III. once wished to urge upon him a sum of money, which he, however, immediately returned. Michael Angelo was certainly plain-spoken here.

"You know" — thus begins a letter of his respecting the building * — "you know that I have told Balduccio, he is not to furnish any thing but the best cement. He has brought some of bad quality, and without a doubt he must take it back. It is more than probable that there was an understanding between him and those who had to receive the cement. He favored those whom I have dismissed from the building, from similar circumstances. He, however, who receives the necessary materials of a bad

* See Appendix, Note LXXXI.

quality, and such as I have forbidden to be received, makes those his friends whom I have made my foes. A new conspiracy seems again preparing; and justice is to be evaded with fees, promises, and gifts. I, however, by virtue of the power bestowed on me by the pope, request you to receive nothing for the building which is not good and suitable. Even if it were to come down from heaven, it shall not be done. It shall not appear as if I took part in these machinations.

"Your MICHAEL ANGELO."

This was distinct. The Cardinals Salviati and Cervini, to whom the care of the building had especially been consigned, had allowed themselves to be gained over by San Gallo's old party, and induced Julius III. to call a council before which Michael Angelo should defend himself. All those who had hitherto been engaged in St. Peter's Church were to meet together, and to give evidence that the building had been destroyed by Michael Angelo's new plan. The gentlemen had a number of complaints. Immense sums had been expended without their having been told wherefore; nothing had been communicated to them of the manner in which the building was to be carried on; they were completely useless; Michael Angelo treated them as if the matter did not concern them at all; he pulled down, so that it was a sorrow to all who saw it. This was what they expressed in a written document. Yet their criticism was not satisfied with such general statements. The special point in question was the transverse arches, stretching right and left from the centre of the church, where the dome was to be raised, and each of which terminated in three chapels. Michael Angelo's adversaries asserted that by this arrangement too little light reached the interior; a fact which even the pope confidentially communicated to him. He replied, that he wished those with whom the reproof originated to answer at the spot. The cardinals now came forward, and Cervini declared that it was he who had made the assertion. "Monsignore," replied Michael Angelo, "I intend placing three other windows above those already there." — "You never gave a hint of that," answered the cardinal. To which Michael Angelo rejoined, "Nor was I bound to do so; nor will I bind myself to give your lordship, or any one else, information of my intentions. Your office is to furnish money, and to take care that it is not stolen. As regards the building plan, that concerns me alone." And then, turning to the pope, "Holy Father," he said, "you know what I get for my money, and that, if my work does not tend to the saving of my soul, I shall have expended time and trouble in vain upon it." Julius placed his hand on his shoulder. "Your eternal and temporal welfare," he said, "shall not suffer from it. There is no fear of that." The conference ended; and Michael Angelo had rest from his adversaries, so long as Julius III. lived.

3.

Instead of this, the building of the church was interfered with by external affairs: the war which the Strozzi wished to wage against Cosmo was at length brought about, and for the last time blood was shed in Tuscany for the freedom of Florence.

In the year 1552, the German Protestants had compensated for the injury they had received five years before at the hands of the emperor. Charles was now the yielding party, who was obliged to agree to conventions. Encouragement and support had reached the Germans from France; and, after things in the North had taken such a favorable turn, the same good fortune was now to be attempted in the South. French troops landed in Tuscany; and the contest began, upon which the old liberty party still placed their hopes.

It does not appear to me, that Michael Angelo took part in the old ideas. He was too old, and knew the motives too well which served as the incentive. But when we hear that a Soderini declared himself in Rome for Pietro Strozzi, when the latter appeared there; that Bindo Altoviti, a rich man, head of the Florentine community in Rome, and an intimate friend of Michael Angelo's,[*] did the same; that Asdrubale dei Medici, a natural son of Ippolito's, appeared; and that with him sixty Florentine noblemen, all exiles, young and old, arrived in Rome on the tidings of the great undertaking, and awaited with enthusiasm the contest in which they hoped to free their country, — when we hear all this, it is almost impossible to suppose that Michael Angelo's heart was not touched by the sight of these preparations, and by the thought of the possible issue of the war. More he could not do, now that

* See Appendix. Note LXXXII.

he saw death so soon before him, and no earthly future any longer in view. But that he was yet capable of feeling in his own breast the welfare and woe of the world, is evidenced by his reply to Vasari's letter, when the latter congratulated him on the birth of a great-nephew.

Vasari, in the first edition of his Biography, finds fault with Michael Angelo for never having his relatives with him. From an early period, as his letters testify, he held himself from them as much as possible, — first from his brothers, and then from his nephews. It may have been because he wished to devote himself to his work without interruption. How thoroughly, however, he did for his family in other ways all that lay in his power, is evidenced by his letters to Leonardo, from which it appears that he sent considerable sums of money to Florence for the enlargement of the Buonarroti estate. He wished to place his nephew in as brilliant a position as possible, so that he might make a good marriage, to the honor of his family. He unceasingly alludes to this affair, which, however, only came to a satisfactory conclusion in the year 1553. And when his nephew at last communicated to him that he had gained his object, the sympathy with which Michael Angelo replies, shows the love which he cherished towards his own belongings, and his desire to make it evident to them.

" LEONARDO," — he writes, — " From your last letter, I see that you have brought your wife home, and that you are happy, and that she wishes to be remembered to me,

and that you have arranged nothing yet about the dowry.
As regards your happiness, it fills me with the greatest
joy, and I feel that we cannot sufficiently thank God for it,
as far as we men are able to do so.   With regard to the
settlement of the dowry, let it rest as it is, and keep your
eyes open; for, in such money matters, quarrels are likely
to arise.   I know not how things are; but it seems to me,
that you would have done well to have arranged every
thing before the wedding.   With respect to your wife's
remembrances, remember me to her back again, and say
all the love and kindness to her you can in my name; for
you will do this better by word of mouth than I should in
writing.   My wish is, that she should not be the wife of
my nephew for nought.   I have been able to give her no
proof of this at present; but I expect soon to do so.   They
tell me that a beautiful and valuable pearl ornament would
please her well.   I have already looked for such a thing
at a goldsmith's, a friend of Urbino's; and I hope to get it.
But say nothing to her about it; and, if you think of any
thing else, let me know.   With this I will conclude.
Live prudently, and take care of yourself, and do not
forget that there are more widows than widowers in the
world.   The 20th May, 1553.

"MICHAELANGELO BUONARROTI."

Soon after this, he sent rings, and promises other
things acceptable to Cassandra, — for such was the
name of Leonardo's wife, — to whom at the same
time he sends his thanks for shirts which she had
given him; and, in March, 1554, he expresses his
hearty satisfaction to Leonardo that the birth of a
child was expected.

His handwriting here appears unsteady for the
first time.   He was eighty years of age.   It is only

a few lines that he sends. Writing fatigues him.*
His wish is, he says, that, if it be a boy, he should
receive the name of Buonarroto, as that of his grandfather, a name which had now been three hundred
years in the family. The baby appeared at last.
"Leonardo," — writes Michael Angelo, — "You tell
me that Cassandra has given birth to a beautiful
son; that she is going on well; and that you will
name him Buonarroto. All these things fill me with
the greatest joy (*grandissima allegrezza*). Thank
God! may he grant that the child may thrive, so
that he may do us honor, and maintain the family
aright! Give Cassandra my thanks, and remember
me to her." †

These were just the darkest times for Tuscany.
In the midst of them, Leonardo arranged a magnificent christening. A splendid train of noble Florentine ladies conveyed the child to the Church of
San Giovanni. Vasari wrote to Michael Angelo
about it. This was, however, going too far for him.
He could not conceive, he replied, that such a noise
should now be made at the birth of a child. A man
ought not to give way to joy when the whole world
was in tears (*l'huomo, non dee ridere quando tutto
il mondo piange*). Perhaps in the reproach which
he thus expresses, a far more serious thought lay
concealed. He saw Tuscany convulsed by the saddest events, and, in spite of this, unconcerned joy
in his nephew's house at the birth of a son. He
meant to say, that the times were at hand in which
the fate of the country was no longer that which

* See Appendix, Note LXXXIII.   † *Ibid*, Note LXXXIV.

raised or depressed her citizens; that an indifferent generation was living, no longer capable of feeling that patriotic transport and despair, which would formerly, under such circumstances, have agitated the breast of a Florentine. In earlier times, in war, the liberty and the honor of every citizen was at stake. Now, only the advantage of the dynasty is involved. There is no more hopeless spectacle than to see such sentiments arising in the course of centuries; there is nothing more despicable than the outward peace and order which begins with it. All individual and hearty interest in the glory of the country is destroyed; indeed it is almost considered as criminal. Men have to suffer, to be silent, and to obey. They are not to concern themselves about things they do not understand. Such are the people who now appear; who, beside themselves at the heavenly presence of His Excellency the duke, implore permission to be allowed to kiss his sacred hands. So says even Vasari; and yet he is a character and an independent man, compared with those who were the servants of the duke a hundred years later.

The revolt of Siena against the Spanish garrison began the war. Cosmo ought to have come to the help of the Spaniards, his allies; but matters were so unfavorable for the emperor at that time, that he remained neutral. Siena now entered under the protection of the French. Cosmo still stood well with France, until, after some time, owing to a change of circumstances, it seemed fitting to bring the Spaniards by force back again into Siena. Piero Strozzi then went to Siena; he arrived on the 1st

January, 1554, and began to fortify the city. Still, war was not yet declared. Cosmo considered it advantageous to strike the first blow.

For four days, Florence was kept shut up, so that no tidings might reach Siena. For it seems that the quiet adherents of liberty began to rage in secret. Even in San Marco, the monks still clung to the liberty prophesied by Savonarola; and they had their believers among the citizens.

During these four days, the attack of Siena was prepared: ten thousand men were assembled, and, marching past Florence by night, they moved forward unobserved; and while the Sienese were celebrating a festival, and Strozzi was accidentally absent, the scaling-ladders were placed. The plot, however, failed. Still the war was begun; the devastation of the land commenced; and, on Good Friday, the tidings of the first defeat of the ducal troops arrived in Florence. A number of dead, a still greater number of prisoners, and ten standards, were lost by Cosmo's troops in this encounter. At the same time, France levied three thousand Swiss, who were to invade the land from the north; and Lioni Strozzi, the second brother, appeared as high admiral with the French fleet on the coasts of Tuscany.

With Lioni's death, however, which was occasioned by an unhappy shot, the fortune began to turn. After long marchings hither and thither, a decisive battle took place on the 2d August, in which four thousand men were killed, and almost all the Florentine exiles engaged in the contest were taken prisoners by the ducal troops. All, however, — and this is a remarkable sign,—were set free again by the soldiers, and only seven were brought to Florence and beheaded. The Florentines in Rome, who had declared for Strozzi, were declared rebels.

A short time after these events, Michael Angelo received fresh offers to return to Florence. The hope of his coming this time rested on the fact, that the money for the building of St. Peter's began to fail. In the four years, from 1547 to 1551, we find a hundred and twenty-one thousand ducats issued for it; in the four following, only half that sum. The war was in nowise at an end. Strozzi was again in Siena with new forces; the French threatened from Piedmont: there was little prospect for Michael Angelo in Rome, that, at such a time, the building would be more vigorously taken up. Still he preferred remaining at his post; and how thoroughly he was resolved, under any circumstances, not to go away, was evidenced in March, 1555, when Julius III. died, and Cardinal Cervini was elected pope in his stead,—the same man with whom he had come into such hard contest, and with whose elevation the attacks of the San-Gallo party would be revived.

Cosmo at once repeated his request. He promised Michael Angelo that he should be troubled with no work in Florence. His presence alone was desired, and that he now and then should give an opinion upon the duke's undertakings. The zeal with which Vasari and Tribolo seconded these proposals, proceeded, it seems, also from the hope of at length triumphing over Bandinelli, whose influence at court was notorious. Bandinelli managed in the old manner,—insulted Michael Angelo, exerted himself constantly to produce works which should place his in the shade, and was not to be suppressed, though he had all the world against him, and, most of all, Benvenuto Cellini, who, whenever Michael Angelo was mentioned, interfered on behalf of his master.

Michael Angelo might perhaps have been attracted this time, had the new pope ruled longer than three weeks, half of which time he was ill. There were special causes for Michael Angelo's remaining in Rome under Cervini's successor, and for his continuing to remain there.

Caraffa now ascended the papal chair. The fanatical old man with the death's-head face, after having labored fifty years for the papal religion, at length obtained possession of the power which no longer imposed restraints upon his will. His predecessor had issued orders for the reform of morals: with fearful severity, these endeavors were now taken up by the new octogenarian ruler; and that the day of his accession to power might be a memorable one to Michael Angelo, he deprived him at once of his pension of twelve hundred crowns. He was to be indemnified for this with one hundred crowns monthly from the funds for the building of St. Peter's: but he persisted in receiving nothing from this quarter; he sent the money back when it was brought to his house, and consequently lost it. Yet all this is said to have taken place behind the pope's back.* For this was the demoniacal trait of Paul IV.'s charac-

* See Appendix, Note LXXXV.

ter, peculiar to him, as it is to all energetic natures
living only in idea, — that he endeavored to carry
out his designs by force, and, at the same time, was
without the slightest knowledge of the men whom
he employed, and who formed his staff and suite.
Michael Angelo was too proud to speak to the pope
of money. He might have done so; for Paul sent
for him, and expressed in the most gracious manner
his hope of seeing the building of the church rapidly
advanced. At the same time, one of the most talented intriguers, Piero Ligorio, a Neapolitan, was
appointed architect of the Vatican; and, in connection with San Gallo's party, he began immediately
to plot against Michael Angelo.

The latter was eighty-one years old when these
new means were applied for removing him from his
office. The report was spread abroad that he had
become childish; that it was necessary to displace
him; that he was too old and weak. But, instead
of closing with the Florentine offers, which grew
more and more honorable and urgent, while his footing in Rome became more and more insecure, he
stood firmly at his post so long as a spark of power
was left in his body.

4.

Paul IV. is one of the characters who stand forth
as monstrous in history. The whole extent of the
horrors perpetrated by Rome, as a remedy for heresy,
are associated with the name of Caraffa. Few
dates are required to show the course adopted. Any
connection with heretics, even accidental meeting

with them, was punished by a fine of five hundred ducats the first time, and by death in case of repetition. A merely lengthened conversation with such as were summoned before justice for any cause in matters of heresy, met with a fine, the first time, of two hundred and fifty ducats, then exile, and then death. It was thus in 1558. Three years later it was enacted that all letters, packets, and luggage should be opened and searched on behalf of the Inquisition. Soon after, the strictest measures of surveillance were instituted over merchants travelling abroad. In 1566, death awaited any in communication with Geneva. In 1568, all foreigners were watched. The number of holy wafers dispensed had to be reported to the duke in Florence. Such was the progress of things. Julius III. was the last pope in the old spirit. With him the age of renaissance terminated, and the century of revival was followed by that of decline.

Still, I think, injustice has been done to Caraffa. He was not cruel by nature: he believed in the good in men, and showed himself kindly where he entertained no suspicion. Moreover, just as he ruled the age, he was nevertheless ruled by it. It is possible that Pole and Morone, who were candidates with him in the election, would have pursued in general no other course. A proof of this is Pole's conduct in England, whither he went as legate, and where he instituted proceedings against the deceased wife of an Italian convert, Peter Martyr, who had long ago belonged to his own and Vittoria's society. Even in its state of decay, her body was to experience the torments and ignominy which had been designed for the soul that had left it. In spite of this energy, the cardinal fell into disgrace, and Morone was imprisoned. Caraffa sat there like a skeleton : filled with fire, he would have liked to have burnt up at one blaze every heretic. And, while he thus thought and continued the mortifications which he practised throughout his life, his relatives misused their position in the most brutal manner, under his very eyes. Paul, for a long time, surmised nothing of this ; but, when his eyes were opened, he punished like a madman. And, in the same ideal frenzy, he began the mad war against Philip II., who, as successor to Charles V., had taken possession of Spain, Milan, and Naples, and held Rome so completely fettered, that the military movement, with which he brought the Vatican at length to its senses, is scarcely to be called a campaign.

The pope was deaf to all remonstrances : he felt the unworthy position of Rome with regard to Spain. Upon any condition, it must be broken through : a treaty with France was decided on as usual. The freedom of Florence was once more numbered among the things to be accorded ; the Spanish Cosmo was to be expelled, and the old rights restored to the city.

The Spaniards knew every thing. They warned ; at length they began in earnest. An army under Alba advanced from Naples, and lay around Rome like a great serpent : twice the coil was drawn closer, and was followed by reconciliation, pardon, and hearty understanding. Caraffa becomes almost comi-

cal in the extreme arrogance he exhibited: he would
negotiate with no diplomatist.   He, the simple,
ascetic man, had begun to display immense splendor
as pope, for the sake of the Church alone.   He was
the first prince of the world; his house was to be
ordered accordingly.   Art was indifferent to him;
but St. Peter's Church was to advance rapidly.   He
therefore awarded his favor to Michael Angelo, and
did more for the building than any former pope.

When Rome, too, was placed in a state of defence
against the Spaniards, in aiding which the monks in
their cowls were obliged to carry earth, Michael Angelo's advice was asked; but he had left the city as
the Spaniards approached.   He had just lost Urbino,
his faithful servant, by death, and was in an incon-
solable state of mind.   Had he wished to return to
Florence, the opportunity would have never been
more fitting; but he went into the mountains of
Spoleto, and remained there, until return to Rome
in September became possible.

In the letter in which he tells Vasari that he has
returned, we find for the first time a word about
nature.   It is strange there is not an idea of it hitherto either in letters, conversations, or poems.   As,
when we read Rousseau's confessions, paintings and
statues appear expunged from the series of his experiences; so, when we speak of Michael Angelo,
woods and clouds, seas and mountains, disappear,
and that alone remains which is formed by the mind
of man.   Michael Angelo's solitary journey into the
mountains was the first expedition he made in search
of nature.   " I have had great inconveniences and

expenses," he writes to Vasari, "but great enjoyment also in my visit to the hermits of the mountain : I have left more than half my soul there ; for truly there is no peace but in the woods."

He must now especially have missed this peace ; for the intrigues of Pirro Ligorio had begun, and, by the loss of Urbino, he felt himself more than ever separated from the world. For the older he grew, the more the number dwindled of those whom he had gathered round him in middle age. He had sat day and night by the sick couch of his old servant, to whose widow, as we have seen above, he turned with the most anxious sympathy. The letter which he wrote to Vasari on Urbino's death, is truly desponding. The one hope alone remained to him, of soon meeting his lost friend in another life. He had indeed felt, he says, how Urbino, as he lay dying, had suffered less from the fear of his own death than from the thought of being obliged to leave him behind him thus old and solitary in this false and miserable world, in which nothing now remained for him but ceaseless calamity.

The journey into the mountains had, however, raised him from this sorrow, and had given him new strength against his enemies. He neither flinched nor gave way. The duke again wrote to him in the most affectionate terms, and sent the letter to Rome by his own chamberlain. Michael Angelo remained firm. It would be a disgrace to him, he replied to Vasari, to go away now, when the work had been taken up afresh after having long lain fallow, and now the most important part, which had been preparing for ten years, was to be actually done. Had they worked all along as they had begun to do under Paul III., he might now have ventured to cherish the hope of returning to Florence; but it was impossible. He begged Vasari to thank the duke for such kind letters. He could not answer them himself, his mind was too exhausted, and writing was a hard task to him; but, if he were now to go away, he should be doing nothing but rendering a great favor to some thieves, and causing the destruction of the building, and perhaps its discontinuance for ever.

And in this spirit he answered all subsequent inducements. It would be a sin on his part. He had begun in God's name; he must persevere. It was indeed an alluring thought to lay his weary bones by the side of his father's; but he might not do so. And, as Michael Angelo stood firm, the pope was firm also. His enemies could effect nothing. He asserted that he felt himself too old and feeble to undertake the journey, and to exchange the mild air of Rome, to which he was accustomed, for the keener climate of Florence; and the duke at length left him free to remain in Rome. When Cosmo came to Rome in the last year of Michael Angelo's life, he visited him, made him sit down by him, and showed him reverential respect; while, even previous to this, his son, who had been made a cardinal, had sought out Michael Angelo, and had treated him with similar reverence. Thoughts of politics now passed into the background. All were dead who of old had fought for freedom, —who had indeed only lived to see it; and the new state of things was irrevocable. Michael Angelo

submitted to the honor shown him by the possessors
of the new power. He felt that it did not lie with
Cosmo alone, but that the nature of men was
changed. He had consideration for his family. He
used the due forms of humble courtesy towards
the duke; but what he thought in secret we know
not. The weakness of age had never overcome him;
his wisdom never left him; and he gave constant
expression in some way to his deep feelings. I will
here quote one of his poems, the date of which we
know not, but which might well form a supplement
to that outward obsequiousness, which men like
Vasari reported as a change of mind, because it lay
in their interest to do so:[*]—

> "Not always that which the world holds most dear
> Is that which satisfies the heart's desires;
> For the sweet things for which the world aspires,
> Gall-like and cruel to our hearts appear.
> And often needs it that we passive yield
> To the vain fancies of the foolish crowd,
> Fostering sadness while we laugh aloud,
> And smiling with our tears but half concealed.
> That no strange eye my sorrowing soul may see;
> That no strange ear my whispered hopes may hear, —
> This is the happiness vouchsafed to me.
> Blind to the honor and the praise of men,
> Far happier he, wandering alone and drear,
> Who takes his solitary path again."

> 'Non sempre al mondo e si pregiato, e caro
> Quel che molti contenta,
> Che non sia alcun che senta
> Qualchè lor dolce a se crudo, ed amaro.

---

[*] See Appendix, Note LXXXVI.

Ma spesso el folle volgo, al volgo ignaro
Convien ch' altri consenta,
E mesto rida, dove si ride e gode
E piange allor che più felice siede.
Io del mio duol quest' uno effetto ho caro,
Ch' alcun di fuor non vede
Chi l' alma attrista, e i suoi desir non ode.
Ne temo invidia, o pregio onore, o lode
Del mondo cieco, che rompendo fede
Più giova a chi 'l scarso esserne suole;
E viò per vie men calpestrate, e sole."

It is not necessary that these verses should have been written upon the Duke of Florence; but the sentiments expressed in them are sufficient to refer them to him. Of one who kept so secret what he thought, and who brought himself even to the apparent acknowledgment of the contrary, it may be supposed, that, in a matter which had been the most sacred thing to him all his life, he would rather feign a change of sentiment than allow himself actually to change. And this would have been the case, had Michael Angelo actually resolved to return to Florence, not for the sake of his native city, but because his adversaries in Rome did more and more to make it impossible for him to remain there. For, at that time, old as he was, many years and experiences still lay before him in the future.[*]

5.

In the year 1558, he witnessed the death of Caraffa, and the uproar in Rome, when the head of the statue of the pope on the Capitol was broken off by the furious multitude, kicked liked a ball through

[*] See Appendix, Note LXXXVII.

the streets, and thrown into the Tiber, and the prisons of the Inquisition were stormed and burnt down! Under the following pope, he witnessed new attacks upon himself, to which he now replied by offering to lay down his office.

"I heard yesterday," — he writes on the 16th September, 1560, to Cardinal di Carpi, — "in what manner Your Lordship had expressed yourself as to the building of St. Peter's, — that matters could not go worse with it than they had done. This deeply pained me, in the first place, because Your Lordship was not informed of the true state of things; and then, because I, as becomes my office, cherish the wish beyond any man on earth, that it should all progress well. But as perhaps my self-interest or my old age deceive me, and I may be doing injury to the building, against my will of course, I will, as soon as I am able, request His Holiness for my dismissal: indeed, that there may be no delay, I entreat your lordship to release me immediately from my labor, which, as you know, I have undertaken for seventeen years without any compensation; and what I have executed during this time is evident to all. I repeat, in granting my request you will be rendering me a great favor; and I tender my humble submission to Your Lordship.   MICHAELANGELO BUONARROTI."

The new pope, Pius IV., did not agree to this. On the contrary, the income was repaid to Michael Angelo, which he had lost under Caraffa. In the sense of not living to see the dome completed, he made in his own house an accurate model in clay, — after which, under his direction, the larger one in wood was executed, — which contained every proportion most accurately, and, as the vault of the dome

was begun many years after his death, only required
to be copied on a colossal scale. Pius IV. was well
inclined to Michael Angelo. Under him the arts
were again encouraged. He was a Medici, though
springing from the Milanese family who wrote themselves Medichi, and who only subsequently made
their name similar to that of the Florentine branch.
Michael Angelo designed for him the monument
erected in the Cathedral of Milan to his brother the
Marquis of Marignano, who had commanded Cosmo's
troops in the late war.

But the drapery which Caraffa had had painted
over the figures of the Last Judgment, Pius could
not venture to remove. Paul IV. had at first wished
to destroy the entire picture. The drapery which
was finally decided on, thus appears almost out of
consideration for the great master. When the matter
was suggested to him, — for it seems even that the
task of painting the drapery was offered, as it were,
to himself, — he answered ironically, "That is soon
done. The pope has to put the world in order: it
is but a small trouble as regards pictures, for they
keep still." Daniele da Volterra did the work; and
what was thus accomplished is only the small beginning of subsequent endeavors. Volterra would not
have been with Michael Angelo up to the last, had
this painting of the Last Judgment been undertaken
by him against his will: indeed, he would not have
applied himself to such a task.

Michael Angelo was in his eighty-sixth year when
he wrote that letter to Cardinal di Carpi. The
language he used shows how little right his enemies

had in calling him childish and feeble with age.
The course which the affair took, proves still more
plainly how firm he could appear. The committee
inspecting the building imagined they had found in
one of his arrangements an opportunity for setting
him aside, when, after the death of an architect
whom he was accustomed to send as his representative when prevented from coming himself, he
appointed a young but capable man, Luigi Gaeta,
to this post, which he was to fill till a more suitable
person should be found. The committee dismissed
this Gaeta, without asking Michael Angelo; and
Michael Angelo declared, upon this encroachment
on his rights, that he would visit the building no
more.

This was just what they desired. An architect,
Nanni Bigio by name, had long ago reckoned upon
Michael Angelo's position. He was a flattering,
false man, who had got the ear of the committee,
and had made them see that he was just the man
to be employed. Every thing from henceforth was to
be performed according to their wish, especially in
money affairs.

Nanni Bigio belonged to San Gallo's party. In
earlier years, he had succeeded in obtaining the
building of the bridge of Santa Maria, which had
been assigned to Michael Angelo; and he had produced a work, which, as Michael Angelo rightly prophesied, would be soon carried away by the stream.
Nanni had ventured to write to Cosmo himself, and
to solicit him for his patronage, when Michael An
gelo's post should be next filled up; a request which

the duke had simply declined. He was now produced as the man to whom the direction of the building was to be entrusted temporarily, and every thing was managed in the most crafty manner. Michael Angelo was left completely out of the whole affair. He had declared he would come no more, and he came no more. He had said. it was asserted by one of the cardinals, that he would no longer be burdened with the building of St. Peter's.

Michael Angelo, however, now sent Daniele da Volterra to this prelate. He certainly wished, he said, for a deputy; and Volterra alone was to undertake it. The cardinal expressed himself delighted; but, as if nothing had happened, he had Nanni Bigio, instead of Volterra, installed at the building, which he began to conduct immediately; removing beams, altering scaffolding, and coming forward completely as master. Michael Angelo had hitherto taken the matter easily. When they spoke of it to him, he replied, — " He who contends with the worthless achieves no great victory" (*Chi combatte con d'appochi non vince a nulla*). When matters, however, now became too bad, he bestirred himself. The pope was on the square of the Capitol. Michael Angelo appeared before him, and made so much noise, that His Holiness was obliged to let him come into the palace. He then declared his intention of leaving Rome at once, and going to Florence, where the duke made him the most splendid offers, if some change was not immediately made here. The pope quieted him, and called together the committee, who explained that the building would be ruined under Michael Angelo's direction. Pius, however, instead of taking their word, sent one of his suite to St. Peter's to convince himself how the matter lay. The truth now came to light. Nanni Bigio, who was now upbraided with the ruined bridge, and the unfortunate harbor at Ancona, besides what he had spoiled in St. Peter's, was shamefully dismissed; and a brief was issued by the pope, decreeing that, for the future, Michael Angelo's arrangements should not be departed from in the smallest particular.

He who thus came forward was no dying man. And, about the same time, Michael Angelo sent magnificent plans to Florence for a church to be built for the Florentine community in Rome under the duke's patronage. Not only one did he send, but a whole succession of plans for selection, which, as his hands would no longer do his bidding, he had drawn by a young sculptor, Tiberio Calcagni, the same man who had executed the model of St. Peter's dome, and to whom he had given his last work in marble. At that time also, the model of the government palace at Florence, which Vasari was arranging into a ducal residence, was sent to him, that he might give his opinion; and his advice was asked by the young Cardinal Medici, respecting the bridge Santa Trinità, in the same place. The last thing he did for Rome was the transformation of an immense hall in the Baths of Diocletian into a church, which has, however, subsequently been so altered, that, as it now stands, it no longer corresponds with Michael Angelo's designs.

The reason why they had latterly specially wished

to have him in Florence, was on account of the completion of the Laurentian library and the sacristy, both of which stood unfinished and neglected. He arrranged the building of the flight of steps for the library; the chapel he gave up. It is strange how a feeling of interest arises everywhere for something new. The utmost was done to obtain a new plan of Michael Angelo's. The chapel of St. Lorenzo, however, was left, and no one cared. The clergy had fitted it up with an open fireplace, and dust and ashes lay on the figures. Vasari made a plan for distributing among the young Florentine artists the statues and paintings still lacking for its completion; but nothing came of it. Instead of having it finished, the duke made it a meeting-place for the Academy of the Fine Arts established by him, to the honorary directorship of which he appointed Michael Angelo. This happened a year before his death. Not a single artist of importance is indebted for any thing to this institution, the first director of which was Cosmo himself. When the old Lorenzo, placing Bertoldo at the head of the school of art which was working under his own eyes, had wished to appoint himself its first director, the mere idea had made the Florentines smile. It was now otherwise. The time for titles of honor had arrived, when princes stood as demigods upon whom Heaven had bestowed at their birth, for nought and without effort, all those gifts which even the most extraordinary minds among their subjects were not able to acquire without the intense labor of a life.

One alone in Florence, who, low as he stands in

power by the side of Michael Angelo, appears high in comparison with others, from the originality with which he worked and fashioned his own fate, — one alone, and this was <u>Benvenuto Cellini,</u> — produced works at that time which have an existence of their own second to Michael Angelo's. His Perseus, under the Loggia dei Lanci, obliquely opposite the David at the gate of the palace, is the only statue, perhaps, of that time which is free from Michael Angelo's influence. Cellini was a powerful independent nature, and his Perseus is a splendid work. We need only compare the style in which he has written his life, with Vasari's mode of writing, to feel how far he surpassed the latter. Michael Angelo held him in great esteem. He saw the bust in Rome which Cellini had made of Bindo Altoviti, and he wrote him a flattering letter respecting it. It still stands in the palace belonging to the family, close by the Bridge of St. Angelo; but it was not shown to me. The bust of the duke, however, standing in the Uffici, shows how Cellini executed his work. Strictly adhering to nature in details, — exactly representing her, and yet placing the general impression above detail, — he has produced a masterpiece. <u>He cultivated all the arts except painting.</u> He cut the most beautiful dies for coins; he made ornaments, coats of mail, and sword-blades, and at the same time colossal statues when required; and, if the times demanded that also, he could work as an architect. In the last war against Strozzi, the duke had assigned him one of the gates of Florence, and was satisfied with what he did. And yet it is by comparing such a man with Michael Angelo, that the gulf which separates the two becomes apparent, — Cellini, working away with power and genius, but without plan, with no ardent desire for mental elevation, without an idea of the influence which Dante can exercise on the soul of an artist; while Michael Angelo's works, again to use the words of Vittoria Colonna, stand all together as if only one.

6.

At length the day approached so long expected by Michael Angelo, even in times when he had never dreamt that it was so far distant. "The course of my years is finished," begins one of his sonnets, which he wrote when many years still lay before him. His poems show how unceasingly the thought of death engaged him. For the great part they belong to this latter period. Their purport betrays it; often, also, the old, large handwriting in which they are still to be read in the Vatican manuscripts, the great number of a religious and philosophical tendency, and their omission from the published edition of the poems. I would insert many of them, if a translation were possible. All attempts, however, end in nothing but imitations, which lose the peculiar force of Michael Angelo's style. The sorrow which he expresses over past days, and his doubt respecting the future, often rises to despair: —

"The fables of the world have robbed my soul
Of moments given for the things of God;
And, gladly following on sin's evil road,
I missed the step that should have been my goal."

Thus begins the sonnet, "Le favole del mondo m' hanno tolto — il tempo dato a contemplar Iddio." It was not possible to preserve the force of these words in a foreign language.

In the letter in which he congratulates Leonardo on the birth of a son, there is an unfinished sonnet, in which he says that neither painting nor working in marble can now calm his thoughts; and the Vatican manuscripts contain many other verses, in which the things of this world are mentioned with contempt and loathing, and thoughts on God and immortality are marked as the only thing worthy of the soul. It is astonishing to see the tender feeling with which he, who had done every thing for others alone, and who throughout his life had never claimed the smallest grain of honor that did not belong to him, accuses himself of the passion with which he clung to earthly things. All is lost, he exclaims; he feels it. He had done nothing for his soul; nothing has given him a right to heaven but his ardent longing to tear himself away from self, and he knows that he is too weak to do this alone. And yet, much as this anxiety for the world to come corresponded with the spirit of Christianity, it failed to lead Michael Angelo even here to Roman Catholicism. He presents himself alone before Heaven, and seeks to find in his own thoughts that consolation which was perhaps vouchsafed to him when he gave vent to his feeling in these true and beautiful words : —

> "Borne to the utmost brink of life's dark sea,
> Too late thy joys I understand, O earth!
> How thou dost promise peace which cannot be,
> And that repose which ever dies at birth.

The retrospect of life through many a day,
Now to its close attained by Heaven's decree,
Brings forth from memory, in sad array,
Only old errors, fain forgot by me, —
Errors which e'en, if long life's erring day,
To soul-destruction would have led my way.
For this I know, — the greatest bliss on high
Belongs to him called earliest to die."

"Condotto da molti anni all' ultime ore
  Tardi conosco, O mondo, I tuoi diletti;
  La pace, che non hai, altrui prometti,
  E quel riposo che anzi al nascer muore:
    La vergogna, e 'l timore
  Degli anni, che or prescrive
  Il ciel, non mi rinnuova
  Che 'l vecchie e dolce errore,
  Nel qual, che troppo vive,
  L' anima ancide, e nulla all' corpo giova.
  Il dico, e so per pruova
  Di me, che 'n ciel quel sol 'ha miglior sorte
  Che ebbe al suo parto piu pressa la morte." *

The idea expressed by Sophocles also, in his last tragedy, μὴ φῦναι τον ἅπαντα νικᾷ λόγον, of birth being yet to come, surpasses all wisdom. In both men, such words evidence that they had indeed reached the bounds of human life. Their day's work was finished. Their thoughts refused the task of applying themselves longer to earthly things. So close before their view stood the vast future which awaited them, that the greatest thing earth could afford them appeared small; and, looking back, the whole labor of life seemed only a protracted period filled with transitory works, pointing to that which now, as the sole thing

* See Appendix, Note LXXXVIII.

of importance, inspired them with impatience to reach it. And yet so strong was Michael Angelo's vital power, and natural love for those to whose circle he still belonged, that such thoughts only took hold of him at times; and, so long as his hands could move, he worked on to carry out his old plans.

In the beginning of 1564, symptoms appeared which made a speedy end probable. It was extreme old age which terminated Michael Angelo's life. He began visibly to fail, and was attacked by a lingering fever, the issue of which was foreseen. Daniele da Volterra and Tommaso Cavalieri were with him; Federigo Donati was the name of the physician who attended him. Da Volterra sent Leonardo Buonarroto uninterrupted tidings. At Easter, the latter intended to come to Rome under any circumstances; but, in February, Daniele wrote to him suddenly that he must hurry, for the end was approaching. And now death came so speedily, that Leonardo did not find his great-uncle alive. On the 18th February, 1564, between three and four o'clock, in the afternoon, Michael Angelo died, in the ninetieth year of his age. Daniele da Volterra and Cavalieri were with him. To them and to the physicians, he then, for the first time, expressed his last will,—My soul I resign to God, my body to the earth, and my worldly possessions to my relations. And last of all came the wish, that his body should be carried to Florence, and buried there. We fancy the earth must pause a moment in its course, when such a power is snatched away from it. Happy those whose fate in life allows them to have once felt this.

For great as is the loss which they suffer when such a heart suddenly ceases to beat, and the eyes are closed which had penetrated and surveyed every thing, the remembrance of what the man was, gives them for ever a higher view of things. Those who knew Goethe, form, even at the present day, in Germany, a sort of invisible church. Those who had seen Michael Angelo, had it been only the most cursory meeting which brought them in contact with him, must have done so at that time.

We possess the report made by one of the physicians to the Duke of Florence.

"This evening," — he says, — "the distinguished Messer Michael Angelo Buonarroti, a perfect prodigy of nature, departed to a better life; and as I attended him during his last illness, with the other physicians, I heard him express the wish that his body should be taken to Florence. Moreover, as none of his relatives were present, and as he died without a will, I venture to inform Your Excellency of this, as you have so highly valued his rare virtues; so that the wish of the deceased may be carried out, and that his noble native city may acquire greater honor by containing the bones of the greatest man the world has ever produced.

"GHERARDO FIDELISSIMI of Pistoja,

"Doctor of Medicine by Your Excellency's favor and liberality.

Rome, 18th February, 1564."

Michael Angelo had intended before his death to convey his personal property to Florence, where Leonardo was to purchase a house to receive them. This had not been done. The Florentine ambassador in Rome had been charged by the duke, in case of

Michael Angelo's death, to have every thing sealed up at once, so that nothing might be lost, as in such cases was not unusual. We have, too, the report of the ambassador. There was nothing to be found beyond some trifling household furniture and some marble works. Michael Angelo had burnt his drawings. A sealed chest was opened in the presence of Da Volterra and Cavalieri, and a sum of eight thousand crowns found in it. The ambassador ordered at once two of the statues to be packed, and sent to Florence. The trifles which had been found in the atelier were afterwards conveyed there also: all sorts of antique figures of terra-cotta and such like, which are now in the house of the family, where his sword also, and the stick with which he walked, are preserved as touching remains, not to mention his papers, the fate of which is not yet decided.

When Leonardo arrived, the third day after the death, the funeral ceremonies in Rome were already over, having taken place in the Church of San Apostoli. All the Florentines, and all persons in the city of intellectual importance, had attended. It was now necessary to convey the mortal remains to Florence. Opposition was feared from the Romans. It was asserted, that Michael Angelo's last wish to be buried in his native city was not true. They went secretly to work. The coffin was conveyed as merchandise out of the gates.

On the 11th March, it arrived at Florence. After thirty years of voluntary exile, Michael Angelo returned, when dead, to his native city. Only a few knew that it was he who entered the gate in that covered coffin. The duke seems to have given orders that there should be silence. Untouched as it arrived, the coffin was carried to the Church of San Piero Maggiore, and deposited there.

The next day was Sunday. Towards evening the artists assembled in the church. A black velvet covering, embroidered with gold, lay over the body; and a gold crucifix was placed upon it. All formed a close circle round it; torches were lighted, which were carried by the older artists, while the younger took the bier on their shoulders, and so proceeded to Santa Croce, where Michael Angelo was to be interred.

All this was done privately. The artists had assembled one by one in San Piero Maggiore. But the rumor spread through Florence, that the body had arrived. When the procession left the church, a great dark multitude met it, and marched quietly with it through the streets to Santa Croce.

Here in the sacristy the coffin was opened for the first time. The people had forced their way into the church. There he lay; and, in spite of three weeks having elapsed since his death, he seemed unchanged, and bore no symptom of decay; the features undisfigured, as if he had just died.

They carried him from the sacristy to the church, to the place where he was to be interred. But the crowds who now streamed in were so great, that it was impossible to close the tomb. Each wished to see him once more. Had it not been night, says Vasari, they must have let it remain open. But, as it had all been prepared secretly, and only those

came who had heard of it suddenly, the people at
last dispersed.

What interest had the people in Michael Angelo?
They were Florentines no longer, who understood
why he had gone away, and would not return.
The anxiety of the duke, lest the corpse of the great
man might call forth a political commotion, was
needless. They gazed at him, secretly lamenting,
perhaps, the weakness and the loss of liberty with
which they had fallen; like a people looking into
the tomb of an old emperor, under whom all was
long ago great and glorious, and who scarcely feel,
in that decayed body, a remembrance of the times
in which that hand had wielded a sword. They
stand before him; they contemplate him; a feeling
passes through their minds, which as quickly dis-
appears; and they go home, and pursue their daily
duties.

The preparations made by the artists for the
funeral ceremonies were only ended in July. Vasari describes them in an extensive report: he relates, in detail, how the Church of San Lorenzo was
decorated; what emblems and inscriptions were
employed; and by what artists every single thing
was executed. Varchi delivered the funeral oration. Benvenuto Cellini, the only man who at that
time understood Michael Angelo in Florence, was
not present. Various things must have fallen in
his way. In the reports of the academy, it is stated
that he did not wish it. Vasari says he was astonished at his absence; but, in another place, that
he was ill. Leonardo Buonarroti had a monument

erected in Santa Croce, for which the duke gave the marble: Dante's, Alfieri's, and Macchiavelli's monuments are in the same church. Michael Angelo's house, too, in the Ghibelline street, is still standing. Not unchanged; for, with our memory filled with him, we adorn it with paintings and with the works from his own hand, which are now in the possession of his family.

The duke expressed his intention of having a monument erected to Michael Angelo in Santa Maria del Fiore; but he did not do it. Among the statues of great Florentines, which now adorn the court of the Uffici, his also stands, but in a row with others, and without prominence.

All Italians feel that he occupies the third place by the side of Dante and Raphael, and forms with them a triumvirate of the greatest men produced by their country, — a poet, a painter, and one who was great in all arts. Who would place a general or a statesman by their side as equal to them? It is art alone which marks the prime of nations.

CONCLUSION.

MICHAEL ANGELO had lived to see, in the last year of his life, the issue of the Tridentine Council, which separated after having accomplished its task of satisfying Catholic Christendom in its demand for a reform, and making some new statutes. It lay in the nature of things that this assembly — whose original object was, by the common deliberations of Catholics and Lutherans, to find a confession of faith embracing the whole world — should, as its final result, produce a series of propositions, by which the power of the Romish Church, and of the clergy subject to it, was elevated into a system of police, working with boundless authority. The education of youth was now given completely into the hands of the clergy; and they exercised such a thorough control over riper minds, whether expressing their thoughts by letter or in print, or only in conversation, that we should not have been astonished if the history of the second half of the sixteenth century, and that of the seventeenth, exhibited a complete pause in mental activity, except that the human mind possesses an ungovernable sagacity for finding its way to light and truth through a rocky soil. The same spirit of torpidity appeared all the more speedily in the Protestant lands; and while the sphere in this case was more limited, and the relations smaller, the spectacle presented is still more miserable.

But the Church could have done nothing without the good-will of the princes, who now saw in religion one of the effective means for maintaining their authority over nations. We hear henceforth little more of hostility between temporal rulers and the clergy. A cordial understanding took the place of the old disputes. What had occurred in Florence may be regarded as a model for what was going on now throughout Europe: the freedom of the citizens was everywhere disappearing, that exercised by the cities as well as by the nobles; and, instead of constitutions which allowed princes to be considered only as ideal heads of the State, — their executive power being linked closely with legal conditions, — there were absolute monarchies recognizing two agents alone: a prince on his throne, who, as the living representative of God upon earth, was not able himself to sin, or to foster human weaknesses; and a band of subjects, standing, it is true, on different steps, higher or lower, yet possessing no other rights than such as their prince could deprive them of again at any moment. And this was the state of things in Protestant lands as well as Catholic; and, where it had not been carried out, there was at least a tendency to establish it.

Yet even this was not perhaps the result of a common conspiracy of princes against the freedom of their people, but, as in Florence, the natural pro-

gress of circumstances. It has been said how the
dukedom became possible there: the number gradually increased of those who, without belonging to
the old established families of either class, wished
to rise, and join themselves to princes, who were
alone able to open a career to them. This course
became more and more general, and was soon
adopted even by those who had at first despised it.
Those by whom princes were thus made an instru-
ment for advance, fell themselves at the same time
into their hands as instruments for their own elevation; and a new nobility appeared in the lands, less
free than the old, but interfering with more power
and activity, and soon becoming the one element
which represented the people and the land : the civil
functionaries and the army forming the basis on
which the power of the prince rests, both of them
genuinely democratic institutions, by which the old
division of classes was destroyed. And so completely
did this new organization prevail, that only now,
when we begin to return to a more natural order of
affairs, is the impartial consideration of this state
of things possible.

Michael Angelo's career exhibits that stage in the
work of artists when they left free art for court
painting. He himself ended almost as a court architect, Titian almost as a court painter. Whatever
great things were produced in art after their time
has almost alone in view the one aim of satisfying
the orders of pomp-loving princes, — religious pictures for the spiritual lords, secular for the secular
nobles. More and more colossal was the size stipu-

lated, more limited the time allowed, more admirable
the skill of the artists in surpassing both. And
hence Titian in painting, and Michael Angelo in
architecture, were the highest models in succeeding
times, — Titian, with his technical skill, producing
an unusual effect by pure pencil-strokes closely
placed together, Michael Angelo, from the abundance of his positions, making the imitation of nature
almost unnecessary to the sculptor, and from the
grand style of his buildings rendering original ideas
almost needless to the architect. To a great extent,
Michael Angelo and Titian influenced the artists
that followed them, and almost all that has been
produced may be traced back to their agency.

From this time, works of art no longer expressed
the peculiar ideas of the artist. Religious pictures
corresponded neither with the inner feeling of the
master who painted them, nor with that of the laity
or clergy who ordered them. The works were no
longer personal confessions, but were produced by conventional feelings. Triumphs of skill·were praised;
but warmth was to be seen only in cases when a
portrait, painted with love, allowed the heart of the
painter to appear in the coloring. Yet even here
the false fashion spread of making insignificant faces,
by a kind of romantic conception, represent characters not belonging to their possessors; of improving
features and figure; of painting the eyes more
brilliant, the checks more blooming, the lips more
tender, the hair more luxuriant, than nature had
made it. These were portraits which flattered those
who ordered them, but which pass from our memory

like running water. But who could forget a portrait of Raphael's? It is not to be denied, that painters appeared in the seventeenth century who have produced extraordinary things: it would be unnecessary to enumerate them. Not a single one, however, among those by whom the art was cultivated, inspires that alluring feeling, which, up to the middle of the sixteenth century, breathes forth from the works of artists, delightfully fascinating us, and making us imagine the quiet in which they worked, their abstraction in their tasks, their delight in their completion, and the conscientiousness with which it was slowly reached. In the best things of the seventeenth century, we feel that they were quickly executed, that it was of consequence to the master to have finished soon, and that he lost sight of the opinion of those for whom he worked.

This superficial character of modern work corresponded, however, with the increased excitement of men, and the more rapid changes of fate; and the want of concentration in the artist runs parallel with the more superficial enjoyment of the public. The plastic arts ceased to serve as the representation of ideas which moved the world, because the settled habits of men ceased; and without these there can be none of that deeper influence exercised by paintings, sculptures, and buildings. Less firmly rooted to the places where they had grown up, they adorned them with less care; and wandering about, the victims of universal fate, they endeavored in other ways than hitherto to satisfy their yearnings for that highest beauty, of which art is the medium.

2.

Ariosto wrote for the times in which Michael Angelo worked. It can almost with certainty be conjectured that they met each other. But I have mentioned neither his name, nor that of other poets, as they exercised too slight an influence upon the intellectual condition of their times. We are accustomed to rank Leo X. as the liberal patron of poets, scholars, and musicians; but their works had little influence on their age. The ancient authors were understood: the comedies of Plautus were performed and imitated in Italian; but it was the amusement of the nobles. Ariosto and Macchiavelli, the only men who knew how to write good Italian, were neglected by Leo X.

Macchiavelli, in his prose writings, might be regarded as the beginning of a literary era; but his works were not estimated until a later period. The works of the other Florentine historians remained hidden, until, many years after, the manuscripts were found, and made public. Music was an appendage to poetry: it was simple in style, and without the fascinating power it now possesses. All this might have been dispensed with: the plastic art alone was capable of exciting enthusiasm. It alone they understood: every one looked upon its creations; and cities boasted with rapture of their possessions in buildings, statues, and paintings. A flood of sonnets were poured forth when the sacristy of San Lorenzo or the Perseus of Cellini were exhibited for the first time, whilst a poetic storm of contempt broke forth

at Bandinelli's works. Not only did artists stand
foremost at all festivals, but they were deeply inter-
woven with the whole life of the time. No mental
creation of the same period can be pointed out as
equal to the ornaments of the Vatican, the paintings
of the Sistina, and the statues of the sacristy. They
stand as high above the other productions of their
century, as Dante's verses do above the paintings of
Giotto.

From the excitement, however, with which the
Reformation filled all minds, language obtained a
power which made her soon appear as the only
mirror, as it were, for the feelings of nations; and
in the same measure in which what had been produced by language hitherto had held a lower rank
by the side of works of plastic art, from henceforth
all ideas represented by art stood inferior to that
which was written. Raphael and Michael Angelo
ruled the sixteenth century; in the seventeenth,
literature stood supreme. All efforts in the seventeenth century were directed to the one aim of
escaping from the oppression of political and theological tyranny: men's minds turned to the examination of nature, which for a time seemed to come
least into contact with religion; and the domains of
poetry were entered, for there earthly authority had
no power. And it is from this, that, in the three
centuries which have elapsed between Michael Angelo's time and our own, language has risen to such
power, that it would seem utterly impossible for a
painter or sculptor to make that impression by his
works on a people, that Goethe or Schiller made by

their verses and their prose. And this superiority of literature showed itself at the very outset of the new period: Zurbaran, Murillo, Velasquez, are great painters; but they stand far behind Cervantes, Lope de Vega, and Calderon. Lesueur and Lebrun are not to be named by the side of Molière and Corneille; and Rubens, the Shakespeare among painters, and Vandyck, — what are they compared to the actual Shakespeare, from whose verses beings rise before us, in comparison with which Rubens' most charming heads appear monotonous and dumb?

If, however, in the seventeenth century, plastic art and literature still balanced in the scale, in the eighteenth the equipoise was lost, and the superior power of the written word became so evident, that, compared with literature, art almost disappeared. The last remains of that capability for restful enjoyment which was brought from the sixteenth to the seventeenth century, and of that aspect of things which draws comfort from the beauty rather than the freedom of life, were entirely lost, and the efforts of the mind were aimed at casting off the trammels of political relations, the material disadvantages of which began gradually to appear. The money began to fail which had before flowed in for the luxury of the fine arts. Men began to compare the value of money, time, and labor, with the capacities of the lands which they needed and cultivated. The natural sciences engrossed more and more attention. Italy, as the fatherland of the fine arts, sank back into the position of a country in which pastime was alone thought of. Spain had descended from her all-powerful height; the central authority of Rome in spiritual things began to lack the means of asserting itself, and the initiative in the movement was taken by the French, a people endowed with great capacity for literature, but with no natural creative feeling for the plastic arts. The French character, however, at last so entirely penetrated the intellectual life of nations, that painting, sculpture, and architecture sought their models in France; and, as in the preceding century the personal element had gradually vanished from the works of artists, even nature now also disappeared.

3.

This loss was soon, however, no longer limited to the arts. As years advanced, literature shared it also. The feeling began to be roused in Europe, that not only the political state of things in which they lived was unnatural, but also the means by which they endeavored to rise above it had ceased to be of service. French literature had been powerful so long as it fought against the Roman hierarchy: now, when that power was broken, new and fresh matter was required for mental sustenance; and it was now at last that the Protestant Germanic nations, who had hitherto been unable to do any thing but in connection with the French movement, came forward independently, and began to lead the advance.

The fate of Germany had been dissimilar to that of other lands. Elsewhere, bloody wars, in which nations had taken part, had issued in the preponderance of either Catholicism in France and Spain, or

of religious liberty in England and Holland. By
these contests, which stirred up every passion of the
people, characters had been formed, and a fresh
defensive spirit had been fostered in individual
minds, tending to the advantage of the general state
of things. Without these wars, neither Shakespeare,
nor Corneille, nor the Spanish poets, would have
met with the characters they bring before us.

With the Germans, on the contrary, nothing of
this kind was experienced. They tolerated each
other. No one disturbed the Lutherans to force
them to defend their lives; no one provoked the
Catholics to attack. Both parties were almost her-
metically sealed towards each other. Whilst everywhere violent oppression was concentrating and
strengthening the power of princes, things dragged
on slowly with the Germans without coming to any
grave decision. The infinite division of the land
continued; and even the mighty attack of the Hapsburg dynasty, who incited Italy and Spain against
the Lutheran north to force it to return under the
old yoke, had no result. For thirty years, Germany,
unable as she was as a nation to give the decisive
blow, was the battle-field for the surrounding peoples;
and after the strangers, who thus made war on her
soil, had at length concluded peace, the old state of
things returned again. No one had been victor; no
one remained master of the land, which alone had
lost. Germany as a whole now scarcely existed any
more. The Catholic parts fell under the influence
of Rome; while in the Protestant parts, in secret
imitation of the French Government, that rule of

princes and pastors was established, which is a characteristic of the past century. In other lands, the arts continued to flourish: in Germany they ceased completely in a national sense; and Protestantism, which had been a motive to the Romanic lands for gathering together all their powers, produced, for those whom it ought most to have profited, nothing but sterility and stagnation.

In speaking of Germanic art, we must neither measure it by that of the ancients, nor by that which took place in Italy in the sixteenth century. All this lies separate from German art, and the influence exercised by these forces only operated disturbingly. German art was forced for centuries out of its peculiar course by contact with Italy, and only now has it returned back again to the old track, which, corresponding with the art-instincts of Germany, is alone fitted for further progress. There are many, who, having become great in antique and Italian ideas, consider the impending naturalization of the present day as an error. If they would pursue German art, however, as something authorized in itself from the first, and acknowledge its effort, as an embodiment of German ideas, to give that to the people which the people demand from art, they must, in the great confusion of the present day, see a return to it as nothing but fitting and natural.

At a period when in Italy the plastic arts had not yet been revived, there existed in Germany a painting, sculpture, and architecture, the remains of which intimate the high degree of cultivation which these arts had reached.

Italian sculpture and architecture were revived
by the influence of the antique works which were
either preserved in Rome, or newly brought to light.
Not so painting. Giotto was in Avignon. How far
north he penetrated from there we know not; but
that, in his day, things were to be obtained there
which neither Italy nor Byzantium possessed, is
certain. The strip of Europe between the mouths
of the Rhone and the Rhine, the fruitful valleys of
these two rivers bordering on each other, is the land
in which the antique syle has been preserved and
cultivated more vigorously than in Italy and Byzantium. Here the contest between ancient and modern
times was most natural and fruitful. Here antique
architecture had passed through every phase into
the Gothic. Here, in the old cities, political forms
never suddenly broke up and perished; but they
gradually assumed a modern transformation. Here,
if Giotto came so far, he found an art progressing
from the earliest traditions, spreading through the
lands on the right and left, and one branch of which
— painting — was, I believe, brought by him to Florence. Here, too, independent of what happened
afterwards in Italy, the arts continued to be cultivated, sustained by the riches of the land and the
independent position of its inhabitants, until, in
the time of Charles V., when the political structure
of all Europe was overthrown, the true life of the
land was fettered by Spain and Italy, and art fell
under the influence of the schools of Titian and
Michael Angelo.

Were I to compute what had been produced by

Germany and the Netherlands in painting and
sculpture up to the time of Raphael, it would not
only rank equal to the industry of the Italians, but
would surpass it. The one fundamental difference
alone is exhibited from the first: Roman art is
guided by an ideal feeling for the harmony of lines,
and for the combination of all the figures into a
definite composition; whilst German art, with a self-
limitation often appearing almost like conscious
obstinacy, only strives after accuracy in imitating
what it has in view. However rude Giotto may
appear in his portrait of Dante, no one in the north
could have drawn such an outline. And, therefore,
far inferior as the Italians are in tenderness of
coloring, and in that fidelity with which the Germans paint, in one thing they excel them, — they
know how to elevate their figures above the individual
character. In the Cathedral of Bruges there is a
Madonna's head ascribed to Van Eyck. It represents
the countenance of a woman, who is on the point of
bursting into tears; but, with all the powers she
possesses, she endeavors to command herself, and to
repress the despair, to yield to which would be an-
nihilating. The closed mouth, almost burst open
by sobs; the eyes, which seem to have sucked in
her tears; her pitiful weakness, and at the same
time her strength, — is not to be described with
words. Raphael would never have got so far as to
think of representing it. And it is in the portrayal
of such moments that the masterly power of the
Northern painters lies. They portray the most delicate emotions of the mind. Neither the Greeks

Mona Lisa (La Joconde).

LEONARDO DA VINCI.

nor the Italians can produce an attempt in this
direction.

In portraits also, this national difference is discovered. Antique busts and statues wear the expression of a calm, passionless soul. The eyes seem
to look clearly and steadily into a light distance; the
lips draw regular breaths; the bearing of the body is
as if the eyes of the people were upon them, observing their deportment. Italian portraits exhibit sometimes a slight smile: we feel for the most part that
the masters endeavored to choose the happiest moment. We have said how carefully and ingeniously
Leonardo induced this frame of mind in the beautiful
Mona Lisa. In the portraits of Dürer or Holbein,
on the contrary, there is not a glimpse of a transient
feeling, not a tinge of ideal joy in the expression;
but the man is represented with astonishing care as
he sat there and allowed himself to be painted, not
one spark more excited than usual, but tranquil and
deliberate, just as one sees people looking out of a
window. They intended to give the whole distinct
truth, and they gave it, nothing less, nothing more;
the man as he is to-day, and was yesterday. And,
beyond that, the painters could do nothing: their
capacity ceased.

That this capacity, however, appeared in proportion as the mental character of the times became
freer, is evidenced by the works of Holbein and
Dürer. They were influenced by Italian art as it
existed prior to Raphael. Perhaps, had Germany
had a capital at that time like Rome or Paris, and
could at the same time have kept herself free by an

independent policy, a higher art would have been now developed, which was not possible in the cities, in which, from their oppressed condition and lack of intellectual intercourse, the artists scarcely kept themselves alive. How miserably must Dürer have worked his way, relying upon his profession for a livelihood! Adam Krafft died in the hospital. There was no pope, no emperor in the land, no cultivated nobility. The nation was nothing compared with others: Italian influence made its way, as Romish right made its way, and abolished German customs. Nothing now any longer stood its ground against the immense facility with which they worked in Italy, and the impression made by the Roman and Venetian paintings. Italy became the goal of the German and Netherland artists (of German especially there is soon little further mention), and foreign ideas and foreign style overcame what was national.

Nevertheless, the difference between Romanic and Germanic conceptions was too profound for it not soon again to break forth. The arts which had languished in Germany flourished again in the Netherlands. Rubens is the greatest here. In a strange way, he seemed to combine the opposite styles. In the technical part, he belongs entirely to Italy. It was there he learned to paint and to arrange. The pomp of the Spanish and Roman-Catholic Church furnished him with religious materials, imperial policy with historical. In spite of this, his figures, faces, and every thing belonging to lifeless nature, testify the Germanic conception of his paintings. He painted a dying Christ, which, regarded as a

portrait of him whom we honor under this name,
would be insufferable : a common figure taken from
nature, as though a German peasant, robbed of his
garments, were lying there, the signs of death presenting themselves in his body ; and yet this body,
its position, its flesh, the muscles from the tangled
hair to the sole of his feet, are produced on the
canvas with a truth and ability which makes us say
with admiration that only a great artist could have
painted it. Rubens could do nothing beyond the
bare nature. He painted a Last Judgment : it
would be inconceivable for any man to approach it
with religious feelings. Christ is sitting there with
his beard and curling hair, with an air of noble
superiority, like a prince looking at an execution, —
a Spanish king perhaps, when heretics were to be
burned ; and the condemned rush, in the form of a
cascade of naked women of the fattest kind, *pêle-
mêle* into hell, like a pailful of fishes emptied out.
And yet, what life is there in this colossal piece of
human flesh! What truth in the strange allegorical pictures in the Academy at Brussels! How
graceful even is the mixture of antique divinities
and earthly princes, both dressed in the latest fashion, and designed by Rubens to glorify the deeds of
the royal family of France! His pictures, however,
only afford true enjoyment when they appear at
once as portraits. Thus it is with the Mary in the
cathedral at Antwerp, who steps forward incredibly
gracefully, like a delicate young Flemish peasant
girl ; or the Adoration of Mary in the Church of
St. Jacques, where Rubens painted himself and his

first and second wife, both young and blooming, as
if he had had them both with him at the same time.
These figures, each in itself, or in contrast to each
other, form a charming picture. The one, ardent,
brilliant, bold, energetic, but still tender and lovely;
the other, shy, retiring, and thoughtful. We seem
to see the lips move in the one, as she chatters with
lively animation, and in the other as she expresses
her feelings in few words. And at the same time
there is a gleam over both as if no evil destiny could
befall these women, and the sun must shine wherever they appear.

If Rubens shows the attempt to reconcile the contrary styles, in the works of another master, the
intention of *not* yielding to this is strikingly manifested; and, heightened by this intentional opposition,
the true nature of the Germanic conception comes
forward so forcibly, that, perhaps, never has the
prevailing taste been more sharply opposed.

I have before stated, that, whenever the restraint
of a school has been broken through, a powerful
talent has cast itself forcibly upon nature. After
Titian's last revolution, this attempt had been once
more made in Italy, not exactly against the Venetians, but against the school forming in Bologna
under the Carracci, which fancied it had discovered
a so-called best method, resting on a general knowledge of all that had been hitherto produced, and
by which, whether it were good or bad, all that
was characteristic was abolished, not to mention
individual influence. To use what had been acquired with taste, this was the secret. This was

opposed by Michael Angelo Caravaggio, a master, who, with an unusual eye for lines as well as color, but with no feeling for ideal beauty, has produced works, which, like daguerreotype imitations of natural incidents, surpass every thing executed in this way even up to the present day, and whose influence contributed much to lead subsequent painters back again to nature. But Caravaggio had always Italian nature before him, the charms of which it seems, almost against his will, forced him to portray the tender and the lovely. We, however, are now alluding to a Netherland master, upon whom neither the Italian sky, nor the antique, nor Raphael nor Michael Angelo, exerted their unconscious influence; endowed with the same obstinate adherence to the nature of his country, with all-surpassing talent, with an immense sense of color, a colossal power of invention, and with an industry which appears truly inconceivable,—and this was Rembrandt, to me the greatest painter which his age produced.

Rembrandt, like Michael Angelo, created a world for himself. Whether he painted or etched, he transports us with our whole soul into that which he represents. His portraits are like sudden apparitions of people whom we watch, just as, unseen by night, we might look into a strange room through a window. He likes to heighten this charm by a striking light; but he does not need it. He paints a smiling child stretching out an apple to us, till we could grasp it to take it from him. He etches Adam and Eve under the apple-tree, he a naked, clownish

peasant, she a cow-girl; but we see them living
before us, and hear in fancy their silly chatter.
The acuteness with which Rembrandt observes, the
innocence with which he represents, the romantic
charm which he wraps round his works, make it
almost impossible to regard them otherwise than
with delight, and with the desire to possess them.
From the most insignificant sketch, he elicits something that gives delight.   He etches a strip of water,
a couple of trees, and a cottage beneath them, as
though one had it in view as the object of a walk.
All his Biblical scenes are adorned often with horrible figures, — with a Christ of fearful ugliness, but
yet really so striking, so truly a copy of that which
came into his mind, that we never think of gain-
saying it.   There is no art in it, in the antique or
Italian sense: it is, we might say, a thing of the
imagination; a permanence given by lines and color
to things which pass casually before the eye, or
wander through the mind; a representation which
one feels constrained to gaze upon.   There is nothing to elevate and mould the soul, to excite our
noblest feelings, to calm our passions: but it contains that which art must possess for the Germanic
mind, — not merely truth, but reality; that which
Shakespeare possesses, and all the poets whom we
rank as our best.   We demand situations into which
we can enter; and, where painting represents no
ideas. we want imitations of nature, as illusive as
they can be.

From this there arose subsequently in the Netherlands the school of those who endeavored, by every

employment of art, to represent passive still life.
Exact imitations of the most ordinary household
implements were produced. Flowers, dead or living game, birds, knives, glasses, — in short, any
thing which could be represented ; and, as the prime
of this branch of art, landscape-painting, the true
excellence of the art-productions of the present day.
With landscape, which at first formed only the background of figures, and afterwards, without figures,
represented only the distance, the sky, the sea,
trees, and rocks, all was given up which had hitherto
been designated as art. A landscape would have
been an empty board to Michael Angelo, as the
most beautiful region without man was a wilderness
to him: the Greeks, Romans, and Italians required
men and cities; the Germans, untouched nature and
solitude. Yet, as with increasing civilization the
characteristics of nations began to intermingle, so
the sense of the beauty of still life seems to have
broken upon the Italians and French also ; and,
where the human form had been exhausted in every
position and effect, landscape-painting emerged as
the production of the seventeenth century in the
domain of art. Claude Lorraine, Salvator Rosa,
and Poussin, stood with the Netherlanders as masters
of equal repute with historical painters. And, with
the introduction of landscape, music prevailed instead of poetry. But, though by both the deepest
feelings can be expressed, human language and
human form are alone able to utter and portray
them ; and thus music and landscape denote rather
a weakness than a strength of the age, which would

prefer to dream and forget, than to see and act. Both these, however, in the beginning of the past century alone remained as the arts in which personal feeling found its expression: in poetry, architecture, sculpture, and figure-painting, there was only mannerism. The former delighted the higher circles as amusements to which they occasionally devoted themselves: the latter were consigned to the mechanical hand often of very talented masters, who completed excellent things in their different branches of art, but were so completely subject to the demands of fashion, that no great ideas found their way into their works.

4.

Such was the state of things when, about the middle of the last century, French literature began to influence Germany, and the weapons which had been used against Rome were now turned against Protestantism. Whilst, in the Roman lands, the end of the contest was a kind of moral dissolution, so that every thing existing began to waver and fall into a confusion from which there appeared no escape; in Germany, men arose who asserted their personal influence with so much power, that chaos began to crystallize anew around them. I will mention as some of the leaders, Lessing, Herder, Winckelmann, Kant, and Goethe. What was done under them and by them, in mental work, raised Germany from ruin. Frederick the Great took care that a political focus should be given to this renovated life. And, while the influence thus gradually cultivated spread over the whole earth, that basis was won on which we now stand.

For the first time, the whole human race was conceived as one universal soul-endowed creature, going through its stages of development; and, guided by the natural sciences, the earth was regarded as the theatre of this race, changing likewise according to laws. The ideas of a former age, of cosmogony, of the progress of the world, and of the perfectibility of man as one united nature, began to take root in men's minds. The future appeared as something to be determined by analogy with the past; the moral development of the mind was considered in its full extent, and an historical position only was assigned to Christianity; and the mind, striving after such an elevated view of things, saw itself transported into a realm of freedom. All that had before seemed fixed and immovable, suddenly appeared as a creation of the human will, to which liberty was given to adopt any other course, and over which the powers of earth possessed no obligatory and supreme direction. Man was free. To *will* was all that was necessary to *do*. All that was requisite was only to perceive the highest good, in order to advance towards it. Such were the final results reached by the new critical contemplation of human things.

Even at the present day, these principles form the element of life in which those move who exercise true power over mankind, and to whose knowledge others must submit. We labor to set aside the hinderances which, as outward conditions of life, are still left as remnants of times of less distinctness, and which are tenaciously adhered to by the multitude. What Winckelmann did for art, through the ancients, a whole succession of men have done for other branches of science; all striving towards the same aim, and therefore, consciously or unconsciously, working into each other's hands. A vast arrangement of things began. To him, who considered the world in the old spirit, this activity must have appeared like destruction. The reproach was raised, that they were pulling down, and would not know how to build up. And when the results of this criticism were at length brought about, and a kingdom like France fell to ruin within a few years, it seemed as if the times of general destruction had begun, in which, even in the present day, many believe who see before them the certain ruin of the human race.

Literature had caused this movement: the people had become accustomed to allow themselves to be influenced by it alone. In the domain of literature, the consequences of this revolution in the minds of the people were now exhibited.

When, before, great and startling things had been produced, poets and writers had hitherto always adhered to what had been handed down to them. They had had models before them; they had allowed things belonging to others to influence them; and, while they had gained reputation, a fixed outward form had had a great share in the success. Then Rousseau appeared in France, and wrote his new "Eloise." It was a work perfectly without plan: it was different to every thing that had been hitherto known. It was the regardless communication of a man, who, lonely and thinking only of himself, gave full vent to his passion and to his whole nature in a series of pictures, in the contemplation of which the reader became another man. Touched in every feeling, we obtain a new aspect of things from this book, as though we had lived another life after having taken it in. Never before had a work of art come upon a people with such penetrating power, and made such an immense impression. Rousseau influenced Germany; but he only helped to mature what was taking place there, and he called forth nothing which would not have been produced without him. Goethe began his career: he wrote his "Werther." Without scarcely knowing what he was doing, he brought out a work for Germany,—new as the "Eloise" to the French, equally powerful, a storm of passion couched in words, compared with which every thing before must have appeared cold and calculating. And thus did Goethe besides in his "Götz von Berlichingen;" thus did Schiller in his "Robbers,"—works which, casting aside the restrictions of vague feeling, ridiculed every thing established, and showed a freedom of action such as never before had been laid claim to or attempted. No conditions were henceforth necessary for artistic work. Pure passion seemed to satisfy. Every thing offered itself to her, and placed itself at her service.

In this sense, a revival also of the plastic arts now occurred.

Uninterruptedly since the sixteenth century, antiquity had been held up to view in writings and works of art. The French tragedists were proud of complying with the rules of Aristotle. In schools and universities, ancient culture formed the basis of the instruction. Sculptors and painters spoke of Phidias and Apelles. But all that ancient times had produced had been hitherto conceived in the lump as a whole. Æschylus and Terence, Aristotle and Seneca, Homer and Virgil, works of Greek and Roman artists, all appeared *en bloc* as the mental expression of one single past epoch, which was designated the ancient world. Winckelmann brought a system into this disorder as regards the plastic art; and his opinion that the conditions of its origin may be discovered in every work, thus separating the periods of the past, began to obtain over artists. They learned to criticise works as necessary products of distinct circumstances; they examined appearances with perfect freedom; they disengaged themselves from all that hitherto had seemed an indispensable condition, and began to work anew. Poor young men, who scarcely succeeded in selling or receiving orders, if they could only gain enough to prevent their starving, seized upon painting, in order to give expression to thoughts which had nothing to do with the productions of the old style of painting. Unconcerned as to that which was called art in the world in which they lived, they studied according to their own instincts, and chose their course as it suited their personal feelings. whese urged them to Rome. Her monuments, and the magnificent nature around, equally filled their souls. They endeavored to embrace philosophy, religion, history, and poetry; and the works of the plastic arts, and those of the poets, possessed almost equal value for their aspiring minds as they had once done for Michael Angelo. Ideas were the principal things to them: paintings were only the drapery that clothed them. It was of little moment to them whether their work struck people or no: they only endeavored to satisfy themselves. It had no influence over their course of development, that here or there they met with patrons, even with princes, who helped them forward with money. Equally little did it affect them that they were often forsaken or ill-treated by Germany. They needed nothing but the sense of personal freedom, which was filling men's minds, and which was the creative power in themselves.

It was a new, unprecedented course which they adopted; and new, unprecedented productions were the result.

Carstens, a Schleswig-Holsteiner by birth, who died young in Rome, of consumption, after a life full of misery, is the first great artist in the modern sense; the first who, were a line drawn from the ancients to the Italians, and carried on further at random, would incline in its direction. We become perfectly acquainted with his opinions by reading the letter which he wrote from Rome to the Prussian minister, who, not without a presentiment of what the man was worth, and who, notwithstanding, with all the conceit of a civil functionary, considers his high po-

sition as higher than mind and character, attempted
to prescribe to Carstens from Berlin. This letter
is well known; but the original is said to have been
written in still stronger terms than the copy contained in Fernow's valuable biography. For the
first time, a ray of pride, such as Michael Angelo felt,
burst out again from the soul of an artist. Again,
for the first time, it is an artist over whom Michael
Angelo exercised an influence. Michael Angelo was
at that time always spoken of with reverence, especially in Italy: he stood before all as one never to
be surpassed. But what he had been, no one
dreamt; and the connection between his works and
the times in which he lived, never once awakened
inquiry. Goethe relates, how artists disputed in
Rome whether Raphael or Michael Angelo were the
greater. We can be sure, that, where questions of
such a kind are raised respecting great men, no
spark of true understanding comes into play. It
was not Michael Angelo's buildings and statues that
now exercised an influence, but his art of producing
every thing almost by outline alone, and the manly
independence breathed forth from his works.

Carstens's works were indeed often nothing but
sketches with light shadows, or, when he painted,
pictures which could be produced in the cheapest
manner. Unconcerned at the opposition which was
abundantly raised against him, he endeavored to
express what appeared the highest to him; and the
enthusiasm which these simple expressions of a great
mind excited, is sufficient to prove the deep necessity
for such works which had arisen in men. Carstens

allowed himself to be influenced freely by the antique, by the great Italians, and by nature; and he pressed forwards. He died too young to reach the prime of his labors. All, however, that since his time has awakened enthusiasm in Germany, is to be traced to the course which he took. There were no more portraits, still-life, genre, and landscape: whoever could produce good things in these branches continued to work in them; but above them there again rose an art, animated by a higher spirit, just as an art of poetry, since Goethe's time, has risen above all other literature.

Carstens's great successor is Cornelius, to whom, different to his predecessor, a great age has been granted, and to whom the German original of this work is dedicated. He has become old enough to be himself allowed, like Michael Angelo and Goethe, to enter upon the heritage of his fame. It is possible to speak of him. His works stand before us as historic acts. Carstens was acquainted only with Italian art and antique works; Cornelius received his first impressions from the old German and Netherland masters, who, at the time when he began to work, as if newly discovered, suddenly attained to new honors, and filled his imagination. He afterwards went to Rome. That which had hitherto separated Greek, Italian, and German art, found its reconciliation in Cornelius. Carstens did not live long enough to divest himself of all traces of imitation, and to perfect in himself so satisfactorily his conception of the living human body as to obliterate the remembrance of Michael Angelo and the works of the ancients. To this Cornelius attained. He, freeing himself more and more from extraneous influence, has in his latter works conceived the human body as though he saw it for the first time, and had never seen it painted and drawn by others; and, while adhering thus strictly to nature, he has understood at the same time how to satisfy the peculiar bias of the German mind with respect to exact individual characteristics. The great simple passions of men form the subject of his works. No one, since Michael Angelo's death, has presented such vast problems to art as Cornelius, whose noble conceptions have been more powerfully and grandly embodied with increasing years. He is a painter in the highest sense. Like Michael Angelo and Raphael, he touches the intellectual life of the people on all points, and endeavors to represent that which most deeply affects their minds. Yet, in spite of all, how do his efforts, and all that has resulted from them, tell upon the people?

Let us place Michael Angelo's name instead of his. What would *he* be able to do, were he now to appear? and what proportion would *his* influence bear to that which Goethe exercised, and unceasingly continues to exercise? Goethe's life flows like an indispensable stream through the German lands: Michael Angelo in the present day would have had no more influence than Goethe would have possessed, had he appeared in Michael Angelo's times. What Michael Angelo would have missed in the present day is the cultivation of the people, whose eye had in his time been prepared for him for a century:

what Goethe would have missed at that time is the
extent of the mental horizon, which, as things were
three centuries ago, appears to us now contracted
and narrow.   Countries were at that time like limited
seas, upon which a moderate coast navigation is
carried on : at the present day, all the quarters of the
globe form one single ocean, which is boldly traversed
in all directions.   To effect an influence, we need
stronger means than paintings which do not change
their place.   What is art to us now, when nations
are agitated with unrest?   It hushes not the infinite
misgivings that oppress us, that expectation of a
great destiny which we look for like a revelation.
We press onwards, instead of resting and decorating
places for the quiet enjoyment of life.   The times
are passed, when, as in the days of Michael Angelo,
the ocean surrounded Europe as the great central
land, beyond which lay fabulous regions, and at the
heart of which was Italy, as the centre of creation.
The atmosphere and the firmament of stars are no
longer a fabulous space without limits: science penetrates into the immeasurable ; and the light of the
sun is analyzed, that we may know of what matter
the great luminous ball consists.   All our mental
progress, however, is rather of an analyzing than of
an accumulating nature.   And the further we advance, the more we avoid coming to results.   We
prefer for a time to increase our material.   We lack
the certainty with which we acted in days past.
Then we believed more firmly in the wonderful
legends we regarded as history, than the scholar now
does in the phenomena which he has distinctly before

him, and which he doubts, because unknown and delusive influences have their effect on his mind. And so Winckelmann, from whom modern art dates, was no artist; Lessing, with whom German literature begins, was rather a critic than a poet; even Goethe, if we estimate the whole extent of his works, rather contemplated than created. The uncertainty respecting what was to be achieved, seems everywhere to have overpowered the formative power; the contemplation of works which artists of past ages had executed seems to have satisfied far more than the enjoyment of the newest production. And if the plastic art was valued as the adorning of places to which men clung with affection; in the present day, when almost every one wanders about without a fixed home, either in his native city or in the lands he visits, so that scarcely any one dies where he was born, the main object of all art seems to be lost. To the Athenians, Greece was the only land from the beginning: all round were barbarians, round the barbarians the ocean, round the ocean the infinite heavens. Who now, however much he may cling to his country, cherishes even the idea of such a feeling? The Germans, knowing that Celts or Sclaves first inhabited the soil on which they stand, look upon that almost alone as their country, where their people are. The old Germanic feeling again prevails. They need nothing but a climate somewhat resembling their own: for the rest they only require their people and their friends there. I ask myself, I who regard art as the noblest fruit of human activity, why I can so completely do without it and its works in view of the clouds which drift over the sky, of the woods whose rustling murmur fills my soul, and of the sunshine which moves above the wooded hills. I know that I went from Rome to Florence, quite filled with the thoughts of the things I had seen ; that in Florence, absorbed again with art, I could scarcely conceive returning to a land where art flourished miserably, as a blessing but scantily yielded. I went from thence to Naples. In Livorno I embarked on board a vessel, and had nothing before me but the sky, the sea, and the distant coast. Sitting by night on the deck, I saw, gliding past me, the dusky blue shadows of the islands through which we made our way ; and the day dawned, while the stars became larger and brighter. Suddenly, in the distance, there rose obliquely from the horizon a thin line of light. We came nearer: Vesuvius stood out from the sky, one side of which the streaming lava had thus marked ; and, while the islands round suddenly rose out of the mist, we sailed round the last headland, and the whole majesty of the Bay of Naples lay spread out before me. What then were the paintings and statues and palaces to me?

And where do we find a trace of this all-absorbing feeling among the Greeks, Romans, and Italians of Michael Angelo's day?

And this, too, is to be borne in mind, — what delights us to-day, in the ruins of Rome and the paintings of Raphael, is the enjoyment of memory as well as that of sight. Remembrances of the past hover round us, the feeling of what the times were that produced them, and, at the same time, the pride of living and knowing how to estimate them. Yes: who would envy the times which gave them birth, and wish himself transported to their bonds and fetters? And who, looking upon these works, has regretted the absence of similar creations in his own age? We have wished that Beethoven and Mozart, Goethe and Shakespeare, were present, working still; but that Michael Angelo, Raphael, and Phidias should come and labor on, — such a wish has never risen in my mind. Goethe says, "If Raphael were ever to return, we would assure him of an excess of wealth and honor." But the quiet atmosphere in which he flourished; the carelessness of life under Leo X.; the delight in existence; the happiness; the thoughtlessness of the future, — who could prepare all this for him? And even if Goethe were right as regards his own time, — for his Italian journey occurred at that period prior to the French Revolution, when there was no idea of the doings and disturbances which followed in Germany, — he would have judged differently in the present day. Cornelius's career, had Goethe been his contemporary, would have shown him that he erred. For what has been the end of this mighty power, waited for through centuries, and no successor to which will probably appear for centuries to come? With deep shame, I write the fate awarded to this man in Prussia. He is not, indeed, allowed to suffer want: an honorable, brilliant old age has fallen to his lot. But, while for that which is called official art the greatest sums are fixed and given, not only are there none finished of the paintings ordered of

Cornelius, — the cartoons of which, wherever they appear, eclipse every thing else, unsightly as is their gray paper and charcoal strokes, — but so much cannot even be obtained in Berlin as a couple of simple walls for the cartoons of the paintings executed by him in Munich, which are kept shut up, and the permanent exhibition of which would exercise the greatest influence upon German art! And, worst of all, neither ill-will nor intrigue seem to blame for this: it can only be laid to the perfect absence of feeling for the injury and disgrace inflicted on the people, and called down upon themselves. Perhaps, however, it would have fared little better with Schiller and Goethe, had they written and sung in the days of Raphael and Michael Angelo.*

5.

What made the art of the Greeks so great, was the perfect balance in the cultivation of the people. As poets, as politicians, as animals (we use the term to express physical life alone), they stood upon the same height as they occupied as philosophers, soldiers, and artists. Each of these branches, separately considered, seems to carry the day over the rest. They stand before us like a model body, while other nations have their weak point somewhere. A reflection of this shines forth again in the Italians of the sixteenth century; but it is no more than a reflection. Their culture was endlessly defective; Michael Angelo towered too high above others; and the decline which took place was too sudden, while

* See Appendix, Note LXXXIX.

it required centuries to bring the Greeks from their elevated position. With us Germans, however, this harmony is completely lacking; for although, from the end of the last century, it has been our unceasing aim to bring it about, the prison air of past times presented too great an opposition to the fresh breath of freedom, and many in the present day regard as treasonable the mere wish to aspire after doing that which is the first groundwork of national existence. Without it, however, no art is possible. The mere feeling of what we may be, and the ideal unity to which we have at last attained, is sufficient for literature. Art, however, — plastic art, — requires a surer basis.

What, therefore, is our position at the present day?

In architecture, from the employment of new materials, the outward form has become paramount to the object of the work. The styles hitherto have been arbitrary, outward coverings chosen at will, in the employment of which the architect may show more or less taste, but the true value of which has vanished. The material and its judicious application form for a time the main point to which universal attention is directed.

As regards sculpture, many statues are erected; but it seems as if greater importance was given to the casting, and that the model was considered only as a preliminary to the more difficult task. Statues are no longer the visible link uniting the people to the departed forms of the great men they represent. The statues might one and all not be there, and the

great men would be just as near us.   The feeling for
art as a part of the national consciousness is lacking.
Painters try in vain to work, as it were, in the name
of the people.   They can represent nothing but their
own individual peculiarities.

A work of art is effective in the present day, not
from what it represents, not from the place which it
adorns, nór from the remembrance of the day on
which it is erected; but it makes an impression, because it shows how an appointed artist has conceived
things, and how he has reproduced them.   It must
be he, and no other.   We always wish to know who
has executed it.   That only awakens interest in the
present day which appears to reveal a character.
But, to the creative mind, it matters little what this
or that society or a single city says of him: he will
address himself to all, and work as unconditionally
as possible.

The industry of the sculptor has given place to
that of the writer.   Whoever has any thing to say in
the present day, writes it.   Nor is effort made to
obtain a good style: the aim is to suit many minds.
What is written is then sent forth into the world to
seek unknown friends, with whom it finds a hearing.
Such work would have been inconceivable formerly.
Michael Angelo worked for Rome, Shakespeare for
London, Goethe for mankind.   At the present day,
the man who is conscious of innate talent knows of
only two powers by which he is influenced, — the creative power within him, and the opinion of the universal invisible multitude to whom he communicates
his ideas.   Popes would no longer find men like

Michael Angelo. Living at the present day, he would
not have troubled himself to paint walls and to serve
masters. Very different objects would occupy his
mind. I have said that Carstens preferred to draw,
and painted with the simplest means: in this, too, I
see consolation for Cornelius, that although his cartoons are not finished, yet as they stand he seems to
have completed his work. His true talent is drawing. The walls in Munich, which he painted or super-
intended, are of less value to me than his cartoons.
These, travelling round the world, appearing in Bel-
gium, Austria, and England, have acquired the no-
toriety to which he owes his late fame. Engravings
are taken from them. As photographs, they are in
every hand; and in this way their influence will endure, until perhaps some day a museum worthy of
them may be achieved, where they may find their
true place, not as the ornament of a Camposanto,
but as the memorials of a great man.

In this way, the artists of the present day press onwards. Each represents what is most agreeable to
his own taste, and then leaves his production for an
unknown purchaser. Pictures travel from city to
city, seeking a resting-place. But we are no longer
ambitious of having these works in palaces, and in
the possession of individuals, who, if they choose, can
shut them up; but we desire museums, in which the
best works can stand open to all as public property.
The building is not considered, but its contents,
which can be changed at any moment. And how
natural such an idea is to the people, is shown by the
gifts of private persons, who are incited by a feeling

that a work of art may no longer be a possession which can be withheld. Hence, if the State would do any thing for the arts in the present day, museums must be built; and committees, not selected from officials, but from independent men, the members of which might be partly appointed by the artists themselves, should decide what works should pass into the public possession. A connection with the State would be thus secured to artists, and at the same time the sale of great works would be rendered possible. When any thing superior is produced, it can thus alone find its right position, without wounding the power which created it, by a sense of dependence, and thus interrupting the course of its internal development.

For freedom is the first condition. Why are men in the present day so deeply interested in Michael Angelo? Is it from his paintings, which, half destroyed by time, are only accessible to those who go to Rome; or from his statues, which, still more hidden than his paintings, are in Rome and Florence? The feeling with which he produced them, — that feeling that all his works and deeds are to be regarded only as a single act, emanating not from the artist alone, but from the citizen of his country, from the man who was on all points great and strong and noble, — this feeling awakens him from the dead, and excites in us the irresistible longing to draw nearer to him.

Nor shall we stop here. Times will come again in which peace will return, nations will again begin harmoniously to adorn their lands, and cities will again take pride in the beauty of the buildings occupied by the great. It is certain, that all we accumulate now will one day be fully enjoyed. Those artists who, working in secret, are unappreciated or valued less than they deserve, will be then understood in their works, and will occupy the place befitting them. We know not when this will be : it may be soon, or it may be after the lapse of years. Then, however, and then only, will Michael Angelo also be appreciated as he ought to be.

APPENDIX TO THE THIRD EDITION, 1868.

A YEAR is passed since the death of Cornelius. He died the 6th of March, 1867. What I wrote concerning him while he was yet alive is no longer applicable in the same sense. That which is past is past; we view it from a new standpoint; a career is ended. The end carries our thoughts back to the beginning; a completed whole lies before us, which we view in its entirety.

Even in his last days Cornelius continued to look forward to the hour which should witness the execution of his earlier plans, the great projects which had drawn him to Berlin in other days, when he was the world's first artist, admired by that world. Filled with a sense of the dignity of his calling, he remained rooted there to the last; and though the condition of affairs had completely altered, he continued to regard it as a mere temporary mischance, comparable to the years of waiting an exile must endure until the term of his banishment be ended.

How wonderful was his growth even to the end! Mere sketches at first, his last charcoal drawings begin to become paintings almost, so frequently did he call to his assistance all the soft, delicate gradations of light and shade. His art never remained at a standstill. It progressed steadily and visibly until the work dropped from his hands.

But who remained in those last days to admire his creations? A few of the younger generation, a very few of the older. Cornelius stood alone. This for the most part is the lot of those who have reached the eighties; but compare this man's old age with Michael Angelo's. No world which he had created lay outspread before him. He left, when he went, no gap impossible to fill, save a temporary one. What, then, has he been for us? How will future centuries view the conditions of to-day? They will say, perhaps: "When, after centuries of unproductiveness, a great and prosperous nation brought forth its greatest artist, that nation concerned itself about him as little as if there had been a superfluity of such men. For the grief which it felt at the loss of this man it found no other words than conventional, hesitating ones. It felt no obligation to perpetuate his works." Indeed, when there was discussion merely of the benefit which might result from the bringing them together in some public place, the croaking voice of one man was heard declaring, "There would be too many if we should place all the cartoons in this projected museum; the works of Cornelius would take the place of others better deserving of space!" And, in fact, at the present moment the matter rests there; and although it is possible that the works of the great man may yet occupy the spaces of the building projected for this purpose, it is by no means certain.

I do not speak for the sake of finding fault. Whom would it be possible to censure? I state the fact merely, the present condition of affairs, and it may also serve in some sort as a document for the future historian of the great master, a record of facts vouched for by one who was contemporaneous with him, one who desires only that the truth should be stated. And far be it from me to condemn these times in which we live. Who would dare to do that to-day? I discern in them the noblest germs of spiritual life for the future, and am not so impatient that I cannot await the passing of the few years which must elapse before the shifting sands of politics shall be scattered from the soil which they now overspread and conceal. But no one who knows Germany deeply will allow himself to be misled by the obvious shallowness of the higher spiritual culture which has manifested itself among us. The history of the Germanic people has a continuity, a clearer significance, which make it impossible that even the experience of a revolution such as these last years have brought forth can lead us to believe that all those eternal laws (eternal at least in an earthly sense), those laws in obedience to which the German spirit has flowered and striven onward, should be annihilated, and a nation spring into being for whom art (using the word in its most comprehensive sense) shall no longer be the standard by which we measure the spiritual potency of the times. That day will never dawn. Statesmen and military heroes may bring to pass what they will; we may compare these men with Alexander and Pericles, but the years will surely not be wanting when the impartial verdict of the historian will place Homer and Phidias higher than Alexander and Pericles. The unity of the German nation has been revealed to us through the last war, but that oneness sprang from the efforts of men who, creating a common language, and giving their noblest thoughts through it to the world, first made possible the idea of a united people. I need not here enumerate the men whose names have been for many years the common possession of the German nation, in whose inheritance they have felt themselves one, in whose possession alone they still to-day feel themselves in the highest sense a united people whom no superficial barriers can keep apart.

Do we feel this as we should? The Italians recognize and acknowledge what they owe to Dante, but in Berlin the efforts of twenty years have not yet succeeded in obtaining a fitting site for a memorial to Goethe. It would not do to place one elsewhere, and such sites as are suitable are occupied already, or secured, to celebrate the fame of men more deserving!

Neither is this statement offered by way of censure. Has not Goethe's spirit reigned this many a year over all Germany? The whole land, its plains and its mountains, are his pedestal and his comrades', and if, peradventure, there are generations in this land unable to recognize that mighty figure which, visible enough to the view of other nations, towers into the skies, time will scatter the mists which have obscured their vision. Goethe, Homer, and Dante, whose works are read by men, women, and mere youths, stand upon heights so far above their countrymen that the most favorably disposed can add nothing to their fame, enmity cannot detract from it; kings, generals, and statesmen, on the contrary, receive a posthumous fame according to the pleasure of the historian, who merely reads what is recorded of them in archives.

Cornelius belongs to the numbers of those whose fame is not dependent upon the pleasure of the historian, whom we dare praise without feeling that we are thus conferring a benefit, whom we dare censure without feeling that we detract from their well-earned renown.

It was not the mission of Cornelius to give to the generations among whom his life spent itself that which might have touched all hearts and intellects as an embodiment of the national life. Nature had made him one-sided, solitary, inflexible. A Catholic, he was by preference surrounded by Catholic friends. His active existence had passed in the Rhine country, in South Germany, and in Rome. He did not come to North Germany until he had reached the years when a man ceases to be specially receptive. In Berlin, in his immediate neighborhood, he was surrounded by the chance representatives of another circle. Rome was the atmosphere in which he could breathe most freely, while every German demands freedom of thought with which to withstand an old-established order; the German desires to lift himself above existing conditions, desires to be independent and guarded in his judgments, but much depends upon the nature of the conditions which call forth this feeling. Cornelius more than once expressed in my hearing his reverence for Luther. I remember how in Rome, in 1857, I was at some pains to procure for him a Lutheran Bible which he wished to own. But Protestantism itself he could not comprehend, that blossoming of the life of a nation, whose later growth Luther himself did not foresee. Cornelius was controlled by historical and philosophical ideas which it was impossible to bring into harmony with the life of the new times, as we comprehend that phrase in North Germany to-day.

But how necessary to its growth was this limitation of his nature! He was compelled to realize how little the age in which he lived was capable of recognizing its own ideas portrayed in painting. What impulse stirred Germany most deeply in the last decades? A desire to break chains which had become insupportable. The life of the people felt itself compressed, encased as in an armor; it longed to breathe freely. What have such thoughts as these to do with art, whose true aim is to interpret in enduring forms, to express repose, to seize a formless superabundance of materials, moulding into shape what already exists, to limit the illimitable? In the years of political despair art in Germany was merely an illusive lullaby, with which we hushed to sleep wishes which, too often indulged in, had been a crime. " Patientia levius fit malum, quod corrigere nefas est " was the watchword. Men reached out towards every possible means of doing this, and among these art was not forgotten. But this art did not, as in the days of Michael Angelo, penetrate the life of the people, as though this were the soft, willing clay out of which in days of peace fair forms might be fashioned. Art pacified us now and then, polished off a corner here and there, beautified visibly where it concealed, but it created nothing.

Therefore, when Cornelius, with increasing years, united himself more and more with the one controlling element that makes art in the grand sense of the word possible, the Church, he obeyed an instinct which we must not misunderstand. Here alone he perceived stability, and felt himself borne onward by ideas that were capable of artistic expression. In the days when we first observe him as a young man, he was filled with the enthusiasm of glowing youth, resentful of foreign dominion, throwing itself with creative power into the life of the nation. His thoughts were alienated from all which we to-day term politics in the practical sense, — they were directed towards spiritual things only; and for many years he had the support of a cultivated and intelligent public ; a richer, finer culture had separated itself from the undercurrent of national life, and swam to the surface. But when the entire nation had been stirred to its depths, and saw itself no longer face to face with its past, but with its future, when it took possession of its own history, how soon Cornelius saw his public disappear, himself standing alone ! No altered order of things was responsible for this ; no potentate or parliament had power to make it otherwise, was able only to feel the significance of that which died with Cornelius, the deeper significance of the fact that his loss seems to the nation to-day no loss at all, that he disappeared like some grand old cathedral fallen to ruins, a cathedral in which for years no divine service has been held. It is an historic phenomenon, this turning away of the gaze towards other things, this self-complacent contentment ; — all that opposition could effect against Cornelius has been done.

Cornelius, a man whose keener glance penetrated through the husks of things to their hidden kernel, must have felt this; and in the barren wilderness upon which he saw himself cast, through no fault of his own, the thoughts of the Roman Catholic faith, familiar to him from childhood, sustained him, were at last his only food. But the greatness of his art shows itself in the way he gave himself to these ideas, — dominating them, shaping them to his own purpose, not mastered by them. On the threshold where he had placed himself he remained independent, remained German in the noblest sense.

But who to-day bestows even a glance upon such distinctions? The attention of the people is busied with others, more important, I grant.

But it will not always be so. With each departing year we are a long step nearer the day when the events of our generation also shall have become historic. Others then will weigh the value of that which has been won by a people whose energies this many a year have been directed only to traffic and war. Coming centuries will relate how there dawned suddenly in Germany a day when she realized that there must be a national renascence, or her strength would become mere impotence ; how the attention of Germany turned again to her artists and poets, and then men began to derive from the works of Cornelius all of deathless worth that lies concealed in them.

But who knows when that day will come?

APPENDIX TO THE SIXTH EDITION,
1890.

This book was written in times of expectation unlike those of to-day. Nothing then was known of a war against France, of a German Empire, of the uprising of a social democracy! Yet all these things were in the air.

Since then a national museum has been built by our first Emperor for the cartoons of Cornelius, Goethe's statue has been standing ten years in Berlin, and enormous sums are expended upon art and artists.

It would be difficult to describe the general conditions of the artistic life of to-day in Germany. It is no longer ruled by great artists, who, standing alone, dictate to artistic effort what it shall strive for, to public taste what it shall admire. Certain tendencies dominate, wherein may be observed an onward movement, which, though variable, never retrogrades, — tendencies so powerful that they in themselves form standards by which to measure future effort. We possess a literature rich in influence, in sympathy with the labors of artists and the reception of their works. In our atmosphere there is that which promises perhaps the unfolding among us and the recognition of supreme artistic power.

It is wonderful to note how great is the interest in Michael Angelo's life work and history. New evidences are constantly coming to light; new material is constantly adding to the number of his works, and bringing criticism to bear upon them. We may say almost, "Every one knows about him." We must believe that his influence upon the artistic strivings of humanity will ever remain a growing one.

WEIMAR, September, 1890.

The seventh edition, 1894, is merely a reprint of the sixth.

NOTES.

I. — PAGE 2.

Harford, ii. 3, places the mediation of Tommaso di Prato erroneously in this year.

II. — PAGE 7.

As the question respecting modern imitations of the Laocoon has become a matter of discussion from some recently discovered antique bas-reliefs of this group (about which Professor Emil Hübner at Berlin lectured at the Winckelmann Festival of 1863, before the Archæological Society), I will here quote the passages, which seem to be of importance, besides those already mentioned.

1. Vas., xiii. 72 (Delle Opere di Jacopo Sansovino). Berugheta was probably the "young Spaniard" whom Michael Angelo recommended to his brother (p. 322); and, as the latter left Rome in 1508, the competition may perhaps be placed in this year. It may likewise be supposed, that the head in the Aremberg collection may be a copy of one of the models executed on this occasion. Still, I consider it an antique work, so far as the plaster-cast with which I am acquainted in the Berlin Museum allows me to judge of the workmanship.

2. Fiorillo, i. 137, quotes a passage out of the "Historia von Herrn Georgen, and Casparn von Frundsperg, Frankfurt, 1572," in which it is said, that the Laocoon was destroyed in 1527 by the Germans and Spaniards. Bandinelli's restoration would therefore have been undone, and Montorsoli's renovation would have been necessary. The question now is, how much was destroyed in 1527, and whether the serpents, which now appear to have been several times restored, as well as the arms of the sons, were intact previous to 1527. As regards the latter, they were not thus restored by Montorsoli; but, according to Murray's Handbook, they were added by subsequent sculptors.

Vasari does not say a word of copies of the group in bas-relief, nor a syllable of other smaller copies in bronze.

III.—PAGE 10.

Guicciardini gives the best account of the affairs of the time. He entered most deeply into them, and reviewed them as a politician.

IV.—PAGE 26.

... "ricordo, come più dì sono che Piero di Filippo Gondi mi richiese della Sagrestia nuova di San Lorenzo, per nascondervi certe loro robe, per rispetto del pericolo in che noi ci troviamo, e stasera a dì ventinove di Aprile 1527 v' ha cominciato a far portare certi fasci: dice che sono panni lini della sorella, e io, per non vedere e' fatti sua, nè dove e' si nasconde dette robe, giù ho dato la chiave di detta Sagrestia detta sera."
Further:—
"Ricordo, oggi questo dì venti quattro di Settembre 1528, com' io ho pagato ducati trentasette d' oro larghi, e grossoni tredici, e danari sei per l'accatto che io ho avuto dal commune, e' quali danari portò Antonio Mini che sta meco, e pagògli al camerlingo che è Bernardo Gondi.
"Ricordo, come oggi a dì sette di Maggio 1529 ho pagato a Giovanni Rinuccini lire cinquanta, e soldi undici per conto di braccia cinque, e un quarto di panno nero che m' ha avuto dare per fare una cappa alla spagnuola, e detti danari portò Antonio Mini," etc.
"Ricordo, come oggi a dì nove di giugno 1529 ho comperato otto braccia di panno monachino da Filippo degli Albizzi per uno lucco el quale mi fè tagliare in bottega sua," etc.

V.—PAGE 30.

La Storia di Girolamo Savonarola e de' suoi tempi, narrata da Pasquale Villari. Firenze, 1861. II. lxxi.

VI.—PAGE 32.

No. 47 of the Letters to Buonarroto, in the possession of the British Museum.

"Buonarroto,—Io sono andato a trovare messere Antonio Vespucci. Hammi detto che io non posso secondo le leggi fare fare l'ufficio, che io ho avuto, a un altro, e che, se bene e' si fa fare a altri' che e' si fa per consuetudine, e non per le leggi; che se io mi voglio arrischiare a accettarlo, per farlo fare a altri, che io m' arrischi, ma che io potrei essere tamburato, e averne noia; però a me parebbo di rifiutarlo, non tanto per questo, quanto è per conto della peste che mi pare che la vadi tuttavia di male in peggio, e non vorrei che a stanza di quaranta ducati tu mettessi a pericolo la vita tua. Io t' aiutero di quello che io potrò. Rispondimi prestò quello che ti pare che io facci, perchè domani bisogna che io sia resoluto, acciò possino rifare un altro, se rifiuto.

"MICHELAGNIOLO, in Firenze."

VII. — PAGE 34.

Perhaps the Atlas, which Mariette considered as designed for the top of the monument of Julius II. Goethe, in his translation of Cellini, speaks of the figure as gold.

VIII. — PAGE 53.

A painting of Puntormo's, bearing his name, which is to be seen in Munich: a Madonna seated on the ground, the design of which is wonderfully beautiful; and it seems to me to have been painted after a cartoon of Michael Angelo's.

IX. — PAGE 56.

It is a difficult matter to translate words and phrases containing eulogiums, from one language to another. The mode of address, for example, *padre onorando*, often occurs, and is merely an expression of politeness. Just so when it is said that a prince has treated any one *come un fratello;* it is only intended to express, that he has been condescending. Things of this kind have been often brought forward, as if they afforded proof of very intimate relations. The expressions respecting Michael Angelo, however, seem here to have been intended seriously.

X. — PAGE 56.

We must, however, state what was taking place in Cambray when Florence was abandoned to her fate. Francis I. used the city as if it were a sum of foreign money, with which he paid his debts. It is instructive to see the skilful treachery of this prince, who is always painted and described as an ideal of chivalrous qualities.

The ambassador sent by the city to the court of the king was Baldassare Carducci. Even the choice of this man shows how ill the public were advised. Proposed as gonfalonier in the year 1527, with Capponi, old and therefore claiming respect, passionate and the advocate of a so-called bold system of policy, they sent him to France, rather for the sake of being free from him at home, than because they thought him suited for the post, which had hitherto been held by refined Mediceæan nobles, — men who knew the ground, and were conversant with the manner in which they should choose their course of action. Of all this, however, the old lawyer and popular leader knew but little; and all his energy and his power in leading the multitude at home helped him so little in his new scene of activity, that he allowed himself to be made use of for any thing the king wished.

His dispatches lie before us. At the very first, Carducci, who was mistrust, keenness, and restlessness itself at home, appears delighted with the prospects of a reconciliation between emperor and king, and almost convinced of the prosperous consequences for Florence from the treaties brought about on this occasion. King Francis assured him, indeed, on his oath, and all the great lords at court likewise, that nothing could happen, come what will, without the fixed and certain prosperity and peace of the city of Florence being the first condition. "Ambasciadore," said one of the first personages at court to him, "if you had ever cause to say that the king could enter into any agreement with the emperor than one in which you did not occupy the first and most advantageous position, I will allow you to say that I am no man of honor, because I am a traitor."

Such was the tone previous to the unsuccessful events in Lombardy, and when the pope might have died any day. Then, however, came the defeat and the publication of the treaty of Barcelona, between pope and emperor, the true purport of which was Florence. Now, also, on this side a ruder tone was assumed towards France; and Francis, in his turn, used more general expressions towards Carducci. The latter became apprehensive; even at the French court it was known that the army under Orange was not designed alone against Perugia. Francis I. had at that time, indeed, neither money nor soldiers; and the emperor held his sons as hostages in Madrid. In spite of this, it appeared still to Carducci that the utmost that could happen was, that France might assent to the destruction of Perugia. Thus ends his letter of the 5th July. Then followed that from St. Quentin of the 5th August, the time of Michael Angelo's return to Florence. The city and the whole of Italy will never forget, writes Carducci, what they may expect from French alliances, promises, and oaths. Suddenly, no one knew why, the treaty with Spain was concluded and published, by which the Italian allies of the king were given up to the emperor. Up to the last moment, Francis had drawn in the ambassadors of Venice, Florence, and Ferrara.

and held them firm in the belief that they would be cared for. For, up to the last moment, the king needed his Italian allies, while he strengthened his own importance through them, and at the same time prevented them from concluding a peace direct with the emperor. And then, after he had so thoroughly deceived and misused them, he suddenly disappeared. He was away at the chase, and inaccessible. It was impossible to get an audience. And, when this was at last accomplished, hearty regrets and new promises were made; and he pleaded that he could not have altered matters.

It was an especial disgrace to Carducci, that a high ecclesiastic, a Florentine, who went to Rome with the treaty between the king and emperor, while it was still a matter of secrecy before its publication, sent to ask him whether he had letters to give him for Florence. He might like to send the information home, that all was progressing well for the city. "Such an insult!" writes the enraged Carducci; "the man has always spoken nobly as a citizen of Florence, and now he shows such a difference between words and deeds."

This would not have happened to Macchiavelli. He had died in 1527, soon after freedom had been again obtained, without having held a public office. Carducci did not understand the business. He was a good citizen, but a bad statesman.

He was ignorant at that time of the worst of all, — that Ferrara and Venice had been conditionally included in the treaty, but Florence not. The city had been obliged to be sacrificed without consideration. King Francis — this must be acknowledged — was in the position to yield to the emperor in every thing, whether he would or not. He immediately made secret promises to the Florentines. As soon as it was, humanly speaking, possible, he would help them. Moreover, Malatesta Baglioni still remained general of the Florentine army in the name of the King of France; and the citizens believed now, as ever, in the good-will of the great lord, with whom they would never break their alliance, nor he with them. Venice and Ferrara acted similarly. They were constrained to throw off the Florentine policy. As a kind of pretext, they asserted that the city, by sending an embassy to the emperor without previously acting in concert with them in the matter, had made the first step in perfidy; that they had been abandoned by Florence, and that they must now take care of themselves. Still their ambassadors remained in the city, as well as those of France. We see from this how natural on all sides all that happened, and was to happen, appeared. They remained on the best terms with France, Ferrara, and Venice, and accepted the situation naturally. It cannot, besides, be denied, that an envoy had been sent from Florence to Genoa, even before Carducci's final dispatches had arrived, and against the urgent opposition of Ferrara and Venice. But, on the one hand, the miserable position in which they had resolved upon this step was sufficiently evident; and, on the other, the instruction given to the envoys was so drawn up, that no dereliction from their duty to both powers was contained in it. Not a single practical proposal was contained in these orders,—only general expressions of fidelity. Besides, the way in which the embassy had been formed, even if fixed proposals had been given to them, would have frustrated any result. Four men were chosen out of each party, each thinking for himself, each with special designs, and each so placing himself that that which was done by the others might appear as not acknowledged or supported by him. The emperor, as usual, received them graciously, was delighted to see them, and expressed in general terms the most benevolent intentions as regarded the city. He entered into nothing further.

XI. — PAGE 60.

Guicciardini says, the 28th September. This is an error. It may be an erratum in my edition.

XII. — PAGE 61.

Vasari says the goldsmith Piloto escaped with him. It is not elsewhere mentioned, and it seems untrue.

XIII. — PAGE 62.

Segni writes as though Capponi had seen Michael Angelo. Segni was Capponi's near relative.

XIV. — PAGE 76.

Leonardo da Vinci received the same sum in France, and Cellini also, to whom we owe this notice. Michael Angelo received the same while engaged in the Chapel of San Lorenzo, and double the sum subsequently in Rome. No definite proposals were made by Florence as regards money at a later period.

XV. — PAGE 79.

Michael Angelo's poems appeared hitherto only in the edition which was arranged in 1623 by the grandson of his nephew, a writer in Florence known under the name of *Michelangelo Giovane*. He says in the preface, " Perchè diverse Rime di Michel Angelo Buonarroti e manuscritte e di stampa vanno attorno poco emendate, si fanno consapevoli i lettori che conferitosi il testo che de' suoi componimenti si conserva nella libreria Vaticana, il quale in gran parte è di mano dell' autore, insieme con quanti di essi componimenti si trova appresso gli suoi eredi ed appresso altri in Firenze, se ne sono scelte le più opportune e più risolute lezioni; perchè molto irrisolute, e non ben chiare ve ne hanno, come bozze di penna non sodis fatta, e si sono lasciate da parte quelle opere che citate dagli scrittori spezzatamente e particolamente dal Varchi, non si sono ritrovate intere; con desiderio di farvi vedere anche quelle, quando venga il rinvenirle perfette."

These assertions are false, — in the first place, when they assume to give the text according to the Vatican manuscripts; and, in the second place, as regards the selection of the best readings.

The Vatican manuscript consists of several parts, — of two collections of numbered poems, which Michael Angelo, it seems, had himself prepared and corrected; and a series of loose papers, which are bound up with those first manuscripts. Scarcely one of these poems agrees with the edition of 1623; for which reason, in some later copies of this edition, the different reading of the Vatican manuscript is noticed, and the poems contained in it, and not included in the edition of 1623, have been added.

Any separate papers of Michael Angelo's poems, found elsewhere, never agree with the edition of 1623.

Accordingly, nothing remains but the supposition that the papers in the possession of the family, and which have been hitherto inaccessible, furnish the different reading.

Against this, however, is the fact, that all the differences in the edition of 1623, both as regards the sense and the language, do not appear to improve, but to weaken, often even not only changing the sense of the poem, but destroying it, so that empty phrases take the place of ideas. In spite of this, however, we should not question the assertion of the younger Michael Angelo, that he had worked from papers, which, being in the possession of the family, were accessible to him alone, if the manuscript from which the edition of 1623 was printed, and that in the possession of the British Museum, did not plainly show what was done in the printing. This was evidently the last fair copy, and agrees for the most part with the printed one. It contains, on the other hand, additional alterations in many passages, — the work of a friend, probably, to whom it was given; and the manner in which this criticism was used allows us to conclude how it was in general carried on. Where a phrase did not appear elegantly turned, where words were repeated, where the senso was not quite plain to the editors, an alteration was made; and, when it could not be done in few words, whole passages were remodelled. A series of poems we find marked and omitted as *difficultuosi*, —pieces containing, for the most part, a deep philosophical train of thought. In short, they have been treated in such a manner, that we feel justified in ignoring the edition of 1623 as thoroughly valueless; in considering even those poems published in it, and nowhere else, as retouched; and in only receiving as genuine that which lies before us as authenticated, or written in Michael Angelo's own hand.

In the poem on the death of his father, which unfortunately only exists in the edition of 1623, I have at least given the form in which it appears in the London manuscript before being retouched.

As the rest will appear, without doubt, when the Florentine papers come to light, and in their true form, I omit them here.

Only when the Florentine treasures are brought out, will it be worth the trouble to collect Michael Angelo's poems in a critical edition. It is a pity that Condivi has not carried out his intention to have them printed.

What has been hitherto written respecting Michael Angelo as a poet, on the ground of the edition of 1623, loses weight from the fact that the writers suppose the text before them to be the authentic one. The succession of the poems, too, is throughout arbitrary; and all the conjectures based on the accidental arrangement, contained in editions of the present day, fall to nothing as regards this point. The Vatican manuscript may well furnish a foundation for future editions.

XVI.—PAGE 91.

In the possession of the British Museum.

"Alfonsus Dux Ferrarie Mutine et Regij Marchio Extensis, Rodigyque Comes et Carpi Dominus Col mezo delle presenti nostre Patenti lettere. Noi commandiamo strettamente e sotto pena de nostra gravissima Indignatione a tutti li nostri subditi, stipendiarii e officiali, che lascino andare, e passare securamente, e senza arrestatione alcuna lo exhibitor presente: Il che andando al suo camino, passara per la città nostra di Modena, et per la nostra Provincia di Carsignana, ordinando alli (p⁰ predetti) nostri officiali che trattino esso exhibitor come se fusse un proprio di nostra corte in tutto quello che gli bisognosi per commodita del viaggio di sua persona. Et declaramo che 'l securo transito il che volemo e commandamo che gli sa (sia) con(c)esso e osservato, se intende per quindici giorni futuri da la Data, la qual' e' alli X de Novembre in Ferrara 1529."

Below: Bon:/.

XVII. — PAGE 92.

The Berlin Museum contains Begarelli's works.

XVIII. — PAGE 93.

See Cellini. Antonio di San Gallo led the works; see Nardi, ed. Agenor Gelli, II. 159. Note I.

XIX.— PAGE 110.

Respecting paintings after Michael Angelo's cartoon of the Leda, see Aretino's letters, which Bottari has made use of very unsatisfactorily for his collection. A Leda after Michael Angelo is in the royal palace at Schwedt.

XX. — PAGE 128.

Ferrucci's death is placed by Segni on the 2d August, by Sassetti (Vita di Fr. Ferrucci; Arch. stor. iv.) on the 4th. The 3d is given in Capello's and Gonzaga's reports. Varchi also reckons it so.

These last days of the city form a kind of test of the historians of the period. Nardi's account is the most vague, Segni's the more just; Varchi accumulates detail, but we feel that he was not an eye-witness. Guicciardini alone stands above things. Every word is sure with him, though he belonged to a party. But his judgment is cold.

What a contrast these works present to Capello's dispatches! They are not to be surpassed, as regards the representation of each separate day. But it is impossible to gain a just impression of the whole from these letters. The man who so writes must regard the day on which the dispatch is drawn up as the termination of events. But each letter thus becomes, through the following, a sort of stale goods. Unimportant things are depicted as too weighty: that which is truly of moment is placed too much on a line with the rest. Each grouping falls apart, because the writer knows nothing of the future, which can alone give the artistic balance to the whole.

XXI. — PAGE 135.

Varchi.

XXII. — PAGE 138.

The Tuscan Government considered a drapery necessary.

XXIII. — PAGE 151.

Goethe says, that Ludovisi finds a whole song of Homer in the head of Juno. Hence my plagiarism.

XXIV. — Page 152.

Varchi delivered a public lecture upon this, which he had printed, and sent it to Michael Angelo.

XXV. — Page 153.

Se in una pietra salda, etc. Madrigal.

XXVI. — Page 154.

Casts of the figures of the Medicean tombs have been placed in the new museum in Berlin, but so unfavorably, that they cannot possibly be criticised. They require light from above. Besides this, the plaster is made shining by a sort of saponaceous coating, and has false lights.

Small models of the male figures are at Dresden in private possession. They are considered as original works of Michael Angelo's; but hitherto this has only been conjecture. They are of burnt clay. I know them only by casts.

One circumstance seems to prove their genuineness. In the Biblioteca Trentina, redatta da Tommasa Gar. Dispensa prima, Trento, 1858, there is a life of the sculptor Vittoria, and among the original papers there is a part of his Ricordi : —

"20 Aprile 1562. Ricordo io — come questo di sopr*. comprai un piè del Giorno di Michelangelo che fece ne la sagrestia di S*. Lorenzo di Fiorenza. È questo piede zanco del modelo di sua man, et per suo pagamento et saldo contai a Nicolò Rofino bolognese che vende disegni, scudi tre venetiani trabocanti, et tuti dua si contentò. Val scudi, No. 3."

This left foot, however, is just the one missing in the Dresden model.

XXVII. — Page 157.

Another Giovanbatista Strozzi was a furious adversary of the Medici. He was, however, banished immediately after the surrender of the city. See Varchi.

The first verse was as follows in Italian : —

> "La notte che tu vedi in si dolce atti
> Dormire, fu da un Angelo scolpita
> In questo sasso, e perchè dorme ha vita;
> Destala se no 'l credi, e parlaratti."

Cf. Anthol. iv. 103 : —

> Τὸν Σάτυρον Διόδωρος ἐκοίμισεν, οὐκ ἐτόρευσεν
> Ἢν νύξῃς, ἐγερεῖς. ἄργυρος ὕπνον ἔχει.

And Philost. I xxii. for Michael Angelo's reply : --

Καθεύδει ὁ Σάτυρος, καὶ ὑφειμένῃ τῇ φωνῇ λέγωμεν περι αἰτοῦ,
μὴ ἐξεγείρηται.

We see how the classics at that time penetrated the minds of the cultivated. For although Strozzi, as a scholar, would probably receive his suggestion direct from the Anthology, Philostratus was necessary for Michael Angelo's reply.

XXVIII.—Page 163.

The letter is in Gaye, ii. 228. "Ciesa = scesa."

XXIX.—Page 163.

"L arte."

XXX.—Page 164.

In the possession of the British Museum. From a copy made for me : —

"Amice carissime, havendomi fatto intendere messer Alessandro Guarino, già mio oratore costi in Fiorenza, quello che voi gli avete mandato a dire circa la pittura che avete fatto per me, ne ho ricevuto molto piacere. E perchè già lungo tempo ho desiderato di avere in casa qualchuna delle opere vostre, come a bocca vi dissi, mi pare ogni ora un anno ch' io possa vedere questa. E però mando a posta lo esibitore presente mio servitore chiamato il Pisanillo, e vi prego che vi piaccia mandarmela per lui, dandogli consiglio e indirizzo come l' abbia da condurre salva, e non vi scandalizzate se ora per il medesimo messo non vi mando pagamento alcuno, perchè ni da voi ho inteso quel che voi vogliate, nè da per me lo so giudicare non l' avendo ancora vista, ma bene vi prometto che non avete perso quella fatica che avete durata per mio amore, e mi farete piacere grandissimo se mi scrivete, quando (quanto?) vi piacerà' ch' io vi mandi, perchè sarò molto più sicuro del giudicio vostro il stimato che del mio, e oltra il premio della fatica vostra vi certifico che sempre sarò desideroso di farvi piàcere e commodo, come sapete che meriti il molto valore e rara virtù vostra. E vi fra tanto e sempre me vi offero di buono cuore in tutto quello ch' io possa fare che vi sia grato.—Bene val. Venetiis.

"xxii. Oct. 1530. Alfonsus, Dux Ferrariæ."

XXXI.—Page 165.

Gaye, II. 230.—Soliciterò l'opera refers probably to the Apollo, which Michael Angelo was executing for Valori.

XXXII.—Page 166.

Middle of November, 1531.—The letter in which he informs Aretino of his appointment is dated the 4th December. The position was worth 800 scudi; but 300 he had shared with Giovanni da Udine. ·

XXXIII.—Page 168.

The letter is in the possession of the British Museum. From a copy prepared for me:—

"Carissimo compare (osservandissimo),—Credo vi maravigliarete, sia stato tanti giorni non vi abbia scritto; la cosa è stata, prima per non avere avuto cosa meritasse, e l' altra per l' accidente quale modo oramai abbiate inteso come nostro signore papa Clemente mi ha fatto piombatore. E hammi fatto frate in loco die Fra Mariano, dimodochè se me ne vedeste frate, credo certo ve ne là ridereste. Io sono il più bello fratazzo di Roma. Cosa in vero non modo pensai mai. È venuto moto proprio dal papa. E Dio in sempiterno sia laudato, che pare proprio che Dio abbi voluto così. E così sia.

"Ora, compare mio, gli è venuto a Roma messer Jeronimo Staccoli (*ostaculi*, he writes) da Urbino. E mi è venuto a trovare insino a casa. E non mi trovò. E oggi mi ha parlato in Cancelleria. E mi ha referito tutto quello ha negoziato con il Signore duca di Urbino circa la sepultura di Giulio. E mi ha detto assaissime parole, in conclusione dice avere offerto dei partiti alla eccellenza del duca vostro,* che vi siate disposto fin (ire) l' opera di papa Giulio . . . facendo l'ordine del contratto faceste con Aginensis, cioè l' opera grande . . . che vi segnerà provvedere al instante dei danari. E il duca rispose che il non posseva provvedere al resto dei danari, ma che sua signoria era molto più contenta che vi faceste l' opera del secondo modo, cioè che fusse breviata per la valuta dei danari avete ricevuti. E più, mi disse el detto messer Jeronimo, che partito da Urbino gli mandò dietro uno in posta con una lettera, che a ogni modo d(ovesse) trovare di assettare questa cosa, che a ogni modo la si faccia, ma che 'l duca vorria che gli faceste uno disegno come ha da essere l' opera, che sopra quello ella si rivolveria della sua volontà. Io gagliardissimamente risposi al detto messer Jeronimo, che vi non eri (eravate) uomo da fare pruove di disegni, nè modelli, nè simili frascarie, che questa era la via di non finire mai questa opera, che la cosa del duca si può bene contentare, che vi v' inclinate a volere fare l' opera di quello che s' era disegnato (scia disegno!) e che apprezziate tanto l' onore vostro quanto altri persona apprezzi il suo. E

---

* The *duca vostro* is not distinct; but it can only be Urbino.

mi rispose messer Jeronimo a che modo si potria fare questa cosa. Io gli risposi a questo modo: che eccellenzia del duca con tutti gli eredi di papa Giulio si contentasse di annihilare il contratto che fu fatto per Aginensis, cioè dell' opera grande, e fare un altro contratto, come voi vi contentare di fargli una opera ... della valuta dei danari avete ricevuti, e rimanere a voi in coscienza vostra ogni quantunque cosa quando non mettesti ... che un sasso in opera; che loro si contentasse di ... la vostra volontà. E così, come il migliore tempo della vita vostra gli stato comodo, stiano che vi restituiscano al presente la vostra liberta, e che non vi legano a cosa nessuna, ... solum farvi padrone di ogni cosa come volete voi; che gli metterà molto meglio conto a fare a questo modo che volere la minuzzare, o per altre vie. Di modo chè detto messer Jeronimo confessa che questa è la via, e mi ha detto vi debba scrivere, ch' il farà ch' il duca si contentarà di tutto quello che vorreste voi, e l' ambasciadore suo. E con messer Jeronimo in nome del duca, e degli eredi di papa Giulio annihilarà il contratto, e ne farà un' altro come volete voi nella forma che gli ho offerto io, cioè di fare finire detta sepoltura nel secondo modo intra fine di tre anni, e spendere del vostro due mila ducati, computando la casa, che detta casa si venda, e gli danari di detta casa suppliscano al numero di due mila ducati, e non ho voluto offerire più, e credo questi bastaranno, e si contentano troppo. E gli pare molto bella cosa, che questa opera la vogliate fare senza che bene spendano uno quattrino, e che voi vi contentate spender gli due mila ducati. E messer Jeronimo mi ha promesso di scrivere al duca che faran ... ch' il duca vi scrivera, e rimettera ogni cosa a voi, e voi vi degnarete rispondere al duca quello vi pareva, ma non offerite più danari. Ora mi fare che la cosa stia in buonissimo termine e risoluzione, come avete a fare questo secondo contratto. E mandatemi una forma del contratto, come volete che stia, che non si preterirà parola. E ancora mandatemi una carta di procura, che in nome vostro si possa annihilare il contratto primo, e fare il secondo, e promettere in nome vostro tutto quello mi commanderete, e così credo sarete contento, e starete con l' animo in riposo. E credo, mi ha detto, il faremmo ringiovenire di 25 anni. Altro non vi dirò di questa cosa; fate voi, e state di buona voglia.

"Perdonatemi che ancora non ho finita la testa del papa, ma spero a ogni modo mandarvela quest' altra settimana, le cose di questo ufficio mi hanno impedito (or le cosa — mi ha —). E Dio sa, quanto mi duole non esser possuto venire a Firenze come ... vi aveva promesso. Ma Dio ha voluto così. Spero venirvi a veder questa state. E non mancate della promessa, acciò ci godiamo un poco insieme.

"Pregovi raccomandatemi alla signoria del messer Bartolomeo Vettori, e ditegli che io seguiterò l' opera sua, e sarà servito. E così vi prego ancora raccommandatemi al mio signore messer Giovanni Gaddi, Clerico di camera. E a voi mi raccomando per infinite volte. Cristo sano vi conservi.

"Tutto vostro frate Sebastiano de Lucianis pittore fece scrivere."

He therefore dictated it.

Address: "Dño Michelagnilo De Bonarotis dño meo collendissimo in Firenze. In Firenze."

XXXIV.—Page 168.

Risuscitare morti, an expression frequently used by Michael Angelo, seems only to signify "to undertake something impossible." In the contrast here, *fare figure che pajono vive*, the meaning would seem pointed out by words, if the signification of *fare figure*, etc. (although I have attempted to explain it by painting) was not somewhat obscure. Perhaps between the two, as occurs in all intimacies, a jargon was occasionally used, which we can no longer understand.

XXXV.—Page 169.

The letter is dated from Florence. *Cinquante* is written, but it must in any case mean 1500. In Venice, Michael Angelo only spent 20 lire.

XXXVI.—Page 171.

Not "twice every year," as we find erroneously stated.

XXXVII.—Page 172.

Tribolo subsequently copied the figures of the sacristy on a small scale, — works which, if I mistake not, now stand in the academy "dei belli arti in Florence."

XXXVIII.—Page 172.

"Giuliano" he is naturally called by Vasari.

XXXIX.—Page 174.

Vas., xi. 64.

XL.—Page 175.

Vasari's letter, upon the intended completion, is in the Lettere pittoriche.

XLI.—Page 183.

It still stands in good preservation. The fortifications, on the other hand, which we see in the present day, were rebuilt by Cosmo; so that nothing of Michael Angelo's works, which may be recognized as such, remain. Vauban's studies from them appear therefore doubtful.

XLIL—Page 220.

See Wilhelm Grimm, Die Sage vom Ursprung des Christusbildes.

XLIII.—Page 222.

What I said in Note 77 of the second volume of the first edition of this book, respecting the possibility that Michael Angelo had intended to place Savonarola by the side of Christ, instead of the Holy Virgin, appears to me too doubtful, after close and repeated examination of the original in Rome, for me to repeat it here.

XLIV.—Page 245.

According to M'Crie. As regards the history of the Reformation in Italy, M'Crie's otherwise excellent work is unsatisfactory.

XLV.—Page 257.

Guicciardini, Opere inedite; a highly interesting book.

One more expression of Michael Angelo's: "Inteso che Sebastiano Veniziano aveva a fare nella cappella di San Piero a Montorio un frate, disse che gli guasterebbe quella opera; domandato della cagione, rispose: che avendo eglino guasto il mondo che è si grande, non sarebbe gran fatto che gli guastassino una capella si piccola." Vas. xii. 279. The new editors observe, in a note to this, "E chiaro che Michelangiolo volle alludere al frate Lutero." It seems to me not so clear. He certainly had not such things in his mind, but meant what Guicciardini meant.

What, besides, does the *frate* which Sebastian had to paint mean? It must have been a painting; on which perhaps the portrait of a *frate* was to be exhibited.

XLVI.—Page 258.

Segni, vi.

XLVII. — Page 266.

Nos. 42 and 43 of the letters to his father, in the possession of the British Museum.

XLVIII. — Page 268.

Pierbasso was still with Michael Angelo in July, as is evident from the proofs (Tavola B) which Campanari has added to the paper, in which the portrait of Vittoria Colonna, painted by Marcello Venusti, is represented as a work of Michael Angelo's.

XLIX. — Page 275.

No. 9 of the Letters to Leonardo, in the possession of the British Museum.

" Mi scrive che, sebbene non ha avuto tutte le cose ordinate dalla chiesa, che pure ha avuto buona contrizione, e questa per la sua salute basta, se così è."

In No. 7. Michael Angelo inquires about it.

" Lionardo, — Io ho per l' ultima tua la morte di Giovansimone. Ne ho avuto grandissima passione, perchè speravo ben che io vecchio sia a vederlo innanzi che morisse e innanzi che morissi io ; è piacuto così a Dio. Pazienzià. Arei caro intendere particularmente che morte ha fatta, e se è morto confesso e communicato con tutte le cose ordinate dalla chiesa, perchè quando l' abbia avute, e che io il sappi, n' arò manco passione."

L. — Page 278.

Giannone, xxxii. cap. 5.

" Narra Gregorio Rosso, testimonio di veduta, che in quei giorni dì Quaresima, che l' Imperadore si trattene in Napoli, andava spesso a sentirlo in S. Giovanni Maggiore con molto suo diletto, impero che, com' e' dice, predicava con ispirito grande, che facea piagnere le pietre."

Rosso says that the stones might have wept : it is not the *emperor* who says so, as, in strange agreement, many modern writers upon church history — who, however, only quote Giannone himself — have misunderstood the passage.

LI. — Page 290.

Valdes came with the emperor. Was Vittoria at that time in Naples? I find nothing in proof of it but an intimation of Giannone's.

LII.—Page 291.

El **Arte** en Espagna, Revista Quingenal de las **Artes** del Dibojo, Tome segundo, Madrid, 1863, contains the beginning of an article about Francesco d' Ollanda, to which is added a very life-like portrait of Michael Angelo, in a woodcut, from a drawing of the master's. Unfortunately, what is said in this paper does not touch upon Francesco's early beginning: a manuscript concerning his Italian journey, and undoubtedly containing many important disclosures, still remains to be published. Unfortunately, the manuscript of the record we possess was no longer to be had in Lisbon; Professor Dr. Emil Hübner endeavored in vain to gain a glimpse at it. This is all the more to be deplored, as the passages published by Raczynsky, in his translation, contain many things which allow us to conclude much remodelling and many omissions on the part of the French translator to have taken place. To mention only one thing: at the close of the first day, on his return home, there is suddenly mention made of a fifth member of the company, who had not been alluded to before as present. From this we do not know whether the translator simply misread many names, which we might otherwise suppose Francesco had stated falsely. Thus, for example, with respect to that in note—

LIII.—Page 297.

when the Monte Cavallo is mentioned, at the foot of which Michael Angelo is said to dwell. This could, however, not be the case, as it would have been in the neighborhood of San Silvestro. Michael Angelo lived at the foot of the Capitoline Hill, on the Macello dei Corvi. I could not discover the house itself. Probably Monte Capitolino stood in Francesco's report.

There is a house shown on the other side of the Capitol, close by the ascent to the Palazzo Caffarelli, and even in Fournier's new and extremely faulty book, "Rome and the Campagna," it is so designated. This, probably, rests on an invention of Roman *valets de place*.

LIV.—Page 300.

Francesco d'Ollanda's portrait exhibits Michael Angelo with the felt hat on his head. Gaultier's little engraving of the Last Judgment also gives Michael Angelo's portrait thus, at the place intended for the arms of the Medici.

LV.—Page 306.

Among the Florentine papers, a number of letters from Francesco d'Ollanda's to Michael Angelo are to be found.

LVI.—Page 308.

Campanari (Ritratto di Vittoria Colonna) speaks of these times, and deduces from Michael Angelo's sonnets his connection with Vittoria. It is too full of conjectures. In the recital of their friendship, given by different writers, the poems are, in general, made use of in a manner which cannot possibly be justifiable.

She must have left Rome in September, 1541; for in August she was still in Rome (Visconti, cxxvii.), and in October we see her in Viterbo. According to Visconti and the dates of her letters, we may almost fix, year by year, the places where she sojourned.

LVII.—Page 311.

In the possession of the British Museum.

"Unico maestro Michelagnelo et mio singularissimo amico lo hauta la uostra et uisto il crucifixo, il qual certamente ha crucifixe nella memoria mia quale altri picture, viddi mai ne se po ueder piu ben fatta, piu viva et piu finita imagine et certo jo non potrei mai explicar quanto sottilmente et mirabilmente e fatta per il che ho risoluta de non volerlo di man daltri et pero, chiaritemi se questo e d' altri: patientia: se e uostro jo in ogni modo vel torrei ma in caso che non sia uostro et uogliate fare a quel uostro, ci parlaremo prima perche cognoscendo jo la dificulta che ce e di imitarlo, piu presto mi resolvo che colui faccia un' altra cosa che questa: ma se è il uostro questo, habbiate patientia che non son per tornarlo piu. jo l' ho ben visto al lume et col vetro, et col specchio et non viddi mai la piu finita cosa

" son
          " Al conta da uostro le (?),
                              "MARCHESA DI PESCARA."

From a copy prepared for me. The " Al conta da uostro " I do not understand. I give the peculiar orthography, as it is Vittoria's only letter.

LVIII.—Page 313.

The letter is in Bottari, addressed: al Marchese di Pescara. Ticozzi makes out of it Duke Cosmo. Later writers have omitted the address entirely.

The poem lies before me in three forms: in the first place, that which I have inserted above,—undoubtedly the form in which Vittoria first received it, as it stands on the same sheet

as that on which the letter was written to her. The second is
in Michael Angelo's hand, and is likewise in the Vatican manuscript, but in a series with others.

> " Ora su 'l destro, or su 'l sinistro piede,
>   Variando cerco della mia salute,
>   Fra 'l vitio e la virtute.
>   Il cuor confuso mi travaglia e stanca,
>   Come, chi 'l ciel non vede,
>   Che per ogni sentier si perde e manca.
>   Porgo la carta blanca
>   Ai vostri sacri inchiostri,
>   Ch' amor mi sganni, e pietà il ver ne scriva,
>   Che l' alma da sè franca
>   Non pieghi agli error nostri
>   Mio brieve resto, e che men cieco viva.
>   Chieggio a voi, alta e diva
>   Donna, saper, s' el ciel men crudo tiene
>   L' umil peccato, ch' el superchio bene."

It is the same strain of thought, only with some points more
clearly carried out. The third is in the edition of 1623, and,
up to line eight, it corresponds with the above; after that, it is
as follows : —

> " Ai vostri sacri inchiostri,
>   Ove per voi nel mio dubbiar si scriva,
>   Come quest' alma, d' ogni luce priva,
>   Possa non traviar dietro il desio
>   Negli ultimi suoi passi, ond' ella cade;
>   Per voi si scriva, voi che 'l viver mio
>   Volgeste al ciel per le più belle strade."

These are general forms of expression without any fixed
meaning, by which the poem loses its real ideas. It is impossible that this can be any thing but an invention of the editor.
In the same way, the poem, "Perch' è troppa molesta," has
been robbed of its true meaning by the younger Michael Angelo. The genuine text is as follows : —

> " Perch' è troppo molesta,
>   Ancor che dolce sia,
> Quella mercè che l' alma legar suole;
>   Mia liberta di queste
>   Vostr' alta cortesia
> Più che d' un furto si lamenta e duolo.
>   E com' occhio nel sole
>   Disgrega sua virtù, ch' esser dovrebbe
>   Di maggior luce ch' a veder ne sprone,
>   Così 'l desio non vuole
>   Zoppa la grazia in me che da voi si crebbe,
> Ch' il poco al troppo spesso s' abbandona;
>   Nè questo Agnol perdona.
>   Ch' amor vuol sol gli amici, onde son rari
>   Di fortuna e virtù simili e pari."

"The reward is too handsome, sweet as it is, that holds the soul in fetters. My liberty complains of your kindness, and feels it more painfully than if a theft had been done me. And as the eye feels its power diminished by the sun, while it ought to increase in light, so my wishes demand no hindering thanks from you, which you bestow too largely; for too little often grows out of that which is too much, and (Michael) Angelo cannot suffer this."

LIX. — Page 315.

This poem also is in the Vatican manuscript in various forms.

LX. — Page 322.

Condivi mentions the peculiar form of the cross. It has not elsewhere come before me.

An oil painting of smaller size, only containing the lower half of the composition, i. e., Christ with the two angels, is in the Berlin Museum, where it has been erroneously attributed to Sebastian del Piombo

LXI. — Page 327.

The Macello dei Corvi is sketched differently in the plans to be found in the Barberini Library to that which is pointed out under that name at the present day. In this quarter of the city there are a number of old houses of the sixteenth century; and I am convinced, if the matter were more thoroughly pursued than time allowed me to do during my last visit, the house might be discovered.

LXII. — Page 332.

Instead of *pur sanità* at the close of the letter given by Gaye, I suppose *sua sanità* is intended. We have flattering letters from Aretino to Vittoria Colonna, written during the years 1537 and 1538.

LXIII. — Page 332.

Aretino's letters. Paris edit., 1609, ii. 40.

"To Vasari.

"Enclosed in your letters, I received the two copies, executed at my request, of the monuments of the Dukes Giuliano and Lorenzo. They please me much. In the first place, because you have drawn them so beautifully; and, in the second place, because they are the work of that god of sculpture, from whose divine hands I have seen the sketch of St. Catherine, which he did as a child. (*Lo schizzo della Santa Caterina che disegnò sendo fanciullo.*)

"Even in this early beginning, he shows himself in all his majesty (*tutto pieno di maestà*); and we feel that such gifts are awarded by Heaven but rarely to mortal men. Any one must be astonished to see an ear executed so delicately and accurately with the pencil. All painters to whom I have shown the sheet are agreed that he alone who has done it would have been able to produce it. And I myself, — it was to me as if I now for the first time realized the miracles of this miracle, when I had it thus before me.

"Now, however, when I opened the box, which reached me through the Giunti, and I saw the head of one of those representatives of the glory of the Medici, I stood for a time as if petrified with admiration. How was it possible that the Duke Alexander, only for the sake of showing himself graciously disposed towards one of his servants, could have robbed himself of such a treasure! I am almost afraid of examining and praising this countenance, so venerable and wonderful does it appear. Beard, hair, brow, eyebrows, and eyes, — how they are executed! What an ear! what a profile! and this chiselled mouth! all combining to give expression to the feeling which animates the whole. He seems to see, to be silent, to listen; and over all there is the venerableness of a holy old age; and yet every thing is nothing but clay, formed into a few features by the fingers.

"And with this I will close my letter. The life of art breathes forth from the creative hand of this great man; for what he creates, speaks, moves, and breathes. Not I alone am proud to possess this work which you have sent me by the permission of your master, but the whole of Venice boasts of it. I am too insignificant to be able to requite such a gift by another; it would lessen the value of the gift were I only to attempt it, and therefore no more than my thanks to such a master and to such a friend.

"Venice, the 15th July, 1538."

Aretino calls the head, *uno degli avvocati della gloria dei Medici*. This seems to refer to a Medici himself. Among all, I know of Pope Clement alone as "bearded." It is, however, nowhere mentioned that Michael Angelo executed a portrait of him. Or could it be Ottaviano dei Medici, of whom I have never heard of a portrait at all?

Still, the person whom it represented is the least important part. It appears far more important, that in this head we have the only portrait executed by Michael Angelo as a sculptor.

Could the whole thing, perhaps, be only an error of Aretino's, and the heads sent by Vasari be those of the emperor and Clement VII., executed by Alfonso Ferrarese, and purchased by Vasari for Florence? Vas., ix. 14.

Aretino's letter, moreover, is falsely dated, as Alexander had been long murdered in 1538. His letters are often wrongly dated. They are also, as comparisons with the originals prove, at times altered by him for publication. Thus it is with his letters to Duke Cosmo, which are different in Gaye.

LXIV.—PAGE 333.

The letter concludes: "Attendete a esser scultore di sensi e non miniatore di vocaboli." It is not said unkindly. It is addressed to Lodovico Dolce, and treats of good and bad style in writing.

LXV.—PAGE 340.

The engraving of Enea Vico, of which Vasari speaks, does not bear his name. Bartsch asserts that it does not exist. If we examine more closely the large engraving which Salamanca published in 1548, we see that the different sheets of which it consists have been very differently executed. Some are engraved in small undefined lines, almost as if they were etched; others are done with a strong flourishing point. It is to me beyond a matter of doubt, that different hands were at work on it. Enea Vico might therefore have had a share in it. Perhaps he worked too slowly, and others were brought forward to assist. The good parts of the engraving belong to the best that that period has produced. Before Michael Angelo's time, honor was sought for in work.

Aretino received Michael Angelo's letter of January, 1538, through Nardi. Hence Michael Angelo's connection with this old Florentine democrat was lasting.

LXVI.—PAGE 352.

Nos. 1, 2, 3, 7, 8, 11 of the Letters to Leonardo, in the possession of the British Museum.

The end of No. 11:—

"Vorrei che chi ti vuol dare moglie, pensassi di darla a te, non alla roba tua. A me pare che egli abbi a venir da te il non cercar grande dota. Però tu hai solo a desiderar la sanità dell' anima, e del corpo, e la nobiltà del sangue, e de' costumi, e che parenti ella ha, chè importa assai. Altro non ho che dire."

LXVII. — Page 355.

"Della casa sua." By this his party is meant. It could scarcely refer to the older San Galli, for whom Michael Angelo always had the greatest respect.

Vasari says, in the "Life of Antonio di San Gallo," —

"Facendo poi fare Sua Santità i bastioni di Roma, che sono fortissimi e venendo fra quelli compresa la porta di Santo Spirito, ella fu fatta con ordine e disegno d'Antonio con ornamento rustico di trevertini in maniera molto soda e molto rara, con tanta magnificenza, ch' ella pareggia le cose antiche: la quale opera dopo la morte d'Antonio fu chi cercò, più da invidia mosso che da alcuna ragionevole cagione, per vie straordinare di farla rovinare; ma non fu permesso da chi poteva."

In the first edition, he concludes thus: —

... "dopo la morte di lui, fa chi cercò con vie straordinarie far minare, mosso più da invidia della gloria sua, che per ragione, se' fosse stato lasciato fare da chi poteva; ma chi poteva non volse."

Both times he is intentionally obscure, but the second time still less intelligible than at first. Vasari must have had reasons for taking one iota from the clearness of what he had at first only intimated.

On the other hand, in Michael Angelo's Life (2d edit.), there is the following passage: "Portò disegnata tutta la fortificazione di Borgo, che aperse gli occhi a tutto quello che s' è ordinato e fatto poi; e fu cagione che il portone di S. Spirito, che era vicino al fine, ordinato del Sangallo, rimase imperfetto."

Vasari, as is natural, in truth, always takes the part of those whose life he is writing. He therefore, in San Gallo's life, entirely omits the quarrel about the fortifications of the Vatican suburb which called forth Michael Angelo's interference, and only speaks of the architectural beauty of the gate of S. Spirito. In Michael Angelo's Life, merely the practical question is treated of, and at the same time the point is conceded to him. Who the person indicated in San Gallo's Life may have been, still remains obscure.

LXVIII. — Page 356.

"È stato nel suo dire molto coperto e ambiguo, avendo le cose sue quasi due sensi." Vas., first edit. Vasari has touched upon many personal things in his second edition.

LXIX. - Page 373.

To Bartolommeo Ammanati?

LXX.—Page 378.

It is asserted that Michael Angelo was a member of Tolomei's academy. Poleni, Exercitationes Vitruvianæ primæ, Batavii, 1739, p. 60. Upon the academy itself, see Tolomei's letters. A certain connection of the members with Michael Angelo is a matter of course; but we know of nothing more.

LXXI.—Page 380.

Papencordt, p. 132.

LXXII.—Page 381.

Gamucci's copy differs from the present form of all three palaces, yet it is truly too bad for inferences to be drawn from it.

LXXIII.—Page 393.

In an essay before published by me, I have erroneously referred the poem to Cavalieri to Vittoria, among other errors contained in that paper.

LXXIV.—Page 395.

Vasari mentions the group even in his first edition. It was placed at first, in 1549, in San Spirito, in Florence. Gaye, II. 500. "Nel medesimo anno si scoperse in Sto Spirito una Pietà la quale mandò un fiorentino a detta chiesa, e si diceva che l' origine veniva dallo inventor delle porcherie, salvando gli l' arte ma non devozione, Michelangelo Buonarroti."

He gets upon the Last Judgment. He afterwards mentions *capricci luterani*. He prays that God may send his saints to destroy such like. In his eyes, the painting of the drapery under Caraffa is an extremely mild measure.

LXXV.—Page 407.

New detail is continually coming to light upon these circumstances, so that a new work upon them would be just as desirable as it would be acceptable.

LXXVI.—Page 407.

No. 22 of the Letters to Leonardo, 22d October, 1547, in the possession of the British Museum.

No. 26 also is interesting. 3d December, 1547.

"Lionardo,—E' me venne alle mani, circa un ando fa, un libro scritto a mano di cronache fiorentine, dove trovai, circa

dugento anni fa, se bene mi ricordo, un Buonarroto Simoni
più volte de' signori, di poi un Simone Buonarroti, di poi un
Michele di Buonarroto Simoni, di poi un Francesco Buonarroti. Non vi trovai Lionardo che fu de' Signori, padre di
Lodovico nostro padre, perchè non veniva tanto in qua. Però
a me pare che tutti scriva Lionardo di Buonarroto Buonarroti
Simoni. Del resto, della risposta alla tua non accade, perchè
non hai ancora inteso niente della cosa ti scrissi, nè della casa.
"MICHELAGNIOLO, in Roma."

LXXVII.—PAGE 409.

*No. 32 of the Letters to Leonardo, 15th March, 1549, in the
possession of the British Museum.*

"Lionardo,—Quello che io ti scrissi pu la mia ultima non
accade replicare altrimenti. Circa il male del non potere
orinare io ne sono stato più molto male, ho muggiato dì e notte
senza dormire, e senza riposo nessuno, e quello che giudicano
e' medici, dicono che io ho il male della pietra. Ancora non
son certo, mi vo medicando per detto male e èmmi data buona
speranza. Nondimeno, per esser io vecchio e con un si crude-
lissimo male, non ho da prometterla. Io son consigliato d'
andare al bagno di Viterbo, e non si può prima che al principio
di maggio, e in questo mezzo andrò temporeggiando il meglio
che potrò, e forse arò grazia del male. Non sarà desso. Ho
di qualche buon riparo, però ho bisogno dell' aiuto di Dio. Pero
di' alla Francesca che ne facci orazione, e digli che se la sapessi
com' io sono stato, che la vedrebbe non esser senza compagni
nella miseria. Io del resto della persona sono quasi come era
di trenta anni; èmmi sopraggiunto questo male pe' gran disagi,
e per poco stimar la vita mia. Pazienzia; forse andirà meglio
che io non ne stimo, con l' aiuto di Dio, e quando altrimenti, t'
avviserò, perchè voglio acconciar le cose mia dell' anima e del
corpo, e a questo sarà necessario che tu ci sia, e quando mi
parrà tempo te ne avviserò, e senza le mia lettere non ti muo-
ver per parole di nessun' altro. Se è pietra, mi dicono i medici
che è in sul principio, e che è piccola, e però, come è detto, mi
danno buona speranza.

"Quando tu avessi notizia di qualche estrema miseria in
qualche casa nobile, che credo che e' ve ne sia, avvisami, e che
perinsino in cinquanta scudi, io te gli manderò che gli dia per
l' anima mia. Questi non hanno a diminuir niente di quello che
ho ordinato lasciare a voi. Però fallo a ogni modo.

"MICHELAGNIOLO BUONARROTI, in Roma.
"A dì 15 di Marzo 1549."

He uses subsequently the Roman chronology.

LXXVIII.—Page 409.

No. 42 of the Letters to Leonardo, in the possession of the British Museum.

... " Del mio male io ne sto assia bene e rispetto a quel sono stato. Io ho bevuta circa due mesi, sera e mattina, d' una acqua d' una fontana che è quaranta miglia presso a Roma, la quale rompe la pietra, e questo ha rotto la mia, e fattomi orinare gran parte. Bisognamene fare ammunizione in casa, e non bere nè cucinare con altra, e tenere altra vita che non soglio.

(15th June, 1549, is on the address.)

No. 45 also belongs to this period.

... " A questi dì ho avuto una lettera da quella donna del tessitore, che dice averti voluto dare per moglie una per padre de' Capponi, e per madre de' Niccolini, la quale è nel munistero di Cancandeii, e hammi scritto una lunga bibbia con una predichetta che mi conforta a vivere bene e a fare delle limosine, e te dice aver confortato a viver da cristiano, e debbeti aver detto che è spirata da Dio di darti detta fanciulla. Io dico che l' ha a fare molto meglio attendere a tessere o a filare, che andare spacciando tanta santità. Mi par che la voglia essere un altra suor Domenica, però non it fidar di lei.

" A dì 19 giuglio 1549."

LXXIX.—Page 410.

No. 15 of the Letters to Leonardo, 22d June, 1547, in the possession of the British Museum.

From No. 16 of the letters to Leonardo. 30th July, 1547.

We will insert the following passage:—

... " Vorrei che per mezzo di messer Giovanfrancesco tu avessi l' altezza della cupola di Santa Maria del Fiore, da dove comincia la lanterna insino in terra, poi l' altezza di tutta la lanterna, e mandassimela. E mandami segnato in sulla lettera un terzo del braccio fiorentino " ...

The sendings of wine, etc., continue. See Nos. 50, 51, 52 of the letters to Leonardo.

From No. 52.

... " Messer Giovanfrancesco mi richiese, circa un mese fa, di qualche cosa di quelle della marchesa di Pescara, se io n avevo. Io ho un libretto in carta pecora che ella mi donò, circa dieci anni sono, nel quale è cento tre sonetti, senza quegli che mi mandò poi da Viterbo in carta bambagina che sono quaranta, i quali feci legare nel medesimo libretto, e in quel tempo gli prestai a molte persone in modo che per tutto ci sono in istampa. Ho poi molte lettere che ella mi scriveva da Orvieto e da Viterbo. Ecco ciò ho della Marchesa. Però mostra questa a detto prete, e avvisami di quello che ti risponde.

"A dì 7 di marzo 1551."

The correspondence, therefore, began at Orvieto, whither Vittoria went before Viterbo; and he has *many* letters from her.

Another copy of Vittoria's poems, which was in Michael Angelo's possession, is that which Triqueti (Les Trois Musées de Londres, par H. de Triqueti, Paris, 1861) saw in London in the Kensington Museum. Michael Angelo's name is on it. It is the edition published in Venice in the year 1558 by Lodovico Dolce, which was reprinted in 1559. Dolce was an old *protégé* of Vittoria's, and had probably sent the book to Michael Angelo.

Triqueti's book contains good information respecting the works of Michael Angelo's own hand preserved in the Kensington Museum, — twelve numbers.

LXXX. — PAGE 410.

No. 49 of the letters to Leonardo, in the possession of the British Museum.

LXXI. — PAGE 413.

The letter is given by Fea.

LXXXII. — PAGE 416.

See upon this matter Benvenuto Cellini's Autobiography.

LXXXIII. — PAGE 419.

No. 59 of the Letters to Leonardo, in the possession of the British Museum.

"Leonardo, io ho (inteso) per la tua, come la Cassandra è presso al parto, e come vorresti intendere il parer mio del nome de' putti della femmina, se fia così. Tummi scrivi esser resoluto pe' sua buoni portamenti del mastio quando sia. Io non so che mi ti dire. Arei ben caro che questo nome Buonarroto non mancassi in casa, sendoci durato gia trecento anni in casa. Altro non so che dire, e lo scrivere m' è noia assai. Attendi a vivere.   "Michelagnio (sic) Buonarroti in Roma."

Without date. (April, 1554; cf. Vas., xii. 241.)

LXXXIV.—Page 419.

In the Vatican manuscript of the poems, xcviii. "Lionardo,—Intendo per la tua come la Cassandra a partorito un bel figliuolo, e come la sta bene, e che gli porrete nome Buonarroto. D'ogni cosa n' ho avuto grandissima allegrezza, Iddio ne sia ringraziato, e lo facci buono acciò che ci facci onore e mantenga. Ringrazia la Cassandra, e raccomandami a lei. Altro non m' accade circa questo. Io ti scrissi, più mesi sono, che quando si trovassi da comprare una casa che fussi onorevole e in buon luogo che tu me 'n avisassi, e così ti riscrivo che quando ci uscisse fuori tal cosa che tu mene dia avviso, e se non ti par cosa al proposito adesso non mancar di cercare."

He breaks off. Below is written:—

> "Che fia de' mie pensier già vani e lieti,
> All' una e l' altra morte m' avvicino;
> L' una m' è certa, e l' altra mi minaccia,
> Non pinger, nè sculpir fie por che quieti."

LXXXV.—Page 423.

Among the separate papers and accounts in Michael Angelo's handwriting in the possession of the British Museum, is the following receipt: . . . "Scudi doro chetā . . . mene ori . . . (ho ricevuto) p parte della restitutione dellētrāta di mille dugiēto scudi doro che mi fu tolta del papa Caraffa data mi prima da papa farnese uero e chel porto di piacēza me laueua tol(to) limperadore e ultimamēte il papa Caraff lufitio in romagnia mitolse il primo di che fu facto papa," etc.

LXXXVI.—Page 430.

"Non sempre al mondo è si pregiato e caro." Madrigal.

LXXXVII.—Page 431.

A letter of Cellini's, in the possession of the British Museum, even on the 14th March, 1559, expresses pleasure at Michael Angelo's resolution to go to Rome. The letter seems never to have been printed. There is another in the same place, of the year 1561, in which Cellini recommends to Michael Angelo an artist whose name is not mentioned, whom he wishes to have employed in the building of St. Peter's. This has also not been published, so far as I know. In the first letter he addresses him as "Excellentissimo e divino precettore mio Messer Michelagniolo"

LXXXVIII.—Page 441.

Ora would not perhaps be translated *brink;* but the image is chosen because it has been elsewhere often employed. He compares himself besides to an arrow, reaching its aim.

LXXXIX.—Page 481.

Cornelius, cartoons of the paintings at Munich were purchased after his call to Berlin: they stood there unpacked for twenty years, were then exhibited for a short time, made the greatest noise, and were again packed up. Such a treatment of the works of a man of this importance is an unheard-of fact in the history of art.

Cornelius could have sold the cartoons in England; but he refused these offers, because he wished that his works should remain in Germany, It would have been better had he accepted them; for a journey to England would thus, perhaps, have afforded Germans the possibility of seeing the works of their greatest painter.

Instead of raising the inevitable monument to Cornelius' memory when he dies, we ought far rather, while he lives, to subscribe for the building of a house to receive his works. Such a building would be a better monument for him and for us than a statue.

Supplementary to Page 401.

Superficially considered, it might appear that the two standing female statues on both sides of the statue of Moses, might, as well as that statue, be alleged as Michael Angelo's works. Condivi so designates them, and Michael Angelo appears himself to speak of them as such. They are, moreover, his, just as the whole monument in his; but, nevertheless, not his work in the strictest sense of the word. To avoid misunderstanding upon this point, I will give the whole matter more accurately.

Michael Angelo was not in a position, in the year 1542, to complete the monument. He had so far relieved himself from his engagement, that he was only required to furnish three statues of his own work, — the Moses and two others, which are not more accurately specified. At first, the slaves, now in the Louvre, were understood as these two latter ones: as, however, they would have been too colossal for the diminished form of the monument, Michael Angelo took them back, and supplied Rachel and Leah in their place. These he now wished in 1542 to give up also to Montelupo, who was already engaged in executing three other statues for the monument.

Michael Angelo, in his memorial to the pope, in which he urges this arrangement, calls the two statues (Rachel and Leah) "assai bene avanti di sorte che con facilità si possono da altri maestri fornire." If we take these words in their strict meaning, we may gather from them that Montelupo had not much more to do to the statues; but we may equally well take them as a more general phrase, by which Michael Angelo wished to represent the continuation of the work by Montelupo as possible, feasible, and harmless, as regards the statues themselves, without necessarily inferring from this that the statues were already as good as finished. For if this latter had been the case, so much ceremony would not certainly have been required in assigning their completion to Montelupo. Michael Angelo would have himself finished them, or would have had them completed by others in his atelier. Instead of this, they were now given to Montelupo to complete; and a new contract, as regarded every thing, was concluded with him.

Montelupo's entire work for the monument was, at the conclusion of the new contract, as follows: He had to finish five statues, and to receive 550 scudi for them. Among these were two of colossal dimensions. Reckoning these higher, he may have received 120 scudi for each of them, and 105 for each of the others. For none of these statutes had to be more than "*completed*" by Montelupo, as is expressly declared by Michael Angelo, who calls the pieces subsequently finished by Montelupo, "*fatte ovvero finite di Raffaelo di Montelupo*" — (*Letter to Montanto*, 1545). In 1542, Montelupo had finished one, the Madonna, and received 105 scudi for it. From that time, he appears to have received monthly 25 scudi. According to his last receipt, 450 had been paid him in all; and for this he had executed three statues. 105 scudi remained, for which he had still to furnish work, if Michael Angelo, dissatisfied with his work (the bad result of which Vasari excuses by declaring that Montelupo had been ill at the time), had not taken back Rachel and Leah, to complete them himself. We might now say that Michael Angelo had received these two in the same condition as he had given them, and that what then remained to be done to them he had now done himself. My reckoning above may be false, as they had advanced beyond the others; and a sum of 50 scudi each may have been fixed for their completion, which, as the receipt shows, was now deducted from Montelupo.

Yet this is contradicted by the aspect of the statues themselves in the most decided manner (a fact even pointed out by those who adjudge them to Michael Angelo); and, in spite of

Condovi's evidence, and Michael Angelo's own words, we seek for an explanation of this difference.

It may be drawn from Michael Angelo's own words.

Michael Angelo makes an express distinction between *fare* and *finire*. An example has been already given. If, however, Rachel and Leah now came into Montelupo's atelier " as good as finished," and were afterwards completed by Michael Angelo, having been returned untouched, why does Michael Angelo call them, not *fatte*, but only *finite di sua mano?* He intimated by this, most decidedly, the work of other hands. Let us look at the statues: the fact was, Montelupo had spoiled them (to use the severest expression), and Michael Angelo was obliged at last to take pains to complete them, for the sake of his reputation. That he only succeeded in doing so to a certain extent, is shown by the two statues themselves, which no one would recognize as a work of Michael Angelo's; and respecting which, it seems to me, we are in the highest sense fully justified in denying to be his work. Strictly taken, we might certainly designate this work as nothing at all, as is the case with many a piece of sculpture in the present day which goes into the world as the work of a master, but on which he has not done a hundredth part so much as Michael Angelo did to these two statues, Condivi also, without falsehood, may designate them as works of Michael Angelo's own hand. Condivi's point of view, however, was different to ours. In his Life of Michael Angelo, he had the subordinate aim in view of exhibiting his master as innocent with regard to the mausoleum affair, and of proving that, by executing these two statues, he even did more than he was bound to do by contract. We, however, in the present day, seek to discover Michael Angelo's mind in his works, in which he buried himself, as it were, working at them with slow and thoughtful labor. This he did not do, either in Leah or Rachel; nor would he have done so. And, therefore, among the figures on the monument, I regard the Moses alone as executed by Michael Angelo.

PAGE viii. PREFACE. — COPY OF CONTRACT.

The remarks appended are taken from a periodical entitled "Ueber Künstler und Kunstwerke," by Herman Grimm. January number:—

Dichiaramo per la presente polizza, come Messer Leonardo del già Bonarroto de' Bonarroti, cittadino fiorentino, volendo riconoscere e continuare la amicizia che Messer Daniello Ricciarelli da Volterra ha continuato molti anni seco, etiam et con Messer Michelagnolo suo zio, bona memoria, e mettere a cus-

todia piuttosto che a pigione della sua casa in Roma una persona amorevole, nella quale possa confidare sicuramente, che
debbe non pure conservarla, ma ridurla anche in migliore stato
con li danari della infrascritta moderata pigione : concede dico,
detta sua casa, posta nel rione di Trevi, presso Santa Maria di
Loreto, confinante da una banda con li beni di Giovanni Battista Zannuzi, dall'altra con li beni di Madonna Diana de
Bargellis, moglie di Tarquinio Casale, e della parte di dietro
con lo orto del capitano Papinio Capiciucco e le monarche di
San Giovanni Battista, dinanzi con la strada pubblica incontro
al palazzo del vescovo Zambicaro e altri più vari confini al detto
Messer Daniello Ricciarelli da Volterra, per anni novi prossimi
futuri da comminciarsi a dì primo di maggio detto 1564, e come
seguitò da finirsi con ricognizione piuttosto che nome di prezzo
di scudi trentacinque, di Giulj dieci per scudo all'anno, da pagarsi
di sei in sei mesi, anticipata soluzione, secondo la usanza di
Roma, liberamente e senza alcuna eccezione : con dichirazione,
che per evidente utilità e miglioramento di detta casa, possa il
detto Messer Daniello prevalersi e spendere in essa i detti scudi
trentacinque di pigione all'anno, et di detta spesa tenerne e
renderne fedele conto al prefato Messer Leonardo : quale in tal
caso promette farla buona, e scomputarla sopra la detta pigione :
e con patto espresso, che accadendo che esso M. Leonardo solo,
o con sua famiglia, volesse venire a Roma per suoi negotj, o
per altro, gli siano riservate libere tutte le stanze della Torre,
e luogo anche da potere tenere due cavalcature in stalla, e con
dichiarazione ancora, che detto Messer Daniello non possa
appigionare ad altri le due casette appartenenti e congiunte a
detta casa, se non di anno in anno; una delle quali abitava
Pierluigi Gaita : l'altra Aquina, moglie già di maestro Antonio
muratore, e oggi di Giovanni cavatore di pozzolana, a' quali
già Messer Michelagnolo suo zio aveva concedute dette casette
per abitarle a beneplacito suo : e similmente con patto espresso,
che detto Messer Daniello non possa appigionare ad altri per
alcuno spazio di tempo la detta casa principale, nè meno le
stanze della Torre, che Messer Leonardo si ha riservate quando
gli accorra venire a Roma, come di sopra è detto : e caso che
M. Daniello contravennisse questo patto si intende subito esser
finita la locazione di detta casa, et così delle altre due casette
soprascritte appigionate ad altri come di sopra; e perchè
Messer Leonardo lassa in detta casa diverse masserizie, legna-
mi, e ferramenti, come si contiene in uno inventario sottoscritto
di mano di detto M. Daniello, esso promette averne buona cura,
e rendere conto, e restituirlo tutto, o in parte, ad ogni beneplacito e volontà del pfto Messer Leonardo, quale si contenta
che frattanto M. Daniello possa usarle e servirsene a suo
piacere. — Le quali tutti soprascritte condizioni il pfto M

Daniello promette inviolabilmente al detto M. Leonardo osservare e mantenere senza alcuna eccezione, perchè così sono stati d'accordo: e inoltre promette il detto M. Daniello, finito il detto tempo di nove anni, restituire al detto M. Leonardo la detta casa senza replica, o contradizione alcuna, e così M. Daniello renunzia sopra di ciò a qualsivoglia legge, statuto e decreto fatti e da farsi in favore degli inquilini: laquale restituzione s'intende con porte, finestre, serrature, chiavi e altro pertinente a detta casa: dentro laquale, nè in alcuna parte di essa, non sia lecito, nè permesso al pſto M. Daniello cavare, nè far cavare senza espressa licenzia di M. Leonardo: il quale in evento di sua morte vuole che li suoi eredi siano obbligati mantenere la detta casa nel modo predetto, e per il detto tempo di novi anni al pſto M. Daniello: il quale al incontro vuole, che in evento di sua morte, la detta locazione si intenda subito finita, ancora che non fussi finito il detto tempo di nove anni: e che li suoi eredi non possono per virtù della presente continuare, nè pretendere nella detta locazione, e così si obbligano e promettono ciascuna di dette parti respettivamente osservare inviolabilmente, volendo, che la presente polizza abbia forza di istrumento rogato in ampliore forma, etc. etc. etc.   E per fede del vero, io Diomede Leoni Senese, a richiesta di ambedue le dette parti, ho scritta e sottoscritta la presente di mia propria mano, dì, mese, è anno sopradetti in Roma.

Jo Diomede Leoni ho scritta e sottoscritta la presente di mia mano propria.

Jo Leonardo Bonarroto de' Bonarroti fiorentino sono contento e mi obbligo a quanto in questo si contiene, e per fede o fatto la presente soscrizione di mano propria questo dì sopra detto in Roma.

Jo Daniello Riciarelli da Volterra sono contento e mi obbligo a quanto in questo si contiene, e per fede del vero o fatto la presente di mia propria mano questo dì et anno soprascritti in Roma.

Jo Jacopo del Duca siciliano, fu presente a quanto di sopra.

Jo Jacopo di Rocheti romano, fu presente a quanto di sopra.

The house situated on the Capitol, which has always been pointed out as Michael Angelo's, is thus out of the question. On the other hand, Francesco d'Ollanda's statement, that Michael Angelo lived at the foot of the Quirinal, appears correct.   I had supposed it to have been an error, because the Macello dei Corvi, on which, according to Vasari, the house was situated (and he adds, moreover, " at the foot of the Capitol "), could not at the same time be at the foot of the Quirinal. The matter now assumes another aspect: the Macello dei Corvi stretched in Michael Angelo's day further into the square, in the centre of which Trajan's column stands; and the house thus lay in the valley exactly between Capitolinus and Quirinalis.

The different aspect presented by that neighborhood in Michael Angelo's time is shown by the plan in the Barberini Palace, belonging to the year 1551. The position of the Buonarroti house may here be ascertained with tolerable accuracy. No trace of it now exists: it shared the fate of the Raphael Palace near St. Peter's, which also stood in the way when the square was enlarged, and was pulled down.

Major Kühlen drew my attention to a drawing of the Forum of Trajan in the 16th century, in Du Perac's Vestigj dell' Antichità di Roma. The square looks confined, indeed, compared with the present day. Miserable little houses are crowded round the column on every side. San Maria di Loreto is without the lofty dome which now surmounts the church; and in front of it is that cluster of houses which, we suppose, belonged to Michael Angelo's abode. A little house is to be seen in the corner, with a verandah; this was either one of those which he assigned to his workmen, or the entrance to the stables. We see "the tower" which Messer Leonardo reserved for himself and his family, and which contained the better apartments; and on the level roof, with its projecting parapet, there seems to have been a small garden, or the edge only may have been filled with plants, — we know not. But we see, as the contract informs us, that Michael Angelo's property comprised a group of houses, — dwelling-house, atelier, tower, workmen's lodging, and stabling. And that there was a garden besides, with shady laurel trees, is shown by a letter of Daniele da Volterra's, dated 1565, which is in the possession of the British Museum, and which has only now become of importance, since we find, what no one could have known before, that it alludes to Michael Angelo's house.

The letter is addressed to Lionardo Buonarroti, Michael Angelo's nephew and heir.

Molto magnifico e onorando.

Molto più e con ragione dovete maravigliarvi voi, non vi avendo scritto io già tanto tempo. Ma certo è che la causa di sì lungo silenzio principalmente è stata la mia indisposizione, e anco che io mi son fidato molto del buono offizio che ha fatto sempre per sua cortesia Messer Diomede in fra di noi, che me credo che abbiate fatto voi ancora.

Arò molto caro di sapere i nomi dei scultori che hanno a fare le tre figure del sepolcro, e anco arei caro vedere un poco di schizzo di tutta l'opera, e sapere il nome delle tre statue:

mi piace molto che la cosa cammini in quel modo che ragionammo già insieme, perchè non potrà riuscir se non con onore e utile vostro benissimo, il che desidero di continuo.

Jo ho fatto dibattare (Jo ho fattoti patare) gli alberi dell' orto, e deradare ancora tanti di quei lauri che toglievano il sole agli altri alberi. Feci ancora coprire la scala, siccome fu ragionato; non ho già fatto impianellare il tetto della sala perchè desideravo metter in opera del mio lavoro, e speravo che a quest'ora fusse fatto ogni cosa, ma la lungezza in che mi tengono questi padroni franzesi a far questo benedetto getto è causa che ancora si ha a fare, e similmente è causa che le due teste non son gettate perchè aspettavo di far la lega di certo metallo. Ma se io vedrò che la cosa vadi troppo in lungo, io mi risolverò a gettarle, chè già le forme sono a tal termine che presto presto si possan finire. Non voglio aspettare più altro che una risposta del Signor Orazio Rucellai il quale si trova appresso alla Regina, e spero che faccia buon officio per quest'opera, e che me'n abbia in breve a dar resoluzione, che subito, avuta questa risposta, io non aspetterò più a gettarle, e' sia come si voglia. Quanto alla cosa del metallo non occorre visare (fesare) a cosa nessuna chè v'ogni cosa. Circa al far formare la Madonna di basso rilievo, poichè adesso è in mano di Messer Giorgio, sebben non v'è il Marignello, sarebbe forse bene, innanzi che la renda, farla formare a qualcuno altro, chè non può essere che Messer Giorgio non abbia conoscenza di qualche persona atta a fare tal effetto, chè in vero il formare non vuol altro che diligenzia.

Se voi vedete di poter far che la si facci, a me sarà molto caro. E raccomandate (mi) a Messer Giorgio strettamente, e a voi stesso mi raccomando.

Di Roma il dì 11 di Febbraio 1565 in Roma
Vostro affezionatissimo e vero amico,
DANIELE RICIARELLI.
Al molto magnifico e mio osservandissimo
Messer Lionardo Buonarrota Fiorenza.

This letter agrees with Vasari's statements respecting Da Volterra's last works and death; for the excitement connected with this cast was the cause of his speedy decline.

Daniele begins with lamentations at his state of mind. In Vasari we read how the work, although he was a strong man, enfeebled and depressed him. The work in question was the cast of a colossal horse, which Michael Angelo, not being able to undertake himself, gave to Daniele to execute for the French Queen. Daniele worked at his house, and was one of those present at his death. The cast failed the first time, but the second it succeeded admirably.

INDEX.

THE END.